I0892377

Olympic Airways

Graham M Simons

AIR WORLD

AIR WORLD

Olympic Airways
A History

First published in Great Britain in 2019 by Air World Books,
an imprint of Pen & Sword Books Ltd,
Yorkshire - Philadelphia

Copyright © Graham M Simons
ISBN 9781473883536

The right of Graham M Simons to be identified as Author of this work has been asserted by him in accordance with the Copyright, Designs and Patents Act 1988. A CIP catalogue record for this book is available from the British Library All rights reserved.

No part of this book may be reproduced or transmitted in any form or by any means, electronic or mechanical including photocopying, recording or by any information storage and retrieval system, without permission from the Publisher in writing.

Typeset in 10pt Times by
GMS Enterprises Peterborough

Printed and bound in India by
Replika Press Pvt Ltd.

Pen & Sword Books Ltd incorporates the Imprints of Aviation, Atlas, Family History, Fiction, Maritime, Military, Discovery, Politics, History, Archaeology, Select, Wharncliffe Local History, Whamcliffe True Crime, Military Classics, Whamcliffe Transport, Leo Cooper, The Praetorian Press, Remember When, Seaforth Publishing and Frontline Publishing.

For a complete list of Pen & Sword titles please contact:

E-mail: enquiries@pen-and-sword.co.uk Website: www.pen-and-sword.co.uk

Or
PEN AND SWORD BOOKS
1950 Lawrence Rd, Havertown, PA 19083, USA
E-mail: Uspen-and-sword@casematepublishers.com

Contents

Dedication

As this book went to press the news reached the world of the terrible fires in Attica, centred on the town of Mati, but also involving nearby Rafina and Nea Makri that took nearly one hundred lives. The devastated area is just to one side of the flight path in and out of Eleftherios Venizelos Airport Athens, and it is also the location of the Hotel Myrto on Marathonos Avenue, where I stayed when researching this book.

My wife and I walked the lanes of Mati in the evenings as a break from interviewing OA staff - lanes that were shown today crowded with fire-destroyed cars, with Red Cross teams searching for bodies. We ate in the local pizzeria that was shown a burnt out ruin, followed by loucomades in a coffee shop that suffered the same fate; I bought fresh bread from the bakery - now just a pile of smouldering rubble - and we sunbathed on the very beach where so many fled to and so tragically lost their lives.

To all those people who so freely offered hospitality and friendliness to my wife and I and who now have lost so much I would like to dedicate this book.

Acknowledgements

A book of this nature would not have been possible without the help of many people and organisations.

David Lee; Simon Peters, Ron Lynch, British Airways Speedwing; Gregory Konstantellos; Amy Matra; Antonis Simigdalas, Olympic Air; Martha Kesisoglou, Steve Davies, Rudiger Eilardt, Constantine Siappas, Marketing Director, Olympic Aviation; Liana Vassilaki, Senior Superintendent Olympic Aviation Sales; Panagiotis K Makris, Group Manager, Support Services Heraklion Airport; Mrs Helen Sophia Speronis, Public Relations Manager Olympic Airways Athína; Richard Vandervord and Spiros Papadopoulos for a large amount of photographs and memorabilia from their collections; Mrs Sophie Stylianidis, Sales Support, Olympic Airways London; Elina Pardali, Public Relations and Press Co-ordinator, Aegean Airlines; Olga Vasasaki, Public Relations, Aegean Airlines; Kostas Diassitis; Lizetta Vaya; Pavlo Papadimitropoulos, Vice President, ΠΟΛ.Κ.Ε.Ο.Α.; Detlef Doebberthin; John Hili, Olympic Airways London; Athina Kollias; Rose Robinson, administrator of the We're Mad about Greece and the Greek Language Facebook page; The Alexander S. Onassis Foundation; Eustace Stroumpoúles, Alexandros Onassis' driver; Captain Virgil Komnénó; The Onassis Cultural Centre-Athína; Vasylis Tsatsaragos, President, ΠΟΛ.Κ.Ε.Ο.Α

I am indebted to many people and organisations for providing photographs for this story, but in some cases it has not been possible to identify the original photographer and so credits are given in the appropriate places to the immediate supplier. If any of the pictures have not been correctly credited, please accept my apologies.

Introduction

The Olympic Airways (OA) story has always fascinated me as has the country of its birth.

Since I first visited Hellas in 1970, when even though the country was in the grip of a military dictatorship the people were warm and welcoming, ouzo was a drachma a glass, and the glass kept getting bigger: I became intrigued.

What were its origins? Who was involved? Ellinikon Airport out on the edge of the Athenian Riviera was the bustling hub of the eastern Mediterranean, linking worldwide flights to the mainland then out to a string of emerald islands set in the wine-dark Ionian and Aegean seas.

I soon realised that the history was incredibly involved. It is a story of evolvement, conflict, personality and politics; set upon a background of world and civil war, coup and counter-coup, people personalities and places.

Every time I passed through Athína I visited the press office to collect the latest handouts — and every now and again a pack of papers with either a London or Athína postmark would land on my doormat. I also made the London Hotel on Posidonos Avenue, Glyfada my usual stop-over place whenever I visited. This haunt was known all around the world by aircraft spotters for from its roof garden - and bar - it was impossible to avoid getting excellent pictures of the aircraft movements.

From the mid-1980s onwards, and especially during the later years it became clear that the staff who worked for the Olympic Airways Group or any of its parts were getting metophorically battered from pillar to post by those supposedly in charge. In spite of the roller- coaster ride the employees were forced to travel by their political and financial masters, there was still a tremendous pride and spirit within the airline - that sense of φιλότιμο (philotimo) - which to a Greek is essentially a way of life. It is considered the highest of all Hellenic virtues, the standards for family and social living; the core concept is that of respect and walking in right paths. In its purest form, the term means 'doing good', actions that ensure that a person's behaviour is exemplary and demonstrate his personality and the

Εισαγωγή

Η ιστορία της Ολυμπιακής Αεροπορίας πάντα με γοητεύει όπως και η χώρα της γέννησής της.

Από τότε που επισκέφθηκα για πρώτη φορά την Ελλάδα το 1970, όταν ακόμα και αν η χώρα βρισκόταν στο χέρι μιας στρατιωτικής δικτατορίας, το ούζο ήταν μια δραχμή το ποτήρι και το ποτήρι γινότανε όλο και μεγαλίτερο : μου κέντρισε το ενδιαφέρον.

Ποια ήταν η προέλευσή του; Ο οποίος είχε εμπλακεί? Το αεροδρόμιο του Ελληνίκου στην άκρη της Αθηναϊκής Ριβιέρας ήταν το πολυσύχναστο κέντρο της ανατολικής Μεσογείου, συνδέοντας τις διεθνείς πτήσεις με την ηπειρωτική χώρα και έπειτα σε μια σειρά από σμαραγδένια νησιά που βρίσκονται στο σκοτεινό κρασί του Ιονίου και του Αιγαίου.

Σύντομα συνειδητοποίησα ότι η ιστορία ήταν απίστευτα εμπλεκόμενη. Είναι μια ιστορία εξέλιξης, σύγκρουσης, προσωπικότητας και πολιτικής. που τέθηκε σε φόντο παγκόσμιου και εμφυλίου πολέμου, πραξικόπημα και αντίθετο πραξικόπημα, ανθρωποι προσωπικότητες και τοποθεσίες.

Κάθε φορά που πέρασα από την Αθήνα, επισκέφτηκα το γραφείο Τύπου για να μαζέψω τα πιο πρόσφατα φυλλάδια - και κάθε τόσο ένα πακέτο χαρτιών με σφραγίδα του Λονδίνου ή της Αθήνας θα έφτανε στο πατάκι της εξώπορτας μου. Έκανα επίσης το ξενοδοχείο Λονδίνο στη Λεωφόρο Ποσειδώνος, Γλυφάδα η συνήθη στάση μου όταν επισκεπτόμουν. Αυτό το στέκι ήταν γνωστό σε όλο τον κόσμο από τους παρατηρητές αεροσκαφών από το roof garden του - και το μπαρ - ήταν αδύνατο να αποφευχθεί η λήψη εξαιρετικών φωτογραφιών των κινήσεων των αεροσκαφών.

Από τα μέσα της δεκαετίας του '80 και εξής, και ειδικά κατά τα επόμενα χρόνια, έγινε σαφές ότι το προσωπικό που εργάστηκε για τον Όμιλο ή κάποιο από τα μέρη του έπεφτε μεθοφορικά από πυλώνα σε θέση από εκείνους που υποτίθεται ότι ήταν υπεύθυνοι. Παρά την ασταθή διαδρομή, οι εργαζόμενοι αναγκάστηκαν να ταξιδέψουν από τους πολιτικούς και οικονομικούς τους ιδιοκτήτες, υπήρχε ακόμα μια τεράστια υπερηφάνεια και πνεύμα μέσα στην αεροπορική εταιρεία - αυτή η αίσθηση του φιλότιμου - που σε έναν Έλληνα είναι ουσιαστικά ένας τρόπος ζωής. Θεωρείται η υψηλότερη από όλες τις ελληνικές αρετές, τα πρότυπα για την οικογένεια και την κοινωνική ζωή. η βασική έννοια είναι αυτή του σεβασμού και των σωστών ηθικών αρχών. Στην καθαρότερη μορφή του, ο όρος σημαίνει «κάνω καλό»,

manner in which he was raised.

In my conversations with others it became apparent that little of the fine detail about the group of companies was known outside the region, although everyone had heard about the one towering controversial figure; the 'Megalos' (Greek: Μεγάλος) or 'Big Boss' who oversaw much of the central part of the story: Aristotle Socrates Onassis.

As will be seen, Onassis tended to use the airline as his own personal transport system - often showing little to no regard as to the feelings of paying passengers whom his staff bumped off flights at very short notice in order to make room for him, his family or members of the high echelons of his organisation.

The airline also has its share of industrial disputes through its history which was, as often the case, brought about by instigations and intransigence on both sides. Onassis' management style could be very hands-on and confrontational - he certainly had trouble delegating - but at the same time it should be said, that the unions operated with a mentality that ranged at best from ethereal and delusional to vicious and vindictive.

Many of the problems were brought about because of this use of the airline as his fiefdom - and some of the reasons behind it. The story contains a more significant than usual amount of personal details of him and his son Alexandros - who was appointed in 1971 to oversee the day-to-day operations of Olympic Aviation, under the presidency of Stelios Papadimitriou. Olympic Aviation was a regional subsidiary of his father's Olympic Airways. This book also contains more than just a passing reference to Aristotle Onassis' marriage to Jacqueline Lee 'Jackie' Kennedy. That said, I have done my best to steer clear of some of the more lurid stories that have appeared over the years in the press, for these have no bearing on the Olympic Airways theme.

My research made it clear that the airline's story indeed could not be told in isolation. Olympic did not spring fully formed into being in 1957 as many have tried to say. The named company may have come into being then, but its roots were set much further back in history through a number of predecessor airlines - both national and international - who had been using the Hellenic Republic and Athína as the crossroads of the air for the Eastern Mediterranean since the dawn of aviation.

Alexandros' death on 23 January 1973, at the age of just twenty-four in an air crash in what many still think are suspicious circumstances was a trigger to his fathers decline. Alexandros' death had a profound

πράξεις που εξασφαλίζουν ότι η συμπεριφορά ενός ατόμου είναι υποδειγματική και δείχνει την προσωπικότητά του και τον τρόπο με τον οποίο ανατράφηκε.

Στις συνομιλίες μου με άλλους, κατέστη προφανές ότι λίγα από τα λεπτομερή στοιχεία για την ομάδα των εταιρειών ήταν γνωστά εκτός της περιοχής, αν και όλοι είχαν ακούσει για το ένα περίεργο φιλόδοξο πρόσωπο. τον «Μεγάλο» ή τον «Μεγάλο αφεντικό» που επέβλεψε μεγάλο μέρος του κεντρικού μέρους της ιστορίας: ο Αριστοτέλης Σωκράτης Ωνάσης.

Όπως φαίνεται, ο Ωνάσης είχε την τάση να χρησιμοποιεί την αεροπορική εταιρεία ως το δικό του σύστημα προσωπικών μεταφορών - συχνά δεν δείχνει τίποτα για το συναισθήματα της πληρωμής των επιβατών που ο υπάλληλός του έσπασε από τις πτήσεις πολύ σύντομα, ώστε να του δοθεί χώρος. οικογένεια ή τα μέλη των υψηλών κλιμάκων της οργάνωσής του.

Η αεροπορική εταιρεία έχει επίσης το μερίδιό της στις βιομηχανικές διαμάχες μέσω της ιστορίας της, η οποία, όπως συμβαίνει συχνά, προκλήθηκε από υποκινητικές ενέργειες και αδιαλλαξία και από τις δύο πλευρές. Το στυλ διοίκησης του Ωνάση θα μπορούσε να είναι πολύ πρακτικό και αντιπαραβαλλόμενο - σίγουρα είχε πρόβλημα να μεταβιβάσει - αλλά ταυτόχρονα πρέπει να ειπωθεί ότι τα συνδικάτα λειτουργούσαν με μια νοοτροπία που κυμαίνεται στην καλύτερη περίπτωση από αιθέρια και παραληρητικά έως κακόβουλα και δίκαιη.

Πολλά από τα προβλήματα προκλήθηκαν εξαιτίας αυτής της χρήσης της αεροπορικής εταιρείας ως της φλερτ - και μερικοί από τους λόγους πίσω από αυτήν. Η ιστορία περιέχει ένα σημαντικότερο από το συνηθισμένο ποσό προσωπικών στοιχείων του και του γιου του Αλέξανδρου - ο οποίος διορίστηκε το 1971 για να επιβλέπει τις καθημερινές δραστηριότητες της Ολυμπιακής Αεροπορίας, υπό την προεδρία του Στέλιου Παπαδημητρίου. Η Ολυμπιακή Αεροπορία ήταν περιφερειακή θυγατρική της Ολυμπιακής Αεροπορίας του πατέρα της. Αυτό το βιβλίο περιέχει επίσης κάτι περισσότερο από μια απλή αναφορά στον γάμο του Αριστοτέλη Ωνάση με τον Jackie 'Kennedy της Jacqueline Lee. Τούτου λεχθέντος, έκανα το καλύτερο δυνατό για να αποφύγω κάποιες από τις πιο θορυβώδεις ιστορίες που εμφανίστηκαν κατά τη διάρκεια των χρόνων στον Τύπο, επειδή αυτές δεν έχουν καμιά σχέση με το θέμα της Ολυμπιακής Αεροπορίας.

Η έρευνά μου κατέστησε σαφές ότι η ιστορία της αεροπορικής εταιρείας δεν μπόρεσε να ειπωθεί μεμονωμένα. Ολυμπιακό δεν άνοιξε πλήρως σχηματισμένο να είναι το 1957, όπως πολλοί προσπάθησαν να πουν. Η επωνυμία της εταιρίας μπορεί να έχει τεθεί σε ισχύ, αλλά οι ρίζες της τοποθετήθηκαν πολύ πιο πίσω στην ιστορία μέσω διάφορων προγενέστερων αεροπορικών εταιρειών - εθνικών και διεθνών - οι οποίες χρησιμοποιούσαν την Ελληνική Δημοκρατία και την Αθήνα ως το σταυροδρόμι του αέρα για την Ανατολική Μεσογείου από την αυγή της αεροπορίας.

effect on his father, who never fully recovered from the loss of his son. Aristotle Onassis sought to sell Olympic Airways after his son's death and died two years later in March 1975.

The airline continued under state ownership. The company faced severe financial trouble from the 1980s on, mostly because of management problems amid political interfering. Hellenic politicians and their families travelled for free or token amounts on the airline. Successive Hellenic governments also made Olympic carry the press at a ninety-seven percent discount.

Due to the rising losses and debts, the government decided to formulate a restructuring programme in which all debts were erased. This, as well as all the plans that followed, failed. A few years later, in a further attempt to make Olympic profitable, management was given to a subsidiary of British Airways, Speedwing. The result was even more massive debts and rising losses.

Very soon the losses became excessive, so in 2003 further restructuring was called for. In December 2004, the Hellenic government decided to privatise OA, but the sale process failed as none of the buyers was eager to repay the state almost 700 million euro in state aid, which was later declared illegal by the European Commission in December 2005.

In September 2005, the government signed a non-binding agreement with Olympic investors to buy the airline. By the end of the year, the offer fell through because the massive fine imposed on the carrier by the European Commission had not been dealt with.

In 2006 Olympic was thrown a lifeline, when the courts ordered Greece to repay them almost 564 million euro owed to the airline. The money was owed to OA from legally subsidised routes to Greek islands and costs of the relocation to the new airport. The money would be used to pay back part of the State aid declared illegal by the European Commission in December 2005.

Then, on 12 September 2007, the Luxembourg-based EU court ruled that Olympic should repay an amount of money less than what the EU Commission had ordered. This amount included unpaid taxes on fuel and spare parts, as well as outstanding fees to Athína International Airport. The new amount owed by Olympic was €130 million.

Despite all the lawsuits flying around, the staff continued to provide the travelling public with their unique brand of service - but it could not continue.

On 6 March 2009, Development Minister Kostis Hatzidakis announced the sale of the flight

Ο θάνατος του Αλέξανδρου στις 23 Ιανουαρίου 1973, σε ηλικία μόλις είκοσι τεσσάρων ετών, σε ένα αεροπορικό δυστύχημα σε αυτό που πολλοί εξακολουθούν να θεωρούν ύποπτες, ήταν η αιτία για την παρακμή του πατέρα του. Ο θάνατος του Αλέξανδρου είχε βαθιά επίδραση στον πατέρα του, ο οποίος ποτέ δεν ανέκτησε πλήρως την απώλεια του γιου του. Ο Αριστοτέλης Ωνάσης προσπάθησε να πουλήσει την Ολυμπιακή Αεροπορία μετά το θάνατο του γιου του και πέθανε δύο χρόνια αργότερα το Μάρτιο του 1975.

Η αεροπορική εταιρεία συνεχίστηκε υπό κρατική ιδιοκτησία. Η εταιρεία αντιμετώπισε σοβαρά οικονομικά προβλήματα από τη δεκαετία του '80, κυρίως λόγω των προβλημάτων διαχείρισης στο πλαίσιο πολιτικής παρέμβασης. Οι Έλληνες πολιτικοί και οι οικογένειές τους ταξίδευαν για δωρεάν ή συμβολικά ποσά στην αεροπορική εταιρεία. Οι διαδοχικές ελληνικές κυβερνήσεις έκαναν επίσης τον Ολυμπιακό να μεταφέρει τον Τύπο σε μια έκπτωση από το ενενήντα επτά τοις εκατό.

Λόγω των αυξανόμενων ζημιών και χρεών, η κυβέρνηση αποφάσισε να διατυπώσει ένα πρόγραμμα αναδιάρθρωσης στο οποίο να διαγράφονται όλα τα χρέη. Αυτό, όπως και όλα τα σχέδια που ακολούθησαν, απέτυχαν. Λίγα χρόνια αργότερα, σε μια ακόμη προσπάθεια να κερδίσει ο Ολυμπιακός, η διοίκηση δόθηκε σε θυγατρική της British Airways Speedwing. Το αποτέλεσμα ήταν ακόμη μεγαλύτερα χρέη και αυξανόμενες απώλειες.

Πολύ σύντομα οι απώλειες έγιναν υπερβολικές, επομένως το 2003 απαιτήθηκαν περαιτέρω αναδιάρθρωση. Το Δεκέμβριο του 2004, η ελληνική κυβέρνηση αποφάσισε να ιδιωτικοποιήσει την ΟΑ, αλλά η διαδικασία πώλησης απέτυχε καθώς κανένας από τους αγοραστές δεν ήταν πρόθυμος να αποπληρώσει το κράτος σχεδόν 700 εκατομμύρια ευρώ σε κρατικές ενισχύσεις, οι οποίες αργότερα κηρύχθηκαν παράνομες από την Ευρωπαϊκή Επιτροπή τον Δεκέμβριο του 2005.

Τον Σεπτέμβριο του 2005, η κυβέρνηση υπέγραψε μια μη δεσμευτική συμφωνία με τους Ολυμπιακούς επενδυτές για να αγοράσει την αεροπορική εταιρεία. Μέχρι το τέλος του έτους, η προσφορά έπεσε εξαιτίας του γεγονότος ότι το τεράστιο πρόστιμο που επιβλήθηκε στον μεταφορέα από την Ευρωπαϊκή Επιτροπή δεν είχε αντιμετωπιστεί.

Το 2006 ολυμπιακοί οδηγοί έριξαν μια ζώνη ασφαλείας, όταν τα δικαστήρια διέταξαν την Ελλάδα να τους επιστρέψει σχεδόν 564 εκατομμύρια ευρώ που οφειλόταν στην αεροπορική εταιρεία. Τα χρήματα οφειλόταν στην ΟΑ από νόμιμα επιδοτούμενα δρομολόγια προς τα ελληνικά νησιά και το κόστος της μετεγκατάστασης στο νέο αεροδρόμιο. Τα χρήματα θα χρησιμοποιηθούν για την αποπληρωμή μέρους των κρατικών ενισχύσεων που κηρύχθηκαν παράνομες από την Ευρωπαϊκή Επιτροπή το Δεκέμβριο του 2005.

Στη συνέχεια, στις 12 Σεπτεμβρίου 2007, το δικαστήριο της ΕΕ που εδρεύει στο Λουξεμβούργο αποφάσισε ότι ο Ολυμπιακός θα έπρεπε να επιστρέψει

operations and the technical base companies to Marfin Investment Group (MIG). As a result, after thirty-five years of state control and ten years of failed sales attempts, Olympic once again became a private corporation. The new owners secured approximately 5000 of the 8500 jobs of the Group.

Readers may note the use of different words to what they may be used to seeing. For example, I write Hellas or the Hellenic Republic instead of Greece, because this is the correct, official name for the country, derived, by the way from the ancient name of the nation is Hellas or Ellada (Greek: Ελλάς, Ελλάδα). In English, however, the state is usually called Greece, which comes from Latin Graecia (as used by the Romans) and means 'the land of the Greeks', while the Greeks called their land Hellas and themselves Hellenes, which is something I prefer.

Similarly, I have used the Hellenic versions of islands and place names, as they appear on signs and notices: therefore after the first use, for example, Corfu appears as Kerkyra, Rhodes becomes Ródos and Salonica becomes Thessaloniki. Part of this also includes using the standard Δρχ as the abbreviated version of the drachma which was the official currency until 2002.

Readers may also note that many of the photographs and images used in this book are credited to 'ΠΟΛΚ.ΕΟΑ' which stands for Πολιτιστικό Κέντρο Εργαζομένων Ολυμπιακής Αεροπορίας - the Olympic Airways Workers' Cultural Centre Collection who have been incredibly helpful in ensuring this book came to fruition.

This then is the story.

Graham M Simons
1 August 2018

χρηματικό ποσό λιγότερο από αυτό που είχε παραγγείλει η Ευρωπαϊκή Επιτροπή. Το ποσό αυτό περιελάμβανε μη καταβληθέντες φόρους στα καύσιμα και στα ανταλλακτικά, καθώς και εκκρεμείς αμοιβές προς τον Διεθνή Αερολιμένα Αθηνών. Το νέο ποσό που οφειλόταν από την Olympic ήταν 130 εκατ. Ευρώ.

Παρά όλες τις αγωγές που πετούν γύρω από το προσωπικό, το προσωπικό συνέχισε να παρέχει στο ταξιδιωτικό κοινό τη μοναδική υπηρεσία εξυπηρέτησης - αλλά δεν θα μπορούσε να συνεχίσει.

Στις 6 Μαρτίου 2009, ο Υπουργός Ανάπτυξης Κωστής Χατζηδάκης ανακοίνωσε την πώληση των πτητικών λειτουργιών και τις εταιρείες τεχνικής βάσης στην Marfin Investment Group (MIG). Ως αποτέλεσμα, μετά από τριάντα πέντε χρόνια κρατικού ελέγχου και δέκα χρόνια αποτυχημένων προσπαθειών πώλησης, η Olympic έγινε ξανά ιδιωτική εταιρεία. Οι νέοι ιδιοκτήτες εξασφάλισαν περίπου 5000 από τις 8500 θέσεις εργασίας του Ομίλου.

Οι αναγνώστες μπορούν να σημειώσουν τη χρήση διαφορετικών λέξεων σε αυτά που μπορούν να χρησιμοποιηθούν για να τα δουν. Για παράδειγμα, γράφω την Ελλάδα ή την Ελληνική Δημοκρατία αντί της Ελλάδας, γιατί αυτό είναι το σωστό, επίσημο όνομα της χώρας, που προέρχεται από το αρχαίο όνομα του έθνους είναι η Ελλάδα ή η Ελλάδα, κάτι που προτιμώ.

Ομοίως, χρησιμοποίησα τα ελληνικά κείμενα των νησιών και τα ονόματα των τόπων, όπως εμφανίζονται σε σημάδια και ανακοινώσεις: συνεπώς, μετά την πρώτη χρήση, για παράδειγμα, η Κέρκυρα εμφανίζεται ως Κέρκυρα, η Ρόδος γίνεται Ρόδος και η Θεσσαλονίκη γίνεται Θεσσαλονίκη. Μέρος αυτού περιλαμβάνει επίσης τη χρήση του πρότυπου Δρχ ως συντομευμένη έκδοση της δραχμής που ήταν το επίσημο νόμισμα μέχρι το 2002.

Οι αναγνώστες μπορούν επίσης να σημειώσουν ότι πολλές από τις φωτογραφίες και τις εικόνες που χρησιμοποιούνται σε αυτό το βιβλίο πιστώνονται στο «ΠΟΛΚ.ΕΟΑ», το οποίο αντιπροσωπεύει την Συλλογή Πολιτιστικού Κέντρου Εργαζομένων της Ολυμπιακής Αεροπορίας, οι οποίες βοήθησαν απίστευτα για να εξασφαλίσουν ότι το βιβλίο αυτό θα υλοποιηθεί.

Αυτό είναι τότε η ιστορία.

Graham M Simons
1η Αυγούστου 2018

Chapter One

From The Beginning

From the dawn of time, the human race has dreamed of flying like the birds and the more ambitious even of controlling the 'third dimension'. Like other nationalities, the Hellenes were no exception in having the same aspiration as described in the ancient legends of Phaeton and Icarus. Both characters underline the fact that Greeks understood, that just as in other activities, caution should always be exercised because overestimating one's self in the attempt to conquer the air could be fatal as shown by the tragic ends of the two ancient heroes.

Hellas was fortunate enough to have a lawyer - one of the first theorists of the aeroplane's promising future in peace and war - Alfred Athanasopoulos. He published his opinions in the Hellenic press in 1907, and his views touched the feelings of the nation. At the beginning of the 20th century, in a country humiliated in the Greco-Turkish War of 1897, there was a widespread public belief that the new century with its 'miracles of technology' would allow the new state to have the means to wash away the disgrace of defeat.

In 1908 this feeling became stronger as it seems that Leonidas Arniotis, a circus impresario and showman who, at various times had a performing cat and dog act and was once billed as 'The champion rider of the world' took to the skies. According to the Air Historical Branch of the Hellenic Air Force in their history *'Hellenic Wings'*, Arniotis performed the first successful flight in Greece.

There is, however, another legend that in the spring of 1910 a Russian called Outoskin arrived by ferry at Piraeus, just outside Athína (Athens). He is supposed to have brought with him a Farman biplane.

He erected the aircraft at nearby Neo Faliro, possibly in an area close to where the Karaiskaki Stadium is located. By all accounts, he attracted a large crowd, for the occasion had been well advertised. One of the gathered multitudes did not confine himself just to expressions of admiration but approached the intrepid aviator and offered to fly with him. This was the noted athlete and poet Konstantinos Manos, Of course, Outoskin accepted as his future passenger paid him the not inconsiderable sum of 200 Drachma. So, it seems that Konstantinos Manos went down in history as the first Greek flown by paying ticket!

Hellas was very much influenced by France - not only culturally, but also in matters of science and technology and many times French experts were employed when new skills needed to be imported. Therefore it comes as no surprise that the Hellenic government turned to France for assistance during the early development of aviation in Hellas.

In 1911 six army officers Lieut. Dimitrios Kamberos an artillery officer; Cavalry officer Second Lt. Panoutsos Notaras; First Lt. Michael Moutoussis of the military corps of engineers; Cavalry officer Second Lt. Christos Adamidis; Infantry officer First Lt. Loukas Papaloukas and First Lt. Markos Drakos, another artillery officer were sent to France for training. The first aircraft were ordered from the French aircraft company 'Avions Farman' run by three brothers Richard, Henri, and Maurice Farman.

All six officers graduated from the Farman school in Étampes near Paris, but only four served subsequently in aviation.

The Army Aviation started with six machines, including four purchased from the Farman Aviation Works and assembled by French mechanics: there was one Henri Farman 20 biplane, a Henri Farman biplane converted to a hydroplane, officially named Daedalus, piloted by Kamberos. Three of the Farman machines a Maurice Farman Hydravion plus another Maurice Farman biplane unidentified as a type. There was also one Astra hydroplane, named *Nautilos*, piloted by Moutousis and the Nieuport IV G monoplane, privately owned and piloted by Emmanouil Argyropoulos.

Three of the Farman machines were christened

Aetos, Gyps, and *Ierax*. According to legend, the aircraft were paid for by money donated by a poet named Matsoukis.

Kamberos carried out the first Hellenic military flight during military manoeuvres on 13 May 1912. He later flew the first seaplane in Greece in June 1912 during feasibility tests for the establishment of a naval air service. In September 1912 the 1st Aviators Company was setup in Larissa. The government, always short of funds, relied heavily on the public admiration of 'the new peculiarity of the aeroplane' and exploited for its fundraising campaigns that made possible the building of the first military airfield. Greek air power had finally taken material form.

Emmanouil Argyropoulos was born in 1889 and was the son of diplomat George Argyropoulos, the Ambassador of Greece in Russia. He studied civil engineering in Germany and aviation in France. At the end of January 1912, he acquired his pilot's licence and returned to home to Greece together with a privately owned Nieuport IV.G 50-hp monoplane.

On 6 February Argyropoulos announced in the Athenian newspaper that on two days time on Wednesday 8 February he would make a flight from the Rouf area, located in the west of the Athína' centre, between Piraeus and Petrou Ralli Avenue. On the prescribed date crowds flooded onto the field of improvised airport ready to admire the unprecedented spectacle about to take place. Exactly at 8:10 am Argyropoulos 'lifted' his machine into the air to the cheers of the crowd, among whom were George I, His Majesty the King of the Hellenes, Prime Minister Eleftherios Venizelos and many other VIPs.

Left: Prime Minister Eleftherios Kyriakou Venizelos *b*. 23 Aug 1864, *d*. 18 March 1936. He made a flight with Emmanouil Argyropoulos (below right) in his Nieuport IV on 8 February 1912, after which Venizelos named the aircraft *Alcyone*. *(both via Spiros Papadopoulos Collection)*

So Argyropoulos became the first Greek aviator to perform a flight in Greece, an event widely commented upon in the local and national press. After taking off from the Rouf district of Athína, he performed a 16-minute long flight around the city, including an overflight of the Acropolis. An hour later he carried out a second four-minute flight, this time with Prime Minister Eleftherios Venizelos as his passenger. Venizelos was enthusiastic about the concept of aerial warfare and immediately stated that Greece should take advantage of this newly invented weapon.

Following his second flight, Prime Minister Eleftherios Venizelos with a glass of champagne in hand ceremoniously christened the machine *Alcyone* (Halcyon- Kingfisher) the Ancient Greek symbol of hope. In his speech, during the naming ceremony, he said that: *'The aeroplane is suitable as a weapon of the weak. The audacious and daring nature of the Greek will transform it into a splendid weapon of war, capable of rendering great services'*.

Eleftherios Kyriakou Venizelos was an eminent Greek leader of the Greek national liberation movement and a charismatic statesman of the early 20th century remembered for his promotion of liberal-democratic policies. As head of the Liberal Party, he was elected several times as Prime Minister, serving from 1910 to 1920 and from 1928 to 1933. Venizelos had such profound influence on the internal and external affairs of Greece that he is credited with being 'the maker of modern Greece', and is still widely known as the 'Ethnarch' or governor.

On 12 February Argyropoulos carried out another flight over Paleo Faliro, this time using the zoo as a temporary airfield. Crowds of people from Athína and Piraeus rushed to admire the fearless aviator in an equally successful flight, which resulted in an unexpected celebration - the group picked up Argyropoulos and carried him triumphantly shoulder-high to the royal dais where he received the congratulations of King George.

The Balkan Wars

In October 1912 Greece, Bulgaria, Serbia and Montenegro declared war on the Ottoman Empire and their armies started advancing in the enemy territory. On 5 October 1912, the Hellenic Army started pushing northwards, and Kamberos executed the first aerial reconnaissance in Greek history that greatly aided the Army during the battle of Elason.

According to an order issued by the Hellenic High Command the aircraft had under their wings blue and white stripes (the national colours) to be distinguished from the Turkish aeroplanes. Hellenic airmen never met their Ottoman counterparts in the air, so no aerial combat took

Above: Demitrios Kamberos in an early Farman.

Left: Indicative of the French influence in early Greek aviation is this Maurice Farman 7 Longhorn biplane is seen at Nicopolis airfield, Preveza, Greece in late 1912. *(both via Spiros Papadopoulos Collection)*

Early Hellenic Air Force aviators with their Farmans.

Right: Konstantinos Manos, the first Greek passenger in 1910 and the first Greek to die as a passenger in 1913. *(both authors collection)*

place. They mainly carried air observation and air reconnaissance missions, and on some occasions the attacked the enemy with a type of experimental bomb that had been designed by Kamberos. First Lieutenant Moutousis attacked the Ottoman fortifications at Bizani, but he did not do significant damage. But the attack was executed in full sight of the assaulting Greek Infantry to raise their morale and if possible to lower the psychology of the defenders. While the Hellenic army was assaulting Bizani, a Greek aircraft threw newspapers and provisions to the besieged people of Ioannina in what is probably the first recorded use of air power for both relief and psychological operations.

On 24 January 1913, First Lieut. Moutousis, having as passenger Ensign A. Moraitines flew over the Dardanelles in a Farman hydroplane on an air reconnaissance mission to discover the disposition of the Ottoman fleet. They also dropped bombs that caused minimal damage, but the machine was forced to land on the sea because of mechanical problems. Eventually, the crew were rescued, and the aircraft towed to their base by the destroyer *Velos*. The numerous missions of the Greek pilots over the Asia Minor coastline made the Turkish press complain about the impunity with which they flew over the Ottoman forces.

Somewhat strangely, two of these early aviators were bound together by an inextricable fate when both became the first two Greeks to lose their lives in an air crash on Greek soil. With the outbreak of the Balkan Wars, Argyropoulos joined the military aviation with the rank of Lieutenant. On 4 April 1913, during a reconnaissance mission during which they were flying close to a thunderstorm, his aircraft, a captured Ottoman Blériot XI, broke up and fell from a height of 600 metres while flying over the Langadas region near Thessaloniki. Both Argyropoulos and his passenger Konstantinos Manos who had flown with the Russian Outoskin in Athína during 1910, were killed.

During the second Balkan war Bulgaria, who initially possessed the largest aerial fleet, attacked Greeks and Serbs but was defeated. No recorded aerial conflicts between belligerents exist, and it seems the common observation and bombing missions were the norm.

Immediately after the war, the Hellenic Navy started organising its aerial service with British aid. In 1914 the first five naval pilots were ready for service. They had also trained to take off from the sea and land back there as there was no airfield initially in Elefsis.

While in 1914 the Hellenic Republic enjoyed the advantage of having a naval air service initially, the Ottoman Navy quickly followed suit. Greece declared neutrality in the first stages of the war, and there was a lack of funds that prohibited further development. Despite that Kamberos established a pilot training school in Thessaloniki. The decision to, go or not to go to war at the side of Entente or the Central Empires deeply divided the nation to the effect that there were two governments: one in Athína under the royalists and one in Thessaloniki under Venizelos. Pressure from the Allies brought the resignation of the king to abdicate in 1917 and leave the fate of the country to his son and the government of Thessaloniki. Hellenic Army aviation was reorganised by the French with French aeroplanes and Naval aviation by the British with the English material. The circular markings that the Hellenic Air Force use today were adopted at that time along with the adoption of the parachute. The Army operated the 531 Fighting Squadron as well as the 532 and 533 Reconnaissance-Bombing Squadrons and their war activities comprised patrols and reconnaissance, as well as attacks against enemy trenches. They earned the congratulations of the French HQ for their excellence.

As a reward for their support of the Entente, the Greeks were allowed to occupy Eastern Thrace and the Smyrna enclave in Asia Minor. Turkish leader Mustafa Kemal rejected the capitulation terms and started an armed resistance against the Hellenic Army. The Hellenic Air Force found its self with ageing equipment and inability to operate due to lack of fuel. The issue was partly solved as forgotten German fuel supplies from the Great War were rediscovered, and so three squadrons of the Army and one from the Navy went into action. The Greek pilots executed a broad range of missions such as reconnaissance, strafing and bombing the Turkish forces as efficiently covering a front that reached 700 kilometres in 1921.

Initially, as Kemal struggled to reorganise the Turkish air force, the Greeks enjoyed air superiority but as time passed the air fights increased as the Turks attempted to wrest the skies from the Hellenic Air Force. An unfortunate choice of political moves left Greece unsupported by the Anglo-French, and the Hellenic Army evacuated Asia Minor.

In 1917 a decision was taken to establish a Hellenic aircraft manufacturing company, but the wars that followed delayed its foundation until 1925. The situation was far from ideal as Hellas was smarting from the defeat and had to settle 1,500,000 refugees. From 1925 the air force began upgrading with new equipment and in an attempt to decrease dependency on foreign suppliers set up air aircraft factory with the air of a British company.

The State Aircraft Factory of Greece, usually known by the acronym KEA (Κρατικό Εργοστάσιο Αεροπλάνων) formerly referred to as the EAF (Εργοστάσιο Αεροπλάνων Φαλήρου or 'Aircraft Factory Phaliron'). Based in Phaliron near Piraeus, just outside Athína, with technology and initial management provided by Blackburn Aircraft Limited from the UK, a company selected as a partner by the Hellenic military. The first type produced by the factory was the T3 Velos, designed by the British company.

In 1927 an all-Hellenic Air Force model was introduced (although according to other sources, a

Hellenic Air Force Officers pose by Horace Farman F.40 F.3299. *(authors collection)*

Below: Left to right; the Fairey IIF, Breguet 19 and Letov-Smolik on the ground at Tatoi airfield, Athína.
Top right: the fuselage of IIIF G-AABY negotiates its way through the streets of Athína on route to Phaleron. Right: the tailplane had to be removed on the Athína-Tatoi road to clear the roadside olive trees.
(all Charles Baker)

Below:Below: the Fairey IIIF G-AABY, now fitted with floats for the waterborne tests. It is thought that picture was taken at Hydra during a trip to collect the Chief of the Hellenic Air Services and his wife!

British engineer was a part of the design team), the Chelidon (Swallow) multi-purpose military aircraft. It used a Salmson 120 hp engine and had a maximum speed of 150 km/h. However, only one was built for the Greek Navy, as it was considered inferior to alternative types. Later, the factory produced a series of aircraft types under license, including numbers of Avro 504s, a version of the Armstrong Whitworth Atlas and the Avro 621 Tutor.

In the late 1920s, the Hellenic Government decided it was time to unify the naval and military air branches. In preparation for this, a competition was held in August 1929 to select the best machine for the requirements of the Hellenic Military Commission.

There were five competitors: a British Fairey IIIF and an Armstrong Whitworth Atlas, a French Breguet 19 and a Dewoitine along with a Czech Letov-Smolik S.16. The competition took place at two locations: Tatoi airfield for the land tests and in Phaleron Bay for the seaplane trials. It was from here during the water-trials that a flight was made by the IIIF to the island of Hydra to collect the Chief of the Hellenic Naval Air Service and his wife!

The Fairey IIIF was flown out from the UK by Captain Charles R McMullin, assisted by Charles Baker as the engineer. The journey took three days with some fourteen and a half flying hours involved, the pair arriving at Tatoi airfield where they were met by Fairey's agent in Athína, a Mr Coutroubis.

There followed three days of inspection by a number of Generals and politicians before test flying took place. It was then time to convert the Fairey from landplane to seaplane. The aircraft was partially dismantled, the wings 'boxed' placing them on a pair of lorries and then towing the aircraft fuselage behind a truck on its own wheels. The small convoy passed through the centre of Athína to Phaleron Bay, the Hellenic Naval base where it was re-assembled but now on floats that had previously been shipped out from England.

The whole process was of disassembly, carriage by road and re-assembly was supposed to be reversed after the water-borne tests, but McMullin and Baker had other ideas. Charles Baker: '*We didn't relish the fuss and bother of dismantling the wings a second time and carting everything back to Tatoi by road, so we examined the only alternative, which was to fly it back. Just behind the sheds by the side of the road, there was a piece of waste ground, not more than a hundred yards long, which we considered would be sufficient for a take-off. We lightened the machine as much as we could, left just enough petrol in the tank for the hop, and prepared to go.*

The whole base turned out to see us off - thinking we were crazy - but they saw little until we were soaring above the vast cloud of dust which our slipstream had driven into their faces. We had arranged that some mechanics would hold the machine back until the engine was at full throttle, when, on a signal from McMullin, they were to let go. In a few minutes, we were sailing over the Acropolis and heading for Tatoi.

Looking back, I can't understand why we didn't use the excellent main road itself for our departure. With a little cooperation from the police, who would readily have held up the traffic for a few minutes, we could have left so much more cleanly. However, the Greek Naval Air Service eventually placed an order with the Fairey Company for twelve IIIF seaplanes, so it was all worthwhile. I later heard that it was our take-off from that small corner of wasteland clinched the deal.'

In 1930 the naval and military air branches were unified, and the Hellenic Air Force was officially made the third branch of the Hellenic Armed Forces under the supervision of the Air Ministry. After that, the Meteorological Service and the Air Force Academy were instituted with British help and advisors.

Passenger Air Services

Meanwhile, air services were established across the Hellenic Republic with the country becoming something of an aeronautical crossroads.

As early as 1919 the United Kingdom's Winston Churchill said that the London to Karachi, India air service would become 'the air link that buckled the Empire together'. The planned routes out from London - either to India or South Africa all passed through either Thessaloniki or Athína. A weekly England to India passenger and mail service started on 1 April 1929. However, due to the failure of Imperial Airways to negotiate the rights to overfly Italian territory from France, the flight saw the transfer from an Imperial Airways Argosy landplane - to a Calcutta flying boat at Genoa - for an onward flight to Alexandria.

The carriage of 'Air Mail' was of great importance for some airlines, for the mail brought with it subsidies, which meant increased profits. An early northerly Imperial Airways route was:

Armstrong-Whitworth Argosy I G-EBLO *City of Birmingham* of Imperial Airways. Aircraft like this were used on early Air Mail flights to Ellas from the UK. *(author's collection)*

London - Cologne - Nuremberg - Vienna - Budapest - Belgrade - Uskub (Skoplje) - Thessaloniki - Athína. The machine on the first two flights in each direction was an AW Argosy while the third flight was a Handley Page W10.

From Athína the scheduled route was via Souda Bay in northwest Crete and Mersa Matruh to Alexandria by Short S.8 Calcutta flying boats. However, due to the shortage of flying boats, many of the November services were either by sea or used Italian aircraft and went via Tobruk.

During the latter half of 1929 the Italians demanded a cut from Imperial's receipts from the Genoa-Alexandria service, to which the Imperial Airways Board refused recognition, and so the service had to be transferred and routed via Vienna, Budapest, Skoplje, Thessaloniki and Athína from 31 October 1929.

The winter weather over the Balkans sector proved to be both cold and dangerous to passengers at this time of year. However, the Armstrong Whitworth Argosy G-EBLO renamed *City of Budapest* for the occasion, made two trips early in November before passengers were advised to travel between Paris and Athína by the Simplon Orient Express, while only the mail went by air.

The routes flown by Imperial were almost always changing. One example is this service that departed London via Paris to Basle on Saturday 30 March 1929 by the Argosy G-EBLF *City of*

Imperial Airways' Shorts S.8 Calcutta G-EBVH *City of Athens* is seen on the River Medway on 3 May 1928. *(authors collection)*

Above: Kastellorizo harbour showing Air Orient and Imperial Airways seaplanes 'moored' in its accommodating waters during their stopovers sometime during 1931.

Below: Shorts S.17 Kent, G-ABFB *Sylvanus* of Imperial Airways. This flying boat caught fire while refuelling in Brindisi Harbour on 9 November 1935. The only occupants of the plane were the refuelling crew, who managed to jump clear and escaped injury.

Right: The First Air Mail between England and India, franked in Athína on 1 April 1929. *(all authors collection)*

Glasgow and then by overnight train to Genoa. The flight from Genoa to Alexandria from 31 March to 3 April was by the Short Calcutta flying boat G-EBVH City of Athína. The route was:

- 31 March: Genoa - Rome - Naples;
- 1 April: Naples - Kerkyra (Corfu) - Athína;
- 2 April: Athína - Souda Bay - Tobruk;
- 3 April: Tobruk - Alexandria

In April 1930, flights resumed between London and Uskub via Cologne. The section between Uskub and Thessaloniki remained in operation using the railway; the mail was then flown by Short Calcutta flying boat from Thessaloniki to Alexandria via Athína and Mirabella in Crete.

The mail would be flown to Thessaloniki on 2 August, go by overnight train to Uskub and then be flown on to Vienna via Belgrade, and Budapest. The route changed again in late September 1930 with the mail being flown between London and Nuremberg, by train to Vienna, flown to Nish in Serbia and finally carried by train to Athína. From February 1931, the route was now London - Paris by air and then from Paris to Athína on board the Simplon Orient Express.

On 16 May 1931, the route to Athína was again revised with Naples replacing Rome. The first flight on the new route left London for Basle on the Swiss/French border on 16 May on an AW Argosy. The mail was then sent by rail to Genoa and flown to Kerkyra on 17 May and on to Alexandria via Athína and Mirabella on Crete on 18 May. The aircraft used between Genoa and Alexandria were Short Kent flying boats.

From October 1931, the Brindisi - Paris sector was by rail, and the Kent flying boats now flew from Brindisi to Athína via Kerkyra and then, instead of flying from Athína to Alexandria. That change meant that the Kents now made stops at Ródos and Limassol in Cyprus on the Athína - Kasltelorizo - Haifa section.

KLM - Royal Dutch Airlines operated a similar type of service to Java - known then as Batavia - as Imperial did to India and Australia starting with a series of test flights in late 1929. Their routes followed broadly the same locations, going via

Below: KLM operated Fokker F-VII H-NADP on its Far Eastern service that crossed Hellenic airspace.

Left: the face of the 1930 KLM timetable. *(authors collection)*

Brindisi during the winter months and Belgrade during the summer into Athína before crossing the Mediterranean to Alexandria in Egypt.

The regular service started in 1930 routing Amsterdam - Budapest - Athína - Cairo - Baghdad - Bushire - Jask - Karachi - Jodphur - Allahabad - Calcutta - Akyab - Rangoon -Bangkok -Meda-

Palembang - Batavia.

Air France – in the form of Air Orient SA - passed through Hellenic airspace on the way to the Far East. This airline came into being in 1930 through the merger of Air Union-Lignes d'0rient, S.A. (which had been founded in 1927) and Air Asie, S.A. (formed in Indo-China in 1926); its mission was the continued development of regular services to France's Southeast Asian colonies. In December 1929, the company's Marseilles-Syria mail route started in June of that year was extended to Baghdad.

The seaplane route, as was typical for the time, followed the Mediterranean coast: Marseille/ Marignane, Naples, Kerkyra, Athína, Kastellorizo and Beirut. On 17 January, a ten-day multi-stop route was opened by Air Orient to Saigon with full passenger service from Paris to Baghdad. The Mediterranean segment was flown by LeO 242s and CAMS 53s and the remainder by Breguet 280Ts. On 30 August 1933, Air Orient, S.A. and three other companies joined under the label of Societe Centrale pour l'Exploitation de Lignes Aeriennes, S.A. (SCELA), so as to negotiate with the government, and later merged to form Air France.

Letters posted from Marseilles for the inauguration of the Air Orient service - 17-27 January 1931 - received a purple, rectangular handstamp. The first Air Orient leg was from

Below: a Savoia-Marchetti, S-55 of sister airline Società Aerea Mediterranea, similar to the examples used by AEI.

Left: the face of an Aero Expresso Italiana timetable, showing the Roman column as the symbol of Brindisi, the Acropolis and Parthenon of Athína and, in the distance, the Aya Sofya church in Istanbul. Each landmark denotes a stop on the air route. *(authors collection)*

Marseilles to Athína. From here, a seaplane carried the mail to Beirut and arrived on the 21st. From Beirut, it went overland to Damascus and then onward by air.

The first mail originating from Athína to Saigon travelled via Air Orient service starting on 18 July 1931. A total of 22 covers was carried on the first flight. The first return service Saigon-Marseille that dropped the mail at Athína originated on 23 July 1931.

One of the stopovers across the Mediterranean was on the island of Kastellorizo in the bay of Mandraki, where a hangar and workshops were built. Vassilis Karayiannis, headed up the Air France office on the island, assisted by his younger brother, Panagiotis. They provided refuelling to the seaplanes and facilities for passengers and crew, and in case of any delays, their accommodation on the island. Kastellorizo remained a stopover on the way to Syria until June 1940 when the Air France agency was closed.

With an agreement signed between the British and Hellenic Republic governments in 1931, Imperial Airways were allowed to use the Hellenic Naval stations at Thessaloniki, Phaeleron and in

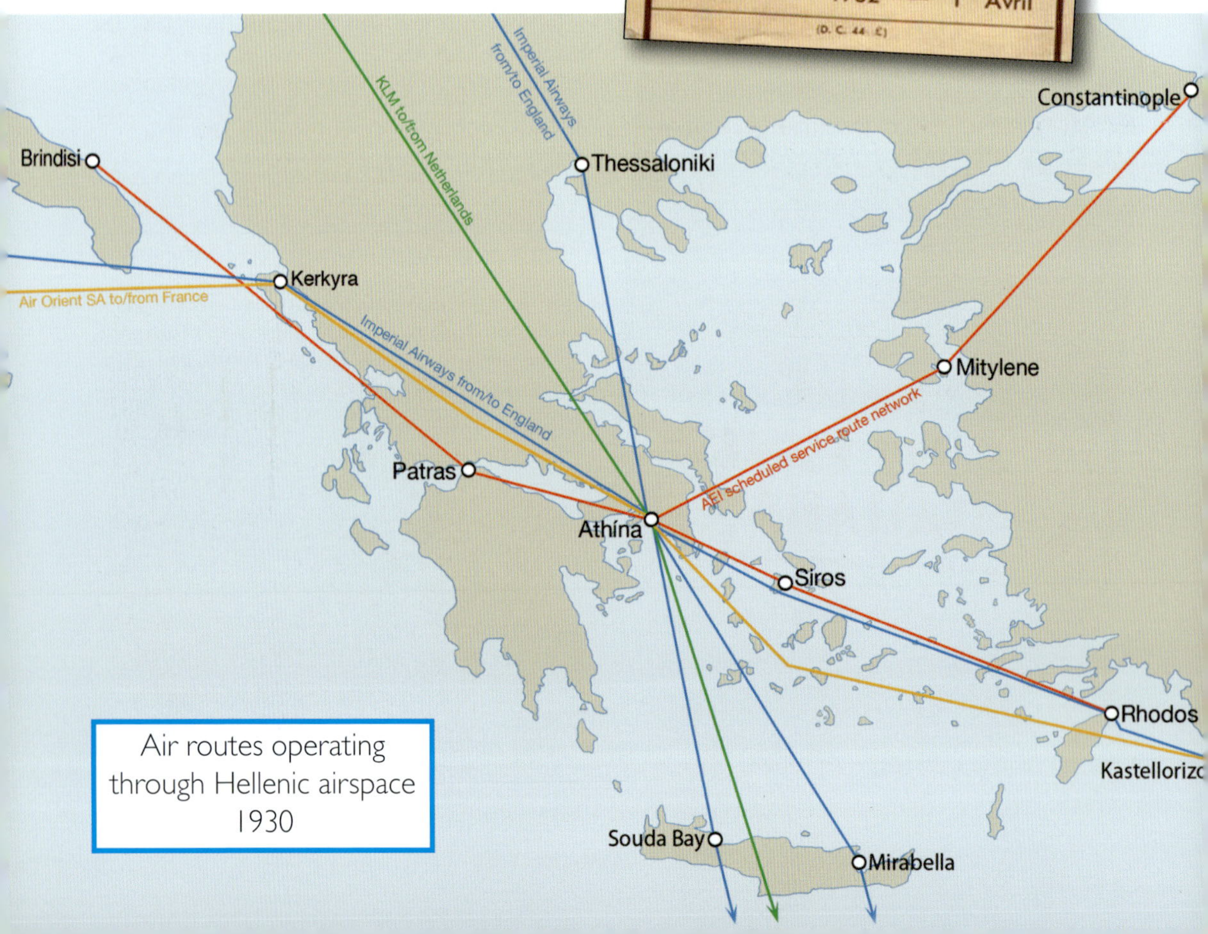

Air routes operating through Hellenic airspace 1930

I-ADZA of AEI wearing fleet number 1 seen during a turn-around. The aircraft was lost off Kerkyra on 25 January 1929.

Below and right: the AEI timetable for March 1933, showing the Brindisi - Athína - Ródos service and the Brindisi - Athína - Istanbul route. *(both authors collection)*

SOC. AN. AERO ESPRESSO ITALIANA

ORARIO PRIMAVERILE - HORAIRE DE PRINTEMPS - SPRING TIME TABLE

BRINDISI - ATENE - RODI

Martedì / Mardi / Tuesday		*Settimanale / Hebdomadaire / Weekly*		Venerdì / Vendredi / Friday
ore 10,45	p.	BRINDISI	a.	ore 13,35
ore 16,45	a.	ATENE	p.	ore 9,35
Mercoledì / Mercredi / Wednesday				
ore 7,45	p.	ATENE	a.	ore 9,30
ore 11,15	a.	RODI	p.	ore 6—

In vigore solo dal 18 marzo
En vigueur seulement du 18 mars
Service in force from 18th march

BRINDISI - ATENE - ISTANBUL

Giovedì / Jeudi / Thursday		*Settimanale / Hebdomadaire / Weekly*		Martedì / Mardi / Tuesday
		Roma	a.	ore 17,50
ore 10,45	p.	BRINDISI	a.	ore 12—
ore 16,45	a.	ATENE	p.	ore 8—
Venerdì / Vendredi / Friday				Lunedì / Lundi / Monday
ore 9,30	p.	ATENE	a.	ore 16,15
ore 16—	a.	ISTANBUL	p.	ore 10,15

Dal 1 al 18 marzo resta in vigore l'orario invernale
Du 1 au 18 mars est valable l'horaire d'hiver
From the 1st. until the 18th March the winter timetable is in force.

A richiesta ha luogo una fermata a PATRASSO fra Brindisi e Atene, a SYRA fra Atene e Rodi, a MITILENE fra Atene e Istanbul
Un arrêt intermédiaire sur demande aura lieu à PATRAS entre Brindisi et Athènes, à SYRA entre Athènes et Rhodes, à MYTILENE entre Athènes et Istanboul
Calls will be made at PATRAS between Brindisi and Athens at SYRA between Athens and Rhodes, at MITILENE between Athens and Istanbul, if inducement offers
Le ore indicate corrispondono all'ora locale - Heures locales - Local standard times

Coincidenze ferroviarie a Brindisi
(Senza garanzia)

- Da Roma, Napoli, Milano (W. L.), Venezia ed oltre: arr. ore 9,07.
- Per Napoli, Milano (W. L.), Venezia ed oltre: part. ore 13,46.
- Per Roma (W. L.) e Napoli (W. L): part. ore 18,50.

Correspondances avec les trains express à Brindisi
(Sans garantie)

- De Naples, Rome, Milan (W. L.), Venise, Paris, etc.: arr. 9 h. 07.
- Pour Naples, Milan (W. L.), Venise, Paris, etc.: dép. 13 h. 46.
- Pour Rome (W. L.) et Naples (W. L): dép. 18 h. 50.

Railways connections at Brindisi
(without responsability)

- From Rome, Naples, Milan (sleeping cars) Venise, London, Berlin, etc.: arr. 9,07. a. m.
- For Naples, Milan (sleeping cars) Venice, Paris, London, Berlin, etc.: dep. 1,46 p. m.
- For Rome and Naples (sleeping cars) dep. 6.50 p. m.

TARIFFA PASSEGGERI (in Lire it.)
TARIF PASSAGERS (en Lires it.)
PASSENGERS FARES (in it. Lira)

BRINDISI	500	700	970	1370	830	920
4	PATRASSO	200	470	900	330	580
4	2	ATENE	270	700	130	380
6	4	2	MITILENE	430	400	650
8	6	4	4	ISTANBUL	830	1000
6	4	2	4	6	SYRA	250
6	6	4	6	8	2	RODI

TARIFFA MERCI (per kg. in Lire it.)
TARIF MESSAGERIES (par kg. en Lires it.)
FREIGHT RATES (for kg. in it. Lira)

Trasporti accessori
Dalle città agli idroscali e viceversa (compresi nella tariffa):

BRINDISI - motoscafo dalla banchina Hôtel Internazionale: partenza ore 10,15.
ATENE - autobus dall' Hôtel Grande Bretagne.
ISTANBUL - autobus dall' Hôtel Tokatlian e Pera Palace: part. ore 9.

Service des autobus
Des villes aux hydrescales et retour (compris dans le tarif):

BRINDISI - à 10 h. 15 un bateau à moteur quittera le quai devan l'Hôtel International.
ATHENES - service d'autobus de l'Hôtel Grande Bretagne.
ISTANBOUL - à 9 h. un autobus partira de l'Hôtel Pera Palace et Tokatlian.

Autobus and Motor-boat services
From the towns to the airports and viceversa (included in the fares)

BRINDISI - Motor boat leaves the pier opposite to the International Hotel at 10,15 a. m.
ATHENS - Motor car from Hotel Grande Bretagne.
ISTANBUL - Motor car leaves Hotel Pera Palace and Tokatlian at 9 a.m.

the Gulf of Heraklion and Mirabello Bay on the north coast of Crete and so thrust forward with their mail service to Australia.

Imperial Airways may have been restricted in their Italian overflights, but that did not mean the Hellenic services were being overlooked. Due to the relatively poor performance and reliability of the aircraft of the times, the flights tended to be over reasonably small 'hops' and avoided high altitude flying for passenger comfort. In the case of the Hellenic Republic, this meant using flying boats that avoided the mountainous central area of the country.

On 1 August 1926, the Rome-based Italian company AEI - Aero Espresso Italiana, or to give the airline its formal name of Societa Anonima Aero Expresso Italiana S.p.A. - started an experimental service from Brindisi to Istanbul via Athína, with intermediate stops at Patras and Mitylene on Lesbos using a Savoia-Marchetti S.55 flying boat flown by Umberto Maddalena. The service, when up to four different flying boats had been employed, lasted until 31 December 1926, possibly as a result of the loss of SA.55 I-APER near Athína a month earlier. The route was suspended until 1 May 1927.

Above: Passengers are helped ashore from AEI's Wal I-AZDH '6'. The somewhat perilous 'gangplank' and rough and ready boarding steps suggest this was at one of the intermediate stops. This aircraft was destroyed by fire in Mytiline Harbour on Lesbos on 10 June 1930.

Left: a poster from AEI advertising the airmail aspect to the service. *(both authors collection)*

AEI had been created in 1923 and initially used a fleet of six SA.55s. The Brindisi - Istanbul route continued until 1930, when on 1 April an extension from Athína to Ródos via Siros was flown, carrying passengers, freight and mail.

AEI also operated a fleet of ten CMASA - Construzioni Mecchaniche Aeronautiche SA - Wal flying boats. As with many other airlines of the period, AEI suffered a catalogue of losses and accidents that included the loss of I-ADZA on a flight from Brindisi to Athína on 27 January 1929 when the aircraft encountered a heavy thunderstorm en route and all eight people on board were lost at sea off Corfu. The same year, on 24 December, I-ADZB crashed into the Aegean and was destroyed. Then, on 10 June 1930 another Wal, I-AZDH was destroyed by fire during take off from Mitylene on Lesbos during a flight from Istanbul to Athína. As far as is known, all the occupants survived.

Three years later, on 18 July 1933, Wal I-AZEE was operating the scheduled passenger service from Athína to Ródos. The aircraft took off from Phaleron Bay at 3:10 pm and the crew proceeded to transmit their position by radio every ten minutes, but the transmission of signals stopped half an hour after departure while the aircraft was flying over the channel between Cape

Sounion and Makronissos island, where it was observed by ships passing by there.

At first, nobody was alarmed as the wireless apparatus could well have suddenly stopped functioning or the aircraft might have entered into what was sometimes called a 'zone of silence' where the short waves can be absorbed. Only after the Ródos Station reported no contact with the machine was received, uneasiness started to spread out but, again, the three-hour limit for the complete trip to Ródos was left to pass before any action was taken. Finally, when that time expired, and as the Syros Station - located seventy-eight nautical miles south-east of Athína - confirmed that the aircraft did not pass over the island, an alarm was issued at Phaleron.

Every effort of the Hellenic Air Force, warships and seaplanes failed to locate the flying boat or the two passengers and four crew members on board. The aircraft, mail, passengers or the crew was never found.

There was great speculation in the press as to the cause of the disappearance, especially in the daily Greek newspaper *Vradyni,* which insisted that the accident was caused by old engines and that the aircraft was operating at too low a level. Aero Espresso rejected both accusations.

It was into this environment that the forerunners to Olympic Airways was created.

Above and below: During the 1930s flying boats make use of the sheltered moorings offered by Castellorizo harbour. The houses and hillside behind make photographic identification easy. *(authors collection)*

Chapter Two

Birth Of The Hellenic Airlines

Ellinikí Etaireía Ennaréon Synkinitón AE (EEES)

The name may be somewhat difficult to pronounce, but in English it means Hellenic Aerial Communications Company and was also known as either Hellinki Etairea Enaerion Synhoinonion – HEES, or the French name Société Hellénique de Communications Aériennes – SHCA. The company was founded by the initiative of the Greek State on 9 July 1930 as a result of the Law 4809 of 5 June 1930.

The law was a confirmation of the agreement between the Hellenic State and the aviation company Ikaros, which had been formed in November 1925, almost certainly as a handling company in the first instance for some of the foreign airlines who were about to enter the Republic. The new law gave information regarding the development of aviation in Hellenic Republic. It also gave the company permission to purchase aircraft from abroad.

EEES was bought for 1,000,000 drachma (Δϱχ) from Ikaros N. Kampanis & Co. The general concession, which had a validity of sixteen years, granted the privilege to transport passengers, goods and mail not only over Hellas, but also to Crete, Egypt, Yugoslavia, Italy, Albania and Bulgaria.

The basic air routes were awarded to EEES were:

1. In co-operation with the Yugoslavian airline Aeroput: Athína – Thessaloniki – Beograd (Belgrade) – Budapest service.
2. In co-operation with the Romanian airline company a service from Thessaloniki – Sofia – Nisch – Bucuresti.
3. In co-operation with the Turkish- Italian airline company Aero Expresso Italiana SA Brindisi – Thessaloniki – Constantinople– Ankara – Adana – Alexandrette – Aleppo.

If the partners were not able to pool with EEES, the Greek company had the right to fly the service alone. The stock capital was 28,500,000 Δϱχ. fully paid and mainly supplied by the Army's Pension Fund, the Post Office's Saving Bank, the Railways of Thessaly, Junkers Flugzeugwerk AG and the National Bank of Greece. In total there were 19,000 shares, worth 1,500 Δϱχ. each. The Hellenic Parliament passed Law No. 82462 on 24 December 1930 which accepted the articles of association of EEES.

Nikolaos Kampanis, the owner of the Ikaros company, joined EEES as the General Manager and remained in post until 5 September 1936, when a Mr Vizas succeeded him. Chairman of the Board of Directors was the Governor of the National Bank of Greece, Jean Drossopoulos, Vice-Chairman, Nikolaos Carolou and Managing Director, Theodore Bogdanos. Directors were General A Frandjis, General C Mazarakis Enian, Admiral A Gonatas, Const Isailloff, E Lambrinoudis, D Lykiardopoulos, P Macris and E Paparighopoulos.

By October it became clear that the National Bank of Greece wanted to keep Junkers Flugzeugwerk AG off of the Board of Directors. It wanted the company to be Greek owned and run.

In November the Elliniki Etaireia Enaereon Synhinoion AE was granted its first subsidy: an annual sum of 660,000 Reichmarks from Germany depending on the kilometres flown per year. Once the company was formed salesmen from the Ford Motor Company who were agressively marketing their aviation products in Europe, offered the new concern a deal to obtain four Ford 5-AT tri-motors. There had been a whole range of legal problems between Junkers and Ford over the tri-motor designs. So similar were they that Junkers sued and won when Ford attempted to export an aircraft to Europe. In 1930, Ford countersued in Prague, and despite the possibility of anti-German sentiment, was decisively defeated a second time, with the court finding that Ford had infringed upon Junkers' patents.

The Board of Directors of the EEES was now at the point to make a decision regarding equipment, and not surprisingly it turned out to be a political one. On 17 January 1931, the Board decided to purchase four Junkers G.24he monoplanes. Dr Adolf Kottmeier contacted Junkers Flugzeugwerk AG and informed them of the final victory over the Ford Motor Company. The deal was mainly thanks to a favourable trade treaty with Germany and financial support by the Hellenic government.

All these aircraft were equipped with three 280 hp Junkers L.5 engines. Junkers Flugzeugwerk AG's Swedish sister company, AB Flygindustri in Limhamn near Malmö, constructed the parts of the four G.24s and transported them to Dessau for assembly. By mid-April the German pilots started the transfer of the aircraft from Germany to Hellas.

First to arrive was Flugkapitän Waldemar Koeder, who flew the first G.24 to Greece which had been allocated the Hellenic registration SY-BAM but this was never used, SX-ACA being applied instead. The second machine, SX-ACB, was flown out two weeks later by Flugkapitän Georg Jüterbock. Flugkapitän Walter Rotbe flew over the third aircraft, SX-ACD, on 28 and 29 May. The first leg of the flight was from Dessau via Wien to Budapest where he nightstopped. The next morning it was to Belgrade and Thessaloniki for customs clearance before flying on to Athína. In June the last Junkers G 24he, SX-ACE, was flown over by Flugkapitän Neuenhofen.

Right: the face of the EEES timetable.

Below: Junkers Ju.24he SX-ACB *Thessalonki* rests between flights, possibly at Tatoi. *(authors collection)*

On 1 June the air service Athína (Tatoi Airport) – Thessaloniki (Sedes Airport) was started up. The service was daily (except Sundays). Elliniki Etairea Enaerion Synkoinonion AE had not yet trained its own pilots; so four Germans pilots flew the aircraft, while training four Greek second pilots. The 370 km long air route was interesting, if not only because of the saving of time. By train the trip took ten and a half hours, but by air it was just over two hours. Furthermore, in Thessaloniki the Yugoslav airline company Aeroput offered a connection to Skoplje and Beograd (Belgrade).

On 23 November Elliniki Etaireia Enaereon Synhinoion AE opened a new three times a week new service running from Athína to Agrínio and Ioánnina.

Organisation of the air services was divided into three areas of responsibilities: the air force was in charge of communication, the Post Office was in charge of the weather reports and the company itself was in charge for the emergency landing grounds along the route. This organisation was perfect for the service to Thessaloniki, but on the second service to Agrínio and Ioánnina this was worse. Latter city was situated in an area surrounded by mountains. A service to this city was however regarded as vital. The city of Pátrai was to be included as well, but due to the difficulties in constructing an airfield here, this stopover had to be dropped.

The company had a financial year running from 1 July – 30 June, thus the results presented in printed material were either given for a calendar year or for a combination of two half years (1931-32, 1932-33, etc.). The financial year, figures for the first months of operation (up to 31 December 1931) were: 3,058 passengers, 21,558 kilogrammes of luggage, 9,061 kilogrammes of merchandises and 4,337 kilogrammes of mail. Regularity was 74.5%. The four aircraft flew a total of 131,074 kilometres (on 336 flights). The subsidy by the Hellenic

State was in 1931-32 14,549,000 Δρχ., being 42 Δρχ. per flown kilometre.

In 1932 the Elliniki Etairea Enaerion Synkoinonion AE network received specific numbers that related to specific flight as published in the Bradshaws International Air Guide: Air Service No. 442 for Athína – Agrínio – Ioánnina and Air Service No 443 for Thessaloniki – Athína. In the German Luftkursbuch timetable published in Germany for 1932 the schedules were published for the services during the summer month (1 May-15 October):

442 Athína – Agrínio – Ioánnina: Weekdays

08.45 am	dep	Athína	arr	4.05 pm
10.15 am	arr	Agrínio	dep	2.35 pm
10.45 am	dep	Agrínio	arr	2.05 pm
11.35 am	arr	Ioánnina	dep	1.15 pm

Left: Agrinion civil airport at Dokiki, was one of the oldest Hellenic airports. It operated mainly as a stopover for the Athína-Ioannina-Kerkira flight. Here passengers pose in from of Junkers G.24 SX-ACA *Athínai.*

Centre: The interior of a G.24, looking towards the rear of the aircraft. Of interest is the curved roof, the 'fishing net' area on both sides of the fuselage for the hat and light luggage stowage and the single, leather-covered seats.

Below: Junkers G.24he SX-ACD Ioannina

Opposite page: an EEES luggage label that shows one of the few known examples of their logo. *(all authors collection)*

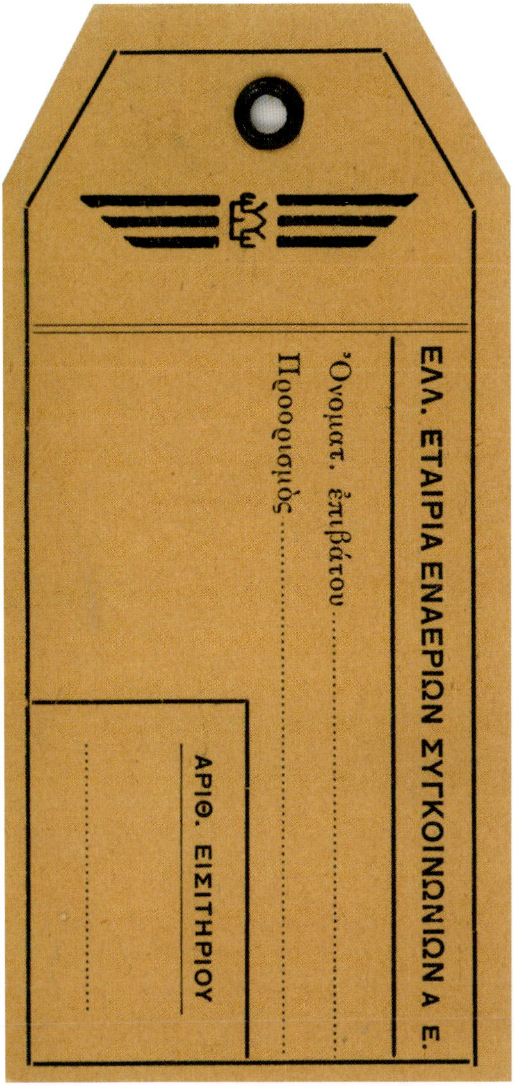

443. Thessaloniki – Athína: weekdays

5.20 pm	dep.	Thessaloniki	arr	09.10 am
6.30 pm	arr	Athína	dep	07.00 am

For Air Service No 442 the departure time for Ioánnina was in the period 16-30 September set at 1245 pm. On the other service there was a change in the schedule on Thursday (period 1 June-31 July). The Junkers G 24he departed at 4.30am. Prices were reasonable and kept just under the prices of a railway ticket, including seat- or sleeper reservations. Thessaloniki – Athína was Δϱχ.822 one-way and 1,545 Δϱχ return. The price for the service to Agrínio was Δϱχ. 450 one-way and return Δϱχ. 825. From Athína to Ioánnina one paid Δϱχ. 716 one way and return Δϱχ.1,331.

In 1932 1,110 flights were made and 414,010 kilometres flown. The number of passengers rose to 7,892 an increase of 157%. The aircraft carried 79,540 kilogrammes of luggage, 98,061 kilogrammes of merchandise and 6,637 kilogrammes of mail. The regularity went up to 89% and that meant 988 flights went without any delays. As in 1931, no accidents occurred.

Between 1 January and 14 March 1933, air traffic in Hellas was paralysed due to flooding of the major airfields. On 15 March the EEES re-opened its network and continued to fly until 20 December of that year. Both Ioánnina and

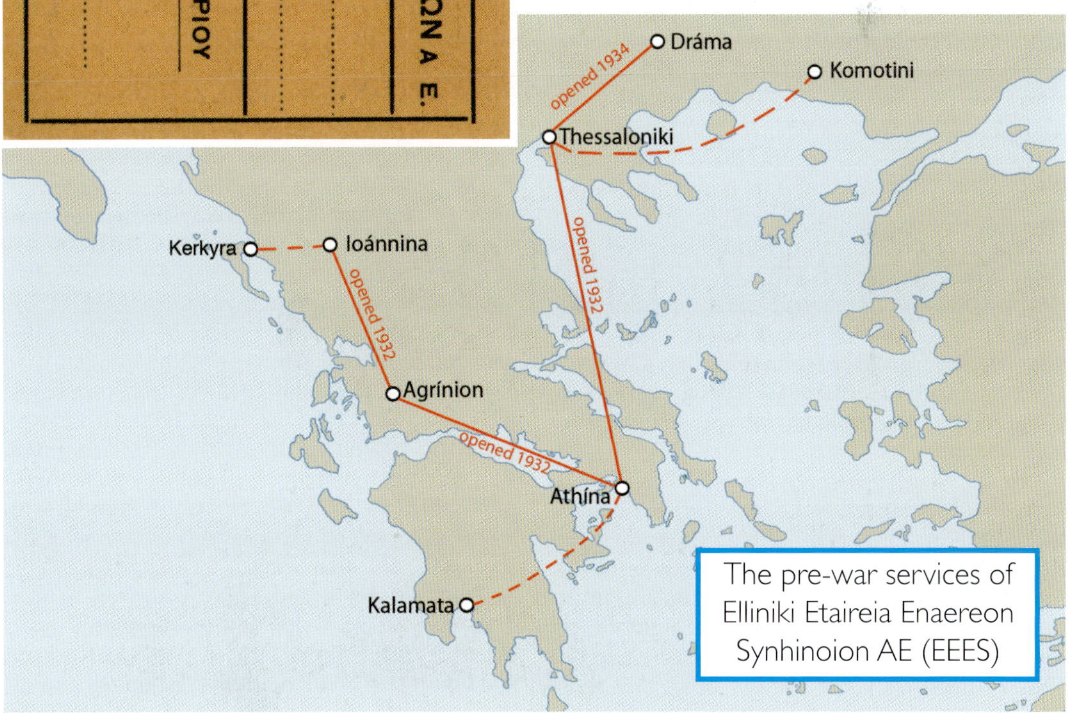

The pre-war services of Elliniki Etaireia Enaereon Synhinoion AE (EEES)

A 1936 aerial view of the flying boat base at Gouvia Bay, Kerkira. The facility had been built in 1931, for the use of Air France, and later Ala Littoria. The giant aircraft hangar was acquired by Technical and Aeronautical Exploitations (TAE), dismantled and moved to Athína as a maintenance facility. The structure was later used by Olympic Airways and is still in existence in 2018! (*ΠΟΛΚ.ΕΟΑ*).

Thessaloniki were regularly served, but the city of Agrínio was only served on demand. The shorter season also meant a decrease of the traffic results. With the four aircraft 376,629 km were flown on 1,007 flights. 6,498 passengers were transported, as well as 64,126 kilogrammes of luggage, 135,675 kilogrammes of freight and 9,985 kilogrammes of mail. It is worth noticing that the transportation of freight and airmail increased. Also the regularity increased to 94.5%.

In April 1934 EEES's Junkers G 24hes had flown 1,000,000 kilometres since their delivery in 1931. The Chief Pilot of the company, the German Georg Jüterbock, and the Chief of Operations, the German Mr Illner, were both congratulated by Junkers Werke AG for this achievement.

On 23 May 1934 the Athína – Thessaloniki service was extended to Dráma, 140 kilometres north-east of Thessaloniki being flown three times a week. This was the only change in the schedule that year, but due to the increase of the number of passengers, and the number of kilometres flown, the Hellenic State increased the subsidy. Previously, for the year 1932-33 it went up to 5.9 million Δρχ, 1933-34 to 7.9 million Δρχ, and 1934-35 to 9.9 million Δρχ. The Government had great interest in the EEES and supported it all the way. This made it very easy for EEES to increase its business. For the year 1934 the results were again satisfying: 1,119 flights performed, 370,961 kilometres flown, and 7,763 passengers, 309,789 kilogrammes of merchandise and 12,658 kilogrammes of mail transported. Again no accidents occurred on any of the services.

On 1 April 1935 the representative of the Greek Government at EEES, M Papadopulos, became Technical Director of the company. In November of that year the majority of the shares, then in hands of the National Bank of Greece, were transferred to the Army's Pension Fund. This was done by request of the EEES and made it possible to increase the stock capital with 500,000 Δρχ. The increase and the move of the shares should also lead to an extension of the network to Egypt and Turkey, as well as new domestic air service. New destinations under planning were Peloponnese (Kalamata), Kerkyra, Alexandropoli and Komotini. The opening of air

Junkers Ju.523m, thought to be SX-ACH *(authors collection)*

routes to Kerkyra and Kalamata were planned for the 1936 season. Together with the change of the shares, Mr Papadopulos changed his position within the company and became General Manager.

By now most of the flight staff were Greek: pilots were Ioannis Theologis, Zissis Linos, Konstantinos Loukidis, Evangelos Papadakos, Ioannis Stathis, Ioannis Tsoukas, George Fragistas and Patroklos Hampas. The flight engineers were: Charalambos Makris, Dionysios Metaxas, Nikitas Bazaios, Athanasios Rizos and Konstantinos Stathis. The radio operators were Petros Garyfalakis, Loukianos Gortsidis, Dimitrios Leonis, Panagiotis Michhopoulos and Evangelos Makris.

The Hellenic and Italian Governments signed in 1935 a new Air Agreement, which would lead to an extension of the service Athína to Brindisi to Napoli and Marseille (France). On the other side the Italians were allowed to continue from Thessaloniki to Sofija.

Regularity on the EEES-routes stayed constant around 90 %. The Athínai – Thessaloniki service had a regularity of 98%, Thessaloniki – Dráma 90% and Athína – Ioánnina 93%. In 1935 1,372 flights were performed and 413,000 km flown. The company was approaching the 10,000 passengers per year. In 1935 a total of 9,075 passengers were reached. The four aircraft still flew without any incidents on the two routes and transported that year 90,346 kilogrammes ofluggage, 217,583 kilogrammes of freight and 15,930 kilogrammes of mail. This year a profit of Δϱχ 5,530,545.50 was made.

In 1936 the service to Thessaloniki was flown twice a day, with three times a week a connection to Dráma. The Ioánnina service was flown four times weekly, with twice weekly a stopover at Agrínio. No new services were opened this year either.

Another view of Junkers G.24he SX-ACD *Ioannina*. It is interesting to note the markings on the tail, and the way the fin is outlined. *(authors collection)*

Junkers Ju.52/3m SX-ACH of EEES in the hangar at Tatoi. *(authors collection)*

The Greek State and the Elliniki Etairea Enaerion Synkoinonion AE signed that year a new agreement in which the above-mentioned increase of the stock capital was regulated and the company was allowed to trade its five years old Junkers G 24he for the more modern Junkers Ju-52/3m. It was to order two Junkers Ju-52/3mges for delivery in 1938. Meanwhile, 196 flights (covering 72,520 kilometres) were made by a hired Junkers Ju-52/3m of Deutsche Lufthansa AG. The aircraft flew on the Athína – Thessaloniki service on which a regularity of 96% was achieved. In addition 510 flights were made by the Junkers G 24he on the line, flying 190,004 kilometres. On the air route Thessaloniki – Dráma 217 flights (30,380 km) and on the route Athína – Agrínio – Ioánnina 420 flights (114,069 kilometres) were made. On 3 special flights 1,365 km was flown. Some of the results suffered a small decrease: 8,207 passengers, 89,785 kilogrammes of luggage, 141,740 kilogrammes of freight and 17,034 kilogrammes of mail. As mentioned before, Nic Kampanis left the company on 5 September and was succeeded by Mr Vizas. In April a meeting headed by the Prime Minister and the Minister of Aviation, J Metaxas, had a special mission to discuss the possibility of extending the services to Kerkyra, Sofija, Beograd and Egypt, and to order the two Junkers Ju-52/3mges. According to the Director of Aviation, Mr Photopoulos, EES could easily extend its network without burdening the National Budget if it co-operated with foreign airline companies. Poland's LOT and Deutsche Lufthansa AG were willing to co-operate when the Greek Government gave permission to the airline companies to fly to Athína. In 1937 negotiations started with Rumania to come to a similar agreement for a service to Bucuresti. After the meeting it was clear that the

The German Luftwaffe operated an inter-island mail and essential item service around the Aegean as a forerunner of what was to come. Here a Luftwaffe Ju.52/3m equipped with floats operates a mail flight in the harbour at Vathy, on the island of Samos. *(authors collection)*

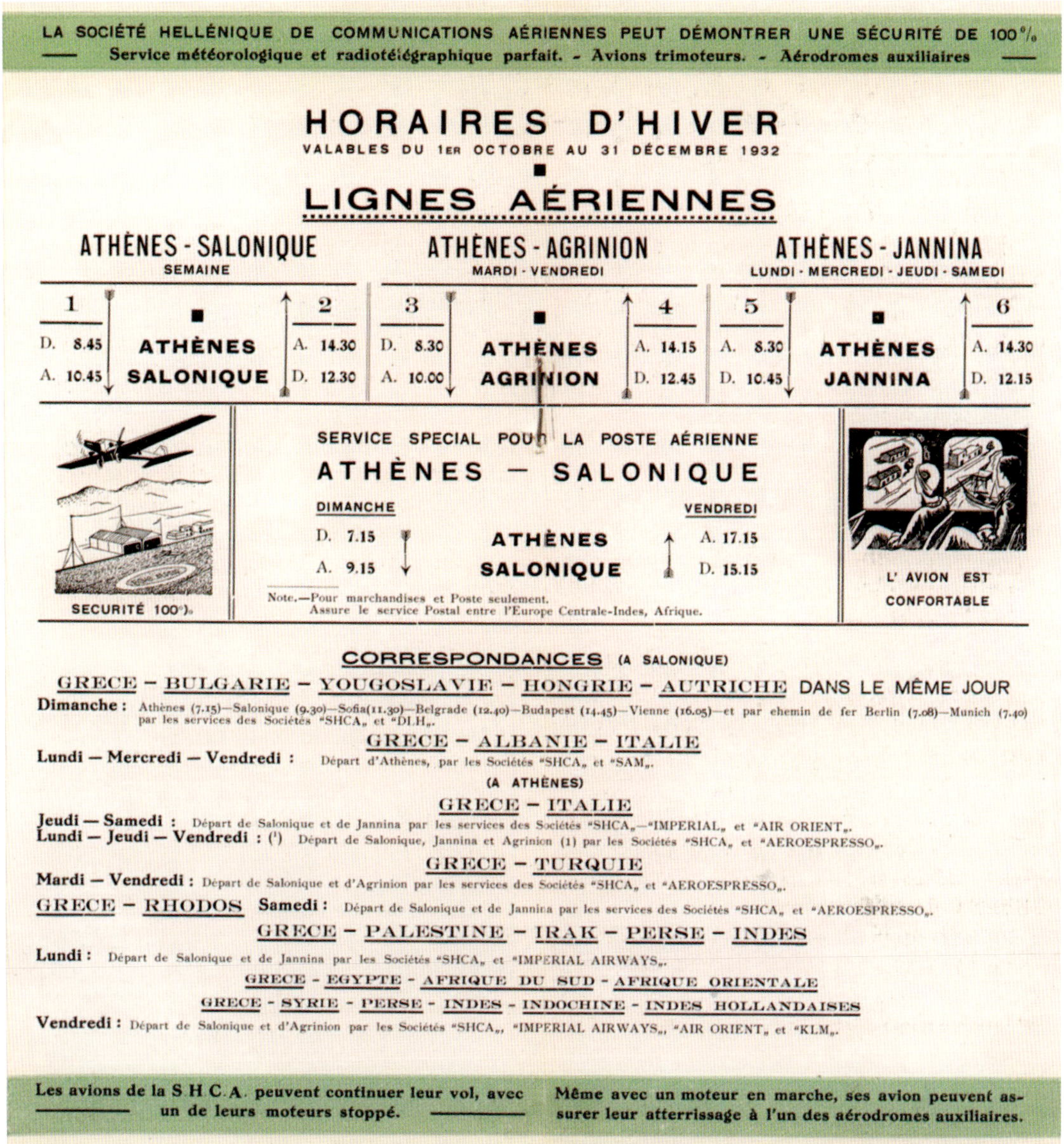

LA SOCIÉTÉ HELLÉNIQUE DE COMMUNICATIONS AÉRIENNES PEUT DÉMONTRER UNE SÉCURITÉ DE 100 %

Service météorologique et radiotélégraphique parfait. - Avions trimoteurs. - Aérodromes auxiliaires

HORAIRES D'HIVER

VALABLES DU 1ER OCTOBRE AU 31 DÉCEMBRE 1932

LIGNES AÉRIENNES

ATHÈNES - SALONIQUE
SEMAINE

1		2
D. 8.45	ATHÈNES	A. 14.30
A. 10.45	SALONIQUE	D. 12.30

ATHÈNES - AGRINION
MARDI - VENDREDI

3		4
D. 8.30	ATHÈNES	A. 14.15
A. 10.00	AGRINION	D. 12.45

ATHÈNES - JANNINA
LUNDI - MERCREDI - JEUDI - SAMEDI

5		6
A. 8.30	ATHÈNES	A. 14.30
D. 10.45	JANNINA	D. 12.15

SECURITÉ 100 %

SERVICE SPECIAL POUR LA POSTE AÉRIENNE

ATHÈNES — SALONIQUE

DIMANCHE		VENDREDI
D. 7.15	ATHÈNES	A. 17.15
A. 9.15	SALONIQUE	D. 15.15

Note.—Pour marchandises et Poste seulement.
Assure le service Postal entre l'Europe Centrale-Indes, Afrique.

L' AVION EST CONFORTABLE

CORRESPONDANCES (A SALONIQUE)

GRECE — BULGARIE — YOUGOSLAVIE — HONGRIE — AUTRICHE DANS LE MÊME JOUR

Dimanche : Athènes (7.15)—Salonique (9.30)—Sofia(11.30)—Belgrade (12.40)—Budapest (14.45)—Vienne (16.05)—et par chemin de fer Berlin (7.08)—Munich (7.40) par les services des Sociétés "SHCA" et "DLH".

GRECE — ALBANIE — ITALIE

Lundi — Mercredi — Vendredi : Départ d'Athènes, par les Sociétés "SHCA" et "SAM".

(A ATHÈNES)

GRECE — ITALIE

Jeudi — Samedi : Départ de Salonique et de Jannina par les services des Sociétés "SHCA"—"IMPERIAL" et "AIR ORIENT".
Lundi — Jeudi — Vendredi : (1) Départ de Salonique, Jannina et Agrinion (1) par les Sociétés "SHCA" et "AEROESPRESSO".

GRECE — TURQUIE

Mardi — Vendredi : Départ de Salonique et d'Agrinion par les services des Sociétés "SHCA" et "AEROESPRESSO".

GRECE — RHODOS **Samedi :** Départ de Salonique et de Jannina par les services des Sociétés "SHCA" et "AEROESPRESSO".

GRECE — PALESTINE — IRAK — PERSE — INDES

Lundi : Départ de Salonique et de Jannina par les Sociétés "SHCA" et "IMPERIAL AIRWAYS".

GRECE - EGYPTE - AFRIQUE DU SUD - AFRIQUE ORIENTALE

GRECE - SYRIE - PERSE - INDES - INDOCHINE - INDES HOLLANDAISES

Vendredi : Départ de Salonique et d'Agrinion par les Sociétés "SHCA", "IMPERIAL AIRWAYS", "AIR ORIENT" et "KLM".

Les avions de la S.H.C.A. peuvent continuer leur vol, avec un de leurs moteurs stoppé.

Même avec un moteur en marche, ses avion peuvent assurer leur atterrissage à l'un des aérodromes auxiliaires.

Government wanted to open up the sky above Greece and allow as many airline companies as possible to open services to Hellas.

The domestic services continued to be flown by EEES. In 1937 the service to Dráma was not operated. The planned extension of the service Athína – Ioánnina to Kérkira was not opened either. In the season 1936-37 the Junkers G 24he, SX-ACE *Patras* flew 769 hours and this was the best performance of the company's aircraft up to that date.

On 21 December 1937 the Greek Air Ministry and EEES signed a new agreement replacing the old one of 1936. EEES was to receive a subsidy for the purchase of three Junkers Ju-52/3ms and could keep its present fleet of Junkers G 24he. The latter aircraft would not have to be changed for Junkers Ju-52/3m. EEES ordered therefore with Junkers Flugzeug- und Motoren Werke AG three brand new Junkers Ju-52/3mges for delivery in 1938. The first two Greek pilots were sent to Germany for training and could start flying on the aircraft upon their return in Greece.

During1938 the same routes as previously have been operated. The result for the year 1937-38 are known and given here: 627 passengers carried, 63,995 kilogrammes of luggage, 205,140 kilogrammes of freight and 8,071 kilogrammes of mail transported. The aircraft made 246 flights and flew 346,060 km on the domestic services.

A set of new legislation replaced the Law 4809 from 1930. Now the EEES was given a subsidy per flown kilometre of Drs 36.33 with a maximum of Drs 16,311,000 per year. Of this subsidy Drs 900,000 was used for the purchase of spare engines for the Junkers Ju-52/3mge, which were to be delivered that year. The Greek Government paid for the three Junkers Ju-52/3mges.

In January 1938 EEES signed a pool agreement with the Egyptian Misr Airworks for the air route Thessaloniki – Athína – Kreta – Alexandria to be flown twice weekly.

On 30 June 1938 the first Junkers Ju-52/3mge, SX-ACF was handed over to the EEES at Dessau, Germany and flown to Athína, where it arrived one day later. In July and August the next two Junkers Ju-52/3mges were delivered to Athína. They were allotted SX-ACH and SX-ACI. The fleet consisted out of four Junkers G 24hes and three Junkers Ju-52/3mges. The Greek Junkers Ju-52/3mge had three 525-550hp 9 cylinder air-cooled BMW Hornet engines which gave it a maximum speed of 315 kilometres per hour. The network in 1938 had a length of 1,228 kilometres on which 1,419 flights were made and 375,049 kilometres flown. The company transported 7,410 passengers, 312,007 kilogrammes of freight and luggage and 7,552 kilogrammes of mail. Regularity stopped at 90.2%. The occupancy was 70.4%.

On 12 or 15 April 1939 the new Junkers Ju-52/3m SX-ACF opened the new air service from Athína to Megalokastron (or Heraklion, the information is confusing on this point) on the island of Kreta (Crete). It was flown three times a week. Misr Airwork started the service from Megalokastron to Alexandria (Egypt) and thus

Right: Lt Col Charles A Gibson, from Sacremento California chats with local children after giving them candy. He was one of the pilots who had just flown in to Kalimaki Airfield with British paratroopers bringing glider-towed infantry in to the area after the Germans had been routed.

Below: C-47s bring in troops and supplies for the people of Athína. The TAE hangar, originally built on Kérkira can be seen on the extreme right of the picture. *(both USAAF via authors collection)*

EEES's first international route was in operation. In 1939 the service Athína – Thessaloniki – Dráma was split up in two separate services with one flight daily (except on Sundays) to each destination. The Thessaloniki service used the new Junkers Ju-52/3m while Dráma was served by the older Junkers G 24he. In Dráma there was a connecting bus service linking the flights to Kavala.

On Monday, Wednesday and Friday the direct service Athínai – Ioánnina was operated mainly by Junkers G.24he. On Tuesday, Thursday and Saturday EEES flew the Athínai – Agrínio – Ioánnina service. Again the opening of a service to Kérkira was planned, but due to the poor drainage at the Kérkira landing ground the service could still not be started. The French airline Air France also served Kérkira, but this was by flying boats. Unfortunately EEES had no flying boats and so had to wait until the airport was suitable for use by landplanes.

Any services for 1940 have not been found, but it is likely that the air route operated in 1939 were continued in 1940. Results are however not known. Italian forces attacked Greece in November 1940 and the Greek Government confiscated the seven aircraft of EEES. The attack was followed by a German invasion starting on 6 April 1941 and on 23 April the Greece surrendered. The three Greek Junkers Ju 52/3ms were taken over by the German Wehrmacht and handed over to the Luftwaffe.

On 13 June 1941 the Deutsche Lufthansa AG took over the 9,690 shares of EEES from the Greek State at the price of 1,500 Δϱχ per share. Deutsche Lufthansa AG obtained through the buying of the shares 51% of the company. In May 1941, just before the take-over by the Deutsche Lufthansa AG, the EEES had received a new concession for the next twenty years, that is, up to 27 May 1961. On 29 August 1941 Deutsche Lufthansa AG asked for an extraordinary meeting of share holders were the new articles of association were accepted and a new Board of Directors chosen.

When 1941-42 the Greek drachma lost its value, Deutsche Lufthansa AG offered the company a new Junkers Ju-52/3m for its shares, if a new domestic air route was opened. EEES

In the waist position of this 40th Bomb Wing B-17 Flying Fortress, refugees in need of urgent attention are flown by the American Army Air Force into Athína. *(USAAF via authors collection)*

however, never took up its regular services. Nor did the new Junkers Ju-52/3m come. On 13 May 1944 a new agreement replaced the older ones, but this had no further influence. EEES stopped all activities and after the war the company did not return on the scene.

A New airport for Athína; and new competition for passengers.

Construction of a new aiport for the Athína area began in 1938. Known as Ellinikon International Airport, sometimes spelled Hellinikon, was the international airport of Athína, Greece for sixty years up until 2001, when it was replaced by the new Athína International Airport 'Eleftherios Venizelos'. The airport was located seven kilometres south of Athína, almost on the coast and just west of Glyfada. It was named after the village of Elliniko, now a suburb of Athína. The airport eventually had an official capacity of 11 million passengers per year, but had served 13.5 million passengers per year during its last year of operations.

The Germans - in the guise of the National Socialists - invaded Greece in 1941, and Kalamaki Airfield - as the site was then known - was used as a Luftwaffe air base during the occupation. The airfield was attacked by both the Americans and the British.

After the war, the Hellenic government allowed the United States of America to use the airport from 1945 until 1993. The airport underwent another name-change in 1945, when it became known as Hassani Airport, it was used by the United States Army Air Forces as early as 1 October, as a base of operations for Air Transport Command flights between Rome, Italy and points in the Middle East.

Kalamaki Airfield - as Ellinikon Airport was known during the war - before it was attacked by the American Army Air Force on 6 December 1943. The village of Elliniko is towards the top left of the picture; Glyfada is towards the bottom right. Both runways - towards the lower left of the picture - remained in roughly the same alignment for the entire airports' life. Poseidonos Avenue can be seen running along the coast. (USAAF)

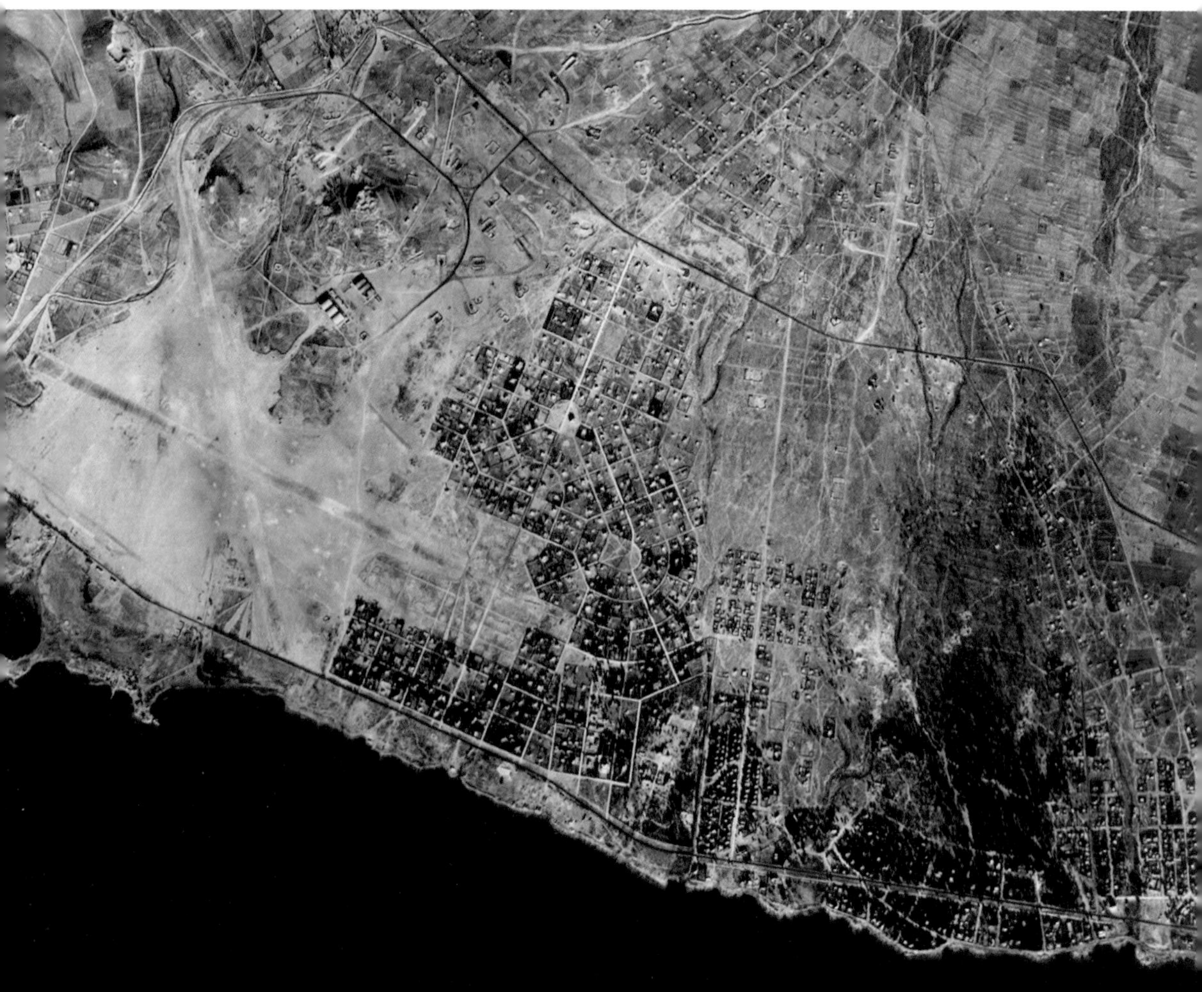

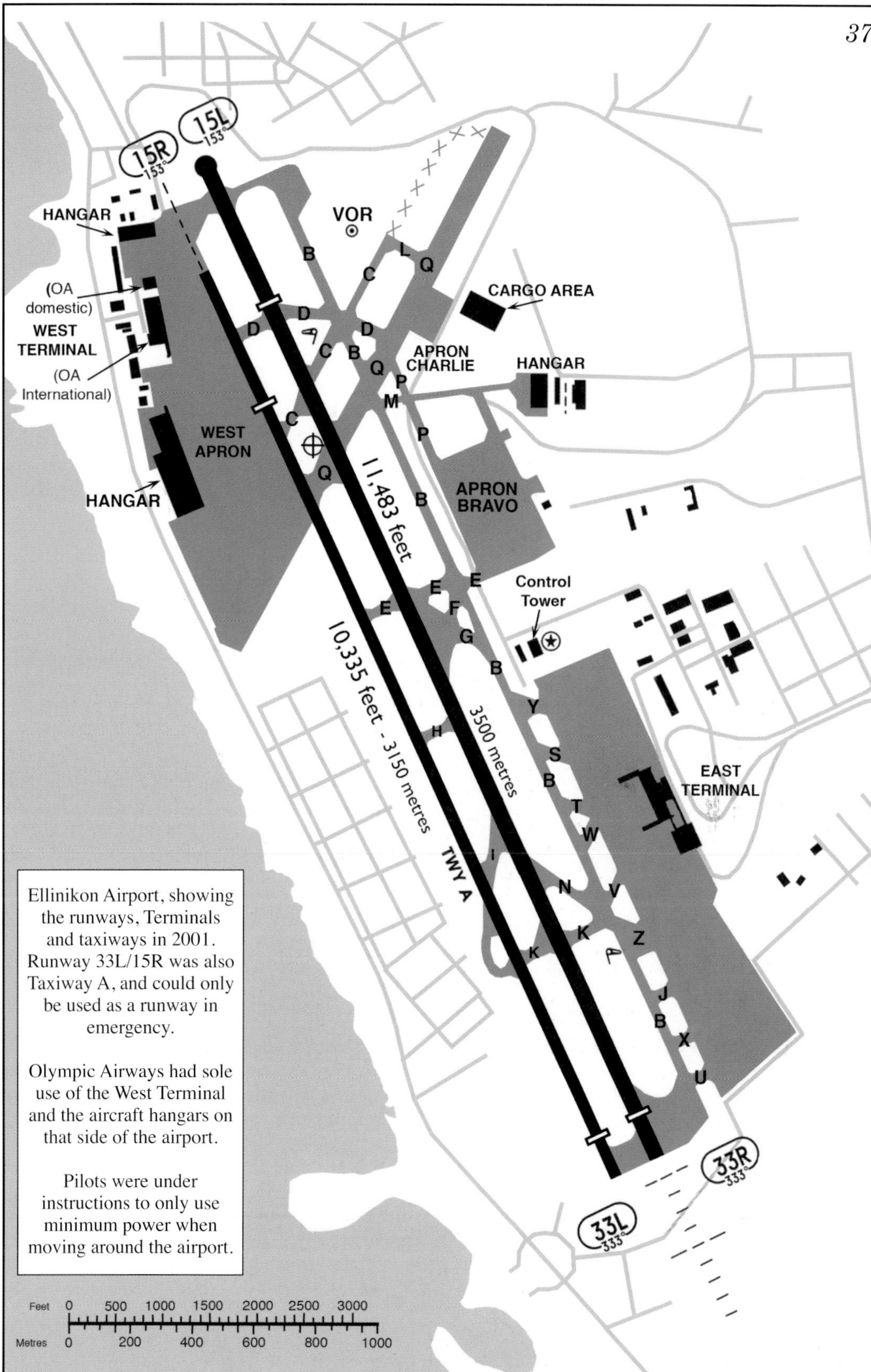

Ellinikon Airport, showing the runways, Terminals and taxiways in 2001. Runway 33L/15R was also Taxiway A, and could only be used as a runway in emergency.

Olympic Airways had sole use of the West Terminal and the aircraft hangars on that side of the airport.

Pilots were under instructions to only use minimum power when moving around the airport.

Ellinkikon Airport as it was in 1998. *(via Spiros Papadopoulos Collection)*

A semi-permanent USAAF presence was established in May 1947 as the facility was being reconstructed to facilitate Marshall Plan aid to Greece and Turkey. On 5 October 1948, the USAF assigned the Military Air Transport Service 1632nd Air Base Squadron to the airport with ten C-47 Skytrain cargo aircraft being based at the airport.

A new control tower opened in 1951, and by 1954 with the end of Marshall Plan, the United States Air Forces in Europe 7206th Air Base Squadron (later Group) was assigned to the airport. Commercial airline service returned to the facility in 1956 with the airport being turned over to Greek civil aviation authorities. The airport was renamed Athína International Airport, and the USAF used a small part of the airport for military cargo use, along with United States diplomatic air traffic.

The tarmac runways were originally 5,900 feet or 1,798 metres long. The northwest-southeast runway, then known as 16/34, was lengthened to 2,250 metres and eventually, as 15L/33R, to 3,500 metres long. The parallel taxiway to the west of the main runway was developed as a second 15/33 runway but was mainly used as a taxiway.

The early terminal area was near the coast road and evntually became known as the West Terminal, used exclusively by Olympic Airways. All other carriers used the East Terminal which was designed by Eero Saarinen and opened on 29 June, 1969. It comprised a main building with 20,225 square metres of floor area, an arrivals building of 3,444 square metres and charter building of 3,400 square metres.

Eero Saarinen (1910-1961) began the design for Athína Airport after his more famous airport terminal buildings for TWA in New York and Dulles in Chantilly, Virginia were already underway. Instead of the soaring, curvilinear forms of these works, Saarinen opted for a more restrained design at Athína. The preliminary sketches show how the columnar rhythm and load-bearing, post and lintel construction of Greek temple architecture served as an initial inspiration. In a letter to Solon Ghikas, the Greek Minister of Communications and Public Works and the project's client, Saarinen admitted that the airport design was '*...a bit influenced by the beautiful monasteries of Athos*.' He probably had in mind the way in which the Mount Athos Monastery buildings descend their steeply sloping site and present their principal façades to the sea. The Athína Airport site sloped gently toward the airfield and Saarinen used this condition to provide entrance at the second floor level, giving users the choice of mounting to the mezzanine level or descending to the departures and arrivals floor below. And Saarinen insisted that the principal façade should face the airfield, welcoming passengers to Greece. Saarinen sought to further link the airport to its location through the planned use of local Pentellic marble (the white stone of the Parthenon) as part of the concrete aggregate used for construction and for the desks and floors on the interior. But that is getting ahead of the story.

In 1947 the Hellenic Parliament determined to bring into existance three additional airlines: Hellenic Airlines (Ελληνικαί Αεροπορικαί Συγκοινωνίαι, ΕΛΛ.Α.Σ.), Air Transport of Greece (Αεροπορικαί Μεταφοραί Ελλάδος, AME) and Daedalus Airlines (Δαίδαλος).

The Scottish Connection - Hellenic Airlines
Scottish Aviation was founded at Prestwick in 1935 by the Duke of Hamilton and Wing Commander D P McIntyre to undertake flying training. During the war, the company operated a very large number of aeroplanes, both single and multi-engined, on various training courses for Royal Air Force personnel, and these courses covered flying training, instrument flying and navigation. The company was also responsible for the development of Prestwick Airport, and after the end of the Second World War Scottish Aviation turned its attention to several other activities, including the design and construction of the Pioneer range of aircraft and to airline operations. Prestwick Airport, though, was taken over by the Ministry of Civil Aviation from Scottish Aviation on 1 April 1946, despite the fact that the private company had very adventurous plans for the large scale development of the airport into a major European airport. Scottish

Hellenic Airlines' SX-DAA *'Maid of Athens'* undergoes maintenance at Prestwick Airport. *(Simon Peters Collection)*

A pair of poor quality, yet historically important images.
Left: King Paul of Greece, who had just ascended the throne, and Queen Frederika accept the delivery of SX-DAA - a civilianised B-24 Liberator to Hellenic Airlines. Reports suggest that this picture was taken at London's Heathrow Airport in 1947, but there is some doubt as to the accuracy of that statement, as Heathrow was undergoing major construction work and airline services were operating out of nearby Northolt.

Hellenic Airlines' SX-DAA at Northolt, London. *(both author's collection)*

Airlines was founded as the airline division of Scottish Aviation in January 1946. The airline was one of the first companies to commence operations after the war, and in order to start these operations a fleet of Dakota and Liberator aircraft was acquired.

The closing months of 1947 saw Scottish Airlines involved in the formation of two new European airlines - Hellenic Airlines and Luxembourg Airlines. On 21 November - although some sources say 13 September - an agreement was signed in Athína between the pension funds of the Hellenic Navy (Πολεμικό Ναυτικό, Polemikó Naftikó), the Hellenic Army (Ελληνικός Στρατός, Ellinikós Stratós), the Hellenic Air Force (Πολεμική Αεροπορία, Polemikí Aeroporía) the Hellenic Civil Service, and Scottish Aviation. This agreement was for the formation of Hellenic Airlines (Ελληνικαί Αεροπορικαί Συγκοινωνίαι) also known by its literal name, Greek Air Transport, often abbreviated ΕΛΛ.Α.Σ. in Greek, in which the

Hellenic Airlines' SX-DAB taxi's past the viewing area at Northolt. *(authors collection)*

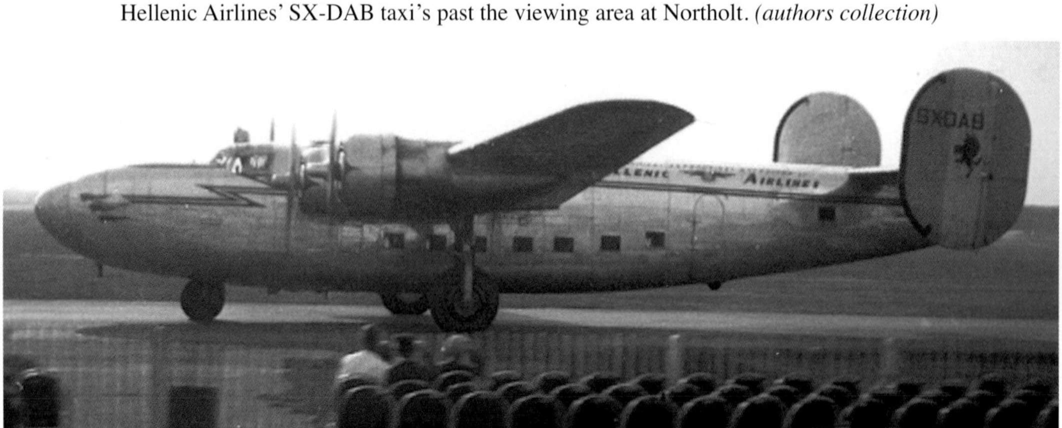

Groundcrew mechanics with Hellenic Airlines' DC-3 SX-BBD. The aircraft was formerly G-AJBD of Scottish Aviation. (*ΠΟΛΚ.ΕΟΑ*).

four pension funds held sixty per cent of the shares, while Scottish Aviation held the remaining forty per cent. Scottish Aviation provided this new Greek company with technical and administrative personnel and aircraft for its services, along with the responsibility for recruiting and training at Prestwick of Greek personnel to take over from British employees at a date some time in the future. Services started in February 1948, and initially Hellenic Airlines linked Athína with Crete, Larissa, London Northolt (non-stop), Ródos and Thessaloniki. The fleet used a pair of civilianised Consolidated B-24 Liberators - termed LB-30s - and six Douglas DC-3s.

Throughout 1948 just one of the Liberators served with Hellenic Airlines but, with the return of the Liberators from the Berlin Airlift in July 1949, Scottish Airlines was able to transfer a second aircraft to its Greek associate. Hellenic's services now linked Athína with Alexandria, Glasgow, Iannina, Kavala, London, Nicosia, Paris and Tel Aviv.

In October 1950, the last of the Liberators was finally withdrawn from service by Scottish Airlines. This aircraft had spent the closing years of its career with Scottish flying the Hellenic Airlines schedule between Athína and Cairo, but was replaced by the more modern Douglas C-54 Skymaster.

In 1951 the poor financial state of the three airlines led to a decision by the Greek state to merge them into a single operator, Greek National Airlines (TAE).

AME

The private company Αεροπορικαί Μεταφοραί Ελλάδος -AME, or Air Transport of Greece -

A low quality, but rare colour photograph of Hellenic Airlines' SX-DAA undergoing servicing during a turnaround. The pale blue and white vertical tail along with the red markings, name and cheat line are shown to advantage against the bare aluminium of the fuselage. The nose hatch is also open for the loading of luggage. *(via Spiros Papadopoulos Collection)*

Above: Sophia Vembo with employees of Hellenic Airlines, alongside one of their DC-3s. She was a leading Greek singer and actress who became best known for her performance of patriotic songs during the Greco-Italian War when she was dubbed the 'Songstress of Victory'.

She began her career in Thessaloniki in the early 1930s. Her reputation skyrocketed after the Italian attack on Greece on 28 October 1940, when her performance of patriotic and satirical songs became a primary inspiration for soldiers and civilians alike, for whom she quickly became a folk heroine. At the same time, she offered 2,000 gold pounds from her fortune to the Hellenic Navy. Following the German invasion and occupation of the country in April 1941, she was transported to the Middle East, where she continued to perform for the Greek troops in exile. After the war, in 1949, she acquired her own theatre, the 'Vembo Theatre', in the Metaxourgeio neighbourhood of Athína. Because of her role in the war and during the Axis occupation, she was awarded the rank of Major in the Greek Army.

Left: mechanics work on a R-1830 Twin Wasp from a DC-3.

(photos: ΠΟΛΚ.ΕΟΑ).

Promotional material from Hellenic Airlines. Above left: the face of a January 1951 timetable, published in London for their C-54/DC-4 Skymaster service. Above right: the face of a 1949 timetable, promoting the Liberator services.

Below: SX-DAA *Maid of Athens* awaiting its next flight. *(all author's collection)*

Sophia Vembo on the steps of an Hellenic Airlines DC-3 with some of the staff. The aircraft is parked on Pierced Steel Planking (PSP) that covered the airfield's operational areas. *(ΠΟΛΚ.ΕΟΑ).*

was founded in 1947, but did not start regular operations until1949 with flights from Athína to Argos Orestiko in Kastoria, using an eight-year-old Avro Anson registered SX-BDA and on short-haul flights from Athína to Kerkyra and Kalamata. This aircraft was the former South African Air Force Anson Mk.1 SAAF 4401/ZS-BRG; according to the few suruving records, it was sold on 24 March 1949 by one Theo Deannis to AME. The aircraft's career was short lived, for on 25 December 1950 it seems it was very badly damaged in a gale at Athína and the aircraft was written off - the remains were everntually burnt on 8 January 1954

One of the first pilots of the company was Panagiotis Kartatos who was later to have a prestigious career later in Olympic Airways, as General Manager.

TAE

Stephanos Zotos, a former Royal Hellenic Navy officer who was transferred to the Air Force in 1925, formed the Technical and Aeronautical Exploitations, known by it's initials, TAE in 1935. He had retired from military service the previous year with the rank of Captain. The new company's first aircraft were a De Havilland DH 87 Hornet Moth SX-AAI, and a De Havilland DH 82A Tiger Moth SX-AAK. Operating from a base at Tatoi Airport north of Athína.

Due to the relatively small number of passengers traveling around Greece in the 1930s, TAE primarily flew routes not covered by EEES. and used its aircraft and pilots as a training school. With the outbreak of World War Two, and the Italian invasion in October 1940, most civilian pilots were mustered into the Royal Hellenic Air Force. However, it was not until the German invasion in April 1941, that the aircraft of TAE were destroyed by the Luftwaffe and the airline ceased operations for the duration of the war.

When Eelliniki Eteris Enaerion Synghinonion ceased operations in 1940, its equipment and routes were assumed by the privately owned TAE. When the Germans invaded in 1941, all company assets are purposely destroyed.

As soon as Greece began re-building its infrastructure after the end of World War Two, Zotos, freshly out of service in the Air Force, looked to re-establish the airline. He worked establishing his company's offices in his home. In early 1946, the prewar company was reformed and on 6 April a contract is signed with Howard Hughes' Transcontinental and Western Air (later

Above left: The first 'passenger terminal' for TAE at Athína-Hassani Airport was a series of tents, with pierced steel planking for a floor. The date was September 1946.

Above right: One of the pioneers of commercial aviation in Hellas was Stephanos Zotos, the founder of TAE. *(both photos: ΠΟΛΚ.ΕΟΑ).*

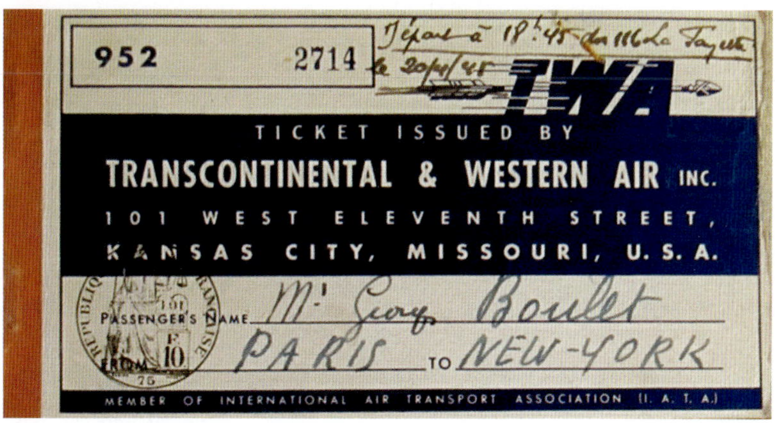

Right: 'Interline' tickets that allowed passengers to purchase a set of tickets in say Kalamata and fly via Athína to Paris and then on to New York. *(authors collection)*

TransWorld Airlines - TWA) for technical assistance. Pilots of the American carrier, which held 35% shareholding, inaugurated domestic Douglas DC-3 services, mainly to Thessaloniki on the mainland and to Heraklion and Chania on Crete; later, overseas routes were begun to Alexandria and Istanbul.

The arrangement allowed TAE to offer ticketed flights to New York and beyond on TWA flights via connections in Paris, France. Frequencies were maintained but services were not financially successful.

Through this partnership, Zotos secured for TAE three ex-US Army Air Force C-47 Dakotas, which were converted into Douglas DC-3s in Egypt during the summer of 1946. These aircraft, registered as SX-BAA, SX-BAB and SX-BAC began service on 30 July 1946 - with the arrival of SX-BAA - from the newly established Athína Hassani Airport south-east of the city on the Saronic Gulf. 'BAB arrived a month later and 'BAC arrived on 15 September. These TAE aircraft represented the first post-war civil aviation in Greece with scheduled service to Thessaloniki and Chania. The airline's passengers waited for their flights in a large tent, until a proper terminal could be built, but the first year of operations the airline carried 11,000 passengers. The airline flew the Greek delegation to the Paris Peace talks on 4 October 1946.

The lack of road and railway networks and the civil war climate in Hellas made air transport look like an expensive but safe means of travel.

In March 1946, elections were held in Hellas. The elections were corrupt and as a result, the victory was greatly in favour of the National Republican Greek League, known as EDES. Therefore, the Communists formed the Democratic Army of Greece (DA), declaring they were fighting to restore Greece to a democracy. During the first year of fighting, the DA was ahead since they were receiving help from Yugoslavia and controlled the northern part of Hellas. The British became increasingly worried and turned to the United States for help. In 1947, the United States agreed so President Truman issued the Truman Doctrine to help Greece fight the Communists.

By the time the US entered, the DA was holding land at the boarders of Yugoslavia and Albania, as well as land in southern Greece. The DA used guerrilla tactics for their warfare whereas the nationalists were receiving weapons from the United States and Britain. Once the United States supported Hellas, the nationalist army greatly increased. Then, Stalin ended his relationship with Yugoslavia's leader, Tito and DA decided to support Stalin. With this factor, and the help from the Americans, the nationalists were able to defeat the communists by the summer of 1949. During the course of the war, more than 80,000 people were killed while another 700,000 were left homeless. The civil war left Hellas in shambles.

It was in this environment that the airlines were trying to operate. The first four months of operation of TAE in 1946 demonstated that air transport in Hellas had good prospects, so the management of the company decided to expand the fleet, and so, in the summer of 1947, TAE secured three additional DC-3s (two from the United States military and one from the British Royal Air Force). The aircraft, registered as SX-BAG, SX-BAH, and SX-BAI respectively, were christened at a celebration on 31 August 1947, attended by the new king, Paul.

TAE actively persued a policy of making the country 'air-minded' encouraging schoolchildren and students from the areas they served to visit the airports and inspect the aircraft. *(ΠΟΛΚ.ΕΟΑ)*.

Left: TAE's SX-BAH, the DC-3 that was hijacked over Evia on 12 September 1948. It is seen here at Croydon Airport, London.

Below: The *'Macedonia'* newspaper reportage of the incident. *(both ΠΟΛΚ.ΕΟΑ).*

ΜΑΚΕΔΟΝΙΑ

Αεροπλάνον τής Ολυμπιακής εξ Αθηνών πρός Θεσσαλονίκην κατέπεσεν είς τό Κακοσάλεσι οι 18 επ' αυτού εφονεύθησαν

ΑΠΕΚΟΠΗ Η ΔΕΞΙΑ ΠΤΕΡΥΞ ΕΝΩ ΕΥΡΙΣΚΕΤΟ ΕΙΣ ΥΨΟΣ 3000 Μ. ΠΡΟΦΑΝΩΣ ΛΟΓΩ ΠΙΕΣΕΩΣ ΑΝΤΙΘΕΤΩΝ ΡΕΥΜΑΤΩΝ ΑΕΡΟΣ Κ' ΕΠΕΣΕ ΠΕΡΙΔΙΝΟΥΜΕΝΟΝ ΕΙΣ ΤΑΣ ΚΛΙΤΥΣ ΤΗΣ ΠΑΡΝΗΘΟΣ

Tragedy struck a few days later when on 3 September 1947, SX-BAB crashed near Voula while on final approach to the Athína-Hassani Airport during an evening training exercise. The training detail called for the pilot to execute a go-around following an aborted landing approach. The DC-3 experienced an abrupt wind change at very low altitude during its approach to the airport. The aircraft fell in the sea and struck a rocky beach, destroying the cockpit. Three crew members in the cockpit, the instructor, the trainee and Hellenic Civil Aviation Authority inspector were killed.

Despite the competition from the new State-created airlines, TAE managed to carry about 66,000 passengers in 1947 and almost tripled that fuigure to 184,000 in 1948.

That year the US Congress passed the Marshall Plan, officially the European Recovery Program, (ERP). This was an American initiative to aid Western Europe, in which the United States gave over $13 billion in economic support to help rebuild Western European economies after the end of World War Two. The plan was in operation for four years beginning on April 8, 1948. The goals of the United States were to rebuild war-devastated regions, remove trade barriers, modernise industry, make Europe prosperous once more, and prevent the spread of communism. The Marshall Plan required a lessening of interstate barriers, a dropping of many regulations, and encouraged an increase in productivity, labour union membership, as well as the adoption of modern business procedures.

Zotos has paid a visit to the US just before the plan became effective on 3 June 1948. With the support of the US Department of Transportation and TWA he secured a four year $US2,840,000 loan for TAE based on the terms of the Marshall Plan.

However, there were limits to the numbers of domestic passengers that the still-shaky Greek market could produce and all of the airlines were constantly in jeopardy of failing. Nevertheless, TAE purchased an additional five DC-3s from the

SX-BAN loads up with freight. (*ΠΟΛΚ.ΕΟΑ*).

RAF in Tehran, registered as SX-BAD, SX-BAE, SX-BAF, SX-BAL, SX-BAK.

One TAE pilot who was to play a huge part in the story of TAE and later Olympic Airways was Paul Ioannidis became a close associate of Onassis. At the beginning of 1943, Paul Ioannidis, aged eighteen, joined the Resistance movement. First, he joined the Nikiforos team in the Greek People's Liberation Army (ELAS) and then FORCE 133, an allied military unit operating in the Greek mountains against the German occupation. In June 1944, following orders from the Middle Eastern Allied Command, he and two British officers escaped from Greece and reached Cairo via Turkey.

He was honoured for his bravery during the War by Great Britain's King George VI with the King's Medal for Courage (KMC) of the British Empire. He was also awarded an honorary diploma by the British Field Marshall Lord Alexander. In the act of protest he returned these distinctions to Charles Peake, then the British Ambassador in Athína, on 10 May 1956, the day that Michelis Karaolis and Andreas Dimitriou, the Cypriot fighters of EOKA, were executed in Cyprus. He stated that these awards no longer meant anything to him as the Cypriots were killed for fighting to liberate their country, just like he had fought for Greece.

Paul Ioannidis received his training as a fighter pilot at the then South Rhodesia RAF Training Centre, and later on, he served in the Royal Hellenic Air Force until 1947. It is thought that during this time Ioannidis flew a number of the eighteen Boeing-Stearman Kaydet fleet supplied by the United Nations Relief and Rehabilitation Administration (UNRRA) They introduced a chemical called dichloro-diphenyl-trichloroethane (DDT), spraying on a nationwide scale, revolutionising malaria control and the idea of disease eradication, and created UNRRA's largest DDT malaria programme. As the Greek civil war unfolded, the fight against malaria acquired a dynamic which immunised it from the political issues of the postwar international scene. As Dr M J Vine, the Chief of the World Health Organisation's Interim Commission in Greece described the process at the time: *'The aeroplanes worked from ten bases, including Elefsina. They were all piloted by members of the Royal Hellenic Air Force, who entered into this dangerous work with enthusiasm. They flew at an altitude of about ten to twenty feet, releasing a fine, oily globular mist. The failure of an engine*

Above: Paul Ioannidis recieved his flight training in Southern Rhodesia. He is seen here about to climb aboard this AT-6 Harvard coded 'N'.

Below: After the war Captain Ioannidis flew Boeing-Stearman Kaydets for the UNRRA as part of the malaria eradication programme in Greece, this machine apparently being UN-7. *(both ΠΟΛΚ.ΕΟΑ).*

Two views of TAE's DC-4 SX-DAC *'Hellas'*, the lower photograph being taken at Northolt just outside London. *(left ΠΟΛΚ.ΕΟΑ, below authors collection).*

Below: Sadly this Hellenic airport is unidentifiable, but it shows the TAE signage over the main entrance. *(ΠΟΛΚ.ΕΟΑ).*

while over a swamp meant a sudden dive and we were fortunate in having only one fatality out of several accidents. Greek wetlands, sparsely timbered and with light vegetation is especially suitable for this method of larval control.

Once discharged, Paul Ioannidis was employed by the Greek national carrier TAE, which consequently became Olympic Airways. At OA he offered his services as Instructor, Chief Flight Instructor, Chief Pilot, Flight Operation Director and finally as Director General until December 1974 when Onassis renounced the contract and handed the company back to the Hellenic State. During his career in the civil aviation, he flew as Captain and Instructor in numerous fixed wing aircraft and helicopters, logging approximately 24,000 hours flying. For twelve years he was flying the Hellenic Royal Family on civil and military aircraft.

In his will, Aristotle Onassis appointed Paul Ioannidis a lifetime member of the Onassis Foundation Board of Directors. Captain Ioannidis was also involved in the business activities of the Onassis Foundation.

Ioannidis flew with TAE for nineteen months before being promoted to the rank of Captain with the support of TAE Captains and Instructors Stratos Xydis and Fanis Spinolas. He was just twenty-five years old.

The Hellenic aviation magazine *'Aviation News'* detailed much of the operations of TAE, which showed that they continued largely without change through the remainder of the decade. The most significant events of this period are tragic. En route on a scheduled flight from Athína to Thessaloniki on 12 September 1948. a TAE DC-3, SX-BAH, with 23 passengers (some accounts say a total of 21 on board) was hijacked by eight

Two snapshots, that although not of the best quality, show some fascinating details.

Above: Although sadly of an unidentifiable former C-47, this is one of the few images that show a TAE Stewardess. It shows that the uniform she is wearing appears to confirm the one depicted in artwork form on the 1952 timetable. Her hat displays the large emblem on the side, and she is holding a cloth-covered tray, presumably containing refreshments for the passengers. The open door has a frame on it that carries the aircraft's next destination.

Below: Just another engine-start before departure of this TAE Dakota. What is of interest here is the apparent emptiness of the background behind - clearly Athína has not yet expanded. *(both ΠΟΛΚ.ΕΟΑ)*.

3.

Timetables from the period tended to be quite artistic and have very stylised images on them.

Above: the cover on the face of this 1952 edition is of interest because although the work of a graphic designer, it does show the colour, style and emblems worn on the TAE uniform by the Air Hostess.

Above right: TAE ground engineers did much of their maintenance out of doors, as this picture of the crew working on the DC-4 shows.

Right: the front and rear cover of the summer 1954 timetable shows artwork depicting the Athenian skyline with Acropolis and Parthenon.

(all ΠΟΛΚ.ΕΟΑ).

Right: the aviation magazine *'Aviation News'* - first published in April 1947 by OTE Financial and Technical Enterprises of 5 Nikas Street, Athína - recorded much of the comings and goings of the civil aviation scene in Hellas, even though there was still a civil war going on!

communists over the island of Evia by six passengers (some sources say eight) who demanded to be taken to Yugoslavia. Some of the hijackers beat members of the crew severely - the radio operator Phivos Xantos was hit over the head with a bottle and then tied up. Details of the hijacking are somewhat sketchy in detail, but one account says that the aircraft commander, Captain Athanasios Igoumenakis attempted to deceive the hijackers to no effect, but following the Axios River he eventually managed to finally land the aircraft on a bombed out airstrip at Burga, some sixty kilometres south east of Skopje, Yugoslavia, where the hijackers deplaned. Captain Igoumenakis contacted the Hellenic authorities and TAE Operations by radio to both report the hijacking and ask for further instructions. After inspecting the aircraft and taking into account the fuel remaining in the tanks, they decided to continue on their journey, landing in Thessaloniki, it's original destination, four and a half hours late! This was the first recorded aerial hijacking in Hellenic history.

1949 proved to be a challenging year for the fledgling airline as it suffered two air crashes. The first was on 23 April 1949, when SX-BAF crashed on landing at Hellenikon Airport. Fortunately, no one was injured but the aircraft was a total loss.

Then, at 6:35pm in the evening of 6 June 1949, SX-BAI, a TAE DC-3 with twenty-two people on board, including Major-General George Kotsalos, the military governor of Kavalla, crashed thirty kilometres northeast of Athína; there were no survivors. The aircraft, along with the flight crew Pilot Captain Karamalegos Eleftherios, First Officer Kandias Christos, Radio Operator Platis Antonis, and flight attendant Levendopoulos Vasiliki - was en-route from Kavala-Megas Alexandros Airport to Athína-Hassani Airport when it entered the core of a cumulo-nimbus cloud during its intial approach to Hassani Airport and crashed on the north slope of Mount Parnitha. It experienced excessive acceleration, causing the separation of the right wing. The aircraft fell to the ground near Malakasa village.

Less than two months earlier, on 23 April, another DC-3, SX-BAF suffered severe damage and was written off during a landing accident at Hassani.

Due to economic recession and improved road and shipping infrastructure, the number of passengers flown by all three airlines reached a plateau at 324,000 in 1949. Pilots flew six days a week, then had a day off.

Technical and Aeronautical Holdings served a number of domestic destinations in Greece on an irregular basis in the period 1935-1941. After the airline was re-established in 1946, it began to operate regular scheduled services. For a period 1946-1951 TAE flew DC-3s to Agrinion, Athína, Chania, Ioannina, Kavala, Volos, Kerkyra, Heraklion, Thessaloniki and further afield to destination such as Alexandria, Beirut, Nicosia and Istanbul.

In 1950, Daedalus Airlines ceased operations. The total number of staff of all three airlines fell to 1,059 people.

Passenger figures for all the airlines showed a decline which was mainly attributed the gradual restoration of the country's road network after the termination hostilities with the civil war. The magnitude of this was demonstrated by their numbers - in 1950 the three companies flew 207,000 passengers, 117,000 fewer when compared to 1949.

This created intense economic difficulties, and the Hellenic government had to act - but how? Without a doubt, Hellas needed to maintain the prestige of a Hellenic-flagged carrier, and so in July 1951, the government forced the merger of all three concerns into TAE Greek National Airlines, and Zotos' airline was absorbed even as the name survived.

On Christmas Eve 1951 a strike by flight staff led to the dismissal of several workers, but it was not long before *Aviation News* revealed that the airlines had carried 19,000 fewer passengers compared to 1950. 1952 saw a further decline in passenger numbers; this time by 11,000.

In January 1953 the only TAE DC-4 was impounded in Amsterdam Schipol due to unpaid debts to Shell. The aircraft was not returned to Athína until 21 April!

The effective 'loss' of the DC-4 forced the company to put DC-3s on the London and Frankfurt services. The only way flights to London could be made was by flying out ground engineers with fuel purchase vouchers as company credit had been suspended for some time. As if that were not enough, when the aircrew arrived in London after about twelve flight hours - not counting time spent on intermediaries stations - they had difficulties in finding a hotel because of the same suspension of company credit!

TAE from the eyes of students

In 1956 TAE, in co-operation with the Hellenic Ministry of Education, announced a writing competition which resulted in a series of flights offered to the student winners. First prize winner

Counter-foil No. 30 as a certificate for fifty shares in TAE issued on 27 August 1951. The image in the centre of the certificate is De Havilland DH87B Hornet Moth SX-AAI that was first registered to Stephanos Zotos, the founder of TAE on 2 November 1938 and sold overseas on 19 April 1941.

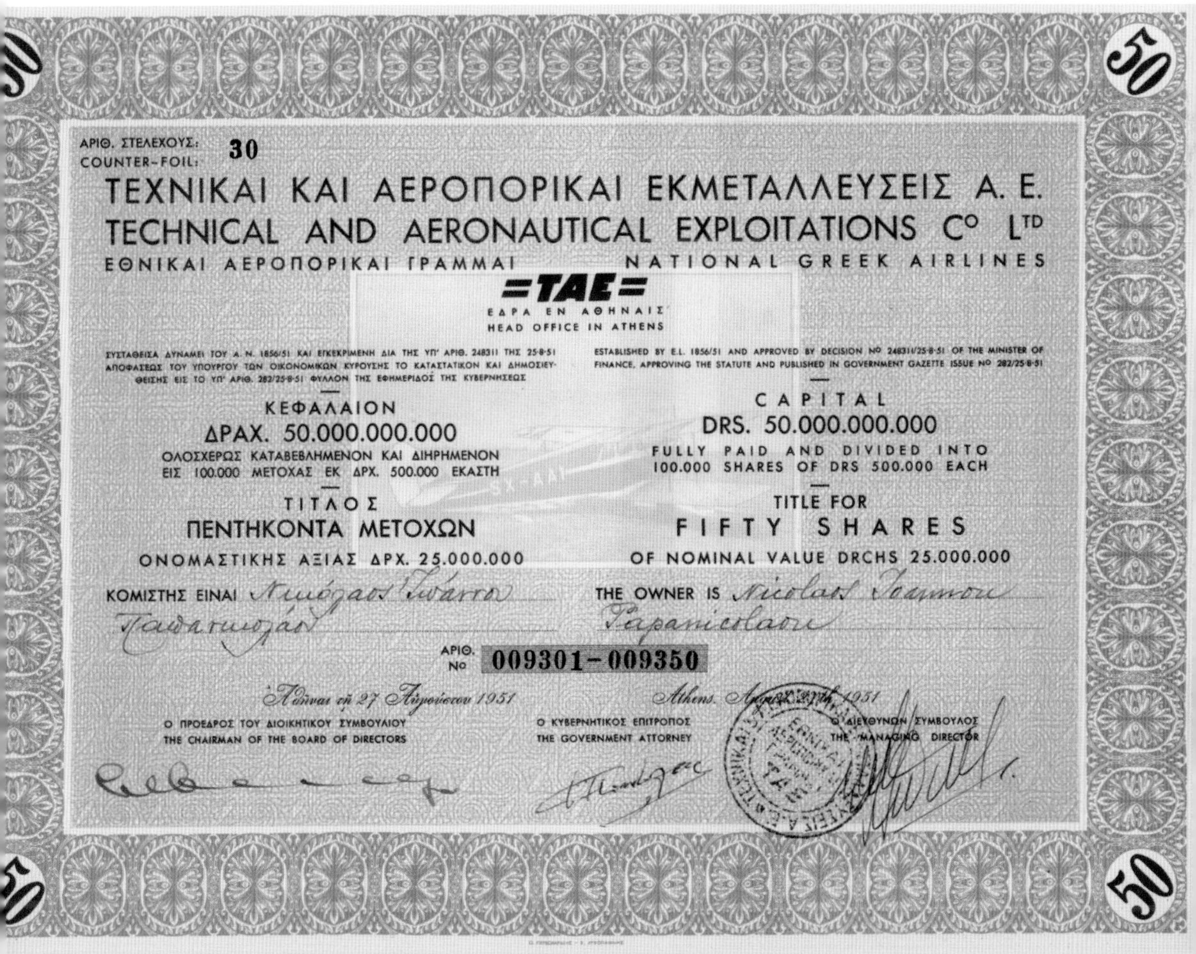
ΑΡΙΘ. ΣΤΕΛΕΧΟΥΣ: 30
COUNTER-FOIL:

ΤΕΧΝΙΚΑΙ ΚΑΙ ΑΕΡΟΠΟΡΙΚΑΙ ΕΚΜΕΤΑΛΛΕΥΣΕΙΣ Α. Ε.
TECHNICAL AND AERONAUTICAL EXPLOITATIONS C^O L^TD
ΕΘΝΙΚΑΙ ΑΕΡΟΠΟΡΙΚΑΙ ΓΡΑΜΜΑΙ — NATIONAL GREEK AIRLINES

=TAE=
ΕΔΡΑ ΕΝ ΑΘΗΝΑΙΣ
HEAD OFFICE IN ATHENS

ΣΥΣΤΑΘΕΙΣΑ ΔΥΝΑΜΕΙ ΤΟΥ Α. Ν. 1856/51 ΚΑΙ ΕΓΚΕΚΡΙΜΕΝΗ ΔΙΑ ΤΗΣ ΥΠ' ΑΡΙΘ. 248311 ΤΗΣ 25-8-51 ΑΠΟΦΑΣΕΩΣ ΤΟΥ ΥΠΟΥΡΓΟΥ ΤΩΝ ΟΙΚΟΝΟΜΙΚΩΝ ΚΥΡΟΥΣΗΣ ΤΟ ΚΑΤΑΣΤΑΤΙΚΟΝ ΚΑΙ ΔΗΜΟΣΙΕΥΘΕΙΣΗΣ ΕΙΣ ΤΟ ΥΠ' ΑΡΙΘ. 282/25-8-51 ΦΥΛΛΟΝ ΤΗΣ ΕΦΗΜΕΡΙΔΟΣ ΤΗΣ ΚΥΒΕΡΝΗΣΕΩΣ

ESTABLISHED BY E.L. 1856/51 AND APPROVED BY DECISION Nº 248311/25-8-51 OF THE MINISTER OF FINANCE, APPROVING THE STATUTE AND PUBLISHED IN GOVERNMENT GAZETTE ISSUE Nº 282/25-8-51

ΚΕΦΑΛΑΙΟΝ
ΔΡΑΧ. 50.000.000.000
ΟΛΟΣΧΕΡΩΣ ΚΑΤΑΒΕΒΛΗΜΕΝΟΝ ΚΑΙ ΔΙΗΡΗΜΕΝΟΝ
ΕΙΣ 100.000 ΜΕΤΟΧΑΣ ΕΚ ΔΡΧ. 500.000 ΕΚΑΣΤΗ

CAPITAL
DRS. 50.000.000.000
FULLY PAID AND DIVIDED INTO
100.000 SHARES OF DRS 500.000 EACH

ΤΙΤΛΟΣ
ΠΕΝΤΗΚΟΝΤΑ ΜΕΤΟΧΩΝ
ΟΝΟΜΑΣΤΙΚΗΣ ΑΞΙΑΣ ΔΡΧ. 25.000.000

TITLE FOR
FIFTY SHARES
OF NOMINAL VALUE DRCHS 25.000.000

ΚΟΜΙΣΤΗΣ ΕΙΝΑΙ

THE OWNER IS

ΑΡΙΘ.
Nº 009301-009350

Ο ΠΡΟΕΔΡΟΣ ΤΟΥ ΔΙΟΙΚΗΤΙΚΟΥ ΣΥΜΒΟΥΛΙΟΥ
THE CHAIRMAN OF THE BOARD OF DIRECTORS

Ο ΚΥΒΕΡΝΗΤΙΚΟΣ ΕΠΙΤΡΟΠΟΣ
THE GOVERNMENT ATTORNEY

Ο ΔΙΕΥΘΥΝΩΝ ΣΥΜΒΟΥΛΟΣ
THE MANAGING DIRECTOR

TAE route network
1949

was Sofia Anastasiadou from the 3rd Grammar School, Thessaloniki, second was Aikaterini Theodore Vettou of the 2nd High School, Kerkyra and third was Christina Pathoulis of the 2nd High School of Athína.

The 'coup de grace' for the company came when passenger figures fell by a further 60,000. Without any state support the company had fallen into dire financial straits. The staff was reduced to 793 people most working 12-hour and 18-hour shifts in order to ensure survival of the company.

Under government supervision, the airlines were amalgamated into a new joint stock company placed under the TAE banner. Shareholding was divided between TAE (30%), Trans World Airlines (TWA) (15%) AME (5%), the Greek Civil Service pension fund (24%), the National Bank of Greece (16%), and the Greek government (10%), Scottish Aviation, which had held interest in one of the merger partners, withdrew from the arrangements.

The airlines were being stifled by the competition, and the lack of cheap loans like the ones they had enjoyed under the Marshal Plan. The Hellenic skies, then as now could not support

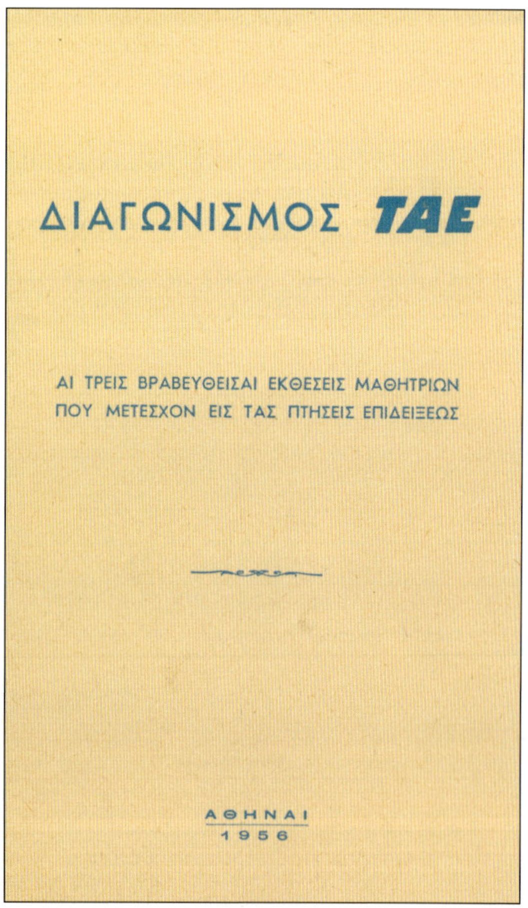

The cover of a TAE/Hellenic Ministry of Education sponsored writing competition for students. *(authors collection)*

Michael Christodoulou Mouskos, known as Archbishop Makarios III was a Greek Cypriot clergyman and politician, who served as the Archbishop and Primate of the autocephalous Church of Cyprus and as the first President of Cyprus. He is seen here deplaning from a TAE DC-3. *(authors collection)*

a large number of airlines. Financial reversals continued and by August 1954 the government which was making good the losses, had been forced to announce that the carrier faced complete privatisation.

The company was also forced to take new loans in order to pay back what it had received. In 1954, the company was under liquidation with an uncertain future, passenger traffic continued to decline, with many of the sailors and technicians fleeing to Middle Eastern companies. As a result, in 1955 the company was auctioned with an initial offer of 60,000,000 drachmas. It was eventually awarded to the Hellenic State for

SX-BAL, seen at Athína in April 1953. The aircraft wears TAE titling with the words 'National Greek Airline' just visible above the window line. Other pictures suggest that this wording was painted in red. This picture was taken after TAE merged with Hellenic to form National Airlines of Greece in July 1951. The aircraft has been obtained from USAF stocks at Payne Field, near Cairo, Egypt and had previously been used under lend-lease by the Royal Air Force. *(author's collection)*

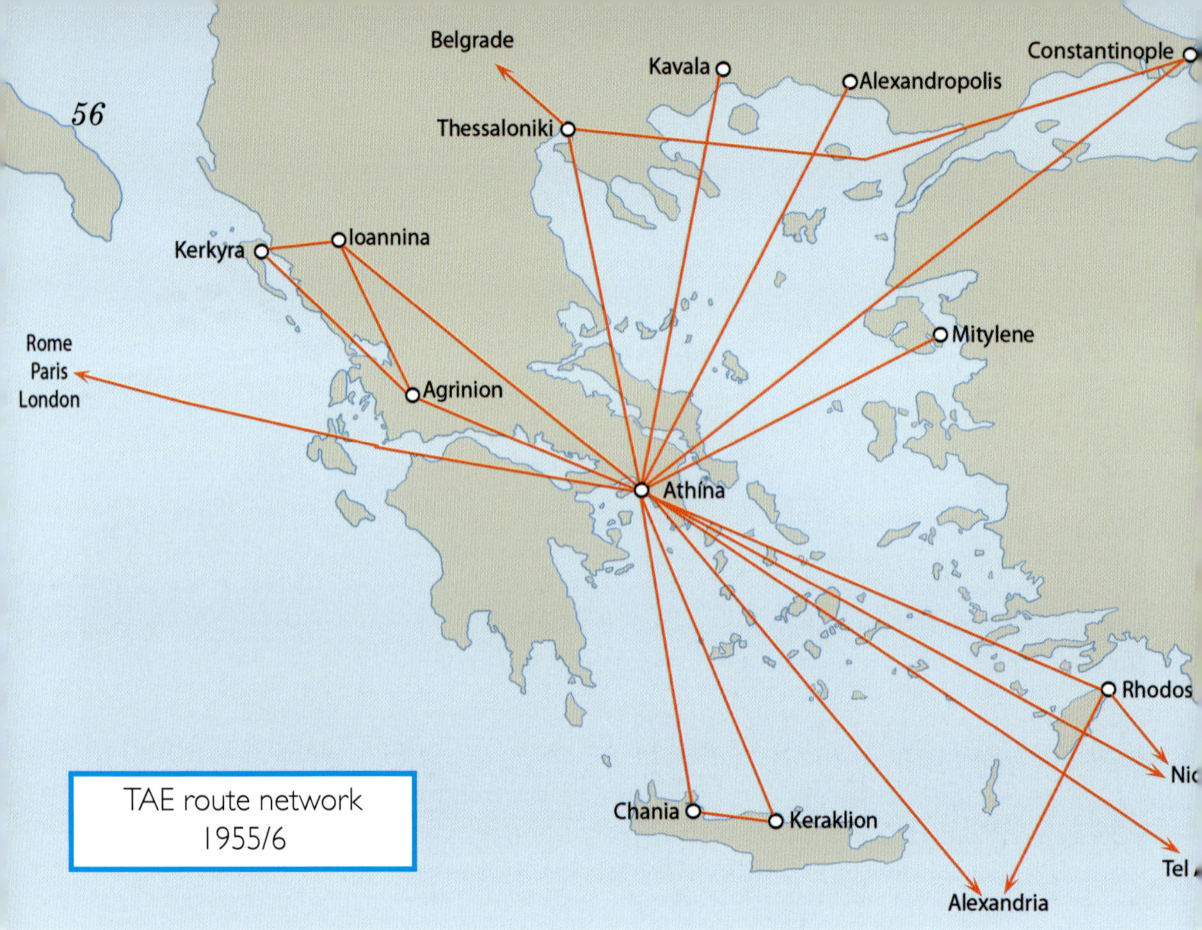

TAE route network
1955/6

lack of other interested parties. The future of the company was uncertain.

On 1 June 1955, the airline was formally taken over by the Hellenic Ministry of Transport, which sold it to shipping magnate Aristotle Onassis on 2 January 1957; Onassis quickly reformed the airline and re-named it Olympic Airways, S.A. on 6 April.

There was one other aircraft owned by TAE that remains something of a mystery. SX-AAJ was ex-HB738, a Fairchild Argus Mk.III of the Royal Air Force. The sole Argus bought in 1946 by TAE as a short range transport. Apparently it was withdrawn from use in 1957, although the registration was transferred to Olympic and left derelict until finally scrapped in November 1975.

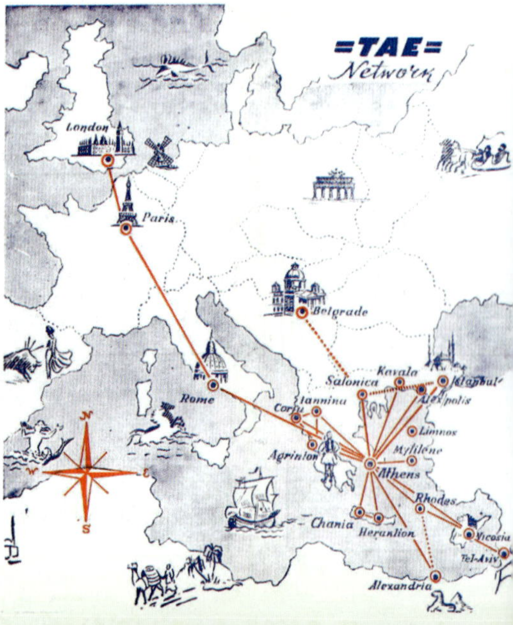

Chapter Three

Onassis and the arrival of Olympic Airways

By the mid-1950s, the political climate in Hellas had improved, and some of the more seasoned politicians began to address themselves to the problems of national development. They were struck by the fact that the richest and most enterprising Hellenic businessmen all seemed to be expatriates. Their success provided a useful quota of stories in the Hellenic press of the local-boy-makes-good variety, but their impact on the economy was negligible. Konstantinos Karamanlis, who became prime minister in 1955, did not think that this should necessarily be the case.

Konstantinos G. Karamanlis (Κωνσταντίνος Γ. Καραμανλής), commonly anglicised to Constantine Karamanlis was a four-time Prime Minister and twice President of the Third Hellenic Republic, and a towering figure in Greek politics whose political career spanned much of the latter half of the 20th century.

He was born in the village of Proti, Macedonia. He became a Greek citizen in 1913 after Macedonia was annexed by Greece, Bulgaria and Serbia, in the aftermath of the Second Balkan War. His father was Georgios Karamanlis, a teacher who fought during the Greek Struggle for Macedonia, in 1904–1908. After spending his childhood in Macedonia, he went to Athína to attain his degree in law. He practised law in Serres, entered politics with the conservative People's Party and was elected Member of Parliament for the first time in the 1936 election at the age of 28. Health problems prevented his participation in the Hellenic-Italian War.

Konstantinos G. Karamanlis;
b. 8 March 1907 – *d*. 23 April 1998)

After World War Two, Karamanlis quickly rose through the ranks of Greek politics, strongly supported by fellow party-member and close friend Lambros Eftaxias, who served as Minister for Agriculture under the premiership of Konstantinos Tsaldaris. Karamanlis's first cabinet position was Minister for Labour in 1947 under the same administration. In 1951, along with most prominent members of the People's Party, Karamanlis joined the Greek Rally of Alexandros Papagos. When this party won power in 1951, Karamanlis became Minister of Public Works in the Papagos administration. He won the admiration of the US Embassy for the efficiency with which he built road infrastructure and administered the American aid programme.

When Papagos died after an illness in 1955, King Paul of Greece appointed Karamanlis as Prime Minister; an act that took the Greek political world by surprise, as it bypassed Stephanos Stephanopoulos and Panagiotis Kanellopoulos, two senior Greek Rally politicians widely considered as the heavyweights most likely to succeed Papagos.

Karamanlis was known as a dynamic if conventional, visionary, and that reputation rested primarily on his ability to cut Gordian knots. Once, when he had been responsible for the public transportation system of Athína, he had promptly terminated a long-standing bureaucratic dispute about its future by the simple expedient of sending squads of workmen to rip up the trolley tracks, thus scoring high on incisiveness but low on sensitivity. Now his solution to Greece's economic problems was equally simple. Massive investment was the answer, and where better to fish for it than among the shoals of wealthy expatriates? Men such as Aristotle Onassis and Stavros Niarchos and all the other shipping magnates, who had little or no involvement with the Greek economy and were seemingly awash with funds; might they prove susceptible to appeals to their patriotism?

First, Karamanlis needed to consolidate his political position. He had become prime minister upon the death of his predecessor, and his parliamentary majority was too tenuous for long-term planning. In the elections of February 1956, his right-of-centre National Radical Union party returned with the overall parliamentary majority he wanted. By way of marking the opening of a new era, he appointed the first woman to hold a ministerial post in a Greek government. Then he invited Aristotle Onassis to lunch.

The invitation was not unexpected, for Karamanlis had already made it known that if he won the elections, he would be anxious to do business with expatriates. Onassis had intimated that an approach at the prime ministerial level would be well received. Only experience and perhaps consciousness of his new international status made him sensitive to protocol, for Onassis was always ready to talk business. Of the ideas which Karamanlis threw out over lunch, the one which excited Onassis most was his proposal for a new national airline.

Everyone knew that the existing state-owned airline, TAE, was a shambles. With its associated lines, it possessed only thirteen DC-3s and one DC-4, and the only international service it could muster was a once-a-week run to Paris and London. It seemed doomed to perpetual loss. What Karamanlis wanted was a profitable airline of international stature, not as a preposterous ambition as it may have seemed. Greece was at an international crossroads, and any national carrier could rely on the important market of emigrant Greeks returning home on holiday, particularly from North America. He reasoned that if Hellenic shipping was an international success story, then why not Hellenic aviation? What was needed, Karamanlis said, was the right man in charge. Who better than Onassis? Why not scrap TAE and create an entirely new Onassis- owned company?

Onassis liked the idea. The prospect of being the only man in the world to own a national airline was practically irresistible. Moreover, aircraft, like ships, were reassuringly mobile assets. He told Karamanlis that, if he cared to submit his requirements, then he would do his best to propose something attractive.

During his lifetime, Onassis was one of the richest and most famous men in the world, with his name becoming synonymous with extreme wealth - and with a style and flair that became reflected in the fledgeling Olympic Airways.

The enigma that was Onassis

It is impossible to study the story of Olympic Airways without looking into the life-history of the person regarded as its founder. According to most official and family records, Aristotle Sokratis Onassis (Αριστοτέλης Ωνάσης) was born on 20 January 1906 and passed away on 15 March 1975. He was commonly called Ari or Aristo Onassis, was a Greek-Argentine shipping magnate, who amassed the world's largest privately owned shipping fleet and was one of the world's richest and most famous men. He was known for his business success, his great wealth and also his somewhat exotic personal life, including his marriage in 1946 to Athina Mary Livanos, daughter of shipping tycoon Stavros G. Livanos, with whom he had two children, Alexander (born 1948) and Christina (born 1950). The marriage would end in divorce when he began an affair with opera diva Maria Callas in 1957 and his marriage in 1968 to Jacqueline Kennedy, the widow of late American President John F. Kennedy.

Regarded by many as something of a lothario, it was also strongly rumoured that he had more than a brief liaison with Eva Perón, the wife of Argentine President Juan Perón.

Onassis was born in Karataş, a suburb of the port city of Smyrna, now İzmir, Turkey, to Socrates and Penelope Dologu who were Anatolian Greeks. It has been suggested that his father had *'...hawked hone-made trinkets around Symrna'*, and that his mother had *'...swept offices and took in washing'*. In later years Onassis did nothing to correct this rags to riches story, but in fact, he was the second child, but the first son of a wealthy merchant and banker.

Onassis had one full-sister, Artemis, and two half-sisters, Kalliroi and Merope, by his father's second marriage following Penelope's death of a kidney infection. His father became a successful shipping entrepreneur and was able to send his children to prestigious schools. When Aristotle graduated from the local Evangelical Greek School at the age of sixteen, he spoke four languages: Greek, Turkish, Spanish, and English.

Smyrna was briefly administered by Greece from 1919 to 1922 in the aftermath of the Allied victory in World War One, but then Smyrna was re-taken by Turkey during the Greco-Turkish War.

The Turkish Nationalist Army, under the command of Kemal Ataturk, attacked the centre of the Greek army on the plateau of Dumlupinar, two hundred miles east of Smyrna, on the morning of 26 August 1922. Within twenty-four hours the Greek front had collapsed.

Aristotle Sokratis Onassis; *b*. 20 January 1906, d. 15 March 1975 is seen here in 1932.

By 2 September the Greek retreat had become a rout; then the Greek fleet upped anchor and sailed away - Smyrna had been left to the Turks. A week later, on 9 September it was occupied without resistance.

For twenty-four hours the city was quiet as the Turks took stock of their prize. On the night of 10 September, a party of Turkish troops entered the Armenian quarter with the aim of finding and killing some prominent citizens hostile to Turkish rule. The government of Ataturk proclaimed that it was no longer a capital crime to kill a christian. The city's churches, crammed with refugees, were sprayed with gasoline and ignited. The wooden walls took fire instantly. Those trying to escape were bayoneted on the church steps.

On the day the Turks arrived in Smyrna, Socrates Onassis had gathered his family around him in his house at Karatassi and closed the shutters. They spent the next four days hiding, watching the destruction of the city through a chink in the curtains. They were in a state of fear bordering on terror. It was clear that their primary source of wealth, Socrates warehouse, had been destroyed in the blaze. Socrates was no longer young and suffered from heart problems, but he had more immediate reasons for apprehension. Distance insulated the family from the fire, but it seemed probable that the Onassis family would be singled out by the Turks in any reprisals that might follow the holocaust.

Aristotle's uncle Homer had fled before the arrival of the Turkish troops. Alexander was immediately arrested and interned at Kasaba, where he was executed. Uncles Basil and John were transported to a concentration camp in the interior. Aunt Maria, her husband, Chrysostomos Konialidis, and one of their children had sought sanctuary in a church in Ak-Kissar in the old Greek town of Thyatira. With five hundred other refugees they were burned alive. Finally, Socrates Onassis was arrested and taken to prison, leaving Aristotle, aged sixteen, the only male in the Karatassi house. Although not on the list of 'traitors' himself, Socrates was endangered by the fact that two of his brothers were.

With his father in jail, Aristotle was now acting head of the family, and it seems he was approached by a Turkish friend of his father's, Sadiq Topal, who had left some of his possessions - stocks, bonds, and a box of jewellery - in Socrates' office in Vezir Hane. As a Turk, Sadiq was able to get a permit to retrieve his goods. Accompanied by a Turkish army officer and two witnesses, Sadiq and Aristotle went to the wreckage of Socrates' office. The safe was still intact. Aristotle boldly asked the Turkish oflicer if he could take some of the money which belonged to his father. Although this was against the emergency regulations, the officer was impressed enough with him to allow Aristotle to take several thousand Turkish pounds for his use.

The money posed a problem. All Greek males over eighteen had to register with the Turkish authorities, after which they were either interned or sent to mainland Greece. Aristo was still not seventeen, but his natural precociousness might easily excite official curiosity. If he were interrogated and searched, the money might be

The burning of Smyrna by the Turks in September 1922. It was from this holocaust that Aristotle Onassis and his family escaped. *(authors collection)*

found on his person and confiscated. Aristotle felt torn between the desire to help his father and the feeling that he should leave now and go to the women of his family marooned on Lesbos without funds. His father, too, felt that Aristo should join the family and take them to Greece. Socrates was confident his Turkish friends in Smyrna would protect him. Aristo acceded to his father's wish and secured a passage to Lesbos on board the US destroyer *Edsall*.

Lesbos had become the clearing house for the million or more Anatolian Greeks on their way to the mainland. The seventeen women and children of the Onassis family were living in tents; food was short, and conditions were unsanitary. Three weeks after arriving there, the family disembarked at Piraeus, the port of Athína. There was, however tragic news about his grandmother Gethsemane, she survived the catastrophe of Smyrna, escaped the Turks and arrived in Greece. However, as she was disembarking at Piraeus, she was attacked by a gang of thieves who tried to snatch her purse. In the struggle, she died in a fall from the gangway to the quayside.

Socrates was eventually released from jail and also made his way to Athína via Lesbos. Here, along with his brother Homer, he confronted Aristotle about his acquisition and spending of the family money. What happened next is unclear, but it seems there was a huge family quarrel, and Aristotle began to plan on leaving Hellas; but where to? At first, Onassis considered the USA but abandoned that when he discovered that, under the quota system which then applied to immigrants, it would be years before all the Greeks who wanted passports would be allowed in. Finally, his fancy settled in Argentina. It was a country where Greeks were reputed to be able to make good, and there were also distant relatives there.

Socrates would not advance Aristotle the fare. Aristo turned to his friends for assistance, who pooled their resources and gave him $200. Later, when it became apparent that his son's decision was irrevocable, Socrates gave him another $250.

With this and a booking for Buenos Aires, he left Piraeus harbour in August 1923 on the first stage of his voyage, travelling on a Nansen passport. These were internationally recognised refugee travel documents, first issued by the League of Nations to stateless refugees. They were established by an international agreement reached at the Intergovernmental Conference on Identity Certificates for Russian Refugees, convened by Fridtj of Nansen in Geneva during July 1922 in his role as High Commissioner for Refugees for the League of Nations.

He went first to Naples, where he had to wait three weeks for a passenger ship to the Argentine. Onassis was to later recall with great enjoyment his first experience of lodging completely apart from his family. The cooking of his Neapolitan landlady far surpassed that in his own home, while the landlady's recently widowed daughter advanced his sexual education. When he left for South America, both women were in tears.

The vessel *Tomaso di Sczvoya* was crowded with Italian emigrants travelling steerage and packed into cargo holds converted into dormitories, three hundred men to each hold.

On 21 September 1923, the ship slid up the shallow, muddy waters of the Rio de la Plata to the docks of Buenos Aires. Aristotle Onassis, age seventeen, struggled down the gangplank, through the Latin exuberance of family reunions, to set foot on a new continent. He had a battered suitcase in one hand and a few hundred dollars in his pocket.

He first worked in the Argentine as 'help' in a Boca restaurant and was later a night worker employed by the Post Office and Telephone Companies, along one of his cousins, Nicolas Konialidis in the same capacity. It was not long before Onassis and Nicolas Konialidi, along with his brother Constantine, formed a loose business association.

Onassis then worked as a telephone operator, with the British United River Plate Telephone Company while following studies in commerce and port-duty administration at Aduanas Argentinas. It did not take him long to become an entrepreneur, creating an Argentine import-export company and going into business for himself. He obtained the Argentine citizenship in 1929.

The family quarrel was settled following a visit to the Argentine by a friend of the household and his father, a tobacco merchant, consigned a quantity of leaf to Aristotle for sale in the Argentine. This consignment was followed by others, and business grew, Onassis, obtaining a contract for the supply of Turkish leaf to Piccardo & Company.

The tobacco was sent via Genoa, where it was transshipped, and it appears that Onassis hit upon the idea of spraying the bales with salt water during their stay at Genoa, the resultant collections from the insurance underwriters for sea damage forming a welcome addition to legitimate trading profits. Insurance Agents were involved and, eventually, an employee gave the game away at a time when Nicolas Konialidis was in Genoa, with the result that he served a term in jail. The dossier appears to have been sent to Greece from Genoa but is thought to have been lost owing to a close liaison between Aristotle Onassis and one Michakopoulos, a Greek Minister at that time.

Through the influence of this Minister, Onassis was appointed Greek Consul in the Argentine but, as he was continually travelling, he appointed Nicolas Konialidis as his substitute. This appointment is reported to have become extremely lucrative, since, as consul, Onassis was able to obtain substantial sums of currency at official rates and sold the same in the Black Market, which at that time, was flourishing.

Within the next four years, he was a millionaire, due in part to many of his illegal doings, such as

Athina Mary 'Tina' Onassis Niarchos née Livanos; *b*. 19 March 1929 – *d*. 10 October 1974). When Aristotle married Tina she was 17, he was 46! *(authors collection)*

smuggling tobacco into Argentina to avoid paying duties and manufacturing cigarettes under other brand names without paying royalties. Onassis would also use bribe government officials to obtain favourable consideration for his illegal activities. In 1931, he received Greek tax exemptions for his ships and was given the title of Vice Consul to Argentina, which substantially increased his status in both countries.

After gaining his first fortune on Argentina, he expanded his shipping business worldwide and relocated to New York city, USA, where he built up his shipping businesses empire while keeping offices in Buenos Aires and Athína.

Onassis built up a fleet of freighters and tankers that eventually exceeded seventy vessels. Onassis's fleet had Panamanian flags and sailed tax-free while operating at low cost. Because of this, Onassis could turn a profit in every transaction, even though he charged one of the lowest prices in the merchant navy market. Onassis made significant profits when the big oil companies like Mobil, Socony, and Texaco signed long-term contracts at fixed prices with him for the use of his fleet while having trouble managing their fleets, which operated under US flags and thus at a high cost.

Most of the 'inacuracies' came to light in documents prepared by the American Federal Bureau

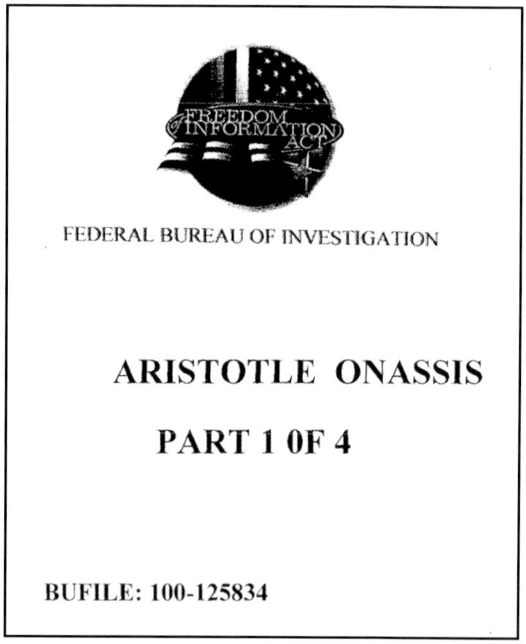
FREEDOM of INFORMATION ACT

FEDERAL BUREAU OF INVESTIGATION

ARISTOTLE ONASSIS

PART 1 0F 4

BUFILE: 100-125834

Aristotle Onassis gained a reputation of being a playboy and a something of a ladies man. As a result, he was often photographed in the presence of glamorous, sophisticated women.

Above: Onassis with *Prima Ballerina Assoluta* Margot Fonteyn in 1955.

Above right: The title page of a huge four part report on Onassis by the FBI. The Americans kept a watch on his activities for many years.

Right: Onassis in the company of Maria Callas at the London Dorchester Hotel in 1959. *(authors collection)*

The chatelain. Aristotle and Tina in the grounds of the Chateau de la Croë near the Cap d'Antibes in the south of France. Onassis rented it from 1954 to 1956, when Niacarios bought it. *(authors collection)*

of Investigation (FBI) and its head, J Edgar Hoover.

Their interest in Onassis seems to have stemmed from his meeting in society social events in Buenos Aires and Montevideo with some Argentinians and others out of favour with the US authorities. The FBI confidential reports are highly entertaining as they seem to include a significant amount of gossip and fallacies provided by the various informants about this 'playboy' that lived between New York, Long Island and San Francisco.

One such document, dated 9 February 1944 was sent by J Edgar Hoover to his field office in Los Angeles, under the heading *'Aristotle Socrates Onassis Espionage - X '*.

The State Department has advised that on 11 January 1942, Onassis made an application for a non-immigration visa, at which time he set out the following information:

He alleged that he was born in Salonica, Greece, September 21, 1900. His nationality was given as Argentine. At the time of the making of the application, he was in possession of a valid Argentine passport No. 701014 issued June 9, 1942, by the police department of Buenos Aires, Argentina, valid for two years. He listed his address as Legal-Reconquista 336, Buenos Aires, Argentina; United States address-Ritz Towers Hotel, 57 Park Avenue, New York City. He said that his business was shipping and indicated that he intended to stay in the United States from five to six months. He stated in his application that he has previously visited the United States on July 10, 1940, and on April 17, 1942.

The FBI files on Onassis are somewhat voluminous, and contain some instances of the phrase that he '*...reportedly expressed sentiments inimical to the war efforts of the United Nations and his activities in the United States should be observed*' or that he '*...possessed fascist ideas*'. It was also noted that '*...He is known to be extremely shrewd and unscrupulous with large investments in shipping*'.

Inimical, is not a word you often see nowadays. It descends from Latin inimicus, which combines amicus, meaning 'friend,' with the negative prefix in-, meaning not. In modern English, inimical rarely describes a person, however. Instead, it is used to describe forces, concepts, or situations that are in some way harmful or hostile.

By the end of the war, Onassis controlled one of the largest privately owned fleets in the world, and the press began to refer to him as the 'Golden Greek.' His shipping firm would make him one of the most prosperous businessmen in the world, shipping mostly ore and oil around the world.

Onassis arrived in the Mediterranean principality of Monaco in 1953 and began to purchase the shares of Monaco's Société des Bains de mer de Monaco (SBM) via the use of front companies in the tax haven of Panama, and took control of the organisation in the summer of that year. Onassis moved his headquarters into the Old Sporting Club on Monaco's Avenue d'Ostende shortly after taking control of the SBM. The SBM was a significant owner of property in Monaco, and its assets included the Monte Carlo Casino, the Monaco Yacht Club, the Hôtel de Paris and a third of the country's acreage. Onassis's takeover of the SBM was initially welcomed by Monaco's ruler, Prince Rainier III as the state required investment, but Onassis and Rainier's relationship had deteriorated by 1962 in the wake of the boycott of Monaco by the French President, Charles de Gaulle.

Onassis and Rainier had differing visions for Monaco. Onassis wished the country to remain a resort for an exclusive clientele, but Rainier hoped to build hotels and attract a greater number of tourists. Monaco had become less attractive as a tax haven in the wake of France's actions, and Rainier urged Onassis to invest in the construction of hotels. Onassis was reluctant to invest without a guarantee from Rainier that no other competing hotel development would be permitted but promised to build two hotels and an apartment block. Unwilling to give Onassis his guarantee, Rainier used his veto to cancel the entire hotel project, and publicly attacked SBM for their 'bad faith' on television, implicitly criticising Onassis. Rainier and Onassis remained at odds over the direction of the company for several years, and in June 1966 Rainier approved a plan to create 600,000 new shares in SBM to be permanently held by the state, which reduced Onassis's stake from 52% to under a third. In the Supreme Court of Monaco, the share creation was challenged by Onassis who claimed that it was unconstitutional, but the court found against him in March 1967. Following the ruling, Onassis sold his holdings in SBM to the state of Monaco for $9.5 million and left the country.

During the oil boom of the 1950s, Onassis was in final discussions with the King of Saudi Arabia for securing a tanker transport deal. Since the Arabian-American Oil Co. had a monopoly on Saudi oil by a concession agreement, the US government was alarmed by the tanker deal. By 1954, an explicit US policy for Saudi Arabia, in addition to strengthening the US 'special position,' was to take 'all appropriate measures to bring about the cancellation' of an agreement between the Saudi government and Aristotle Onassis to transport Saudi oil on his tankers and 'in any case, to make the agreement ineffective'. The arrangement would have ended monopoly control of Saudi Arabia's oil by American oil companies but was forestalled by the US government.

For this reason, he became a target of the US government, and in 1954, the FBI investigated Onassis for fraud against the US. He was charged with violating the citizenship provision of the shipping laws which required that all ships displaying the US flag were owned by US citizens. Onassis entered a guilty plea and paid $7 million.

Between 1950 and 1956, Onassis had success whaling off the Peruvian coast. His first expedition made a net profit of US$4.5 million. That business ended when The *Norwegian Whaling Gazette* made accusations based on sailors' testimonials, such as one given by Bruno Schalaghecke who worked on the factory ship *Olympic Challenger: '...Pieces of fresh meat from the 124 whales we killed yesterday remains on the deck. Among them all, just one could be considered adult. All animals that pass within the range of the harpoon are killed in cold blood.' The* venture came to an end after the business was sold to Kyokuyo Hogei Kaisha Whaling Company, one of the biggest Japanese whaling companies, for $8.5 million.

A new airline

In late 1955, Hellenic airlines in general faced economic difficulties, whereby companies like TAE were affected by strikes and chronic cash shortages. Over Christmas 1955 TAE suffered a twelve day strike with two main demands: the implementation of collective barganing agreements and the establishment of a suplimentary pension fund.

The Hellenic government decided to transfer the operation of this and the other aviation companies to the private sector and, on 30 July 1956, Aristotle Onassis signed a contract granting him the operational rights to the Greek air transport industry that was ratified by legislative decree on 6 October.

It is not surprising that he chose the name 'Olympic' - already a number of his oil tankers

Above: The deal is done! Aristotle Onassis and the Treasury Secretary of Finance sign the contract transferring the state airline to private control.
Below: Aristotle Onassis (left) the Treasury Secretary of Finance (centre) and Georgios Rallis, the Minister for Transport and Public Works (right) sign the paperwork on 30 July 1956. *(both OA files via ΠΟΛΚ.ΕΟΑ).*

Not the very early days of Olympic Airways, but a classic OA Dakota picture nevertheless. Here SX-BBE gets ready to depart. *(authors collection)*

operated under the Olympic Maritime banner, his shipping company. Also, the names of his ships wore the name Olympic as a prefix: *Olympic Games, Olympic Light, Olympic Palm, Olympic Chivalry, Olympic Explorer* and others.

The government of National Radical Union Prime Minister Constantine Karamanlis also agreed to cover a variety of contingencies, including losses incurred by illegal strikes and losses on transatlantic flights. Other concessions granted to the airline included the right to export profits; the right to import capital goods without customs payments; exemption from corporate taxes and from the payment of landing fees anywhere in Greece; a monopoly on refuelling and handling of foreign air carriers flying into the country; and, if necessary, interest-free loans of $3.5 million.

The First OA Service

By the end of 1956, the ex-government airline had been reorganised and capitalised by Onassis and his three sisters. On 1 January 1957, the concern was given a new name, all the TAE staff were retained, and a small number of additional people were employed: the former UAT French Airlines, S. A. official Francis 'Tom' Fabre was recruited as managing director and Amalia Hadjiargyris as his personal secretary.

The fourteen DC-3s and single DC-4 inherited from TAE were given new livery, and the Olympic symbol of five circles became the company logo.

With Captain Pavlos (Paul) Ioannidis at the controls, a DC-3 inaugurated Olympic's flight operations on 6 April over the route from Athína to Thessaloniki. Captain Ioannidis recalls those early days and Onassis: *'The aeroplane was a new field for him. He wanted to fly all over the world, just as he wanted to send his fleet of ships all over the world. That was it. Cost couldn't stop him; nothing could. Proof of this is that he started with Dakotas and DC.4s and ended up flying jets to five continents.'*

Denise Karagiorga, the sole cabin crew member, along with the captain, the co-pilot and the radio operator, later recalled: *'We didn't serve a meal that day because it was a short flight. Nothing out of the ordinary happened.'*

To some, it was just another airline flight: but not to others. Vassilis Vasilikos, the author and later Hellenic ambassador to Unesco, saw a deeper, cultural significance in Olympic's first flight: *'By inaugurating the link between Thessaloniki and Athína 40 years ago, it succeeded in joining Byzantium and antiquity, the two most important constituents of our national identity.'*

The original Olympic Airways emblem.

Two views of the Olympic Airways offices at 8 Othonos Street on Syntagma Square in the centre of Athína. A fleet of busses picked up passengers for the airport from there, and from the Trans World Airlines offices next door.

Aristotle Onassis deplanes from a OA DC-4. The date on the bottom of the print suggests it was 2 April 1957. *(all authors collection)*

At the time there were few radio navigational aids in Hellenic airspace, and most of the time the pilots were required to fly only under Visual Flight Rules, known as VFR flying.

That led to some innovative flight procedures in bad weather. For example, the approach to runway 09 at Micra Airport, Thessaloniki under low cloud-cover and limited visibility, forcing the pilots to fly about 200 feet above the sea and along the coast. A series of barrels, anchored in the sea, ran parallel to the seashore. When the pilots got to the third barrel, they started to turn right at an angle of about thirty degrees on a 090 degree heading and would soon arrive at the end of runway 09.

Other airports required equally unusual techniques that needed attention and concentration, which appear crazy in today's high-tech digital world, but back then passengers preferred to travel by air rather than make long rail or road journies.

The Saga of the Rings

Legend has it that when Aristotle Onassis heard during the negotiations with the Hellenic Government to obtain what was to become Olympic Airways that he would not be able to use the five Olympic rings in his logo due to copyright issues, he is supposed to have simply said *'...that is not a problem. We will add a sixth ring.'* There is also a widespread belief within Olympic Airways that the airline's aircraft wore this scheme right from the inauguration of services.

There is some doubt as to the truth of this. Certainly, Olympic Airways did eventually use a modified version of the logo of Comité International Olympique (International Olympic Committee). These are five interlocking rings drawn horizontally; three above and two below colored blue, yellow, black, green and red on a white field, known as the 'Olympic rings'. The symbol was designed in 1912 by Baron Pierre de Coubertin, co-founder of the modern Olympic Games. He appears to have intended the rings to represent the five participating continents: Africa,

Early Olympic Airways promotional material.

Left: an early travel poster declaring 'Fly Olympic Airways' and below: the face of OAs October 1957 timetable.

It is interesting to see that neither carry the famous 'six rings' logo, which suggests that Onassis' adoption of the modified Olympic Association design came sometime after the airline was created.

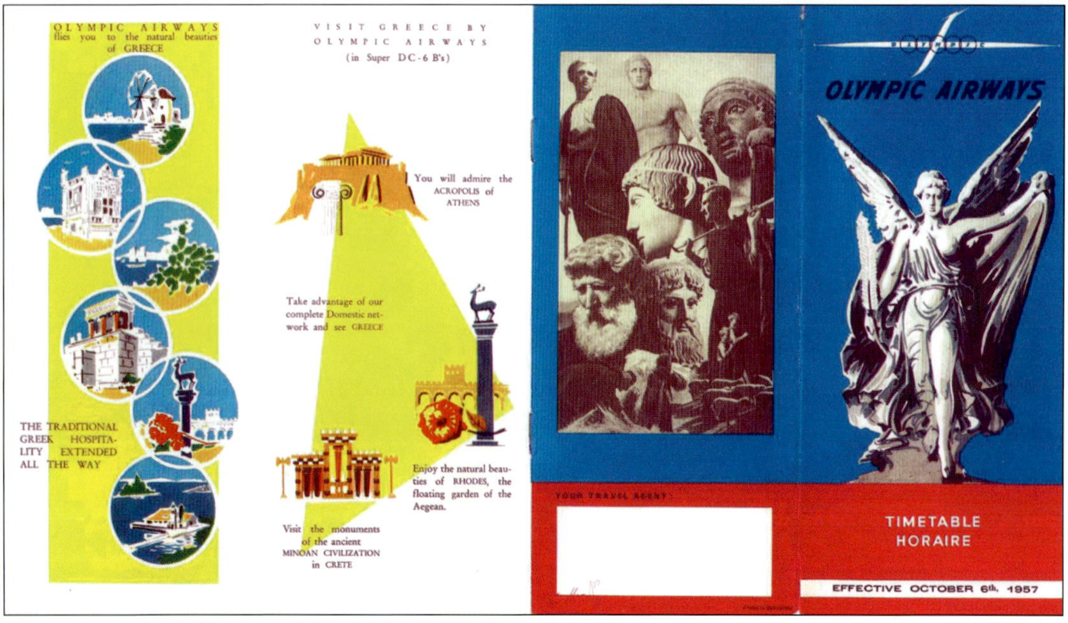

An Olympic Airways postcard showing DC-6B SX-DAE in flight. This rendition shows the aircraft in the so-called 'dark' colour scheme and was used in the very early days of the company, without the six rings on the tail. *(authors collection)*

Asia, America, Australia and Europe.

The Olympic Movement always have been very protective of what it sees as its intellectual property invested in its symbols; as many jurisdictions have given the movement exclusive rights to any interlocking arrangement of five rings, and usage of the word 'Olympic'. They have taken action against numerous groups alleged to have violated this trademark. So it is not surprising that Onassis faced legal objections to what he was planning; however, it appears not to have been instigated at the time that OA was formed.

There is photographic evidence that the early aircraft in the fleet wore a dark blue scheme with an emblem that was 'reversed out' when the need occurred. The only 'rings' were the five white ones surrounding the central part of the Olympic name. It was not until later that the six rings - with one 'broken' and with much more colours - appeared vertically in the tails of the aircraft.

Onassis saw two immediate problems, a shortage of aircraft and a shortage of staff. Straight away he chartered two DC-6s from the French airline Union de Transports Aériens (UTA) and ordered three DC-6s, the latest version manufactured by the Douglas Aircraft Company in the USA. Initially, UTA and Swissair trained the flight crews and technical staff, but Olympic made rapid steps to plan and coordinate the training and hiring of extra employees. They were also not slow in announcing new routes to domestic and foreign destinations while expanding and building the

DC-6 F-BGTY in a hybrid UTA/Olympic colour scheme while on lease from the French airline. As with many of the pictures from the early days, it's not the best of quality, but it does show an important stage of the airlines history. *(authors collection)*

Κυρίες και κύριοι, από το θάλαμο διακυβέρνησης ...
Ladies and gentlemen, from the Flight Deck...

Today inflight announcements starting like this have all but disappeared, replaced by computer screens appearing from the overheads or in the seat-back in front of you. But at a time before those pearls of wisdom issued from the flight deck there used to be sheets of paper - often called 'Flight Status Reports' - that were passed from passenger to passenger down the entire length of the aircraft providing information about the flight. They were often the most transient of items, being looked at briefly - if at all - and then discarded by the stewardess in the galley rubbish.

The Flight Status Report on the opposite page is one such item and is remarkable as it is around sixty years old. It is a DC-3 Dakota flight - the aircraft was SX-BBA - on a journey from Athína to Kerkyra, and is unfortunately not dated, but was discovered in a photograph album with the picture of the aircraft seen below. The Dakota is in the first OA scheme, it previously having been flown by Hellenic and then TAE. This dates it somewhere from 1957 until the aircraft was disposed of to the Hellenic Air Force in 1963. From the markings and the ground the aircraft is parked on - and it is parked, for the control-locks are in place - I would suspect sometime before 1960.

The stewardess was a Miss Vlahoyianni - the aircraft was flying at 8,500 feet or 2,600 metres, just below the level that required oxygen. They were flying at a speed of 144 nautical miles - or 165 miles an hour - which equates to 265 kilometres an hour. At the time it was written, they were either overflying or abeam of Nafpaktos, a small town in nestling in a bay on the north coast of the Gulf of Corinth - close to where the Rio-Antirion Bridge now crosses the Gulf, about halfway between Athína and Kerkyra, the usual distance these type of announcements were made.

Left: DC—3 SX-BBA at Kerkyra.

Below left: on the steps of a DC-3. The sign on the door shows that the aircraft was departing for Athína.

OA operated a whole series of 'Air Experience Flights to give young people the chance to fly. *(all authors collection)*

ΟΛΥΜΠΙΑΚΗ ΑΕΡΟΠΟΡΙΑ
OLYMPIC AIRWAYS

ΠΛΗΡΟΦΟΡΙΑΙ ΔΙΑ ΤΟΥΣ ΕΠΙΒΑΤΑΣ ΕΝ ΠΤΗΣΕΙ
INFORMATION TO PASSENGERS IN FLIGHT

ΑΕΡΟΣΚΑΦΟΣ ΝΤΑΚΟΤΑ ΤΥΠΟΣ DC-3 SX BBA
YOUR AIRCRAFT IS DACOTA TYPE DC-3 SX BBA

Ο ΚΥΒΕΡΝΗΤΗΣ ΣΑΣ ΕΙΝΑΙ:
YOUR CAPTAIN IS: —

ΑΙ ΣΥΝΟΔΟΙ ΣΑΣ ΕΙΝΑΙ:
YOUR CABIN ATTENDANTS ARE:
Δίς ΒΛΑΧΟΓΙΑΝΝΗ
MISS VLAHOVIANNI

ΥΨΟΣ
ALTITUDE
8500 π.
2600 μ.
ΠΟΔΙΑ FEET
ΜΕΤΡΑ METERS

ΘΕΡΜΟΚΡΑΣΙΑ
TEMPERATURE
ΕΞΩΤΕΡΙΚΗ OUTSIDE
ΕΣΩΤΕΡΙΚΗ INSIDE

Η ΤΑΧΥΤΗΣ ΜΑΣ ΕΙΝΑΙ
OUR SPEED IS
144 N.M
Ναυτικὰ μίλια ἀνὰ ὥραν (κόμβοι)
1 ναυτ. μίλι=1.16 στατ. μιλ.=1.85 χμ.
Naut. miles per hour (knots)
1 naut. mile=1.16 stat. mile=1.85 km.

ΚΑΙΡΙΚΑΙ ΣΥΝΘΗΚΑΙ
WEATHER INFORMATION
ΟΜΑΛΑΙ
FINE

Ἡ θέσις μας εἶναι ΝΑΥΠΑΚΤΟΣ
Our position is NAYPAKTOS
Ὑπολογίζομεν ἄφιξιν εἰς ΚΕΡΚΥΡΑΝ 0828 ὥραν Γκρήνουϊτς
Our estimated time of arrival at CORFU is 0828 Greenwich
ἤ 1028 τοπική
or 1028 local

ΠΑΡΑΤΗΡΗΣΕΙΣ
REMARKS

Ὑπογραφὴ Κυβερνήτου
Captain's Signature

ΠΑΡΑΚΑΛΩ ΔΙΑΒΙΒΑΣΑΤΕ
PLEASE PASS ON

Above: From the look of the skyline, this OA DC-3 is landing at Elinnikon. As with most of the OA fleet, this aircraft wore the titles 'OLYMPIC AIRWAYS' on one side, and 'ΟΛΥΜΠΙΑΚΗ' on the other.

Left: Athína in the 1960s, a colourful, bustling place - where 'Olympic Airways' signs proliferated on the roofs on buildings. *(both authors collection)*

required infrastructure in Hellas and abroad to safely and comfortably serve its passengers.

In 1957 OA had one DC-4, two chartered DC-6s from UTA and thirteen DC-3s, operated by a staff of 931 that transported around 244,000 passengers. During the first six months of 1958, twenty pilots and flight engineers were sent to Swissair's flight training centre in Zurich in preparation for operating the new DC-6Bs that were due to arrive the end of August. They would replace the DC-4 and DC-6s for services to Rome, Paris, London, Zurich, Frankfurt, Tel-Aviv, Nicosia and Cairo.

On 29 October 1959, tragedy struck the airline again. DC-3 SX-BAD departed Athína as Flight OA214 at 15:01 local for a flight to Thessaloniki. Following takeoff, the DC-3 climbed to 3000 feet on a 240 degree heading and was then instructed to climb on course to 9000 feet. At 15:20 the crew contacted Tanagra Control, reporting at 9000 feet over Mount Parnis in VMC. This was the last radio contact with the flight; the aircraft crashed near near Avlon Attiki five minutes afterwards.

Officially there were eighteen people on board.

However, postmortem examinations found the remains of a nineteenth victim.

Investigations revealed that the accident was caused by the failure of the gudgeon pin bearing of number six piston of the left engine, which resulted in the sudden breaking of that engine.
There were some contributing factors: the inertia of the propeller at the moment of the breaking of the engine caused failure of the propeller shaft. The broken propeller, rotating, caused serious cuts on the left wing. The latter then separated, and loss of control followed.

The 'look' that said 'Olympic.'
It has been said by many who experienced the era that flying in the early 1960s was more like a lifetime adventure, rather than a simple means of transport from point A to Point B.

Once established, Olympic Airways' international cabin service became known around

Above: A pair of Douglas airliners. SX-DAG, closest to the camera was a C-54A-DO, civilianised as a DC-4 with DC-6 SX-DAH behind on the apron at Ellinikon International Airport in June 1965. (*Peter V Clegg*)

Inset: Jean Dessès (*b*.6 August 1904 – *d*.2 August 1970). the designer of the first Olympic airways uniform that was worn until 1966.

Above left: Three Olympic Airways Air Hostesses pose on what appears to be a set of maintenance steps leading up to the rear door of DC-6B SX-DAI.
(both authors collection)

HRH the Crown Prince Constantine II returns from Italy after winning a gold medal in the 1960 Olympic Games. Sailing in the Bay of Naples, His Royal Highness, with his crew Odysseus Eskidioglou and Georgios Zaimis, beat twenty-six other nations to take the gold.

The calmness of the arrival of the King is in stark contrast to the chaos that met the arrival of George Papandreou (below) back at Athína following his parties landslide election victory in 1964. *(both Spiros Papadopoulos Collection)*

the world as one of the most luxurious and of high quality offered at the time - legend has it that Onassis himself ordered the use of gold-plated China in both First and Economy class in response to the secret (or not so secret) attempts of the First Class passengers to acquire some of the china used for their meals. Onassis aimed for every Greek house to have a reminder of the golden era of Olympic Airways. Fine porcelains and crystals along with elegant designer uniforms combined to achieve a result that left a permanent mark in the history of aviation.

The company's luxurious style brought about by Onassis inspired fashion designers around the world to create exclusive uniform collections to dress the stylish fair hostesses. The designs were either revolutionary or clean-cut classic ones while their accessories range included rubber boots and stylish capes that left their mark in the fashion history. The uniforms were both stylish and refined, while at the same time functional, turning each one of the girls into fashion icons of the time.

Jean Dessès was born Jean Dimitre Verginie in Alexandria, Egypt, to Greek parents, but spent much of his life in Paris when not globetrotting. He was Olympic Airways' first uniform designer and a world-leading fashion designer from the 1940s till the 1960s. He became widely known as the 'king of muslin'. His design for the Olympic Airways uniform included a blue skirt suit fitted in the waist, worn with a crisp white shirt and as was customary with many of the airlines, a chic hat. Hats were a mandatory accessory to the airlines that complimented each uniform, marking the luxury and prestige in aviation.

Plans for expansion...

It was on 23 September 1960 that Olympic Airways revealed details as to their plans for the future. The release started with some background history: *On April 6, 1957, a new era began for the National Greek Airlines.*

It was at this date when Mr Onassis took over from the Greek Government the exploitation of the

For 1960, company notepaper did not have a 'header' as such, instead they used this simple 'footer' at the bottom of the page. (authors collection/OA files)

air services of Greece and formed the Olympic Airways. From that time on, a vast program of reorganization begun with zeal and enthusiasm and is still going on.

Orders for modern new aircraft were placed with the Douglas Aircraft Co.; five DC-6Bs were ordered and delivered in the summer 1958 and two DC-8 Jetliners to be delivered in 1961. On July 20, 1959 the first order for three Comet 4B Jetliners was placed with the De Havilland Aircraft Co.

This is of great interest, for it is the first confirmation I have ever seen that Olympic had indeed been in talks with Douglas in California for the acqusition of a number of DC-8 jet airliners and that these negotiation had reached the stage where delivery dates had been put in place for two. The release continues: '*The technical evolution is followed up closely. Crew members are constantly sent abroad for further training. Up to this date thirty-two crew members have been trained in England at the De Havilland Co. for the Comet 4Bs, of which twelve Pilots, ten Co-Pilots and ten flying Technical Personnel as well as fifty-eight ground Technical Personnel. Another group of fifteen Technicians and Pilots are about to complete their training course in a few days. The training of other crewmembers, for the Comet 4Bs, will follow shortly and it is estimated that more than 1,200,000$ will be disposed for the completion of the whole training program.*

Cabin staff also underwent a long training course and those who graduated, form today OA's world-famous cabin attendants. The passenger is ensured of enjoying select food offered in pleasant surroundings with the crew ready to satisfy all demands and wishes.

The great development of this airline has been extended in all fields. Its fleet has risen from 15 aircraft to 21.

5 Comet 4B Jetliners, 3 DC-6Bs, 2 DC-4s, 13 DC-3s. On order: 1 Comet 4B and 2 DC-8 Jetliners.

As Olympic Airways entered the Jet Age new Booking Offices have opened, both in Greece and abroad and the existing ones were furnished and decorated in modern style. The maintenance Hangars at Athens Hellinikon Airport have been extended and staffed with qualified and experienced craftsmen. The latest machinery has been ordered and installed. Under present practice, every aircraft undergoes rigid check-ups before and after every flight.

The information sheets also contained an amount of statistical data: *Since the foundation of Olympic Airways a remarkable increase is noted in the transportation of passengers, cargo and mail, both on Domestic and International routes.*

During 1957 Olympic Airways carried:
- *a) 218,886 passengers.*
- *b) 2,491,000 Kgs cargo and excess baggage*
- *c) 296,000 Kgs Mail*

During 1958 Olympic Airways carried:
- *a) 551,648 passengers*
- *b) 5,507,000 kgs cargo and excess baggage*
- *c) 459.000 kgs Mail.*

What might have been. From a 1958 publication on IATA airlines comes this rendition of a Douglas DC-8 in pre-Olympic rings markings. *(authors collection)*

An Air France Caravelle gets airborne in the background as Douglas DC-6B SX-DAE and Dakota SX-BAD - the registration is just visible through the foliage of the tree by the tail - awaits another service at Ellinkikon. The DC-6 was later lost when it slammed into a mountainside near Cape Sounion on Monday 8 December 1969. *(Spiros Papadopoulos Collection)*

During 1959 Olympic Airways carried:

a) 425,428 passengers
b) 4,595,545 kgs cargo and excess baggage
c) 589,471 kgs Mail

From January 1, 1960 to August 1, 1960 Olympic Airways carried:

a) 312,870 passengers
b) 5,641, 651 kgs cargo and excess baggage
c) 482.282 Mail

The above figures show the continuous preference of passengers for the service both in flight and on ground, as well as the choice of cargo customers to ship their goods by Olympic Airways, due to careful and safe transportation of their shipments.

To-day, in length of network and frequency of flights, Olympic Airways is scheduled among the big airlines of Europe. In respect of the quality of the various services and amenities offered to its clients and particularly the service given on board its

One of Olympic's modernised offices after refurbishment. *(Spiros Papadopoulos Collection)*

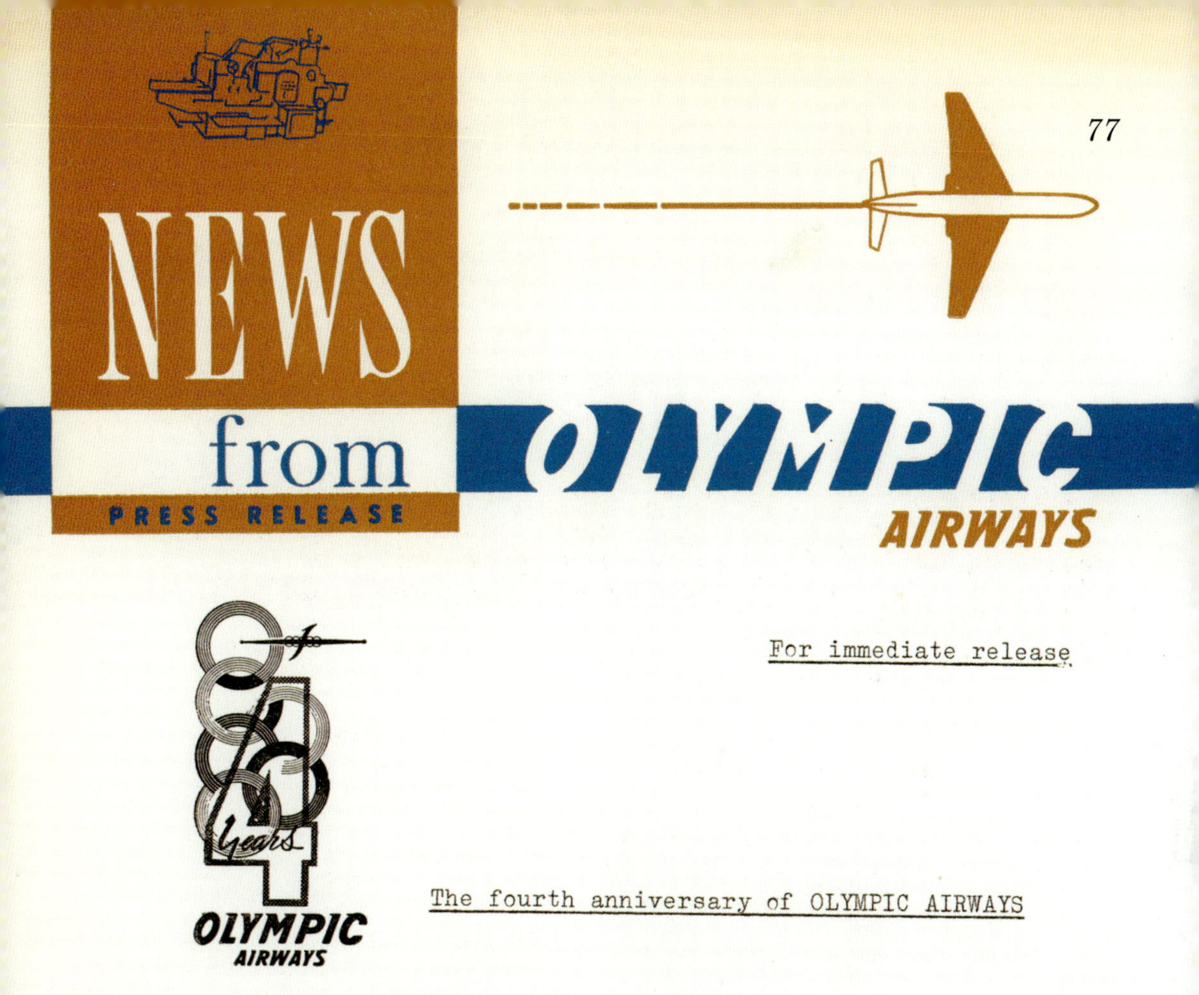

NEWS from OLYMPIC AIRWAYS

PRESS RELEASE

For immediate release

4 Years OLYMPIC AIRWAYS

The fourth anniversary of OLYMPIC AIRWAYS

The header of a Press Release from Olympic dated 4 April 1961 that features the so-far only located design of the 4 Years logo. *(Authors collection/OA files)*

aircraft, it is considered among the best in the world.

Olympic Airways which is now serving fifteem cities in twelve countries in its International Network and links 14 Greek cities and islands with Athína in its Domestic Network, transported high personalities and world known film stars as well as the most difficult and exigent category of passengers.

...and problems with Taxes

By all accounts, Onassis made only one serious error in the concession game. Ironically, it was the concession that aroused most public criticism - Olympic's exemption from taxes. It had come about as a result of his original negotiations with Karamanlis when the airline had been proposed. Onassis had explained his antipathy for tax collectors and his aversion to people riffling through his books.

'Never mind…' Karamanlis has been quoted as saying. *'… Will you settle for a percentage of turnover instead - not much, something entirely nominal?'*

'Of course' Onassis replied, appreciating Karamanlis's need for some return and that the establishment of turnover did not involve any indecently deep probing of the accounts. *'How much had you in mind?* Karamanlis suggested two percent, and Onassis had promptly agreed.

Olympic's first few years of operation were at a genuine loss. It was then that Onassis appreciated his rashness in offering a percentage of revenue in exchange for tax exemption. One did not pay taxes when suffering losses. Onassis, for the first and only time in his life, was seized by an overwhelming desire to be liable for tax. He went to confess this to Karamanlis, sincerely pleading to be treated like everyone else. For once Onassis was outmanoeuvred. Karamanlis, realising that Onassis's accounting techniques could make Olympic a profit or loss-maker more or less at will, refused his request for 'equal treatment.' He did, how ever, offer to reduce the percentage of the take to half a percent and facilitated a 100-million-drachma, low-interest loan from the public coffer to compensate for past 'overpayments.'

Above: SX-DAI on a stand at Maritsa International Airport on Rodos. The airport has been built in 1935 by the Italians and was the main passenger, commercial and military airport - coded '801' - under the italian occupation of the Dodecanese. The airport was named after a local village, but also had the secondary name of G. Pessi Parvis after the Italian ace of the First World War who was killed in the Aegean. After World War Two, the airport remained in use as a military/civilian airport until 1977, when most of the flying moved to the new airport by the coast. *(Spiros Papadopoulos Collection)*

Left: In recent years there has been a proliferation of art and design - mainly airline posters that proport to be genuine, but often are not. This poster sent to me by a friend in Hellas I have never been sure about. It certainly looks of the time, but why make and pay for a full-colour poster, and then reproduce the central part of the image - the DC-4 in black and white?

It was not long before the fledgeling airline expanded - in a modest way. Three more Douglas DC-6Bs were ordered, and on 2 May the first of these operated a regular scheduled service between Athína - Rome - Paris and London.

Battle of the Titans

Stavros S. Niarchos, whose name means 'master of ships,' was, quite simply, a master at seizing the moment and turning it to his advantage, especially if it involved the complex world of shipping. What others may have perceived as a disaster, he recognised as nothing but an opportunity, whether it be an economic depression, war or a shortage - or glut - of oil. The secret of his shipping success was deceptively simple: buy cheap and buy big.

Niarchos, also spent much of his life locked in an endless battle his arch-rival Aristotle Onassis for supremacy on the high seas, in conspicuous consumption and at the altar; he also continually battled with Onassis over Olympic Airways.

Niarchos, who was conceived in Buffalo, New York - where his Greek-born parents had become naturalised American citizens - but was born in Athína on 3 July 1909, three months after his parents had returned from the United States. Growing up in the adjacent port city of Piraeus, he developed a lifelong love of the water, swimming frequently and sailing his first boat at the age of nine.

Although he earned a law degree from the University of Athína when just twenty, his father's financial reversals forced him to seek a more immediately promising career; he joined a flour-

OA DC-3 SX-BBF awaits another load of passengers at Ellinkikon. *(Spiros Papadopoulos Collection)*

milling operation operated by his maternal uncles. Their business imported grain from Argentina, and trying to keep costs down in the 1930's, Niarchos recognised that the family could save freight fees by operating its own ships.

At his urging, his uncles bought seven battered freighters at the Depression-level prices of $20,000 each, and the Niarchos fleet was born. He soon added to the holdings, always buying the largest ships available.

World War Two proved a bonanza for him. He leased his ships to the Allies in 1941 and spent the rest of the war in the Greek Navy. When the war ended in 1945, Niarchos, who had become the assistant Greek naval attache in Washington, did not grieve over the loss of six of his ships to German bombs and submarine attacks. He took his $2 million in insurance proceeds and began buying up surplus Liberty and Victory cargo ships and some T2 tankers that had been mass produced during the war.

To avoid US restrictions on the sale of such vessels to foreigners, Stavros Niarchos formed a company in which his American-born sister and some American friends owned a three-quarter interest. But after Niarchos compounded his audacity by leasing the ships to a Panamanian company to avoid American taxes, the

The café outside the original terminal building at Ellinikon. It was not long before it became an area where the many celebrities who were passing through the airport posed for photographs, becoming something of a hotspot and hang out for the paparazzi. The structure survived right up to the closure of the airport, incorporated into the front area of Olympic Airways' domestic West terminal. *(Spiros Papadopoulos Collection)*

The apron at Ellinikon International Airport, with an OA DC-3 and DC-6B. From the cars, it is thought that the picture dates from around 1965. (*Peter V Clegg*)

Government sued, and he agreed to pay a $12 million penalty, give up some of the ships and have three supertankers built at American shipyards.

As usual, the settlement ended up to his advantage. It came as Stavros Niarchos, who had foreseen the post-war boom in trade, was beginning a shipbuilding spree. Not only did the three large tankers prove far more profitable than the smaller ships he had to surrender, but he also ended up commissioning others, each bigger than the one before.

Stavros Niarchos was one of the first ship owners to grasp the economies of scale: this was that a ship that could carry twice as much oil at twice the fees did not cost twice as much to build or to operate. But he was not the only one to understand the concept. So did Aristotle Onassis, and in the decade after the war, the two began a rivalry that amounted to what was to evolve into a global game of one-upmanship.

If Aristotle Onassis built a 30,000-ton ship, Stavros Niarchos was sure to respond with one of 31,000 tons. The shipbuilding competition continued until 1956 when Niarchos launched the 47,750-ton *Spyros Niarchos,* then the largest tanker afloat.

The owner of Olympic Airways that never was: Stavros Spyros Niarchos; *b*.3 July 1909 – *d*.16 April 1996)

And Niarchos, who became a hero in Greece by building the country's first shipyard after the war, found himself upstaged when Aristotle Onassis became an even bigger national hero in the jet age by creating Olympic Airways.

For Niarchos, who savoured his title as the owner of the largest private tanker fleet, 1956 was to prove the high-water mark in his competition with Aristotle Onassis. Curiously, his very success caused his setback. When the Suez crisis of 1956 closed the canal, this created an enormous new demand for tankers and doubled shipping rates, much of his vast fleet was tied up in long-term contracts to the pre-crisis rates. Onassis meanwhile, who had mostly been locked out of the market by Niarchos, was able to take advantage of the crisis and cash in on the higher rates.

But the Onassis advantage proved short-lived. Niarchos only bullied his way out of the

Above: DC-6 SX-DAD on the ground at Heraklion, Crete in 1963. *(Spiros Papadopoulos Collection)*

Right: A poster advertising the Athína to Alexandria service using the DC-6B.

old contracts, arguing that conditions had changed.

Although Stavros Niarchos lost the opening battle for Olympic, he never abandoned the war. Indeed, one consequence of Niarchos's and Onassis's 'return' to the Hellenic economy was a new level of absurdity in their rivalry.

In reality, whenever Onassis, as a negotiating ploy, threatened to abandon Olympic, Niarchos would immediately offer to take it over. His proposals were invariably accompanied by letters of guarantee from foreign banks, always a potent inducement since money in foreign banks always impressed the Hellenic politicians more than money in Hellenic banks.

There was also what Onassis called 'my salvation, my key to escape.' This was clause 25a of his frequently revised concession to operate Olympic, which allowed either side to terminate the agreement on six months' notice without giving any reason. In games of dare and double-dare with the government, it was a useful threat to have in reserve.

In March 1965, while doing battle with the government of George Papandreou, Onassis explicitly threatened to use the escape clause. 'I feel like a woman who has given birth,' he exclaimed at the time, after a celebratory night out. But as soon as he heard that there were others ready and willing to take over Olympic, he eagerly reassumed responsibility for the airline.

It was, however, a technique that was bound to create enemies. One of the most powerful of these became Air Marshal George Doukas, a former head of the Hellenic Civil Aviation Authority. Doukas submitted a report on Olympic to the government in August 1967. It appeared to be a highly damaging document alleging numerous failures by Olympic to honour its obligations or to act in the national interest and characterising Onassis as 'a cancerous growth on Greek society'.

His credo consisted of having no feeling of being bound by his signature, and of buying people and favours by the classic method of corrupting consciences.' Doukas went on to describe Onassis's method of extracting concessions as

In the 1950s and 1960s, the aircraft and air hostesses all tended to have colour schemes and images that worked together. Here SX-DAI, OA's DC-6B is seen at London Heathrow, with the BEA hangars in the background wearing the classic blue and white scheme, which matched perfectly the Jean Dessès outfits worn by the Olympic Airways stewardesses. The finishing touch, of course, was the white gloves.

Below: passengers are escorted out to what appears to be DC-3 SX-BAL at what is thought to be Tripoli Airport on the Peloponnese.
(all Spiros Papadopoulos Collection)

A typical Ellinikon Airport scene in June 1965. The DC-3 on the left is SX-ECD which belongs to the Hellenic Civil Aviation Authority but was under the care of OA Maintenance. The Olympic DC-3 parked in the hangar mouth is SX-BAH. Behind the photographer is what became Olympic's Domestic Terminal, and off the top left, behind the DC-3s is the Leoforos Posidonos road. *(Peter Clegg)*

Right: a group of seven Olympic hostesses on the steps leading up to the main cabin of DC-6 SX-DAM. *(via Spiros Papadopoulos Collection)*

exhibiting, '*...even under the most charitable of interpretations, the culmination of an entirely brigand-like hunger, the absolute negation of any moral element in his dealings, and the base insolence of his approach*.'

Onassis sued for defamation of character, the only time he ever did so, and it emerged that Doukas's indictment was thin on concrete facts (though those he produced were in the main correct) and faulty in its deductions. Doukas eventually withdrew the allegations, and the case was dropped.

The Niarchos camp quickly learned to maintain close links with Air Marshal Doukas. When Onassis's monopoly was extended until the year 2006, Niarchos challenged the decision in the courts. The concession, he claimed, should not have been renewed before its expiration, and then only as a result of an open competition. His suit was rejected because he had suffered no material damage as a consequence of the new concession and that, whatever his present interest in Olympic, there was no evidence that he would still be interested when Onassis's original authorisation expired.

Throughout the 1960s and into the early 1970s, Onassis maintained a headquarters building at 8 Othonos Street on Syntagma Square, right in the centre of Athína. In the lobby, there was a doorman who ushered visitors to an elevator, with another guard upstairs directing those to wherever the guests wanted to go. 'Megalos', or 'Big Boss' as many of the Olympic Airways employees called Onassis - but never to his face - had an office on the fourth floor, carpeted by a thick blue and grey pile; the windows were also one-way tinted, preserving the inherent anonymity of those inside. By all accounts though, Onassis' office was wherever Onassis was, for he seemed to run the airline and his shipping empire from a series of battered notebooks, held together by a multitude of elastic bands - luxurious office suites were for others and for show!

A more rarefied level of farce was achieved by the plot to thwart Onassis's plans for a prestigious new headquarters for Olympic Airways. Onassis had his eye on what was, without doubt, the most desirable development site in Athína, - the corner of Syntagma Square, opposite parliament and the

Right: 1965 Domna Touli and Moschos Koniaris show off their new uniforms.

Below: Passengers board an unidentified DC-3 of OA. The date is thought to be sometime in 1960.
(both Spiros Papadopoulos Collection)

Hotel Grande Bretagne, once the site of the Athína police headquarters. It was a narrow site of 1,300 square metres, and whoever rebuilt it was obliged to landscape it with flower beds. Thus it was not regarded as economical for a hotel, so the previous owner had offered it as embassies to the Italian and the Yugoslav governments, both of which declined the offer. The owner subsequently died, bequeathing his site in a manner sophisticated enough to guarantee lucrative employment for Athenian lawyers. He left fifteen percent to his niece and divided the rest into ten and five percent units, which he left to such varied institutions and persons as two municipalities on his native island, the Athína Home for the Blind, the Parnassos (a philological association), the Navy and the Air Force Funds, and two lawyers.

Onassis had succeeded in buying out only one of the lawyers before Niarchos, getting wind of his plans, snapped up the other. Score: Onassis five percent of the site, Niarchos five percent.

Onassis beat Niarchos to the Home for the Blind's ten percent, but Niarchos lodged a protest with the Homes board of governors because he was prepared to offer more. The board then called for bids, and Onassis shrewdly submitted one for one drachma more than anyone else might offer. Niarchos cried foul, and the board reconsidered the matter. 'Being composed mainly of Thessaloniki

Politicians...

Above left: Prime Minister George Papandreou and Minister Amynos P. Grusoulios pass through Ellinikon, watched by a military Guard of Honour. Above right: M. Glezos and G. Pspodimitres at the Kavolos (Kavala) Airport with OA flight sometime in 1958.

Bottom left: 1959. Spyros Merskezinis boards an OA flight to Thessaloniki. In 1955 Markezinis founded the Progressive Party in Hellas, but failed to win seats in the 1956 elections. Markezinis's Party eventually won a seat in parliament in the 1958 elections. Below right: February 1964. G. Mouros and A. Papandreou arrive with OA. At the airport of Hsinia for the funeral of Sofoklis Venizelos (Σοφοκλής Βενιζέλος 3 November 1894 – 7 February 1964) a Hellenic politician, who three times served as Prime Minister of the Hellenic Republic. (photos: ΠΟΛΚ.ΕΟΑ).

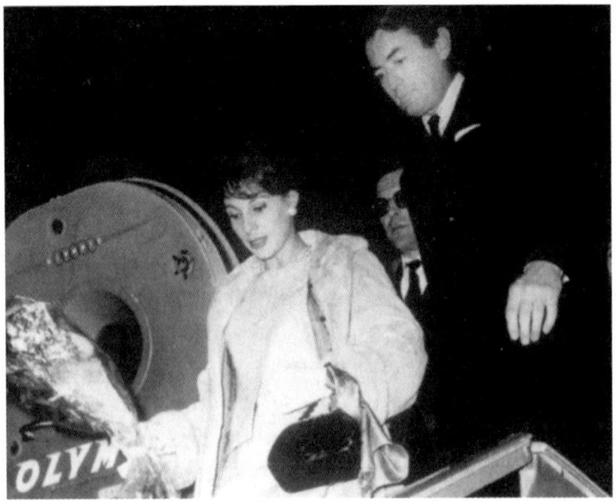

...and celebrities!

Above left: American film star Gregory Peck and his wife Veronique Passani disembark from an OA Comet. Above right: Jayne Mansfield arriving in 1965. She was an American actress in film, theatre, and television, and also a nightclub entertainer, a singer, and one of the early Playboy Playmates, so it is not surprising she was much photographed by the Hellenic paparazzi!

Bottom left: It was August 1970 when movie star Christopher Lee and his family were photographed arriving on an Olympic 707. Bottom right: Dame Elizabeth Taylor, DBE the British-American actress, businesswoman, and humanitarian. She began her career as a child actress in the early 1940s and was one of the most popular stars of classical Hollywood cinema in the 1950s. She continued her career successfully into the 1960s and remained a well known public figure for the rest of her life. She was also a regular visitor to Hellas with her sometimes husband Richard Burton as guests of Aristotle Onassis: she is seen here leaving the West Terminal of Ellinikon, having just arrived on an Olympic flight - first class of course! (photos: ΠΟΛΚ.ΕΟΑ).

University professors who regularly commuted to Athína on Olympic Airways,' said a Niarchos man, 'they opted for Onassis.' Score: Onassis 10, Niarchos 5.

The Navy Fund, which had been following the proceedings with keen interest, then decided to auction their share of the site. Bidding started at 64,000 drachmas ($2,112) per square metre. The Niarchos side learned that Onassis had given his men a bidding ceiling, which they guessed was 75,000 drachmas ($2,475). Since the bidding was required to go up by not less than one percent increments, the Niarchos men cautiously manoeuvred their offer to 74,000 drachmas, which meant that the Onassis men could not top it if their deduction were correct. It was. Niarchos then rapidly snapped up part of the niece's share and all the remaining shares, save that of the Air Force Fund and another 5 percent which the niece kept for sentimental reasons. Score: Niarchos 70, Onassis still only 15.

Before he could do anything with his prize, Niarchos had to fight a two-year court battle to oblige the other owners - Onassis included - to sell. The court ordered a compulsory auction of the entire site on 8 March 1970, winner to take all. To the consternation of the Niarchos men, Onassis did not appear to be represented. Instead, representatives of the Seamen's Pension Fund (NAT) turned up and started bidding vigorously for the site. The Niarchos team had an open line to their boss's erie in Saint Moritz and were under orders to get the site at all costs. The men from the NAT, seemingly oblivious to their determination, continued to force the price ever upward until even Niarchos began to have second thoughts. Only the nagging suspicion that the NAT might be a front for Onassis, and that he had made a deal with the seamen which would give him the entire site after all, meant that Niarchos held his resolve. Now it was the turn of the men from the NAT to start sweating, which they did with repeated requests for recesses so that they could consult amongst themselves. Finally, at 116.1 million drachmas, roughly $3,600 per square metre, they caved in. The site was Niarchos's at last, for a record price. Niarchos might well have wondered who in fact had been the winner since Onassis had made a handsome profit at his expense. For a while, he toyed with the idea of erecting an office building, but his interest in the site died with his pyrrhic victory. At least he got his money back by selling the site to the National Bank of Greece for 120 million drachmas. Onassis

Left: Aircraft engineers are engineers the world over, somewhat overweight, sleeves and trouser legs of their oily overalls rolled up to fit, baseball caps on the back of the head - Olympic's were the same, as seen in this 1961 picture.

Below: the Olympic Domestic Terminal at Ellinikon in the early 1960s. (both (ΠΟΛΚ.ΕΟΑ).

Heraklion Airport, Crete around 1960. *(ΠΟΛΚ.ΕΟΑ).*

built the new Olympic Airways headquarters at 96-100 Syngrou Avenue.

By then the personal rivalry between the two men had extended beyond the world of commercial shipping. Onassis, for example, was jealous at glowing magazine reports pointing out that Niarchos, who maintained numerous palatial homes around the world, preferred to run his business from the 190-foot Creole, invariably described as the world's largest and most beautiful sailing vessel.

The Onassis response was to commission the 325-foot Christina, formerly a Canadian anti-submarine River-class frigate called HMCS *Stormont,* launched in 1943. It was not long until Niarchos abandoned the *Creole* in favour of the motorised *Atlantis,* fifty feet longer than the *Christina*.

And when Niarchos bought the Aegean island of Spetsopoula and stocked it with rare plants and game, making it a hunting paradise where he entertained royalty, heads of state and members of the jet set, Onassis bought an island of his own, Skorpios, six years later.

Niarchos's good sense of timing saved his fortune. He sold off most of his fleet of tankers before the bottom fell out of the industry in the 1970's. But he and Onassis were both bruised by the protracted downturn. In 1970 they even entered into a rare joint venture, to build an oil refinery in Hellas.

Niarchos stayed in business, but the fleet of

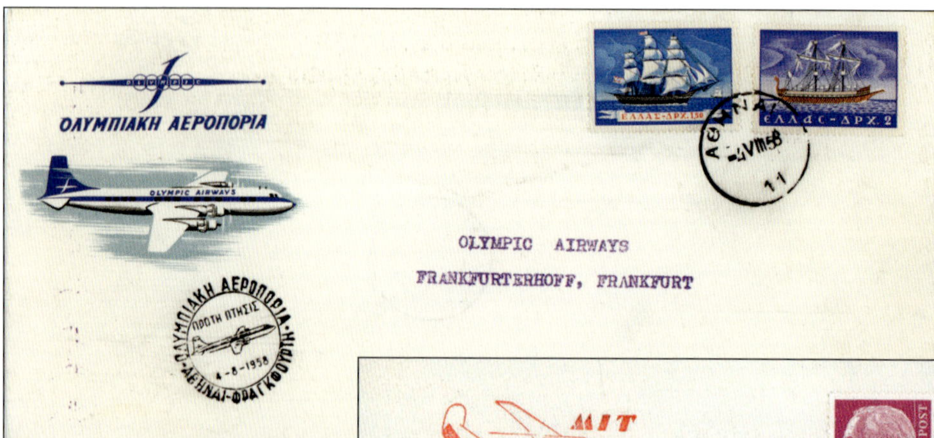

Two first day covers from 1958.

Above: the launch of the Athína - Frankfurt service.

Right: - Frankfurt - Zurich - Athen - Kairo.
(both authors collection)

Above: the Olympic International Terminal and Transit at Ellinikon in 1957....

...about the same time this picture of the OA ground engineers in front of a DC-6 was taken. *(both (ΠΟΛΚ.ΕΟΑ).*

Then, below, the same area a few years later.

DC-3s and Mercedes-Benz busses -it has to be the West Terminal of Ellinikon. (OA Files)

Niarchos Ltd. whose offices were in London became a mere shadow consisting of about eight oil tankers. His family had remained deeply involved in the business, including his three sons, who were expected to continue managing the fleet.

In their rivalry, when Onassis scored a social coup by marrying Tina Livanos, the daughter of the long-reigning Greek shipping czar Stavros Livanos, Niarchos, who had been married and divorced twice, responded by marrying the other Livanos daughter, Eugenie.

It was a rivalry Niarchos was destined to lose, but he had his moments. In 1965, for example, he divorced Eugenie and at the age of fifty-six married Charlotte Ford, the twenty-four year-old daughter of Henry Ford II, the American automobile industrialist. She gave birth to a child a few months later, and they were divorced in 1967.

The next year Aristotle Onassis played his own matrimonial trump card by marrying Jacqueline Kennedy, the widow of the slain American President, John F. Kennedy, and widely regarded as the world's most admired woman, but I am getting ahead of the story!

Since the Hellenic Church had not recognised Niarchos's Mexican divorce, he blithely resumed his marriage to Eugenie. After she died of an overdose of sleeping pills in 1970, Niarchos obtained some consolation by marrying Aristotle Onassis' former wife, Tina.

Her death in Paris in 1974, also from an overdose of sleeping pills, created something of a scandal when her daughter, Christina Onassis, demanded an autopsy with the implication that Stavros Niarchos may have had a hand in her death. The investigation cleared him.

It is clear that Aristotle Onassis enjoyed his battles with Nairchos, and also the exercise in mystification, but the complexities of his airline business were far from being accidental. For Olympic Airways under Onassis was not unlike the creation of some maverick astronomer who, refusing to concede that the earth revolves around the sun, is thereby obliged to create ever weirder, more convoluted, and perilous mechanisms in order to make everything agree with his highly personal view of the cosmos. Onassis had approached Olympic with two unshakable convictions: should the red revolution come (and the chances of it have always seemed fair-to-good in Hellas, especially during the 1960s and 70s), there would be nothing to grab if someone had a mind to nationalize the airline; and Olympic should at all costs avoid the appearances of profitability, which could only make the government reluctant to grant future concessions. These convictions gave Olympic its underlying business logic. By their very nature they were not ones that he could readily impart to the authorities or the courts.

Chapter Four

Into The Jet Age

Aristotle Onassis eyed the forthcoming introduction of the De Havilland Comet 4 jet airliner by British European Airways - scheduled to start in April 1960 - with considerable envy. The world was becoming jet-conscious, and Onassis knew that he had to look well ahead to the use of jet equipment if Olympic was to progress at a rate that would make it a truly commercially successful airline. These were, however, early days, and the airline had much ground work to perform to consolidate its position. By way of doing this services were opened to Zurich and Frankfurt, with the DC-6Bs, and then to Tel Aviv.

Looking to the future, Olympic opened a ticket office in New York in 1958, its primary purpose being to 'sell' the airline to American travellers to Hellas, for TWA had operated a New York-Athína service since 1946. By opening a New York office, it did much to make the American businessmen and travelling public that they might be able to fly around the country on a visit to Hellas.

1959 saw airlines like Air France and SAS begin to start using twin-jet Sud Aviation Caravelles which in America Delta, and United were flying their domestic routes with four-engined Douglas DC-8s. In Europe, British Overseas Airways Corporation had re-started their De Havilland Comet services.

BEA planned that from 1960 until 1964 roughly one-quarter of their capacity would be produced by Comet 4Bs. The target for aircraft utilisation was 2,400 hours per aircraft per year, a work rate almost equal to the figure achieved by the Corporation's turboprop Vickers Viscounts already in service.

The use of jet airliners on services into and out of Athína was going to create a huge threat to Olympic's market, and so Onassis started to look for a way of countering it. Onassis had always been one who wanted to be at the cutting edge of progress and the obvious solution was 'if you cannot beat them, join 'em', but Olympic's finances were not that great to buy a big enough fleet of jets to make and sustain an impact in the marketplace.

Onassis needed to come up with a plan, and on 20 July 1959, it was announced by De Havillands that Olympic was to purchase a pair of Comet 4Bs. There was one more announcement: Aristotle Onassis and Lord Douglas of Kirtleside, the Chairman of BEA

An 'artists impression' of a De Havilland Comet 4B, marked 'S-DAX' in the proposed OA colour scheme. *(DH Hatfield)*

Above: Olympic's first Comet 4B on test from Hatfield - still bearing it's British registration of G-APYC - prior to it's delivery on 25 April 1960. *(DH Hatfield)*

Left: As part of the acceptance proceedure, a team of technicians and engineers from OA visited Hatfield for a number of training courses on the new airliner. *(ΠΟΛΚ.ΕΟΑ)*

Below left - pre-delivery advertising.

stated that a consortium agreement had already been signed between Olympic Airways and BEA providing for joint operational and commercial exploitation of their route network between the UK, Hellas and the Eastern Mediterranean. Each concern was to maintain its identity, no sale or purchase of stock was involved, and both expect to continue to work in close collaboration with all other airlines as they have in the past.

Both airlines hoped for a major increase in their traffic as the outcome of their co-operation, the introduction of Comets in the Spring of 1960, their significantly increased provision of the first-class service, and their joint drive for lower fares.

The large-capacity Continental Comet 4B, seating eighty-seven mixed-class passengers typically, suited both Olympic and BEA equally well. At the time they provided the fastest and best jet travel across Europe. Athína was to come within 3½ hours flying time of London; Beirut, Tel Aviv and

Cairo within 4½ hours. Olympic spoke of possible extensions into the Middle East, to such cities as Damascus, Teheran, Doha, and Kuwait.

Onassis also signed an agreement with BEA for them to provide technical support and training to Olympic's flight crew and technical staff.

The first flight crew-training course, was held at BEA's training centre at London Heathrow. Four people attended the course:BEA's flight operations director, Captain W. Baillie and from Olympic, Captain P. Kyrtatos, Chief Flight Engineer A. Papageorgiou, and Captain Paul Ioannidis.

All the Olympic employees involved did everything possible to conduct the scheduled flights

Left: Captain Paul Ioannidis and the crew deplanes from *Queen Frederica* after the first arrival of the Comet from London (*ΠΟΛΚ.ΕΟΑ)*

Below: The bay of Glyfada, on the outskirts of Athína, seen from a circling DH Comet. Ellinokon Airport is just out of shot on the left. *(DH Hatfield)*

on time and to complete the necessary training programme in light of the upcoming incorporation of the Comet 4B into the fleet. The three Olympic Flight Crew who had been trained helped by conducting flights from London to Paris and back to London in the evenings after their classroom training sessions.

In preparation for the opening of the Comet services, some fifty engineers from Olympic took a series of technical courses with De Havillands at Hatfield. Starting in November 1959, these courses covered the maintenance of Comet airframes, engines, instruments and electrical apparatus. Olympic Airways aircrews also underwent short ground familiarisation courses at Hatfield as part of their training.

The consortium integrated the schedules of each airline's Comet 4Bs, Viscount 806s (BEA) and DC-6Bs (Olympic), and so established Athína as a 'hub' of the Eastern Mediterranean.

The broad strategy was for two of BEA's Comet 4Bs and Olympic's two 4Bs to operate on a daily basis into Athína from London, Paris and Rome. From the Greek capital, they will fan out to Istanbul, Nicosia, Beirut, Tel Aviv and Cairo. At the same time, BEA's Viscount 806s and Olympic's three DC-6Bs would regularly connect London, Frankfurt, Rome, Milan, Geneva and Zurich with Athína, fanning out thence to the Middle East areas mentioned above, including Ankara.

Athína would thus be the consortium's 'junction

The BEA/OA consortium operated jointly marked Comets: BEA machines with 'Olympic' painted in the cheat line, as seen on G-APMC. *(authors collection)*

Olympic machines flew with the Red Square BEA logo near the aircraft's doors, as shown on SX-DAK *Queen Frederika*. *(DH Hatfield)*

box' for connections from eight major European cities to six big Middle East cities and vice versa. Each airline would have significantly enlarged scope for inter-line and interchange opportunities. BEA aimed to increase their revenue over these routes in 1960-61 by 30 per cent. Already BEA's East Mediterranean routes, being long-haul and relatively non-seasonal were the Corporation's most profitable. Now, with the Athína 'booster station' providing more payload to points in the Middle East, these routes would sustain this profitability by providing the traffic for the Comet 4B fleet.

For Olympic the economic advantages of the consortium were a minimum jet fleet, to be maintained by its partner and the maximum of traffic. At the same time, the schedules of Cyprus Airways - connecting Nicosia and Athína with Istanbul, Ankara and Beirut - were fully integrated into the BEA-Olympic consortium.

The first BEA Comet, G-APMA, commenced certification trials on 27 June and had flown about 100 hours by 13 August. On 11 July 1959, it made a day return trip to Athína, taking about 3½ hours each way and giving travellers from England 5½ hours in the Greek capital; yet they were back in time to dine in London.

While the London passengers were enjoying the delights of Athína, two passenger demonstration flights around southern Greece occurred. Professor Theodore Garofalides, President of Olympic Airways, and Costas Konialidis, Managing Director, were present.

The flights were of technical interest because of the runway in use; the long since disappeared 'Zero Three/Two One'. The Comet was using Zero Three,

Right: One of the early 'Comet Girls' for Olympic beside the tail of SX-DAL. Her hat shows the continuation of style with the rosette' that harked back to the days of TAE.

Below: The airside area of the West Terminal in the 1960s. *(both Spiros Papadopoulos Collection)*

Above: the face of the January 1960 British European Airways/Olympic Airways timetable that almost for the first time was advertising Greece as a holiday destination.

PROPOSED COMET 4B SERVICES FROM LONDON – SUMMER 1960

London (Paris, Munich) to Rome, Athens, Istanbul, Cyprus, Cairo, Tel Aviv and Beirut

(British European Airways, Olympic Airways and Cyprus Airways)

Daily	Tue.	Tue. (c) Thur.	Mon. We. Sat.	Wed. (f) Fri. Sun.	Wed. Fri. Sat. Sun.	Mon.	Tue. Thu.	Tue. Thu.	Sat.		Frequency		Sun.	Wed. Fri.	Wed. Fri.	Tue.	Mon. Thu. Sat. Sun.	Wed. (f) Fri.	Mon. Th.(d) Sat.	Tue. Thu. Sun.	Wed.	Daily
OA410	OA402	OA514	OA602	OA371	BE130	BE134/ CY134/34	BE126	BE136/ CY136/6	OA420/ 614		Flight No.		OA429/ 615	CY7/137 /BE137	BE127	CY35/135 /BE135	BE131	OA515	OA372	OA603	OA403	OA409
10.30*	—	—	—	—	12.10*	12.10*	12.10*	22.10*	22.10*	dep	LONDON	arr	06.00*	06.00*	16.10*	16.10*	16.10*	—	—	—	—	17.40*
11.20	—	—	—	—	Daily Comet service to Rome and Athens			—	—	arr	PARIS	dep	—	—	Daily Comet service from Athens and Rome			—	—	—	—	16.50
12.05 From 18 May	—	—	—	—				—	—	dep	PARIS	arr	—	—				—	—	—	—	16.05 From 18 May
—	—	—	—	—				23.45	—	arr	MUNICH	dep	—	04.20				—	—	—	—	—
—	—	—	—	—	—	—	—	00.30 Wed. Fri.	—	dep	MUNICH	arr	—	03.35	—	—	—	—	—	—	—	—
13.55	—	—	—	—	14.20	14.20	14.20	—	Sun. g00.20	arr	ROME	dep	g03.40	—	13.50	13.50	13.50	—	—	—	—	14.10
14.40	—	—	—	—	15.05	15.05	15.05	—	g01.05 From 21 May	dep	ROME	arr	g02.55 From 21 May	—	13.05	13.05	13.05	—	—	—	—	13.15
17.25					17.50	17.50 CY134	17.50	03.55 CY136	03.50 OA614	arr	ATHENS	dep	02.05 OA429	02.05 BE137	12.15	12.15 BE135	12.15					12.25
OA814 18.35	18.35	18.35	18.40	18.40	18.35	18.35	18.40	04.40	04.40	dep	ATHENS	arr	01.20 Sun.	01.20 Wed. Fri	11.25	11.30	11.30	11.30	11.20	11.25	11.30	OA815 11.30
Sun. only	19.40	—	—	—	19.40	—	—	—	—	arr	ISTANBUL	dep	—	—	—	—	10.20	—	—	—	10.20	Mon. only
20.00 From 24 July	— From 24 May	20.00 From 19 May	— From 18 May	— From 20 May	—	20.00	—	06.05	06.05	arr	NICOSIA	dep	23.45	23.45	—	09.55	—	09.55 From 20 May	— From 21 May	— From 19 May	— From 25 May	09.55 From 25 July
—	—	20.45	—	—	—	CY34 20.45	—	CY6 06.50	06.50	dep	NICOSIA	arr	23.00	CY137 23.00	—	CY135 09.10	—	09.10	—	—	—	—
—	—	—	—	21.20	—	—	—	—	—	arr	CAIRO	dep	OA615	CY7	—	—	—	—	10.30	—	—	—
—	—	—	20.30	—	—	—	20.30	07.40	07.40	arr	TEL AVIV	dep	22.10	22.10	09.30	—	—	—	—	09.30	—	—
—	—	21.25	—	—	—	21.25	—	—	—	arr	BEIRUT	dep	Sat.	Tue. Thu.	—	CY35 08.30	—	08.30	—	—	—	—

Left: details of the April 1 to 31 October 1960 timetable showing the consortium's London to Athína service with the linked destinations. BE flight number are BEA, OA are the Olympic flights and CY is for Cyprus Airways, another BEA associate company.

which started close to the Glyfada road and the coast. This runway was only 5,705 feet, or 1739 metres long and obstructed by hills up to about 3,000 feet, 900 metres high within three to four miles - one hillock, 75 feet, 23 metres high was in line with the runway and within 1,500 feet, 457 metres from its end.

De Havilland's publicity machine made much of the event: '*All this means no problem for the Comet. No other jet airliner approaches its airport capability, as the following facts make clear. Using the reverse thrust fitted to two of its Rolls-Royce jet engines the Comet made all its Athens landings without even applying wheel brakes - a remarkable enough performance for airliners of half its speed. The saving in wear on wheel brakes and tyres is quite an item in itself.*

The Comet's take-off from Athens was

The BEA/OA consortium heavily promoted the UK/Hellas services for the summer of 1960. The fares for the time are of particular interest!

De Havilland Comet 4B SX-DAN *Queen Sophia* is prepared to start up on another service. *(authors collection)*

spectacular, as it is everywhere. On the second flight, with many technical people of Olympic Airways aboard, one engine was cut back at 95 knots during the take-off run. Nobody on board could have noticed it, and the other three engines were throttled back from take-off power to normal climb power in the usual way just after leaving the ground. Still, the climb was most impressive to everyone on the aircraft and to the citizens of Athens who, like people everywhere, want the noise of jet aircraft to be lifted up high and away above their built-up areas.

By January1960 OA staff had completed their training. Almost uniquely at the time, not only did they have to satisfy the requirements of the Hellenic Civil Aviation Authority, the flight crews also had to sit examinations with the British CAA in order for the HCAA certificate to be recognised due to Olympic's agreement with BEA that in certain instances OA crews would fly BEA aircraft. Olympic also increased their order for Comets, first to three on 18 March, then to four aircraft on 4 April.

The first Olympic machine, SX-DAK *Queen Frederica* arrived at Athína from the UK with no passengers on board in a record-breaking block-to-block time of three hours thirteen minutes on 30 April. After consultation with both the British and Hellenic Aero Clubs it was declared a new record for that route. Paul Ioannidis was the Captain, with Costas Antachopoulos as co-pilot and Demetris Michailidis as flight engineer. On 14 May a second machine arrived, allowing the first service to be flown on 18 May.

The Comets of Olympic Airways, working in conjunction with BEA, linked Athína with London, Rome, Paris, Zurich, Frankfurt, Brussels, Amsterdam and Istanbul, also Tel Aviv, Nicosia, Beirut and Cairo. The OA machines were similar to those in service with BEA, equipped with seats for twenty-two first-class and sixty-four economy class passengers.

Jets attracting the jet-set

Before the Second World War air travel was for the wealthy few or government officials travelling on state business; after the war, there was the growing emergence of a new travelling public - those travelling for pleasure. Originally it started with a

Olympic's Comet service also went to Nicosia in Cyprus. *(authors collection)*

Above: One of the jet-set! Maria Amalia Mercouri, known professionally as Melina Mercouri, was a Hellenic actress, singer and politician. She is seen posing here in front of OA Comet SX-DAN *Queen Sophia*. A political activist during the Greek military junta of 1967–1974, Mercouri became a member of the Hellenic Parliament in 1977 and became the first female Minister for Culture of Greece in 1981.

Below: the same aircraft, about to depart on another service. *(Spiros Papadopoulos Collection)*

continuation of the pre-war wealthy elite, but slowly and inexorably the demand expanded so that the middle and working class began to consider air travel to reach destinations regarded as suitable for holidays.

In Europe, this tended to be something akin to the migration of the swallows: flying south for the winter. Those in the more northern climes - Scandinavia, Germany, Great Britain, The Nederlands and Denmark headed for the Mediterranean countries. Initially, this was towards Spain, and its islands, Italy and the Adriatic, but by the end of the 1950s the airliners used for tourist travel were starting to have longer range and higher speeds, enabling them to fly to the further reaches of the Mediterranean without it being too long a trek. Hellas then became just within reach, but many considered the country as being well off the beaten track.

It was not long before Aristotle Onassis, and his Olympic Airways team realised the potential both of increased passenger numbers in their aircraft and of increased aircraft handling across the country, both of which benefitted the company. As the travel brochures of the day said:

If you have ever dreamed - and who hasn't? - of the perfect holiday paradise, then you must visit Greece. You will discover a spectacular fulfilment of all your dreams - sparkling turquoise seas, unspoilt beaches, magnificent mountain and forest scenery and beautiful towns as old as time, all shimmering under the magic of the southern sun.

"This is really some flying!
How far are you going?"
"ATHENS—and you?" "TEL AVIV—
but I can't resist a few days in
Athens on the way! Been before?"
"Often—and always OLYMPIC!
There's something about..."
OLYMPIC AIRWAYS
TO
PARIS · ROME
ATHENS
STANBUL · NICOSIA
BEIRUT
TEL AVIV · CAIRO
Indeed there is! They really know how to look after you!
It's speed, comfort and Greek hospitality all
along the line. Prove it! If you're planning
a visit to these places, fly OLYMPIC!
You'll jet there in a trice by
COMET 4B! What better?
All information from
Travel Agents or
OLYMPIC AIRWAYS
141 New Bond Street, London, W.1. HYD 7262
—and the associated services of
OLYMPIC & BEA
provide a high frequency of flights
through and direct, to most destinations.

Greece makes you welcome...
In this glorious setting, you can mingle with gay, friendly crowds or find beauty and peace in solitude. Wherever you go, the hospitable Greeks will welcome you. The Greek word for foreigner means 'guest' too - so it's not surprising that the standard of hospitality is high to-day in a country where the arts of civilisation have flourished for over 3,000 years.

In Greece you will find good roads, restaurants and hotels — many of them modern and lavish. There are holiday camps too, 'Tourist Pavilions' (special hotels run by the Greek National Tourist Office) and the friendly Tourist Police to answer all your questions— in English!

...all the year-round!
The very weather of Greece breathes a welcome - for many people the country's greatest attraction is its sweet, kindly climate with clear blue skies, invigorating air and constant sun. Yes, constant - Greece averages only 25 days without the sun a year, and that means it's perfect for an off-season holiday, too. You can swim from April until December, and even the coldest months of January and February have an average temperature of 50 degrees fahrenheit!

So much to enjoy!
You'll discover, that there's more to Greece than ruins, beautiful and unique as they are. Athens and its nearby resorts offer modern pleasures—as well as the incomparable Parthenon. All over Greece, there are lots to see and enjoy—from skin-diving to night clubbing, donkey excursions to modern steamer cruises—and all at favourable Greek prices.

Want to get away from it all?
Yes, you really can in Greece. Peaceful olive groves, wild pine-clad hills, solitary and inviting beaches - which do you prefer? Then there are the islands, each one different, set in the blue waters of the Aegean and Ionian Seas. You can even find an uninhabited one all your very own!

Link this kind of evocative advertising in with the speed and luxury of the De Havilland Comet and it is not surprising that within a year of announcing the consortium deal with BEA, Olympic released figures that showed that it had carried 494,568 passengers in 1960 compared with 425,428 in 1959, an increase of

Left: The Olympic hostesses liked to have their photographs taken in front of Comet 4B SX-DAN *Queen Sophia*.

Below: In the early 1960s, the De Havilland Comet was seen as the height of high technology, and drew crowds whereever it appeared. *(authors collection)*

16.2%. Their cargo, baggage and excess baggage rose from 4,595,543 kilogrammes to 11,974,000 kilpgrammes, an increase of 260.5%. Their mail loads increased from 589,471 kilogrammes to 805,000 kg., an increase of 35%.

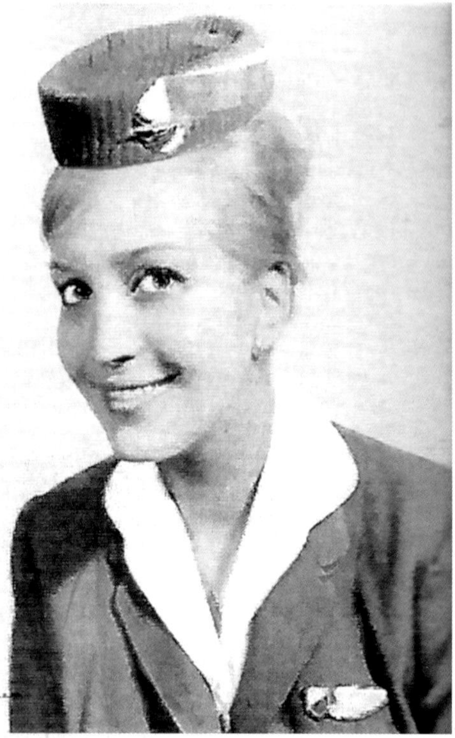

In announcing these remarkable load figures, OA made it clear that there was no doubt that the introduction of the Comet 4B jet service had contributed to the uplift of last year's traffic, although Comets did not operate until May, and although other jets offered competition between Athína and north-west Europe increasingly during 1960. Use of the Comet did much to raise OA's international profile.

Olympic received a third Comet in July 1960, and the fourth in March 1961. *'This new type of jetliner…*

Left: From a 1965 Press Release:
OUR GIRL IN MIAMI
Miranda Pallikaropoulou was chosen to represent Olympic Airways at this year's 'Miss International Airline Stewardess' Contest in Miami beach. Miss Pallikaropoylou was successful in ranking fourth among the five finalists of the contest making her eligible for many prizes and awards. Miranda is a 21-year-old beauty, 5' 6" tall and weighing 123 lbs. She has blonde hair and light brown eyes. She has been an air hostess with Olympic for the past eighteen months. Before that, she studied beauty culture in London and Paris.

Below: The French movie star and heart-throb Alain Delon departs the West Terminal at Ellinikon on an Olympic Airways Comet for Rome. Delon became one of Europe's most prominent actors and screen sex symbols in the 1960s. *(authors collection)*

' A spokesman for the airline asserted '.. *Not only has met with the full appreciation of the travelling public but has been proved as well profitable to the company.*'

With the addition to their fleet of the fourth Comet, Olympic Airlines began operating a new summer schedule which included forty-eight flights a week between London and Athína, routed via either Paris, Rome, and Milan, or Amsterdam, Frankfurt and Zurich. There were also eleven flights a week between London and Istanbul, and twelve flights between London and Nicosia; thirteen flights a week between London and Tel Aviv; five flights a week between London and Cairo, and two a week between London, Bahrain and Doha.

The average daily flying time during the summer of 1960 for each Olympic Comet was 6½ hours, a figure that OA planned to exceed considerably during 1961.

BEA described the consortium partnership with OA as *'...the biggest commercial and operational deal we have yet done'*.

The Olympic Comets had passenger appeal, as shown by a postcard sent from father to son in 1966 records.

'17 October 1966 - 15.15 hours GMT 16.15 Eastern European Time.

Dearest Richard - Am writing this as we fly over Italy and the Adriatic Sea at about 33,000ft and 520 m.p.h.We recently passed over the Swiss Alps and Mont Blanc which was all covered in snow. Have just had quite a nice lunch. The weather is very sunny, and it gets warmer the further east we fly. We are now just over half way and are due at Athína in about 1½ hours. This plane is only about half full - not like our holiday flights. Will send another card from Greece'.

During the era of the Olympic and BEA consortium, there were two fatal Comet accidents,

The arrival of HRH King Constantine of the Hellenes in Amsterdam for the Royal Wedding of Princess Beatrix in March 1966, the arrival on Olympic Airways De Havilland Comet SX-DAN *'Princess Sophia'*. Seen behind the King on the stairs is Queen Anne - Marie and Princess Irene.

both involving BEA machines, neither of which were the fault of the aircraft. The first was on 21 December 1961 when twenty-seven passengers and crew on board G-ARJM lost their lives, although seven passengers survived, following a stall shortly after take-off from Ankara in Turkey. An instrument fault caused the pilot to pull back more and more into a climb too steep even for the high powered Comet, and it stalled, falling near the airport boundary.

The second crash was in mysterious circumstances on 12 October 1967. Comet 4 G-ARCO left London-Heathrow Airport at 21:45 hours on 11 October 1967, operating as BEA flight BE284 to Athína. It carried thirty-eight passengers and 2154 kilogrammes of freight, including 920 kilos for Nicosia. The aircraft arrived in Athína at 01:11 hours on 12 October. Six passengers disembarked, and twenty-seven passengers joined the flight, now changed to Cyprus Airways flight CY284 to Nicosia. As usual, it was refuelled and serviced by Olympic Ground Handling in preparation for the trip to Nicosia.

The aircraft taxied out at 02:27 hours and was airborne on schedule at 02:31; it was cleared by Athína Control to Nicosia on Upper Airway Red 19 to cruise at Flight Level 290. After takeoff, it climbed to 4000 feet on the 180 radial of Athína VOR and then turned direct to Cape Sounion, which it reported crossing at 02:36 hours.

At 02:46 hours, the aircraft stated that it was passing Red 19 Bravo at Flight Level 290 and was estimating Ródos at 03:03. At 03:16 hours the crew reported passing Red 19 Charlie at Flight Level 290 and expected to pass abeam of Myrtou, Cyprus, at 03:40 hours. This message was not received by Athína direct but relayed to them by a westbound Comet aircraft. G-ARCO was then

Rightt: From 1966 until 1969 the French couturiere Coco Chanel (inset) 'dressed' the Olympic Airways stewardesses in this elegant outfit.

Below: British registered De Havilland Comet 4B G-ARJL in full Olympic Colours and markings taxies past another Olympic Airways comet at Ellinikon Airport. *(all authors collection)*

'OLYMPIC AIRWAYS COMET 4B. BUILT BY DE HAVILLAND POWERED BY ROLLS-ROYCE' So said the postcard distributed to passengers about Olympic Airways' Comet services. *(OA via authors collection)*

Right: Κυρίες και κύριοι, πρόκειται να ξεκινήσουμε την επιβίβαση ... ..Ladies and gentlemen we are about to start boarding... An Olympic Ground Hostesss prepares the passengers for boarding another flight. Note the seat allocation boards behind her that match with the boarding card stubs below.

cleared by Athína to change to the Nicosia FIR frequency. Immediately after contacting Nicosia, there was silence.

It was later determined that at that moment a high explosive device detonated within the cabin under seat 4A or 5A. The explosion severely damaged the aircraft causing an out-of-control condition followed by structural break-up at Flight Level 150. The wreckage fell into the sea.

Searchers recovered fifty-one bodies from the sea within a day of the crash, most wearing life jackets and some wearing wristwatches that had stopped at 5:25. Investigators concluded that the aircraft had suffered some form of damage during the initial radio call to Nicosia ATC at about 5:15 am and had broken up in flight about eight minutes later. They estimated the aircraft's wreckage to be scattered on the seabed over an area of about 35 square miles at a depth of 9,000–10,000 feet below the surface.

An aircraft drop tank found floating led investigators to hypothesise that the airliner crashed due to a mid-air collision with a military aircraft. However, searchers also found a cushion from one of the Comet's passenger seats floating on the surface of the sea. The Forensic Explosive Section of the Royal Armament Research and Development Establishment in England received the seat cushion and other recovered objects from the Comet's passenger cabin and on examination was found to have evidence of an explosion. Analysis of the seat cushion showed traces of a military plastic explosive. There had been a bomb on board.

Much suspicion at the time focused on General

Georgios Grivas (Γεώργιος Γρίβας; 6 July 1897 – 27 January 1974), leader of the EOKA guerrilla organisation and EOKA B paramilitary group as being the obvious target. Grivas, however, had switched to another flight at the last minute. Whoever was responsible for this atrocity was never caught.

Politics of the Flight Deck

Since before Olympic had come into existence, there had always been a strong political streak running through the company.

Often this took the form of political action from the Civil Aviation Pilots Association - the pilot's trade union. On 15 August 1966 - at the height of the travel season - the Association called a strike over economic demands. This was an action that dealt a severe blow to the company at a particularly sensitive time. Fifteen days of negotiations followed before the demands of the strikers were partially met.

Throughout the 1960s this tension aggravation and uncertainty within the airline evolved into something of a war of attrition between the Pilots Association and the higher levels of management, in particular with Captain Hondros, Director of Flight Operations. Kyrtatos and Paul Ioannidis, the Chief Pilot. The situation was not helped by Onassis' 'hands-on' style of confrontational management. Unfortunately Onassis had a habit of getting involved in any negotiations right from the start which had the unfortunate effect of damaging his image. It was clear that this antagonised the pilots union regarding their interpretation of the agreements that they had signed uo to. Onassis should have left the negotiates to the appointed company officials and only get

Left: Olympic Airways colours, British Registration G-ARDI and Swissair steps.
Passngers board this DH Comet for another service.

The central signage says 'ΚΡΑΤΙΚΟΣ ΑΕΡΟΛΙΜΗΝ ΑΘΗΝΩΝ', which literally translates as 'Athína State Airport'. The Olympic ground transport is particularly interesting.

involved when there were difficulties or an impassé.

The day-to-day operation of the airline's flight schedule became severely obstructed, and passengers and travel agents alike started to lose faith in the airline. This became even more pronounced every time the trave season reached its peak. The uncertainty of flights taking place began to affect the travel agents, who would advise their clients to travel on other airlines, even if the passengers requested flights on OA. The suggestion that a travellers flight would not take place at the appointed time, or even just be delayed, would lead tourists to form a poor opinion of the airline today termed as 'negative brand identity' in the language of public relations gurus which, once established was difficult to overcome.

Expansion into the USA

There were two areas of the world that had large Hellenic populations - the USA and Australia - so it made good commercial sense to Onassis that Olympic should operate services to these regions from the home country.

By now Olympic had a team of eleven sales representatives: Steve Athanassiades, Andrew Malamis, Nick Pelekanos, George Mitakos, Stergios Karalis, George Koldakis, Peppo Salmaggi, Claude Stylianoudis, Constantinos Kotoulas, Evan Valentis and Nick Laskas.

Olympic were opening sales offices across the USA at a tremendous rate: after New York, came Chicago, then in March 1961, Los Angeles, California. 1962 saw a sales office open in San Francisco.

1965 was a big year for Olympic Airways; it was the year the airline announced an order for three Boeing 707-384s during the first quarter of the year, and the number of sales offices in the USA increased from five to nineteen. The new North American Sales Headquarters on Fifth

Olympic Airways Press Release from New York City in March 1965

FLOATING UP FIFTH AVENUE

Olympic Airways featured prominently in the annual Greek Independence Day parade up Fifth Avenue in New York, with a float made up of fluffy clouds, pretty girls and the Parthenon. Next year, New York will be linked to Athens, via Rome or Paris, with regular Olympic flights by Boeing 707-384C. (authors collection)

Avenue between 51st and 52nd Street in New York opened amid much fanfare.

Much of this publicity and image-making went some way towards demonstrating the enigma that was Aristotle Onassis, for he had made more than business decision when he acquired and set about creating Olympic. He had committed himself in some ill-defined way to the country of his distant ancestors - and this reflected in many ways as to how the airline marketed and promoted itself.

Perhaps a fascinating question about his character is the extent to which he was a Greek. It was something that often preoccupied Prof. Yanni Georgakis, the man whom he eventually appointed managing director of Olympic Airways. Professor Georgakis believed that Onassis had a chameleon-like quality.

'In Greece, he behaved like a Greek, in England like an Englishman. He had this facility for adaptation. When he was in an international forum among global ethics, then he was superb, dignified and controlled. In Greece among Greeks, he adopted the conduct of the market place.'

That is perhaps another explanation for Onassis's occasionally hysterical style of conducting the business of Olympic Airways.

For the opening of the New York Office Olympic invited Alexander Matsas, the Greek Ambassador to the United States to 'cut the ribbon' on 20 April, assisted by two Olympic Airways hostesses wearing what appeared to be a traditional Hellenic dress. Also present of course was Aristotle Onassis,

The costume looked familiar but strangely 'wrong' After much research things fell into place. Ever the marketing man, Onassis linked Hellenic pride of the American immigrants in 'the old country' with selling Olympic Airways to the American market by taking as a loose theme for the girl's outfits from that of Queen Amalia, the first Queen of the Greeks.

Known as 'the Amalia dress' it is an Hellenic traditional folk costume created by Queen Amalia, who ruled as the wife of King Otto from 1837 until their expulsion following an uprising in Athína in 1862. The outfit is the result of an attempt to establish a unifying symbol of Greek identity. It is not until I discovered a brief history of the Amalia costume and its historical significance in the fashion culture of Greece that I realised why Aristotle Onassis selected a version of it for his purposes.

The young modern Hellenic Republic established on 3 February 1830, by the Protocol of Independence, was in need of its own identity after being under the Ottoman rule for roughly 400 years. As such, the newly appointed royal couple of German descent – King Otto and Queen Amalia – accepted the complicated task of reigning over

The streetside view of the Olympic Airways offices in New York. *(authors collection)*

Below: Aristotle Onassis, with Alexander Matas, the Hellenic Ambassador to the USA opens the new Olympic Airways offices in New York, escorted by two hostesses in traditional outfits, which were based on an authentic Amalia dress (left), like this one displayed in Museum of Traditional Greek Costumes in Kalamata. (Author)

At the same time as the opening of their new offices in New York Olympic took the chance to promote their ordering of three Boeing 707s. Here Aristotle Onassis is seen with Alexander Matas, the Hellenic Ambassador to the USA, Archbishop Iakovos and, looking much older than his years an eighteen-year-old Alexandros Onassis. *(authors collection)*

The sales and reservations team in the new Olympic Building on Fifth Avenue, New York.. Left to right are : Sophia Stroubos, Calliope Thomas, Jacqueline Schuh, Meral May, Hellas Mergus with George Nicolaidis and Wilson C. Hunter. *(authors collection)*

the new country with gusto when they arrived in the Greek capital (then located in Nafplio) dressed in traditional costumes. The king proudly wore the fustanella while the Queen wore a romantic folksy dress, influenced by Western European fashion and combining details from Greek traditional costume. For them, the creation of a national attire was necessary to ensure and create a unified identity.

Amalia wore the dress on formal occasions and requested that her female court wear it as well. The costume includes a long dress – called foustani or kavadi – inspired by the Biedermeier style, a central European silhouette popular in Germany and the surrounding countries, with a bodice based on the model of the traditional Hellenic kavadi (a local long-sleeved dress). The dress was open to the front to reveal an embroidered chemise. The kontogouni or zipouni is the short, tight-fitting velvet jacket worn over the foustani, usually embellished with intricate gold patterns. The ensemble ends with a final flourish – the red fez always adorned with a tassel of braided gold threads.

Possibly another deciding factor was the name of his personal secretary - Amalia Hadjiargyris!

On the day, Arisotle Onassis welcomed the assembled guests: '*It is a happy event for all of us. It goes back ten years ago, when the greek government invited a number of Greeks residing abroad, of whom I had the privilege to be one, to think and see what we could do in our small way - a modest and humble way - to contribute to the large and vast way the Marshal Plan was aiding our poor and wounded country.*

Some of my colleagues picked other fields in the industry and economy of our country. Destiny probably made me pick this field, which was the field of aviation. We had to struggle. Struggling in this business is a general rule, like in any other business, but especially this one.

And like the big fellows, we also lost money for a good many years. We struggled, but our testing ground was the testing ground for all great airlines - the linking of the four greatest cities in the history of European civilisation: London, Paris, Rome and

Princess Margrethe - later to become Queen Margrethe II of Denmark - arrives at Ellinikon's West Terminal by Olympic Airways Comet in 1966. *(authors collection)*

Athens - not to mention Amsterdam, Frankfurt and Zurich.

This network, so to speak, is the show window of any aspiring airline. We suffered, We were wounded, but we came out pretty well. And this is what gave us the courage to apply to become a member of the most exclusive club, which is called 'The North Atlantic Club of Aviation.

I hope we have all your good wishes, your friendship and sympathy in our endeavour.'

By all accounts, it was a large, high profile event as this press release from OA stated:

INAUGURATION OF THE OLYMPIC BUILDING IN NEW YORK

On April 20, the new Olympic Building on Fifth Avenue was inaugurated in the presence of the Archbishop Iakovos of North and South America, the Greek Ambassador to Washington, the President of the Greek National Tourist Organisation and many other personalities including members of the press.

They were received by Mr Aristotle Onassis, founder and owner of Olympic Airways, and Mr. Constantin Konialidis, the Managing Director.

The dedication ceremony was conducted by the Archbishop Iakovos' after which the Greek Ambassador, Mr Alexander Matsas, cut the tape and read a message from H.M. King Constantine of the Hellenes.

He was followed by Professor John Georgakis, President of the Greek National Tourist Organisation, who read a message from the Prime Minister, Mr Stephanos Stephanopoulos, and then addressed the assembly in his capacity as official representative of the Greek Government.

The company headed notepaper from 1963. *(authors collection)*

OLYMPIC AIRWAYS

TSD/Publ./17/32

ATHENS: 6, OTHONOS STR.
TELEPHONES: 30.991 — 30.999
CABLE ADDRESS:
HEAD OFFICE: "OLYMPIC"
AGENCIES: "OLYMPAIR"

Athens, September 16th 1963

Finally, Mr Onassis spoke briefly and thanked the guests for attending the inaugural ceremony.

Boeing Boeing...

With the undoubted success of the Comets - designed as they were for middle distance services - it became apparent that Olympic needed larger, more extended range machines. At the time there were only three types of airliner suitable, and they were all American - the Douglas DC-8, a pair of Convair designs, either the CV-880 and 990, and the Boeing 707/720.

With an international network radiating throughout Europe and a domestic service offering air links to nineteen cities and islands, Aristotle Onassis and his management felt by 1965 that the time had come to activate the plan for the long-cherished trans-Atlantic service. By this point, the company had an excellent reputation and a powerful 'image' abroad as the air carrier of Greece, and its Olympic rings were a familiar sight among the fin symbols of various airlines at many international airports. Equally important, of

Right: Passengers de-plane from the rear door of SX-DBA *City of Athens,* the first 707 for Olympic.

Below: A typically misty winters morning at John F Kennedy Airport, New York with an Olympic Airways 707 parked with a pair of TWA 707s behind.

«ἡ Ὀλυμπιακὴ Ἀεροπορία
ἀναγγέλλει
τὴν ἀναχώρησι τῆς πτήσεως
ΟΑ 471
διὰ ΜΠΑΓΚΟΚ - ΣΙΓΚΑΠΟΥΡΗ - ΣΥΔΝΕΫ
μὲ ἀεριωθούμενο BOEING 707
Ἄμεσος ἐπιβίβασις»

Ἡ ὥρα εἶναι 01.00 π.μ. 3 Μαρτίου.
Εἶναι τὸ πρῶτο τακτικὸ δρομολόγιο τῆς ΟΛΥΜΠΙΑΚΗΣ πρὸς τὴν ΑΣΙΑ καὶ τὴν ΑΥΣΤΡΑΛΙΑ.
Εἶναι ἡ ταχύτερη πτήση ἀπὸ τὴν Ἀθήνα.
Ὅπως σὲ ὅλα τὰ ἀεροσκάφη μας θὰ βρῆτε ἔμπειρο προσωπικό, ἐκλεκτὴ κουζίνα, γνωστὴ φιλοξενία. Θὰ νοιώθετε «σὰν στὸ σπίτι σας».
Προσφορὰ γνωριμίας μὲ τὴν ΑΥΣΤΡΑΛΙΑ:
ἐκδρομικὸς ναῦλος δρχ. 21.720*
Ἀθῆναι — Σύδνεϋ μετ' ἐπιστροφῆς
μὲ δικαίωμα παραμονῆς ἀπὸ 45 ἡμέρες
μέχρι 6 μῆνες.

* ὑπόκειται εἰς κυβερνητικὴν ἔγκρισιν.

ΟΛΥΜΠΙΑΚΗ
ΑΕΡΟΠΟΡΙΑ

Διὰ περισσοτέρας πληροφορίας ἀποταθῆτε εἰς τὸν ΠΡΑΚΤΟΡΑ ΣΑΣ ἢ τὰ Γραφεῖα τῆς ΟΛΥΜΠΙΑΚΗΣ ΑΕΡΟΠΟΡΙΑΣ

course, was that the airline was now on a financially sound enough footing to be well placed to absorb the considerable costs of mounting a service to New York.

As Trans World Airlines had been a long-time operator to Athína, it was legislated that Olympic held the reciprocal operating rights, and the formalities of proving its competence for such a service were the only licensing requirements required. The New York office opened in 1958 now really came into its own.

For the Atlantic operation, Olympic ordered three Boeing 707-320Cs on 22 April 1965, which Olympic's advertising department termed 'Super Fan-Jets', in the style of the day. Crew training began soon after, and pilots who were flying

Pierre Cardin, above left, Italian-born French fashion designer, created uniforms for Olympic Airways from 1969 to 1971. Known for his avant-garde style and Space Age designs, he preferred geometric shapes and motifs, often ignoring the female form. Cardin set another new trend: 'mod chic', all the iconography of which appears in the OA uniform.

Below: Boeing 707 SX-DBF *'City of Mycenae'* sets off for the start of another service from Ellinikon. *(Richard Vandervord)*

Above: With engine covers on, Boeing 720 SX-DBH *'Achelios River'* is parked at Ellinikon *(Richard Vandervord)*.
Above left: theee Olympic hostesses at the first Hellenic Fashion Institute showing old Olympic styles. Maria Fassoli, Elini Vlachopolis and Pandelia Kostandoudakis represented the airline, and were photographed for *Vogue* magazine.
Above right, tails and ground services making use of the unbiquitous Ford Transit vans. *(both OA/ authors collection)*

Comets were given conversion training onto the big Boeings at Seattle and later at the TWA Training Center in Kansas City, which continued through to January 1966. Concurrently, route planning and promotion of the new service began, and activity occurred in such diverse locations as Athína, New York, San Francisco and Shannon,

These three airliners, along with following orders, were designated model —384Cs by Boeing, but called 707-320s by Olympic, and registered as SX-DBA to DBC and named *'City of Athens'*, *'City of Corinth'* and *'City of Knossos'* respectively. As with all the Olympic fleet, the names appeared in Hellenic on one side of the aircraft, and in English on the other.

This was the intercontinental model of the Boeing 707, designed to carry a full load of passengers (typically 131 first class or 189 tourists) across the Atlantic. Pan American had placed the first order for this variant on 24 December 1955 when they changed their initial order from twenty -121s to six -121s and fourteen - 321s. Wingspan increased and the shape altered near the fuselage, both of which contributed to an increase in wing

Above: If the café at Ellinikon was the place to celebrity-watch in the 1960s, then the rooftop of the Hotel London on Posidonos Avenue, Glyfada was the place where it was impossible to avoid the jets landing. Here Boeing 707-320 SX-DBO fills the camera lens. *(Richard Vandervord)*

Left: As with all the other airlines, the hostesses had 'summer' and 'winter' uniforms that were usually the addition of a coat. In Olympic's case with the Pierre Cardin outfit, this took the form of a stylish cloak. The white tights, chisel-toe shoes and overall length were very '1960s'!
(OA via Spiros Papadopoulos Collection)

area over the -120 and -220 of almost 20% - the span of the horizontal tailplane also increased. More powerful, (when compared with the 707-120), JT4A-3 turbojets of 15,800 pounds thrust were fitted, and these more efficient engines along with increased fuel capacity of 96,360 litres enabled the aircraft to fly full payload 7,435 kilometres non-stop.

The -320B as ordered by Olympic was fitted with a further improved and larger wing and JT3D-3 turbofans of 18,000lb thrust. The wingspan increase of 1.01 metres led to other improvements including the fitting of wider leading-edge flaps, improved trailing edge flaps while the leading edge of the wing, outboard of numbers 3 and 4 engines, was moved 130 millimetres forward. These improvements led to a 15% increase in range over the -320.

The hand-over of the first Olympic 707 was made at a presentation ceremony in Seattle, USA. Those present gives an insight into just what went in to the introduction of a new type: S. Keremenos (OA inspector), K. Lambadaris (Boeing of Athína), K. Katsanos (Hellenic Embassy advisor), S. Portinos (Hellenic CAA), E. Pantazatos (OA representative at Boeing), E. Horsefall (Boeing Sales Manager), K. Konstantinidis (Safety Officer of the Hellenic Air Force), Phill Chanderter (Boeing), Tryfon Koutalidis (OA Legal Division)

Delivery of the second 707 for Olympic happened on 25 May, and the third at the end of June 1966, a fourth aircraft scheduled for delivery

in June 1968 and two more in 1969.

Immediately afterwards, Olympic began intense line training along the New York-Shannon-New York route, with P. Kyrtatos, C. Hondros, and Paul Ioannidis as instructors.

This training was necessary because all the pilots had to get further familiarised with the Boeing-707 as well as with the new electronic navigational equipment - Doppler and Loran - we would use to cross the Atlantic without a flight navigator. Olympic was going to be the first airline in the world to conduct trans-Atlantic flights using Boeing-707s without a flight navigator, in contrast to all the other carriers, which still used navigators on Atlantic crossings.

The training had to finish on time for the Athína-New York-Athína service to debut on 1 June 1966. A few days before the commencement of this service, Olympic's engineers discovered a fuel leak in the main fuel tank of one of the B-707s; repairs could only be made at Boeing's factory in Seattle.

Top: Boeing 720 SX-DBI sits on the stand alongside Posidonos Avenue, Glyfada. *(Richard Vandervord)*

Above: OA had booking offices all over the mainland and islands of Hellas, most of the staff wearing uniforms designed by Pierre Cardin.

OA girls 'off duty' but dressed to perfection at a company event in 1970.*(OA via Spiros Papadopoulos Collection)*

Once there, the belly fuel tank was found to be leaking and was replaced, and the aircraft returned to New York thirty-six hours later for the inaugural New York- Athína flight with the 707 on schedule as planned. The Athína-New York flight took off with Hondros as captain, with Paul Ioannidis as the captain of the first flight leaving New York for Athína.

It was a memorable day for Aristotle Onassis. Both flights were full and included paying customers and guests of the airline. New York's Club 21 - an American traditional cuisine restaurant and former Prohibition-era speakeasy, located at 21 West 52nd Street in New York City - prepared the inflight meals for the New York - Athína service

Behind the scenes, many employees were concerned about the venture going off smoothly. Many other airlines were wary of Olympic, to the point of looking down on the new upstart company attempting to join the elite trans-Atlantic club. The lack of a flight navigator on the route to and from New York was worry from the beginning, and the problem with the fuel tank did not help, and there were also problems reported with the Doppler

Below: Olympic's promotional team never missed a chance to get photographs to promote the airline - here a party of soldiers pose in tradition dress before boarding for a flight to New York.

Right: a promotional poster in Dutch advertising the sharing agreement with Air France for an Amsterdam - New York service using the 707. *(both OA via Spiros Papadopoulos Collection)*

Passenger announcements, Pierre Cardin style! An Olympic Airways Ground Hostess makes a passenger call. Her outfit, unlike the blue and white of the air hostesses is deep yellow - some called it 'mustard' - and white. The flight departure board behind her is fascinating in style and content!

Two Olympic Airways Ground Hostesses in what appears to be winter wear assist passengers checking in at Zurich aiport for a flight to Athína. *(both OA via Spiros Papadopoulos Collection)*

antenna. But everything went off smoothly.

The trans-Atlantic service was opened on 1 June 1966, on a daily basis, and with stops in Paris and Rome. At Kennedy Airport aircraft stands and passenger gates were required, so an arrangement with American Airlines allowed the use of facilities in its terminal. For technical handling, Lockheed Aircraft Service Company undertook to act for the airline, while a flight planning service was provided by Trans World Airlines, which had already given navigational training to Olympic crews, and had performed engine overhauls for the airline.

Within a month from the start of operations, Olympic was able to increase the frequency of its trans-Atlantic service to nine flights a week in each direction. A further increase to ten flights weekly happened, with three of them being non-stop. Five flights were by way of Paris; two through Rome.

Since the commencement of the trans-Atlantic service Olympic's three Boeings carried more than 50,000 passengers, thus creating an average load factor for the twelve-month period ending 31 May 1967 of 44.4 percent, which, while regarded by Olympic as '...quite satisfactory', was seen by many to be very good indeed. It is perhaps worth noting that a 707 broke even at a 40 percent load factor.

By 1967 Olympics fleet comprised of three 707-320s, five Comet 4Bs, five DC-6Bs and six DC-3s. Its staff had increased to 3300, and by now had 76 offices in thirty-five countries across five continents; in Hellas alone offices and representatives totalled eighty towns and islands. It was also time to start looking for eventual replacements for the DC-6s and DC-3s - there was also scope to replace the Comets with more fuel-efficient aircraft.

During the second week of October 1967, Olympic Airways was asked to supply a Boeing 707 for a special flight on 26 October to transport Ecumenical Patriarch Athenagoras I, the head of the Orthodox Church to Rome for a historic meeting with Pope Paul, the head of the Roman

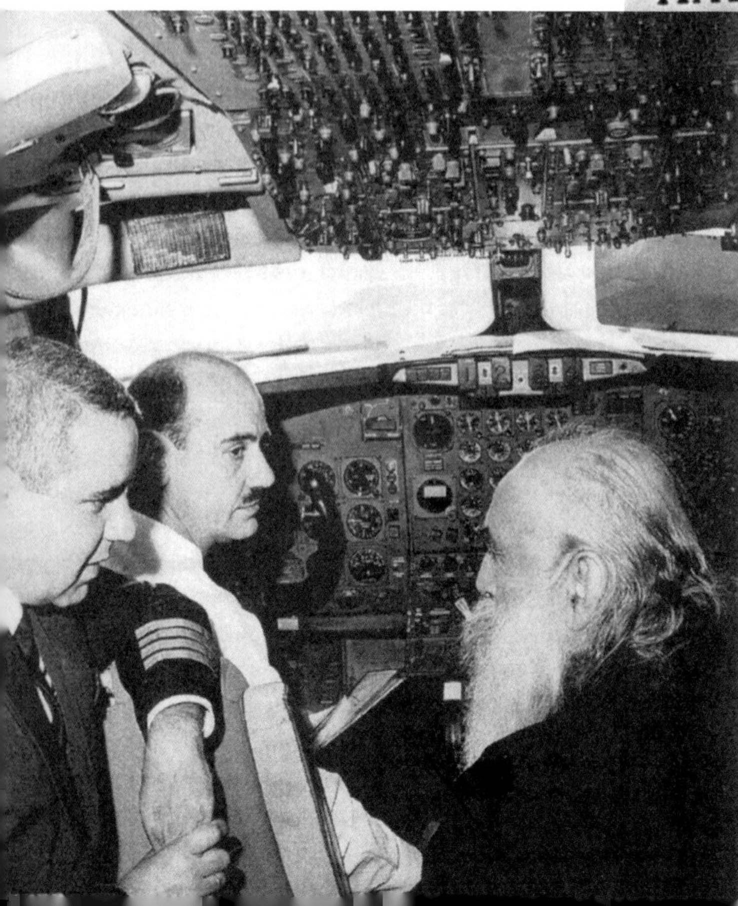

Top: Captain Paul Ioannidis sits above the two insignia - that of the Vatican and the Ecumenical Patriarch on the Olympic 707 which carried Ecumenical Patriarch Athenagoras I to Rome on 27 October 1967

Above: Aristotle Onassis with the Ecumenical Patriarch during the flight.

Left: Captain Paul Ioannidis in the left-hand seat, with Captain C Fikardos behind talks with Ecumenical Patriarch Athenagoras I during their flight to Rome.
(all Olympic Airways Archive)

Catholic Church.

A Boeing 707, captained by Paul Ioannidis was prepared for the event. '*The dividers in the first class seats were covered in purple velvet, and a Byzantine icon was placed in the front divider to the right. The insignia of the Ecumenical Patriarchate and Vatican were placed on the front part of the fuselage, with the word 'Peacemakers' inscribed below.*

The flight was originally scheduled to arrive in Rome from Zurich. However, due to the forecast for dense fog at Zurich airport, it was decided that the Ecumenical Patriarch and his entourage should depart from Amsterdam, where they were waiting, and where the weather conditions were more favourable.

This way, we could ensure their arrival at the scheduled time for their reception in Rome.

On October 26th, I stood in front of the staircase leading to the aeroplane entrance and welcomed the Ecumenical Patriarch and his entourage. Aristotle Onassis and John Georgakis accompanied him. The Patriarch truly made an astonishing impression with his appearance. He came to the cockpit during the flight and stayed with us for a while, talking to us about our jobs and families.

The flight landed normally at Rome's Fiumicino Airport at 09:30 for the start of the three-day visit, where a grand welcome was held for the Patriarch.

According to Olympic Marketing, the upward and onward trend continued. In 1968 OA set new records in traffic. 1,264,499 passengers on international and domestic services, travelling 1,296,660,000 passenger-kilometres, with new route opening from Athína to Nairobi, Kenya and Johannesburg; non-stop flights from London to Ródos were inaugurated; new flights between Beirut and Nicosia; Thessaloniki was added to the Athína-Frankfurt route, with a unique new service

The great and the good! Passengers de-plane from an Olympic 707, while a ground hostress checks the ships paperwork with a ramp agent.

Right: Aristotle Onassis acts as Senior Steward, offering a menu card to King Constantine while on a special flight. It looks like an argument going in in the background!
(both OA via Spiros Papadopoulos Collection)

Above: with everything down and out, Boeing 707-320 SX-DBC *City of Knossos* sweeps in for another landing. *(Richard Vandervord)*

Right: from the days before political correctness, three Olympic 'Coffeee, Tea or Me' girls share a joke and a snack 'down the back'. *(Spiros Papadopoulos Collection)*

that introduced helicopters from Athína to Skiathos, Chios, Mykonos, Santorini and Spetsai.

Olympic had received another DC-6B and a B-707-384C by mid-1968. They were also set to receive another 707-384C and a 727-284 from Boeing's factory in December. Also, the airline had ordered four 727-284s and one 707-384C that were due to be delivered in January 1969. Olympic faced huge problems, regarding the coordination of the training programmes for the crews for these aircraft and the increased number of flights operated for the summer season. Pilot shortages had arisen because their only source of Hellenic crews came from the military and, apart from the fact that there were not enough of them, those who were interested were relatively old.

The solution that was adopted was to send hand-picked young men to CSE Aviation in Oxford, England for their complete training.

The Four Kings of EMI...

On 22 July 1967, much to the delight of everyone who knew about it, Olympic Airways carried possibly the four most famous people in the world at that time from London Heathrow to Athína.

The trip was supposed to be secret, but somehow the details were leaked to the media and the Western Terminal at Ellinikon was besieged by hundreds of press photographers and paparazzi.

George Harrison, Ringo Starr, John Lennon, his wife Cynthia and son Julian, along with Paul McCartney, Jane Asher, Pattie Harrison's 16-year-

First Flight covers: Athína - Chicago - Montreal 11 July 1969. *(authors collection)*

old sister Paula Boyd, Mal Evans and NEMS (North End Music Stores) employee Alistair Taylor arrived at Ellinikon to look at a set of Greek islands that The Beatles were considering buying to live on.

However, their hired yacht was delayed due to a storm off the Cretan coast, leaving them stuck in Athína for several days. While they were waiting, Paul McCartney and George Harrison chose to stay at the Athína family home of their Greek host Alexis 'Magic Alex' Mardas, while John Lennon and Ringo Starr went shopping for musical instruments.

The yacht - the MV *Arvi* had twenty-four berths and a crew of eight, including the captain, a chef and two stewards. The party set sail the on 25 July, to look at suitable islands.

As Ringo Starr was later to recall: *'It came to nothing. We didn't buy an island; we came home. We were great at going on holiday with big ideas, but we never carried them out. We were also going to buy a village in England - one with rows of houses on four sides and a village green in the middle. We were going to have a side each'.*

George Harrison remembered it somewhat differently: *'We rented a boat and sailed it up and down the coast from Athens, looking at islands. Somebody had said we should invest some money, so we thought: 'Well, let's buy an island. We'll just go there and drop out.'*

It was a great trip. John and I were on acid all the time, sitting on the front of the ship playing the ukuleles. Greece was on the left; a big island on the right. The sun was shining, and we sang 'Hare Krishna' for hours and hours. Eventually, we landed on a little beach with a village, but as soon as we stepped off the boat, it started pouring with rain. There were storms and lightning, and the

The Beatles arrive in Ellinikon on 22 July 1967.

Above: Julian Lennon being carried, with his father John behind. Paul McCartney is second from the right.

Right: Jane Asher, Paul McCartney, Julian Lennon, John Lennon.
(both via Spiros Papadopoulos Collection)

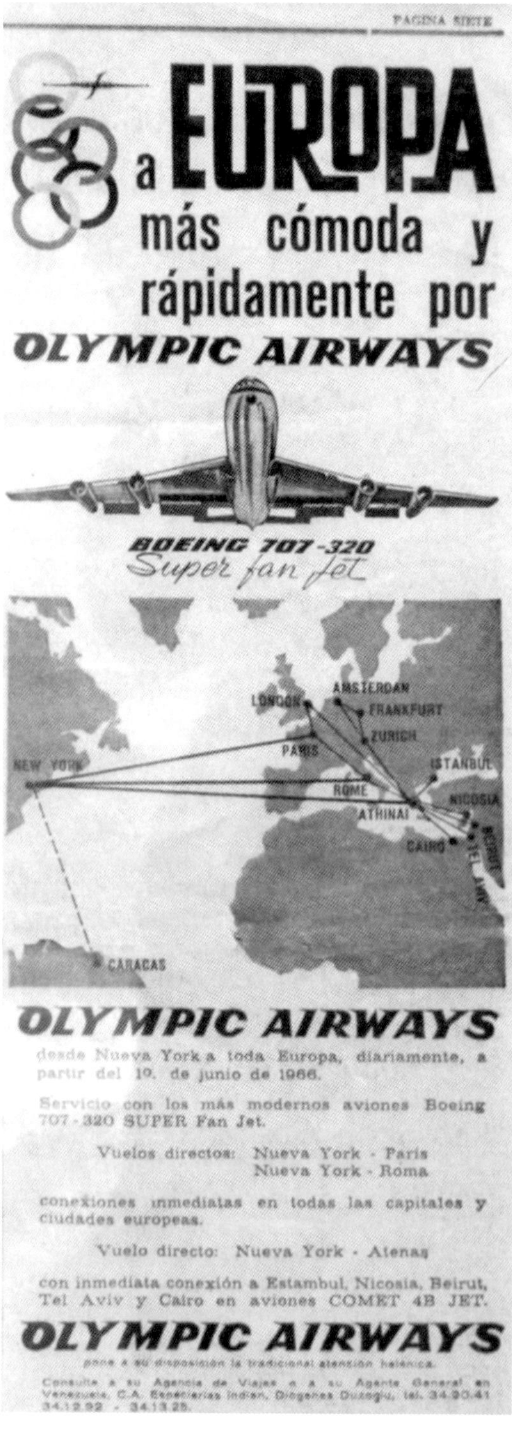

Often the labours of an airlines Marketing Department is only seen in the country where the viewer lives. Few realised that the airlines advertising was global and appeared in many languages. This one, in Spanish, relates to the linking service from Caracas, Venezuela. (authors collection)

only building on the island was a little fisherman's cottage - so we all piled in: "Scuse us, squire. You don't mind if we come and shelter in your cottage, do you?'

The island was covered in big pebbles, but Magic Alex said, 'It doesn't matter. We'll have the military come and lift them all off and carry them away.' But we got back on the boat and sailed away, and never thought about the island again.

The airline kept growing. It hired thirty-six pilots and seventeen flight engineers precisely for this purpose in 1968. It sent thirty-eight pilots and twenty flight engineers to Boeing's training centre to receive training on the B-727-284. At the same time, several training courses were operating at the Olympic's own training centre for stewards and stewardesses. Also, Olympic launched a new route to Johannesburg and Nairobi on 1 November 1968.

In early 1969, after Olympic received the remaining four Boeing 727-384s, it retired its four Comet 4Bs. The Comet 4B was an excellent aircraft in its day and offered passengers a comfortable flight, with less flight time, while providing pilots, flight engineers, and mechanics with substantial experience in jet airliners. These aircraft had logged a total of 97,052 flight hours in Olympic service.

In 1969, the company hired another six pilots, four flight engineers, sixty stewards, and twenty-one stewardesses in preparation to start up the Athína-Montreal-Chicago and Athína-Vienna-Brussels routes.

The Enfield Olympic – a digression into electric car rentals.

In the early 1970s Enfield Automotive a British company with history in production of rifles, motorcycles and boats owned by the Greek shipping mogul John B Goulandris set out to develop an electric car – a concept that was well ahead of its time. The result was the Enfield-Neorion 8000 with production planned on the island of Syros in the Aegean, where Goulandris owned the Neorion shipyard after production in the United Kingdom was deemed too expensive.

A specialised car factory was set up on Syros in a former clothing warehouse with the equipment moved from England. Shipyard staff trained in vehicle production and additional specialist auto workers hired. What the team lacked in experience they made up by enthusiasm for what they were going to produce.

Production started in late 1973 and lasted until early 1976. During this period around 120 cars were built. The Electricity Council purchased almost half of them in England, and the rest sold around the world to various individuals that must have been seen as being quite eccentric for the time. That is because the car had limited capabilities being strictly a city car and its price was two-and-a-half times that of a comparably sized vehicle such as the popular Mini. And of course, environmental sensitivities should have been running much lower than today.

Construction of the little car used aluminium panels for anti-corrosion protection and lighter weight (which eventually was not that small considering the size of the batteries of the time). It could carry two passengers at a maximum speed of 40mph (with only 8hp engine power which however was tested to cope with the challenging terrain of the Greek island). It had a range of 35-55 miles depending on driving conditions and used components of other cars (brakes and suspension) to reduce development and production cost. It was recharged using a typical household 220V power outlet.

Apart from the standard 8000 version (produced in bright colours (white, orange, blue, yellow) at least three other versions designed and prototypes built, but did not go into production. There was an open top called the Bicini, the buggy, known as the

Three views of the Enfield 'Olympic' taken from a sales brochure. The lack of doors - just a strap used instead, plus the woven straw seats make for an 'interesting' ride. It seems that the back seat passengers faced to the rear. Olympic planned to rent out these small electric cars to customers on the Hellenic islands. Location of the airport picture is something of a mystery - the cars appear to be British registered, but the airport seems to be Ellinikon. (authors collection)

Boeing 707 SX-BDF *City of Mycenae* climbs away from Ellinikon. (*Spiros Papadopoulos Collection*)

Enfield Olympic and a commercial van version called the Miner.

Goulandris had previously moved to New York in 1941 and later married Maria Lemos, a member of another prominent Greek ship owning family and long-time friend of Jackie Kennedy. So, it is not surprising that at some stage, discussions must have taken place with the management of Olympic Airways - or was it Olympic Aviation? - for according to the surviving records - with photographs to back them up - there were plans for Olympic to have a fleet of the open top buggy version, complete with four back-to-back woven-straw seats out at the island airports to hire out to passengers. Nothing came of the idea.

OA and airport staff parade airside at the new airport of Iraklion, on Kreta which was officially inaugurated on 5 May 1972 Compare this to the earlier picture1 (*Spiros Papadopoulos Collection)*

Chapter Five

Politics, Disasters and Financing

Coup and counter-coup - the Military Junta

It is impossible to tell the story of Olympic Airways without briefly describing the military coup d'elat of 1967 what led up to it and how OA managed to survive.

In 1947, the United States formulated the Truman Doctrine and began to support a series of authoritarian governments in Greece, Turkey, and Iran to ensure that these states did not fall under Soviet influence. As already mentioned, with American and British aid, the civil war ended with the military defeat of the communists in 1949. The Communist Party of Greece (KKE) became outlawed, and many communists either fled or faced prosecution. The American Central Intelligence Agency (CIA) and the Hellenic military began to work in close collaboration, especially after Hellas joined the North Atlantic Treaty Organization (NATO) in 1952. This cooperation included the placement of notable CIA officers Gustav Lascaris Avrakotos and Clair George. Avrakotos acceded to the CIA in 1962, and his assignments included an anti-communist mission in Greece and duty in the CIA's Langley, Virginia, headquarters. Allegedly Avrakotos was the link between the CIA and Greek Secret Service (KYP) and that he met Georgios Papadopoulos and other military men who played a part in the Greek military junta of 1967–1974. Allegedly Avrakotos also played a role in encouraging the Brigadier Ioannidis coup against Cyprus President Makarios, which was the pretext for the subsequent Turkish invasion of Cyprus.

Greece was a vital link in the NATO defence arc which extended from the eastern border of Iran to the northernmost point in Norway. Greece, in particular, was seen as being at risk, having experienced a communist insurgency. In particular, the newly founded Hellenic National Intelligence Service (EYP) and the Mountain Raiding Companies (LOK) maintained a very close liaison with their American counterparts. In addition to preparing for a Soviet invasion, they agreed to guard against a left-wing coup. The LOK, in particular, was integrated into the European stay-behind network.

After many years of conservative rule, the election of the Center Union's Georgios Papandreou, Sr. as Prime Minister was a sign of change. In a bid to gain more control over the country's government than his limited constitutional powers allowed, the young and inexperienced King Constantine II clashed with liberal reformers, dismissing Papandreou in 1965 and causing a constitutional crisis.

After making several attempts to form governments, relying on the dissident Centre Union and conservative MPs, Constantine II appointed an interim government under Ioannis Paraskevopoulos, and new elections called. There were many

The official portrait of His Majesty King Constantine II of the Hellenes.

The landside aspect to the airport buildings at Kerkyra in the mid-1960s. (*Peter V Clegg*)

indications that Papandreou's Centre Union would emerge as the largest party, but would not be able to form a single-party government and so were forced into an alliance with the United Democratic Left, suspected by conservatives as being a proxy for the banned KKE, something which became a pretext for the coup.

Before the scheduled elections of 28 May 1967, with expectations of a wide Center Union victory, some conservative National Radical Union politicians feared that the policies of left-wing Centrists, including Andreas Papandreou (the son of Georgios Papandreou, Sr.), would lead to a constitutional crisis. In 1966, Constantine sent his envoy, Demetrios Bitsios, to Paris on a mission to persuade former prime minister Constantine Karamanlis to return to Greece and resume his role in politics. As it turned out, the constitutional crisis did not originate either from the political parties, or from the Palace, but from middle-rank army putschists.

On 21 April 1967, just weeks before the elections, a group of right-wing army officers led by Brigadier General Stylianos Pattakos and Colonels George Papadopoulos and Nikolaos Makarezos seized power in a coup d'etat. The Colonels were able to seize power quickly by using elements of surprise and confusion. Pattakos

General Pattakos (left) with Colonels Papadopoulos (centre) and Makarezos (right) in May 1967. *(ΟΑ/ΠΟΛΚ.ΕΟΑ Collection)*

Olympic Aviation's area of the western side of Ellinikon with the TAE hangar - in blue - that was transferred from Kerkyra in the centre of the picture. *(OA/ΠΟΛΚ.ΕΟΑ Collection)*

was the commander of the Armour Training Centre based in Athína.

The coup leaders placed tanks in strategic positions in Athína, gaining control of the city. At the same time, a large number of small mobile units were dispatched to arrest leading politicians, authority figures, and ordinary citizens suspected of left-wing sympathies, according to previously prepared lists. One of the first to be arrested was Lieutenant General Grigorios Spandidakis, Commander-in-Chief of the Greek Army. The Colonels persuaded Spandidakis to join them, having him activate a previously-drafted action plan to move the coup forward.

By the early morning hours, the whole of Greece was in the hands of the colonels. All leading politicians, including acting Prime Minister Panagiotis Kanellopoulos, had been arrested and were held by the conspirators. At 6:00 a.m. EET, Papadopoulos announced the suspension of the eleven articles of the Greek Constitution. A consequence was that anyone could be arrested without a warrant and brought to trial before a military court.

Georgios Papandreou was arrested after a nighttime raid at his villa in Kastri, Attica. Andreas was stopped at around the same time after seven soldiers armed with fixed bayonets and a machine

An Olympic Airways stewardess checks passengers boading this company DC-6B. *(OA/ΠΟΛΚ.ΕΟΑ Collection)*

Olympic Airways' offices on Othonos Street, with a typical Hellenic street kiosk, a periptero outside. The first kiosks appeared at the end of the 19th century, as a form of financial assistance to the war-wounded. At first, the only products found in a kiosk were tobacco and newspapers. In the 50's and the 60's, the kiosks had telephones. At this time, the Greek households did not have land-line phones, so the kiosks played an important role in the communication of people and they became very popular. From the suitcases outside, the offices also served as a pick-up point for busses out to Ellinikon. *(ΟΑ/ΠΟΛΚ.ΕΟΑ Collection)*

gun forcibly entered his home. Andreas Papandreou escaped to the roof but surrendered after one of the soldiers held a gun to the head of his fourteen-year-old son George Papandreou.

When the tanks came to the streets of Athína on 21 April, the legitimate National Radical Union government, of which Rallis was a member, asked King Constantine to mobilise the state against the coup immediately; he declined to do so and swore in the dictators as the legitimate Hellenic government.

The three plot leaders visited Constantine in his residence in Tatoi, which they circled with tanks, effectively preventing any form of resistance. The King argued with the colonels and initially dismissed them, ordering them to return with Spandidakis. Later in the day, he took it upon himself to go to the Ministry of National Defence, located north of Athína city centre, where all the coup leaders had gathered. The King discussed the coup with Kanellopoulos, and with leading generals. It was a pointless exercise since Kanellopoulos was a prisoner while the generals had no real power, as was evident from the shouting of lower and middle-ranking officers, refusing to obey orders and clamouring for a new government under Spandidakis.

The only concession the King could achieve was to appoint a civilian as prime minister, rather than Spandidakis. Konstantinos Kollias, a well-known royalist and a former Attorney General of the Areios Pagos (supreme court), was chosen. Kollias was little more than a figurehead, and real power rested with the army, and especially Papadopoulos, who emerged, as the coup's strong man and became

Minister to the Presidency of the Government. Other coup members occupied key posts.

Up until then, constitutional legitimacy had been preserved, since under the then Greek Constitution the King could appoint whomever he wanted as prime minister, as long as Parliament endorsed the appointment with a vote of confidence or a general election was called. It was this government, sworn-in during the early evening hours of 21 April, that formalised the coup. It adopted a 'Constituent Act', an amendment tantamount to a revolution, cancelling the elections and effectively abolishing the constitution, which would be replaced later.

In the meantime, the government was to rule by decree. From the outset, the relationship between Constantine and the colonels was an uneasy one. The colonels were not willing to share power, whereas the young king, like his father before him, was used to playing an active role in politics and would never consent to being a mere figurehead, especially in a military administration.

The King finally decided to launch his counter-coup on 13 December 1967. Since Athína was militarily in the hands of the colonels, Constantine decided to fly to the small northern city of Kavala, where he hoped to be among troops loyal only to him. The vague plan that Constantine and his advisors had conceived was to form a unit that would invade and take control over Thessaloniki, where an alternative administration would be installed. Constantine hoped that international recognition and internal pressure between the two governments would force the junta to resign, leaving the field clear for him to return triumphant to Athína.

In the early morning hours of 13 December, the King boarded the royal aircraft, together with Queen Anne-Marie, their two baby children Princess Alexia and Crown Prince Pavlos, his mother Frederika, and his sister, Princess Irene. Constantine also took with him Prime Minister Kollias. At first, things seemed to be going according to plan. Constantine was well received in Kavala, which was under the command of a

'Olympic 456, you are cleared for take-off'. The glasshouse atop the the West Terminal at Ellinkikon in the mid 1960s. *(OA/ΠΟΛΚ.ΕΟΑ Collection)*

Passengers deplane from DC-6B SX-DAC alongside the manicured lawn area at Kerkira Airport in 1965. *(Peter V Clegg)*

general loyal to him. The Hellenic Air Force and Navy, both strongly royalist and not involved in the junta, immediately declared for him and mobilised. Another of Constantine's generals effectively cut all communication between Athína and northern Hellas.

Constantine's plans were overly bureaucratic and somewhat naive. He assumed that orders from a commanding general would automatically be obeyed. Further, Constantine was obsessive about avoiding bloodshed, even where the junta would most likely respond with violence. Instead of attempting to drum up the widest popular support, hoping for spontaneous pro-democracy risings in most towns, Constantine preferred to let his generals put together the necessary force for advancing on Thessaloniki in strict compliance with military bureaucracy. The King made no attempt to contact politicians, even local ones, and even took care to include in his proclamation a paragraph condemning communism, lest anyone would get the wrong idea.

In the circumstances, middle-ranking pro-junta officers neutralised and arrested Constantine's royalist generals and took command of their units, and subsequently put together a force to advance on Kavala to arrest the King. The junta, not at all shaken by the loss of their figurehead premier, ridiculed Constantine by announcing that he was hiding from village to village. Realising that the counter-coup had failed, Constantine fled Greece, taking his family and the helpless Kollias with him. They landed in Rome early in the morning of 14 December. Constantine remained in exile all through the rest of military rule. Even though he would return to Hellas, the country's abolition of the monarchy in 1973 stripped him of his status as King.

Throughout all of this chaos, Olympic Airways somehow continued operating. Since 1966 when Olympic opened a transatlantic service with the first of a fleet of Boeing 707s, the airline embarked upon a series of new operations which led to an expansion of both the network and fleet. Furthermore, transactions have become more

Boeing 727 SX-CBB *Mount Pindos* taxies out for another service. *(Richard Vandervord)*

With everything down and out, Boeing 727 SX-CBE *Mount Athos* comes into to land at Ellinikon. (*author*)

Right: the face of the 1971 summer schedules that included the USA, Canada, Europe, Middle East and Africa.

varied, and this is reflected in the composition of the aircraft fleet.

With the opening of the transatlantic service, the Greek national carrier appeared to have a set of clearly-defined plans. The 707s worked the North Atlantic, and the Comets used on the European routes until the introduction of a new type of aircraft. On the home front, DC-3s and DC-6Bs soldiered on over the domestic network. At the beginning of 1967 when the 707s had completed a first year of operation for Olympic, and the airline was even more pleased with this fleet than it thought likely.

Due to the success of the big Boeing, the airline's mind was made up when it came to replacing the ageing Comets on the European sectors. While BEA operated Tridents, any pressure that there might have been to operate a like aeroplane on the London-Athína pool was relieved for Olympic with the termination of that pool agreement.

1968 was to be a monumental year for the airline. Traffic increase was marked; a total of 1,264,499 passengers - both domestic and international flew OA in 1968, travelling 1,286,680,000 kilometres, with a number of new routes opened. On 1 November from Athína to Nairobi, Kenya and Johannesburg, non-stop flights from London to Ródos and new flights between Beirut, Nicosia; Thessaloniki was added to the Athína - Frankfurt route.A new, unique service that made use of helicopters was introduced between Athína to the islands of Skiathos, Xios, Mykonos,

Two views of the Civil Super Super Frelon SA 321F F-OCMF that was chartered to Olympic Airways as part of the test campaign in Hellas. The aircraft was regularly flown by pilot-in-command Gérard Henry with his friend Pierre 'Tito' Maulandi. *(both Spiros Papadopoulos Collection)*

Left: Gérard Henry on the left with Pierre Maulandi. *(Sud Aviation)*

The Civil Super Super Frelon SA 321F F-OCMF was leased to Olympic Airways as part of the test sustained use of this civil version in regular airline use. *(Spiros Papadopoulos Collection)*

Santorini and Spetsai. That same year another 707 was acquired, two more ordered along with five Boeing 727-200 trijets.

On its own now, the Greek airline opted for Boeing 727s and ordered a fleet of five. Such was the carrier's rate of growth that they ordered the long-bodied version to provide, with seats for 144, the capacity that the Trident could not.

The Boeing 727 was a mid-size, narrow-body three-engined jet aircraft built by Boeing Commercial Aircraft from the early 1960s to 1984 and was a compromise among United Airlines, American Airlines, and Eastern Air Lines; each of the three had developed requirements for a jet airliner to serve smaller cities with shorter runways and fewer passengers.

Later 727 models were stretched to carry more passengers and replaced earlier jet airliners such as the Boeing 707 and Douglas DC-8, as well as ageing propeller airliners such as the DC-4, DC-6, DC-7, and the Lockheed Constellations on short- and medium-haul routes.

It could carry up to 189 passengers, and later models could fly up to 2,700 nautical miles nonstop. Intended for short and medium-length flights, the 727 could use relatively short runways at smaller airports. It has three Pratt & Whitney JT8D engines below the T-tail, one on each side of the rear fuselage with a centre engine that connects through an S-duct to an inlet at the base of the fin. The 727 was Boeing's only trijet aircraft.

The 727-100 first flew in February 1963 and entered service with Eastern Air Lines in February 1964; the stretched 727-200 flew in July 1967 and entered service with Northeast Airlines that December. The 727 became a mainstay of airlines' domestic route networks and was also used on short- and medium-range international routes. Passenger, freighter, and convertible versions of the 727 were built.

On 9 July 1968 Olympic took another huge step forward with the arrival of an Aérospatiale (formerly Sud Aviation) SA 321 Super Frelon ('Super Hornet'). This was a three-engined heavy transport helicopter produced by aerospace manufacturer Sud Aviation (later Aérospatiale) of France. It held the distinction of being the most powerful helicopter to be built in Europe at one point, as well as being the world's fastest helicopter. Registered F-OCMF it was to stay in Hellas for eighteen months.

The Wedding of the Century

Rumours were abounding that Aristotle Onassis was about to get married again, and not to just anyone, but to Jacqueline Lee 'Jackie' Kennedy, the wife of the 35th President of the United States, John F. Kennedy, and former First Lady.

On 16 October 1968, the *Boston Herald-Traveler's* front-page story upgraded the Jackie - Onassis rumors to hard news. The newspaper confidently expected a marriage announcement shortly. There was still nothing official from the Kennedy family, but the paper had questioned Cardinal Cushing about the rumors, and he could not tell a lie.

Besides, Onassis was in Athína for most of October, engaged in delicate business discussions with the Greek military dictator, George Papadopoulos. It seems that Jackie called Onassis with the news that the secret could not be contained much longer. She thought they should marry quickly.

Professor Georgakis, the only person in Athína, thoroughly acquainted with Onassis's plans, received an early morning summons to the Glyfada villa. Onassis told Georgakis that Jackie insisted the marriage take place with the utmost speed.

They discussed possible locations for the ceremony, Onassis's first choice was the American embassy, and, although Georgakis warned him that Greek marriages had to be performed in churches to be legal, he was nonetheless induced to try to 'fix things up' at the embassy. 'Supposing,' Georgakis asked a US official, 'a distinguished Greek should wish to marry a prominent American widow. Could they for reasons of speed and modesty do it here?' The official only repeated what Georgakis already knew.

It was decided that the chapel on Skorpios was the most suitable place since Jackie was insisting on the sort of privacy that only the island could provide. Onassis was reconciled to a Greek Orthodox service, but he demanded that Georgakis find some way of minimizing the impression of exoticism it might have on the Kennedy children. Georgakis was urged to find a priest 'who could speak some English and not have too long a beard;' a task which presented difficulties, because the hirsute and unilingual bishop of Lefkáda, whose diocese included Skorpios, had already cast himself in the role. After several rounds of ecclesiastical negotiations, Georgakis secured the services of an Athína University chaplain.

The news of the marriage was a shock to Onassis's family. Artemis alone reacted with enthusiasm. By nature a matchmaker, she considered Jackie the 'number one,' a bride worthy of her beloved brother. Onassis's children - Christina, then eighteen, and Alexander, twenty - were appalled. Both nourished the hope that their father might one day remarry their mother, whose

Very few photographs of the Onassis-Kennedy wedding were taken, let alone survive due to the high level of security surrounding events. The only one that I know of is this telephoto lens shot, taken at Ellinikon on 18 October, showing Mrs Artemis Garofaufailidi on the steps about to board, with her brother Aristotle Onassis just obscured by the head of a security official board OA's DC-6B SX-DAR *Isle of Samos* ready for the short flight to Andrivida to meet the OA 707 carrying his bride-to-be Jacqueline Kennedy. Onassis' son Alexandros is on the left, framed by the cab of the ground vehicle. *(Spiros Papadopoulos Collection)*

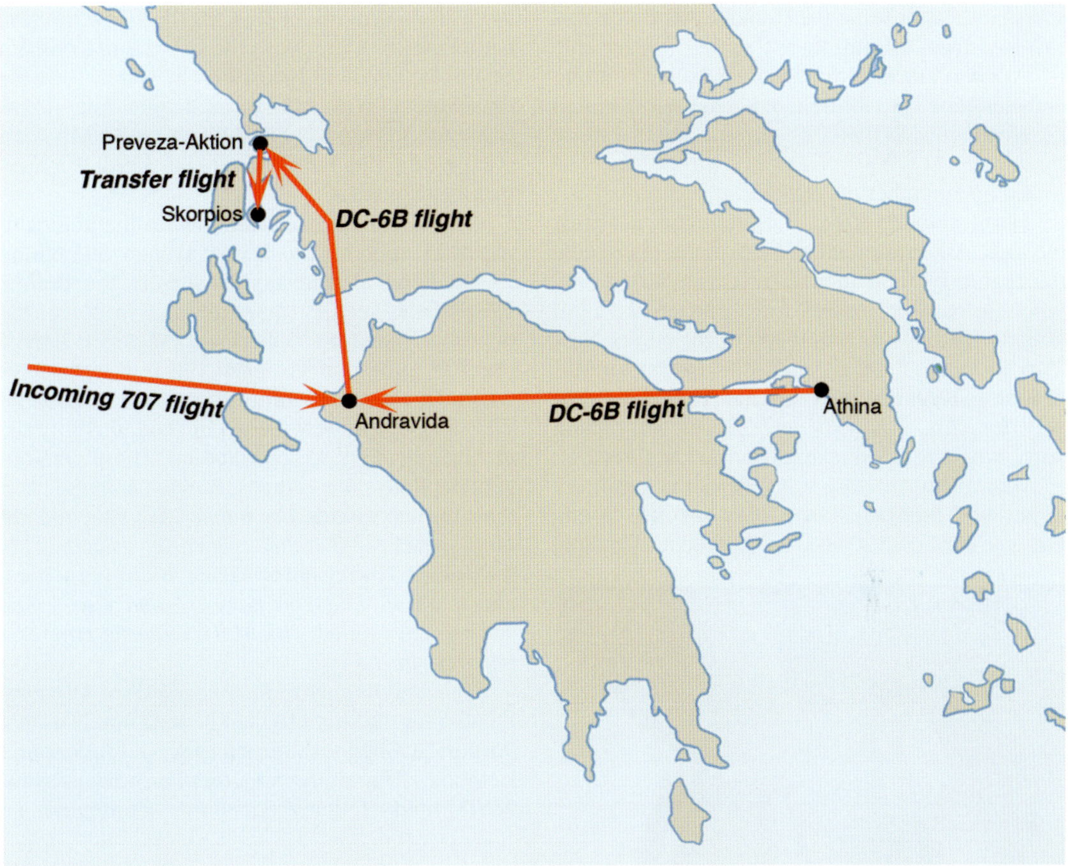

Olympic Airways staff worked hard behind the scenes co-ordinating the timings, routes and transfers between the three aircraft used to get the guests, principals and officials to Scorpios for the wedding or Aristotle Onassis and Jacqueline Kennedy. Initially all descended on the remote military airfield at Andravida in the Peleponnese, Onassis and his party arriving by DC-6D from Athína, with Mrs Kennedy and her party arriving by Boeing 707 from New York. From Adravida, all boarded the DC-6B for the short flight to Aktion airport near Preveza, where they transferred aircraft yet again, this time to the Super Frelon for the twenty-six kilometre flight to the private island of Skorpios.

marriage to the Marquess of Blandford did not seem destined to last. Onassis had occasionally mentioned this possibility to his son, but it appears to have been a device to reassure the boy rather than a real intention.

The marriage was officially announced in New York at 3:30 P.M. on Thursday, 17 October by the curious expedient of a message from Janet Jennings Auchincloss Rutherfurd, an American socialite, and Jackie Kennedy's half-sister that was relayed to the press by Nancy Tuckerman, Jackie's social secretary. Miss Tuckerman said, *'Mrs. Hugh D. Auchincloss has asked me to tell you that her daughter, Mrs. John F. Kennedy, is planning to marry Mr. Aristotle Onassis sometime next week. No place or date has been set for the moment.'*

The Press immediately went into a feeding frenzy, for information, quotes, photographs; all and everything was fair game. Onassis was in a taverna when the official announcement of his marriage reached Athína. He got a good night's sleep at Glyfada, and he was rested and cheerful for his first confrontation with the press as Jackie's fiancé when he arrived at Athína airport with his sister and a secretary. *'I am going to marry her tomorrow or within three days at the most,'* he said expansively. *'I can't say exactly because I must see and talk to her.'* He said the honeymoon would be spent on Skorpios *'...unless Jackie wants to make a tour of the Mediterranean on the Christina.'* He brought the conference to a close with: *'I have so many family problems to settle on my head. Please leave me alone and give me your blessing.'*

Behind the scenes, Olympic Airways staff were frantically planning and arranging what amounted to a covert military operation; indeed there are strong indications that the Hellenic Air Force was involved from the outset.

At six o'clock in the evening, Jackie, smiling and clutching her children, made her way through the crowd outside 1040 Fifth Avenue into a waiting limousine. At John F. Kennedy Airport she was joined by a number of relatives.

Here, Captain Donald McGregor, a senior Olympic Airways pilot had been preparing to take the regularly scheduled 707 service to Athína, when he received orders for a particular flight. Ninety-three passengers listed to fly on his New York to Athína flight are shifted to another aircraft at John F. Kennedy International Airport to make way for Mrs. Kennedy and her eleven-person party, who he was to take to Andravida, Greece.

Andravida Air Base was and still is a military airport 192 miles west of Athína operated by the Hellenic Air Force, located 2.5 kilometres from the town of Andravida in Elis, Hellas. Construction had begun in 1955, with the first air detachment established there in June 1960. In March 1961 the detachment was transformed into the 117th Combat Group (117 Σμηναρχία Μάχης), comprising the F-84F-equipped 339th Fighter-Bomber Squadron.

The legitimate press along with the hordes of paparazzi tried to cover every avenue, attempting to 'shadow' all the key players in the drama. Despite the secrecy measures put in place, the newsmen managed to work out the destination of the 707 and soon besieged the remote airfield where Onassis's DC-6B met his bride's incoming 707. The newsmen were given short shrift by the authorities - they were locked up. Those who did get telephoto shots of the scene on the tarmac had their film confiscated by the police. They did not miss much. *'Welcome, darling,'* Onassis is supposed to have said to Jackie after giving her a chaste kiss. *'Did you have a good trip?'* She smiled and replied: *'I had a wonderful trip, and it's a wonderful day.'*

The wedding party then boarded the Olympic DC-6B for the flight to then new Aktion National Airport that had just opened to serve Preveza and Lefkada. The airport was then, as now, used by NATO and Hellenic Air Force Command, so

Right: An Olympic Airways publicity poster that was so common around the airports of Ellas, this one showing a hostess in a the Pierre Cardin uniform. The girl is standing on the bottom step of the rear airstair of an Olympic 727. *(OA via author)*

Below: Boeing 727 SX-CBF *Mount Taygetus* taxies out to the runway hold point for the start of another service. *(Richard Vandervord)*

Above: Flagship of the Olympic 727 fleet, SX-CBA *Mount Olympus* climbs away. all the Olympic 727s were named after Hellenic mountains *(author)*

Left: a truly stunning publicity picture of a girl in the Pierre Cardin Olympic uniform. *(OA via author)*

again, security from press attention was not a problem. At Aktion the leased Super Frelon helicopter was already waiting for the arrival of the DC-6B; a quick transfer and they were off on the short twenty-six kilometre hop to the helipad on Skorpios.

Back in New York, the American Civil Aeronautics Board, the agency of the federal government charged with regulating aviation services, including scheduled passenger airline service, were frantically trying to probe the mass passenger 'bumping' case. However, they were hamstrung in being unable to take action unless any complaints were made; and mysteriously, none ever were.

In the meantime, some two hundred fifty journalists, all eager to cover 'the wedding of the century,' homed in on the tiny fishing village of Nidri on the island of Lefkáda, less than two miles from Skorpios. They hired a fleet of caiques and besieged Onassis's island. On the afternoon of 19 October, the eve of the wedding, Jackie agreed to a brief press conference. She made a valiant attempt to touch the newsmen's hearts, saying, '*We wish our wedding to be a private moment in the little chapel among the cypresses of Skorpios, with only members of the family and their little children. Understand that even though people may be well known, they still hold in their hearts the emotion of a simple person for the moments that are the most important we know on earth—birth, marriage, and death.*'

The wedding eventually took place amid scenes of utter chaos

Incidents and accidents.

In all the midst of trying to exist in what was something akin to a totalitarian military state, Olympic ran into a spate of political incidents, and tragic accidents that severely complicated its day-to-day operations.

On 16 August 1969 a company DC-3, on a domestic flight from Athína to Agrinion with 31 aboard, was hijacked by a Dr Vassilis Tsironis, with his wife and two children in tow. With the help of two guns and two knives smuggled on board, the family highjacked the airliner, forcing its pilot to land in Albania. During the flight, he

Olympic DC-6B SX-DAF seen against a stormy backdrop on the ground at Bierut. *(Spiros Papadopoulos Collection)*

revealed that he had been jailed by the military regime and apologised to the passengers for their inconvenience, saying he has acted to save his family. It seems that he had managed to get a few days of leave from the prisons of the regime, and took advantage of the chaotic tourist season, boarded an Olympic Airways DC-3 airliner for the Greek city of Agrinion.

The Albanian authorities initially arrested Tsironis believing he was a spy, but then organised a banquet for the family, the crew and the passengers in what the pilot later described as a cinematographic feast. Faced with the Stalinist regime in Albania, however, the Tsironis family soon opted to seek refuge in Sweden, the destination of hundreds of political refugees at the time, where, according to obituaries published after his death, the Swedish authorities imprisoned the doctor until the end of the junta. In an attempt to prevent further hijackings, on 23 September the company brought in a new rule that required all passengers on domestic flights to present identification cards or passports before travel.

A few months later, on 8 December 1969 - DC-6B SX-DAE with five crew and eighty-five passengers en route from Chania on Crete to Athína with slammed into Mount Paneion near the Sounion Non-Directional Beacon, during a thunderstorm. The aircraft was just twenty-one nautical miles from its destination, and there were no survivors.

2 January 1969, and there was another highjacking. - The Hellenic Government identified the hijacker of the Olympic Airways DC-6 from Crete to Athína as 30-year-old Cretan bricklayer George Flamourides, also known as George Paravolidakis. Officials said the terrorist fired a revolver shot that missed the pilot's head by inches, smashing a cockpit window then demanded to be taken to Cairo, Egypt.

The flight, Olympic Airways 944, had a crew of five. The passengers included Americans, Greeks and Italians. The airline refused to release passenger names, but the press got details anyway. *'I saw him rush to the captain's cabin,'* said George Xilouris, He said he had not heard the shot, but did see the man rushing up to the pilot's cabin a few minutes after the airliner took off from Iraklion airport. *'When the stewardess went to open the door, the man stuck a pistol in her stomach and pushed her aside.'* Elizabeth Petersen of Seattle, Wash., apparently did not see this because she said: *'I haven't got the foggiest idea how it happened. All we knew, was that suddenly we were flying over the Nile Delta instead of Athens'*.

The plane's Greek captain, Dionysis Mavrokefalos-Robotis, 36, told the Egyptian officer who interviewed him: *'I tried to alert Athens Airport to inform them but he shot at me and the bullet passed behind my head and struck a window.'*

Flamourides told Egyptian newsmen he was a Communist and had fled Crete to escape the present regime. He said it had jailed him for five months on a political charge and subsequently 'harassed' him. *'I came to Cairo because there is grand democracy here under Nasser,'* he was quoted as saying in English. He said he sought asylum but hopes to move on to Moscow.

The ninety-seven passengers on board later

resumed their flight to Athína after on another Olympic aircraft. Flamourides was later imprisoned in Egypt for eight months, and then sent to Sweden on the initiative of the UN Refugee Commission.

On 22 July 1970, an Olympic Airways Boeing 727 with sixty-one passengers and crew en route from Beirut to Athína was hijacked by seven members of the Popular Front for the Liberation of Palestine (PFLP). As the airliner - operating as OA Flight 255 - was flying over the island of Ródos, a man entered the cockpit armed to the teeth and stated that he was a Palestinian and was taking over the aircraft along with four of his comrades, which included a woman believed to be named 'Mona' and thought by some to be the infamous PFLP highjacker Leila Khaled. A little while later, a second hijacker entered the cockpit. Their goal was to secure the release of seven of their comrades held in Greek jails.

The airliner landed at Ellinikon and parked in a spot that was far from the airport terminals. One of the hijackers walked down the rear airstair holding a machine gun. The other four remained inside the airliner, except for 'Mona', who went up and down the aisle several times.

Aristotle Onassis happened to be in Athína. As soon as he heard about the hijacking, he hurried to the airport. The authorities communicated with the hijackers over a frequency belonging to the Civic Aviation officials. The kidnappers demanded that the airliner was refuelled and said they would give up the eighty passengers they were holding as hostages in exchange for their imprisoned comrades. The negotiation lasted several hours. Meanwhile, the 727 was refuelled, and the passengers started being released gradually with women, children, and the elderly going first.

At some point during the negotiations, Onassis offered to go out and speak directly with the terrorists: everyone tried to change his mind, but he was adamant. He wanted to propose to the hijackers that they release all the passengers and take him instead, with the promise that the authorities would allow them to take off. By doing so, Onassis was risking his own life in an effort to achieve the release of all passengers. He headed over to the 727 with his hands outside of his

Original caption: *The accused hijacker of Olympic Airways DC6, identified by the Greek government as George Flamourides, 30, sits between two security guards at Cairo airport today. The plane was hijacked after takeoff from Crete on its way to Athens today. A Greek man rushed into the cockpit, fired a warning shot through the window, and forced the pilot to fly to Cairo. The 97 passengers later resumed their flight to Athens (Spiros Papadopoulos Collection)*

pockets. As he approached the hijackers,'Mona' came out too. They spoke for quite some time, and then Onassis returned. He was astonished and disappointed that they refused his offer.

The negotiations continued until the evening, with talks being mediated by a representative of the International Red Cross. The hijackers finally allowed the remaining passengers to disembark. Afterwards, the plane took off for Beirut, but landed at Cairo after Beirut's refusal to permit landing with the five terrorists and the Red Cross representative on board. Onassis wondered why the hijackers had opted to take the official instead of him.

Much later it was learned that the Greek Minister of Interior, in charge of the matter, agreed to allow the International Red Cross Middle East representative Andrée Rochat to mediate. Finally, an agreement was reached providing to free, one month later, their seven fellow hijackers imprisoned in Hellas and the airliner returned to Athína on 7 September.

On Nov. 8 two Italians seized an Olympic Airlines plane flying from Paris to Athína. They forced it to return to Paris and later declared they had been trying to 'sabotage' the military regime in Greece by frightening off potential tourists.

5 November 1970 - the nosegear of DC-6B SX-DAI collapses after the plane's landing at Kerkira, Corfu, causing the Douglas to run off the left side of the runway 35 and come to a stop 450 ft. out; there are no fatalities.

16 October 1971 - En route from Kalamata to a YS-11A is hijacked to Beirut by a lone gunman, Constantine Yannopolos, who claimed to have planted a bomb on board. A few days later, on 26 October, another YS-11 en route from Athína to Crete, is diverted to Rome by a single assailant who is overpowered on the ground at the Italian capital.

There was yet another hijacking on 28 May 1972; a Boeing 707 from Heraklion to Athína with 153 passengers. The aircraft was commanded by Captain Lambros Kanelliopoulos. It seems that a

October 1, 1970

OLYMPIC messenger

VOL. 2 No 3. PUBLISHED FOR THE OLYMPIC FAMILY

ARISTOTLE ONASSIS SUCCESSFULLY NEGOTIATES RELEASE OF OA PASSENGERS FROM SKYJACKED PLANE

Mr. Aristotle Onassis shares a laugh with Peter Mellas, of NEWSWEEK Magazine, during a special press conference held at Ellinikon Airport following the skyjacking of an OA Boeing 727.

Aristotle S. Onassis, founder and owner of Olympic Airways, made international headlines again in July, but this time the front page banners were not of any social or financial significance. Rather, Mr. Onassis played the real-life role of a hero.

Six Arab commandos, five men and one girl, skyjacked a Greekflag Boeing 727 bound from Beirut to Athens by threatening to blow it up with its passengers and crew aboard. After landing at Ellinikon Airport, the guerillas demanded the immediate release of seven commandos held in Greek jails pendings trial for bombings in Athens.

At one stage of the eight hours of negotiations, the presence of Mr. Onassis was requested by the outlaws. They stated that he was one man whose word they would trust.

The founder of Olympic rushed to the airport to see what he could do to safeguard the lives of the passengers and crew.

He met with the leader on the tarmac and offered himself as a hostage to replace the 53 passengers. His offer was politely turned down.

During his dialogue on the runway, a tommy gun was pointed at Mr. Onassis from inside the aircraft.

At his special press conference, Mr. Onassis answered all questions as to what happened during the tense moments when he negotiated with the skyjackers. The world press hailed him as a man possessed of heroism matched with his success in the business world.

Airline Public Relations photographers seem to have been inspired by the American TV series *'Hawaii Five-O'* and their opening sequences that made use of 'fisheye' ultra-wide-angle lenses. So it was also with Olympic...

young man called C Savvakis entered the cockpit brandishing a pistol and had a parcel hanging around his neck. He demanded to be taken to London for medical treatment as he claimed to be suffering from serious debilitating headaches.

Electrical wire was dangling from the package leading to a button in his hand. He told the Captain that it contained dynamite and that he could detonate it at any time by pressing the button.

Captain Kanelliopoulos took no chances and went along with the demands, but managed to convince the hijacker that it would be better to land at Athína first, let the passengers disembark, refuel and then take off for London.

At Ellinikon, the aircraft was surrounded by police and the passengers were allowed off. Captain Paul Ioannidis, the Director-General of Olympic Airways discussed and analysed the situation with the head of the police security team; eventually, Captain Ioannidis boarded the aircraft on his own and convinced the hijacker to surrender to the Greek authorities, thus avoiding any bloodshed.

One condition that Captain Ioannidis agreed to - Director General of Olympic Airways — that after his release by the Hellenic authorities, Olympic would send him to London for treatment. The pistol was real, but the 'parcel with the dynamite,' turned out to be a bundle of wooden sticks tied together. Savvakis was later tried and recieved a two-year prion sentance. This was the fifth hijacking on board an Olympic Airways flight.

The flight of Constantine and Kollias left Greece with no legal government or head of state. This did not concern the military junta. Instead, the Revolutionary Council, composed of Pattakos, Papadopoulos, and Makarezos, appointed another member to the military administration, Major General Georgios Zoitakis, as Regent. Zoitakis then appointed Papadopoulos as prime minister. This became the only government of Greece following the failure of the King's attempted counter-coup, as Constantine was unwilling to set up an alternative administration in exile. The Regent's position was later confirmed under the 1968 Constitution.

In a legally controversial move, even under the junta's own Constitution, the Cabinet voted on 21 March 1972 to oust Zoitakis and replace him with Papadopoulos, thus combining the offices of Regent and Prime Minister. The King's portrait remained on coins, in public buildings, etc., but slowly, the military chipped away at the institution of the monarchy: the royal family's tax immunity was abolished, the complex network of royal charities was brought under direct state control, the royal arms were removed from coins, the Navy and Air Force dropped their 'Royal' names, and newspapers were prohibited from publishing the King's photo or any interviews.

The Colonels preferred to call the coup a 'revolution to save the nation'. Their official justification was that a communist conspiracy had infiltrated Greece's bureaucracy, academia, press, and military, to such an extent that drastic action was needed to protect the country from communist takeover. Thus, the defining characteristic of the Junta was its staunch anti-communism. They used the term anarcho-communist to describe leftists in general. In a similar vein, the junta attempted to steer Greek public opinion not only by propaganda but also by inventing new words and slogans, such as old-partyism (palaiokommatismos) to discredit parliamentary democracy or Greece for Christian Greeks (Ellas Ellinon Christianon) to underscore its ideology. The junta's main ideological spokesmen included Georgios Georgalas and journalist Savvas Konstantopoulos, both former Marxists.

As soon as the coup d'etat was announced over Greek radio, martial music was continuously broadcast over the airwaves. This was interrupted from time to time with announcements of the junta issuing orders, which always started with the introduction, 'We decide and we order'. Long-standing political freedoms and civil liberties, that had been taken for granted and enjoyed by the Greek people for decades, were instantly suppressed. Article 14 of the Greek Constitution, which protected freedom of thought and freedom of the press, was immediately suspended. Military courts were established, and political parties were dissolved. Legislation that took decades to fine tune and multiple parliaments to enact was thus erased in a matter of days. The rapid dismantling of Greek democracy had begun.

The citizens' right of assembly was revoked and no political demonstrations were allowed. Surveillance on citizens was a fact of life, even during permitted social activities. That had a continuously chilling effect on the population who realised that, even though they were allowed certain social activities, they could not overstep the boundaries and delve into or discuss forbidden subjects. This realisation, including the absence of

...who used these images of Boeing 707 SX-DBD *City of Sparta* in their inflight magazine of the early 1970s. *(both Spiros Papadopoulos Collection)*

Above: Boarding an Olympic 707 at Ellinikon, and left: the inflight safety card. *(both Spiros Papadopoulos Collection)*

any civil rights as well as maltreatment during police arrest, ranging from threats to beatings or worse, made life under the junta a difficult proposition for many ordinary citizens. Photography by ordinary citizens was banned in public locations.

The military government was given support by the United States as a Cold War ally, due to its proximity to the Eastern European Soviet bloc, and the fact that the previous Truman administration had given the country millions of dollars in economic aid to discourage communism. U.S. support for the junta, which was violently anti-communist, is claimed to be the cause of rising anti-Americanism in Greece during and following the junta's undemocratic rule.

To gain support, Papadopoulos projected an image that appealed to elements of Greek society. The son of a poor but educated rural family, he was educated at the prestigious Hellenic Military Academy. Papadopoulos allowed substantial social and cultural freedoms to all social classes, but political oppression and censorship were at times heavy-handed. Kostas Gavras's film Z and Mikis Theodorakis's music, among others, were never allowed even during the most relaxed times of the dictatorship, and an index of prohibited songs, literature and art was kept.

Concurrently, tourism was actively encouraged by Papadopoulos' government and, funding scandals notwithstanding, there was a great development of the tourist sector. With tourism came nightlife. However, under Papadopoulos, in the absence of any civil rights these socio-cultural freedoms existed in a legal vacuum that meant they were not guaranteed, but rather dispensed at the whim of the junta. In addition, any transgressing into political matters during social or cultural

Scenes at an airport- 1: loading an OA 707 for another trip Catering is put aboard, suitcases are lined up ready for placing in the holds and the fuel tanks are topped up. *(all Spiros Papadopoulos Collection)*

activities usually meant arrest and punishment. Although discotheques and nightclubs were, initially, subjected to a curfew, partially due to an energy crisis, this was eventually extended from 1.00 a.m. to 3:00 a.m. as the energy crisis eased.

Financing the expansion

Through all the turmoil of the countries political crises, Olympic Airways struggled to carry on normally. When the prestige-conscious military dictators seized power on 21 April 1967, Onassis found himself under severe pressure to turn Olympic into a major international carrier operating a sizable jet fleet. Apart from the two De Havilland Comets and three Boeing 707s it already had, the rest of the fleet was, at best, elderly.

It is clear that Onassis enjoyed the exercise of mystification of his business activities and that the complexities of his airline business were far from accidental. Olympic Airways under Onassis was not unlike the creation of some medieval wizard who, refusing to concede that the earth revolves around the sun, is thereby obliged to create ever weirder, more convoluted, and perilous mechanisms to make everything agree with his highly personal view of the cosmos. Onassis ran OA as his fiefdom and approached Olympic with two unshakable convictions. Should the communist revolution return and succeed - and the chances of that happening always seemed fair-to-good in Greece - there would be nothing to grab if someone had a mind to nationalise the airline; and Olympic should at all costs avoid the appearances of profitability, which could only make the government reluctant to grant future concessions. These convictions gave Olympic its underlying business logic. By their very nature, they were not ones that he could readily impart to the authorities or the courts.

In the late 1950s and early 1960s it was virtually impossible for a company to borrow more than three times its net worth, and in Olympic's case this was a meager $1.5 million. At the time this was traditionally the way either bank loans or stock issues. The obvious solution was to float a stock issue, but Onassis refused this option because he was determined to keep his assets on Greek soil to a minimum. Onassis's consequent unwillingness to add to the elderly piston-engined driven fleet he had inherited was the principal reason for Olympic's unimpressive performance in the first decade of its existence. He muddled through by means of 'subordinated loans' from other Onassis companies abroad, such as Ionian

Ltd, which effectively guaranteed loans much larger than Olympic would otherwise have been able to raise. But there was a limit to the amount of money which could be raised in this manner.

One of the basic problems that these self-imposed limitations presented was how to acquire aircraft. Normally this should not have been a major difficulty, for previous Greek governments had traditionally been generous in underwriting projects deemed to be in the national interest. But taking out a government loan for either OA or Onassis would have involved the kind of accountability Onassis found so repugnant, and it would almost certainly have meant that any assets acquired with the loan would have to be located within reach of the Hellenic government – something that was precisely what Onassis was determined to avoid. The alternative was to raise money on the international money market, but this also went against Onassis's instincts.

Today, there is an obvious alternative, but it was little known or used at the time of OA's inception; that of aircraft leasing. It was however, something that Onassis knew about and made good use of. To give at idea as to just how much of a pioneer in this field he was, as late as 1976, operating leases of jet airliners accounted for less than 2% of the worldwide fleet, then 15% in the early 1990s, 25% in 2000 and 40% in 2017, with lessors involved in 62% of second hand mid-life aircraft transactions since 2000: 42% in Europe and 29% in North America.

Airlines lease aircraft from other airlines or dedicated leasing companies for two main reasons: to operate aircraft without the financial burden of buying them, and to provide temporary increase in capacity. The industry has two main leasing types: wet-leasing, which is normally used for short-term leasing, and dry-leasing which is more normal for longer-term leases. The industry also uses combinations of wet and dry. For example, when the aircraft is wet-leased to establish new services, then as the airline's flight or cabin crews become trained, they can be switched to a dry lease.

A wet lease is a leasing arrangement whereby one airline - known as the lessor - provides an Aircraft, complete Crew, Maintenance, and Insurance (ACMI) to another airline or other type of business acting as a broker of air travel - known as the lessee - which paid by hours operated. The lessee provides fuel and covers airport fees, and any other duties, taxes, etc. The flight uses the flight number of the lessee. A wet lease generally lasts from one to twenty-four months; a shorter duration would be considered an ad hoc charter. A

Scenes at an airport- 2: detail pictures of an OA 707. The flightdeck, nose and undercarriage inspection before flight. *(all Spiros Papadopoulos Collection)*

wet lease is typically utilized during peak traffic seasons or annual heavy maintenance checks, or to initiate new routes. A wet-leased aircraft may be used to fly services into countries where the lessee is banned from operating.

They can also be considered a form of charter whereby the lessor provides minimum operating services, including ACMI, and the lessee provides the balance of services along with flight numbers. In all other forms of charter, the lessor provides the flight numbers. Variations of a wet lease include a code share arrangement and a block seat agreement. In the United Kingdom, a wet lease is when an aircraft is operated under the Air Operator's Certificate (AOC) of the lessor.

A dry lease is a leasing arrangement whereby an aircraft financing entity - the lessor - provides an aircraft without flight or cabin crew, ground staff etc. A dry lease is typically used by leasing companies and banks, requiring the lessee to put the aircraft on its own AOC and provide aircraft registration. A typical dry lease lasts upwards of two years and bears certain conditions with respect to depreciation, maintenance, insurances, etc., depending on such things as the geographical location and political circumstances of the operating region.

A dry-lease arrangement can also be made between a major airline and a regional airline, in which the major airline provides the aircraft and the regional operator provides flight crews, maintenance and other operational aspects of the aircraft, which then may be operated under the major airline's name or some similar name. A dry lease saves the major airline the expense of training personnel to fly and maintain the aircraft, along with other considerations (such as staggered union contracts, regional airport staffing, etc.). In the United Kingdom, a dry lease is when an aircraft is operated under the AOC of the lessee.

There is one further alternative that of a 'Damp lease' whereby there is an arrangement where the lessor provides the aircraft, flight crew and maintenance but the lessee provides the cabin crew. It is also occasionally referred to as a ‘moist lease'.

Right: promotional material showing Olympic Airways' internal and external services for 1973.

Below: 707 SX-DBC departs on another revenue earning service. *(both Spiros Papadopoulos Collection)*

Yannis Tseklenis was born in Athína in 1937 and is an Hellenic fashion designer. In 1967 he founded the fashion company 'Boutiques Tseklenis.'

During 1971, Tseklenis designed the new uniforms for Olympic Airways' hostesses, taking as inspiration for his designs from the olympic rings, while a new maxi and mini version came in use, enriched with complementary accessories like the umbrellas. In 1972, maxi dresses were introduced for the flight attendants in Business Class.

Tseklenis launched an exclusive collection which included all the necessary accessories a flight attendant would need: umbrellas, the dress and the statement boots. The white boots received a lot of positive feedback as they introduced a new fashion era.

He not only designed the uniforms that were worn from 1971 until 1976, but in 1988 produced the designs for the interiors of the Olympic fleet of aircraft.

Olympic had a need for five Boeing 727s and two more 707s and at the time were strongly indicated as being purchased at a publically asked price of $54.1 million. Wether or not that was the actual price Onassis was being asked to pay by Boeing was never revealed, but the publically quoted price and eventual 'done the deal price' were usually two very different things – however, the problem for Onassis still remained. Whatever the price, how he could conceivably raise that sort of money without floating a stock issue?

Onassis adored such conundrums. Making money in itself was no longer enough, unless it also constituted an affirmation of his own genius. Working out how to buy $54 million worth of airliners for an airline which did not have the ability even to borrow the money was the sort of challenge Onassis thrived on.

The solution he finally hit upon and induced the government to accept was something that he claimed was entirely his own creation.

Tryfon Koutalidis, who was to become the head of the legal department at OA went on the record saying that: *'I always say I went to three universities, London University, Athína University, and Onassis University...'* Although many were vehemently against what Onassis did, Koutalidis was one of those who marveled at Onassis's solution and at the interlocking web of companies and financial arrangements that supported it. It went like this: Olympic Airways, though a Greek company, was in reality the wholly owned subsidiary of Victoria Financiera Panama, of which Onassis was the sole shareholder. Onassis duly created another Panamanian corporation, Aircraft Leasing Company, which functioned as a consortium, financed seventy percent by the First National City Bank of New York, fifteen percent by the Boeing Aircraft Corporation, and fifteen percent by yet another Onassis company in Panama.

It should be mentioned that Onassis had a considerable number of Panamanian registered companies, many of which were used by his maritime activities. With regards to aviation, he had a number which he used for this and subsequent Olympic deals, among them Sociedad Maritima Miraflores Ltd, Ionian Ltd, Armadora Aristotelis Panama, and Condor Financiera Panama. Aircraft Leasing bought the airliners from Boeing and dry leased them to Olympic Airways a ten year period. All the Onassis organization had to put up was the fifteen percent – $8 million - and none of the money went anywhere near Hellas. Olympic Airways paid the rental in 120 monthly installments to Victoria Financiera Panama, which then passed on the requisite amount to Aircraft Leasing. It was then remitted, without deductions,

The first Olympic Boeing 727 service to Amsterdam, using SX-CBB *Queen Anna-Maria* was marked with the usual style. *(Spiros Papadopoulos Collection)*

'Κυρίες και κύριοι, καλώς ήρθατε στην Αθήνα. Παραμείνετε καθισμένοι έως ότου ο κυβερνήτης απενεργοποιήσει την ένδειξη ζώνης ασφαλείας. Η τοπική ώρα είναι τώρα πέντε λεπτά έξι το βράδυ. Ladies and gentlemen, welcome to Athens. Please remain seated until the Captain turns off the seat-belt sign. The local time is now five minutes past six in the evening.' Olympic OA260 - operated by 720 SX-DBK on this occasion - arrives from London. The Hellenic Air Force had facilities on the extreme left of the picture, and woe betide anyone caught pointing a camera in that direction! *(author)*

first to First National City Bank, until its seventy percent was paid off with interest, then to Boeing until they had their fifteen percent, and then to the Onassis Financing company.

When details of the deal leaked out, Onassis's critics jumped to what seemed the obvious conclusion: he was renting the airliners from himself for a whopping profit, thus insuring that Olympic lost money, while he raked it in tax free in Panama. He was simply milking the hard-pressed Greek economy for his own personal profit.

Onassis was able to rebut these charges to government investigators, though in public he always preferred to lie steadfastly, asserting that the aircraft belonged to Olympic. It was said that Olympic was paying a rental for the seven aircraft of $60,000 each a month, which compared favourably with the price on the charter market. Even if the rental were not a fair one, Onassis would and did argue, the idea that he could rob Olympic in Greece to pay himself in Panama was ludicrous as long as both Olympic and the Panamanian companies were wholly his, and as long as Olympic neither paid taxes not received subsidies. They were both his pockets, so how could moving assets from one to the other possibly be construed as improper? It was the truth, but not the whole truth.

The least defensible aspect of the deal was what happened to the airliners at the end of the ten years. Again, Onassis was able to answer with complete truth, they did not immediately end up in his pockets but with First National City. If they had been acquired by Olympic on a lease-purchase plan, then they would of course have become an

707 SX-DBD *'City of Sparta'* departs John F Kennedy Airport New York for another flight back to Hellas. *(Richard Vandervord)*

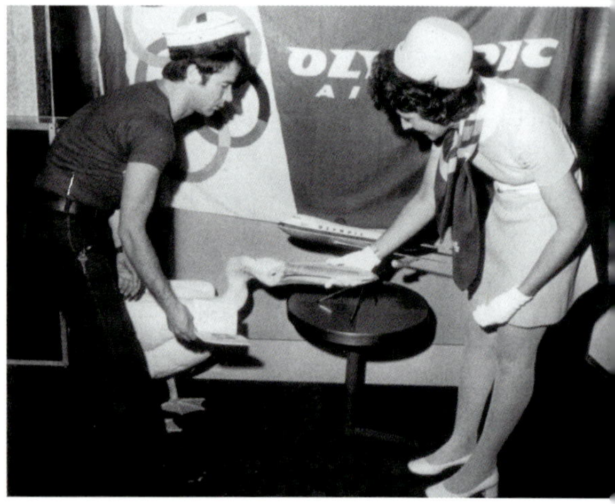

Right: Petros (Peter) the Pelican was a wounded bird rescued and adopted by a Myconian fisherman. In the end, as the island gained destination glamor status, Petros the Pelican managed to generate substantial income for his adopted home. By charming locals and tourists alike – posing patiently for a 'click' alongside kings, hippies and jetsetters – the tireless and docile bird was soon promoted to island mascot. He was unashamably used by OA to promote Mykonos as a destination. *(OA files)*

asset of the airline. Onassis did not explain the personal reason why he wished to avoid this. His explanation to the investigators was that the credibility of Greece - politically and economically - was so low in the eyes of international financial institutions that he would have had trouble raising any money to lease the aircraft, let alone on such advantageous terms, if the lease had stipulated that the airliners were to revert to Olympic at the end of the ten years. What would happen, therefore, was that Aircraft Leasing and its aircraft would revert to First National City. What Onassis did not say was that immediately after that they would revert once more to his own company, Victoria Financiera, which thus got the aircraft and their $8 million back with interest.

Onassis's often reiterated claim that he never received a drachma in subsidy for OA from the Greek government was completely correct. Olympic Airways received no subsidies because Onassis simply did not want them - he did not want them because the receipt of subsidies involved the opening of his books. Concessions were much more convenient, and these could be best obtained by pointing to a dismal annual balance sheet: During his eighteen years of proprietorship, Olympic Airways showed a profit during only three years, and these were explained by Onassis as being the result of capital transfers within his empire.

Olympic's 'losses' were almost invariably outweighed by 'profits' in other Onassis - controlled companies, whose existence was dependent on the airline. George Theofanos, who was appointed the president of Olympic Airways by the government after Onassis's death, explained that '*...most of the planes and buildings belonged to and leased from other Onassis companies. I do not doubt that Olympic was very profitable- for Mr Onassis. The complicated system [of interlocking companies] he had created meant that he personally could not lose money.*'

The first of the 727s entered commercial service in 1969, and since then traffic expansion led to an increase in the fleet with an order for more. This fleet quickly grew, however, and not stop there, for changes on the domestic scene led Olympic closer to Boeing all the time. The last of the DC-3s retired on 1 May 1970 and their successors, the 94-seat DC-6Bs, showed signs of flagging.

Replacing the DC-6

The DC-6Bs, which aircraft operated an average stage length in the Greek Islands of 150 miles on a concentrated schedule, were comfortable even with 94 passengers on board but were destined for retirement. Their replacements were to be a 'mix' of Boeing 727s and, for Europe, the latest and most exciting feeder-liner, the Japanese NAMC YS-11.

The NAMC YS-11 was a turboprop airliner built by a Japanese consortium, the Nihon Aircraft Manufacturing Corporation. The programme was initiated by the Ministry of International Trade and Industry in 1954; the aircraft was rolled out in 1962.

In the mid-to-late 1950s, the Japanese Ministry of International Trade and Industry identified a requirement for a short-haul airliner to replace Douglas DC-3s flying on Japan's domestic routes and encouraged companies in Japan's aircraft industry to collaborate to develop and produce the new airliner. It was a joint venture between Mitsubishi Heavy Industries, Kawasaki Heavy Industries, Fuji Heavy Industries (now better known as the parent company of automobile manufacturer Subaru), Shin Meiwa, Showa Aircraft Industry Company and Japan Aircraft Industry. The company was set up in 1957 and formalised as the Nihon Aeroplane Manufacturing Company (NAMC) in 1959.

NAMC designed a low-winged twin-turboprop monoplane seating 60 passengers. Jiro Horikoshi, the designer of the Mitsubishi A6M Zero fighter, was involved in creating it. The airframe was mainly designed and manufactured in Japan, the engines were built by Rolls-Royce, with the 3,050 ehp Rolls-Royce Dart RDa.10/1s selected for the new aircraft. Electronic equipment, avionics, mechanical and fuselage components were supplied either by Japanese companies or foreign suppliers during the YS-11's production lifetime.

Aristotle Onassis and Olympic Airways sent a lot of time investigating a DC-3 replacement, including on the left, what appears to be a model of the Handley Page Herald.

Below: Hawker Siddeley loaned Olympic their HS.748 demonstrator G-AVRR for a number of test services around the country. *(both Spiros Papadopoulos Collection)*

Olympic certainly gave the Hawker Siddeley 748 serious consideration, leasing two demonstrator examples from the company for a summer season. Nevertheless, the design failed to meet Olympics requirements especailly when compared to the YS-11. *(OA/ΠΟΛΚ.ΕΟΑ Collection)*

The twin-engined YS-11 delivered similar operational performance to the four-engined Vickers Viscount and had 50% more capacity than the similarly configured Fokker F27 Friendship.

The first prototype made its maiden flight from Nagoya Airport on 30 August 1962, with the second prototype flying on 28 December. It received its Japanese Type certificate on 25 August 1964, with American Federal Aviation Administration (FAA) certification following on 9 September 1965.

The first production YS-11 flew on 23 October 1964. At first, deliveries were mainly to Japanese airlines, then NAMC developed the YS-11A, with higher gross weight, to make the aircraft more attractive to the North American and European market, and in particular to meet the requirements of Piedmont Airlines, which ordered ten YS-11A-200s, with an option for an additional ten aircraft.

The YS-11 had been the subject of a very close study by Olympic's operational and commercial departments, and eventually, a fleet of six ordered. The aircraft was selected after comparable studies were made of the Hawker Siddeley 748, Fokker's F.28 Fellowship and F.27 Friendship, and others. The HS 748 was rejected as too small, as was the Friendship, while the Fellowship was not right as a jet. For the rough and in some cases non-existent runways of the Greek domestic island network, only a turboprop would do. Whatever turboprop was chosen, it had to have the correct capacity, and the 64-seat YS-11 suited OA's requirements well.

Two other types considered for DC.3 and DC.6 replacements by Olympic was the Fokker F.27, seen in Aer Lingus colours and the F.28 in Air Anglia markings. Both types failed to meet Olympic's requirements. *(both authors Collection)*

The prototype Nihon YS-11 - seen here undergoing engine runs was fully evaluated by Olympic Airways before the decision to make use of a fleet of them was made. *(Authors Collection)*

June 15, 1970

OLYMPIC messenger

VOL. 2 No 2. PUBLISHED FOR THE OLYMPIC FAMILY

NEW ARRIVALS AT HELLINIKON

The first two (of five) Japanese-manufactured aircraft acquired by Olympic Airways arrived in April at Hellinikon Airport. The Nihon YS-11A 220 series airplanes have been named the Isle of Cephallonia and the Isle of Ithaca. Accommodating 64 passengers each, the turbo-prop planes replaced OA'S DC 3s and partially, the DC 6Bs on domestic operations.

On hand at Athens airport to officially receive the new aircraft were (left to right) Mike Margaronis, OA System Ground Operations Manager, Walter Conrad, newly-appointed General Director of OA in North America, Roger Loubry, Second Vice-President of the Board of Directors, Capt. Shizuo Kikuchi, who piloted the plane from Japan, MITSUI's representative Hiroshi Shirahata and Loucas Grammaticos, Technical Director of Olympic Airways.

How the arrival of the YS-11s were announced in Olympic Messenger, the company newspaper.

Delivery of the Nihons.

Delivery of the YS-11s from Japan to Ellas was a somewhat involved and complicated process that had to follow a slightly tortuous route, as demonstrated by SX-BBR, which was typical of the ferry flights.

This particular aircraft flew for the first time on 12 April 1971, when it made the first of a series of three test flights, the last one being on 24 April. By now it had flown a total of six hours twenty minutes and was declared ready for delivery.

On 30 April Captains Sugawara, Sakasaki and Engineer Fukuba boarded the aircraft at Nagoya for a two-hour twenty-five-minute flight to Kagoshima on Kyushu island where they refuelled for a three-hour fifty-minute flight to Taipei in Taiwan.

Day two of the trip - 1 May - and it was another early start - this time for a three-hour forty-five-minute flight to Manila in the Philippines. The next day they flew for seven hours twenty minutes from Manila to Kota Kinabalu in Malaysia, then on to Singapore. 3 May saw a single flight; three hours forty-five minutes from Singapore to Bankok in Thailand.

4 May was something of a long haul. Departing Bankok, they flew to Rangoon in one hour forty-five minutes, then over the border and on to Calcutta, India on three hours and five minutes. There was a brief stop in Calcutta before a further four-hour ten-minute flight to Dehli. The next day

YS-11A SX-BBH *Isle of Ithica* taxies in to the West Terminal. (*Spiros Papadopoulos Collection)*

it was a further eight hours flying to Karachi and then Doha in Qatar.

Day seven of the journey was planned to be from Doha to Kuwait in one hour fifty minutes, and then on to Damascus after a three-hour twenty-minute flight for an overnight stop before going on to Athnia on 7 May. However, good weather and an early start meant that the crew could press on to Athína on 6 May, arriving at Ellinikon at 14.45 local, having made the three-hour twenty-minute flight in good time.

The first of the Olympic YS-11s entered service in April 1970 and quickly showed itself as a profit-making airliner for the company. The YS-11s were the model YS-11A-220, with uprated Rolls-Royce Dart turboprops. The YS-11A (known locally as a 'Nihon') is probably the heaviest twin-turboprop ever put into production, weighing as much as a Viscount, but also having as much power as a Viscount, provided by only two 3,060 e.h.p. Rolls-Royce Dart 542-10Ks,which give it a good STOL performance plus good economy. The aircraft soon took over from the DC-6Bs on some sectors, which were then disposed of.

A typical Nihon flight for me began, not long after dawn as usual, at the West Terminal of Ellinikon. This trip was, for me something of a special occasion, as it was my honeymoon! Not for my wife and I this trip would we be staying in the

Olympic used to do a trio of aircraft 'rotations' throughout any given day. There was a surge of very early morning departures - mostly out to the islands, that returned like homing pigeons ready for another wave of departures around lunchtime which returned ready for the evening rotation. In the early 1970s when I was island hopping, most of my flights were very early in the morning which gave a lovely golden light, as shown in this picture of 727 SX-CBA *Mount Olympus* as seen from YS-11A SX-BBH en route to Lesbos.(*author)*

Above: Olympic's YS-11A SX-BBG *Isle of Cephalonia* awaiting another load of passengers. In the background, behind the Learjet is Olympic's Operations and Training building.

Right: Boarding Cards and Baggage tags, old style! *(both author)*

London Hotel on Posidonos Avenue, Glyfada; instead we overnighted at the Arethusa Hotel, on Mitropoleos just off Syntagma Square in the centre of Athína, having arrived the early evening before on Olympic OA260 - operated by 720 SX-DBK from London Heathrow.

Flight OA740 was supposedly a forty-five minute trip across the Aegean to Mytilene International Airport 'Odysseas Elytis' on the island of Lesbos, close to the Turkish coast. After braving the rather frantic check-in desks and going through the departure gate, I was greeted by the sight of the what appeared to be entire YS-11A fleet lined up on the ramp. I was soon climbing the steep integral passenger steps into SX-BBH 'Isle of Ithica' and settling into one of the sixty-four large and comfortable seats.

The YS-11A had the almost ugly but purposeful look that typified many Japanese products of that era, with its DC-8 type nose and the engines mounted over the wing above a very large wheel-wells. The passenger cabin was undoubtedly spacious, although the windows were apparently designed for the Japanese passenger; the top of the window was level with my shoulder, and the best way to see out properly would have been to sit on the floor. The toilet on board is also worthy of note as being one of the largest I have ever experienced aboard an aircraft, with its principal equipment surmounted by an enormous square seat!

No sooner seated than we were informed that there would be a fifty-minute delay and that smoking would be permitted for those passengers sitting on the right-hand side of the aisle - I was never quite sure how the smoke knew that it was not allowed to cross the isle! Five minutes later the 'No smoking' sign reappeared, and the Rolls-Royce Dart engines were started up.

In no time now Flight OA740 had begun with the stewardesses giving a demonstration of seat-belt fastening, as a change from the more usual life-belt drill, and we were soon climbing away from Ellinikon's runway 15L, holding a steady, if noisy climb until overhead Cape Sounion, when a left-hand turn was made, setting a direct course for Lesbos at a cruising altitude of 15,000 feet for the five hundred kilometre journey.

Captain Nicolaidis circled the picturesque town of Mytilene and then out along the coast with the island on our right and Turkey on our left passing closely alongside the 14/32 runway before turning again and bringing the Nihon down into the 1200 metre long runway, right alongside the coast. On slowing to taxi speed, we were met by a pair of armoured cars, which stationed themselves behind each wingtip, escorting us back to a small white building which served as the village shop/café cum

Ramp Agent Nikos Vardakidis stands by the airstairs of one of Olympics YS-11As - the famous 'Nihons'. The picture shows two things, the size of the aircraft - it really was big for a twin-engined turbo-propand how low the line of cabin windows were when kooked at in relationship to the top step of the airstairs! *(OA/ΠΟΛΚ.ΕΟΑ Collection)*

airport office and arrival/departure lounge. We had arrived on schedule.

The passenger door of the YS-11 had hardly opened and the built-in airstairs extended when I could hear the airport's public address system; *'Would Meester and Mee-sis Gra-ham Simm-onds, recently arrived from Athína please make themselves known to an Olympic Airways Representative.'*

The return flight, this time aboard SX-BBP *'Isle of Andros'* a few days later was equally memorable. We were joined on board by the local priest who blessed not only the dispatcher but also the stewardesses and the pilots - which did much to reassure the other passengers. It was during the flight back to Athína that I discovered another quirk of the airliner; after nearly spilling my glass of orange juice - another Olympic domestic flight tradition - I found that there are no trays fitted - or carried - on the Nihon and drinks have to be held or put on the floor!

For the longer sectors, the average international stage-length being 500 miles, the Boeing 727s were profit-makers too, while on the

A busy scene on the ramp at the domestic side of the West Terminal, Ellinikon, with Piper Aztec SX-BDL in from of a YS-11 looming behind. *(authors collection)*

domestic services Olympic maintained that these aircraft would at least break even. Their operations are being assisted by a new Government policy aimed at supporting Olympic on the one hand and attracting more tourist traffic on the other. The twenty-one airports in Greece were receiving huge investment money by the Department of Civil Aviation, and much was spent on runway and terminal improvements. Additionally, four new airports were being built with more to follow.

Where runways were lengthened and new airports built, the high-capacity 727s carried the increasing tourist traffic; and as an indication of just how this trade grew, the figures for 1970 showed a traffic increase of fifty per cent, while the forecast for 1971 was twenty per cent above the previous years figures. Both the 727s and the YS-11s were considered responsible for the dramatic improvement in financial results in 1970.

1969, and the passenger traffic figures showed a 23% increase over the previous year. On 1 April Olympic inaugurated new routes to Montreal, and Athína - Vienna - Brussels three times weekly.

In areas where even moderate-sized runways were an impossibility, or almost out of the question,

Top: A sneaked picture of the flightdeck of YS-11A SX-BBK. *(author)*

Above: the ill-fated SX-BBQ taxies out for another service. The aircraft was named 'Isle of Kalymnos' but it does not appear to be carrying the name in this picture.

Left: the aftermath of disaster. The fuselage broke in two either side of the centre-section after the aircraft hit the water, and is seen here beached at Voula with the two sections lashed together 'nose to tail'. *(Spiros Papadopoulos Collection)*

With fixed undercarriage and a rear 'tailgate', the Skyvan found many uses with OA, including dropping parachutists as seen with SX-BBO *Isle of Skiathos* (right) while SX-BBN *Isle of Mykonos* is refueled for another passenger service. (both *Spiros Papadopoulos Collection)*

Skyvan SX-BBO *Isle of Skiathos* lands on the first airstrip at Skiathos, not long after the airport was opened in 1972. (*Spiros Papadopoulos Collection)*

yet another aircraft type has been acquired, the Short Skyvan. Two Skyvans obtained for inter-island services and these rugged little airliners were soon placed on services between Ródos, Kos, Karpathos, Athína, Porto Heli and Sparta, and in the Ionian Isles. The aircraft's STOL capabilities were of considerable value in this difficult, mountainous countryside. With such a varied and far-from-standardised fleet spread across two divisions, Olympic was growing and growing well, claiming at that time to be *'the world's fastest growing airline'*.

Whether this be entirely accurate or not, the airline was indeed offering its passengers a range of services and aircraft types. Witness to this is the fact that a Light Aircraft and Helicopter Division was recently established, with Aristotle Onassis's son Alexander at its head. The point of this new Division, of course, is to make available to travellers who want charter facilities for flights between the islands and the Greek mainland. At its conception, the fleet constituted Piper Najavo, Aztec and Cherokee aircraft, and two S.N.I.A.S. (Sud) helicopters, an Alouette II and III. This division only remained in the experimental stage for a short time; it did not take long to be expanded into something huge.

Towards the end of the year - on 21 October 1972 - Olympic suffered yet another loss when the virtually new YS-11 SX-BBQ *'Isle of Kalymnos'* impacted into the sea off Vouliagameni Beach three kilometres from the end of the runway at Elinikon. The aircraft, operating as Flight OA506 departed Kerkyra at 19.55 with forty-nine passengers and four crew on board. in deteriorating visibility it crashed just before landing at 21.30. Despite an extensive rescue effort, one crew member and thirty six passengers lost their lives.

OLYMPIC - Onassis Likes Your Money Paid In Cash

Athena Kollas, an Hellenic-Canadian, has some fun reminders of OA and the early 1970s at Ellinikon: *My aunt started with OA back in 1972, during the Junta era. When my aunt was accepted for an interview and before she was hired, she had to do a cat walk of sorts, in front of Onassis himself and a few other men, so they could see her legs! She (my aunt) told me that! She spoke English fluently and some French but had no other training except a high school diploma. She was hired as ground staff and ticketing at the East Air terminal, where OA had a small number of staff to help with transfers.*

I used to accompany my aunt to work as she wanted me to get a job with OA, (which is why I came to Greece in the first place), however, during my interview it was explained to me that I had to learn to speak Greek first! We spent endless hours

Below: Masquading as a 'Mini Jumbo' Skyvan SX-BBW is seen undergoing maintenance in the hangars at Ellinikon. *(Richard Vandervord)*

Left: a snapshot of the same aircraft with three OA hostesses beside it. *(Spiros Papadopoulos Collection)*

Seen in the early morning light at Maritsa Airport on Rodos is 727 SX-CBC *Mount Parnassus* about to depart on another service. (*Spiros Papadopoulos Collection)*

during her shift at the East Airport terminal departures hall, at the ticket sales counter, gossiping about her colleagues, people watching and commentating. Every few minutes, there was the Ding Dong and the announcement of a boarding time and gate of different flights and then the tsouk, tsouk, tsouk of the flight board changing flight times and destinations The summers were so busy and there was no air conditioning and there were people sleeping all over the departures hall, on the floors and outside. I remember how rude she and the staff were to tourists and departing passengers. In one instance, two young, long haired guys with backpacks, came up to the counter and asked how much a ticket to Australia (don't remember the city) would cost? My aunt looked at them in a condescending manner laughed and told them 'too much for you!' I nearly fell through the floor in embarrassment but she told them the price. They returned after a few minutes and plunked a pile of drachmae on the counter. My aunt looked up in astonishment and told them to go to the next window to pay…. Never 'judge a book by its cover' came to mind.

A few years later, one friend of mine in Rhodes, needed to get back to Crete for work. The OA

Air Experience flights was a common occurance right throughout the history of OA. Here a gorup of students have their picture taken in front of YS-11 SX-BBI *Isle of Samothraki* (*Spiros Papadopoulos Collection)*

flight was fully booked and she'd arrived late, the gates were closed. In her desperation, (being young and cute helped) she got herself down to the runway, (which was quite easy to do if you were a rep for a travel company in those days,) where the plane was before it taxied and ran in front of the plane, pleading and waving to the Captain to let her on. She was let on the flight and had a jump seat. (I did not witness the scene, but when I asked how she got to Crete, she described what she did and knowing her character, I didn't doubt her for a second!)

Once, on a small plane (I called them mosquito planes) flying from Rhodes to Kos, I don't think there were more than twenty seats, we hit severe turbulence and I saw the Captain (separated from the cabin by a curtain) crossing himself and my fellow passenger grabbed my hand in fear. I didn't feel threatened and found it all quite amusing, the naïve 22 year old that I was back then.

Carrying the Olympic flame

In 1972 Olympic Airways found itself in the world's spotlight: carrying the Olympic flame for the Games of the XX Olympiad of the modern era, otherwise known as the 1972 Summer Olympics. These games were to be held in Munich, Germany from 26 August to 11 September, but the flame set off from its mother country consierably earlier.

On 28 July the flame set off from Olympia for a relay that would cover 5,532 kilometres and involve 6,200 torchbearers. En route it took in Athína and Thessaloniki, made a detour to Istanbul and then headed to Germany via Varna in Bulgaria, Bucharest in Romania, Belgrade in Yugoslavia, Budapest in Hungary and Vienna in Austria.

The Games were largely overshadowed by what has come to be known as the Munich massacre. Just before dawn on September 5, a group of eight members of the Black September Palestinian terrorist organisation broke into the Olympic Village and took nine Israeli athletes, coaches and officials hostage in their apartments. Two of the hostages who resisted were killed in the first moments of the break-in; the subsequent standoff in the Olympic Village lasted for almost eighteen hours.

Above: The lighting of the Olympic flame is held several months before the beginning of the Olympics in the historic site of Olympia, near the temple of Hera. Eleven women dressed in ancient Greek robes represent the priestesses and perform the ceremony. The chief-priestess lights the torch with the use of a parabolic mirror that concentrates the light of the sun.

Left: In 1972 Olympic Airways played its part in the carriage of the Olympic flame.

727-234Adv SX-CBE *Dyonisus* taxies out. (*Spiros Papadopoulos Collection)*

Late in the evening of 5 September that same day, the terrorists and their hostages were transferred by helicopter to the military airport of Fürstenfeldbruck, ostensibly to board a aircraft bound for an undetermined Arab country. The German authorities planned to ambush them there, but underestimated the numbers of their opposition and were thus undermanned. During a botched rescue attempt, all of the Israeli hostages were killed. Four of them were shot, then cremated when one of the terrorists detonated a grenade inside the helicopter in which the hostages were sitting. The five remaining hostages were then machine-gunned to death.

All but three of the terrorists were killed. Although arrested and imprisoned pending trial, they were released by the West German government on 29 October 1972, in exchange for a hijacked Lufthansa airliner.

Larger, Longer, Faster

That same year - on 3 March 1972 - Olympic turned to the important Hellas-Australasia market, a continent that had a vast Hellenic population who had settled there over the years, principally in Sydney and Melbourne. OA began Boeing 707–320 operations between Athína and Sydney twice a week via Bangkok and Singapore using *'City of Athens'* for the innaugural twenty hour flight.

Olympic acquired seven Boeing 720-051B aircraft, a medium-range derivative of the Boeing 707, initially on lease, but later purchased from Northwest Airlines in the USA. The airline also entered the wide-body era by obtaining two new Boeing 747-200s. OA even showed interest in the BAC-Aérospatiale Concorde supersonic airliner, two examples of which visited Ellinikon during 1972 and 1973. On 2 June, 1972, the British-assembled prototype 002 G-BSST made the first

2 June 1972, and Concorde G-BSST lands at Ellinikon on the first stop of a 46,000 mile sales tour. It reached Athína after a two hour thirty-six minute flight from Fairford in the UK. (*BAC-Aérospatiale/ Authors Collection)*

Left: Ramp servicing and technical assistance by Olympic Airways. Below left: Captain Kyratos, OA Director Flight Operations and Captain Grispos, CAA Director of Operations.Below: Concorde F-WTSS seen low over the centre of Athína, with the Parthenon visible under the rear of the aircraft. All these pictures are from *'Concorde Flight News'* which, because it was an internal staff-only newspaper did not have the best of reproduction!

Above left: Concorde low over Glyfada. Above: Mr Panagopoulos, Greek Civil Aviation Minster (left), Mr Loubry, Olympic Airways executive Vice-President and standing Mr Fisher, CAA Director (Certification Standards) and Mr Richards, Aerospatiale's Deputy Sales Director.

Left: Concorde 001 downwind about to be cleared to land at Ellinikon.

stop at Ellinikon International Airport on its successful 46,000-mile tour to the Far East and Australia. While on the ground - all the handing was done by OA with aircraft servicing supervised by representatives from BAC-Aérospatiale - it was inspected by Mr Stylianos Pattakos, the First Deputy Prime Minister of Hellas, Nikolaos Makarezos the Second Deputy Prime Minister and General Odysseas Angelis, Chief of the Armed Forces.

Then, from 4 - 6 January, 1973, the French-assembled prototype 001 F-WTSS carried out four trial flights from Ellinikon, in order to check out a modification involving the nose landing gear setting.

On two of these flights, officials of the Greek Civil Aviation Administration and executives of Olympic Airways were invited to a swift Mach 2 demonstration over the western Mediterranean that finished with low-level flybys over the Parthenon,

A quintet of OA hostesses pose beside the Boeing Company 747 demonstrator at Seattle, WA. The event was the announcement of the OA order for 747s. (*Spiros Papadopoulos Collection*)

Three images from the handover ceremony for the first Boeing 747—200B for Olympic Airways at Boeing's Paine Field facility in Washington State. Somewhat remarkably, for a Hellenic—American event it was low- key and free from much razzamatazz!

There was, of course the traditional Boeing-operated flight out into the Pacific until they were two hundred nautical rr1iles offshore from Paine Field where the change of ownership occurred - meaning that the money changed hands or at least a radio message was transmitted to the banks to allow such an event to take place - before the aircraft changed course to Vancouver in Canada and then returning to the start point. This meant that the aircraft was now technically 'second hand' and thus exempt from taxes in Washington State!

Glyfada and Cape Sounion.

Introduction of the 747 brought forth a flurry of press releases extolling the virtues of flying aboard Olympic's new wide-body:

In the 'Spacious Age' of air travel, a Jumbo-Jet is not merely an aircraft - it's an airborne luxury liner. With an increased number of cabin crew Olympic's 747 - passengers are assured of the ultimate in comfort, service, and convenience. In-flight entertainment is ensured by five movie screens and a selection of musical programs from individual audio channels.

The Boeing 747 is the first wide-body, high-capacity commercial jet, with double the passenger and cargo capacity of previous generation jetliners. Each of its four JT9D-7A engines has two-and-a-half times the power of previous intercontinental jet engines. Olympic's new Jumbo 747-200B model is the most powerful, reliable and advanced of the 747 family. Hand luggage can be stored in new individual overhead closed stowage bins. For passengers' convenience all service units are built in the arm of the chair: individual reading lamp switch, cabin attendants, call button, control units for music and movie soundtrack, seat recliner control and 'Lumbar' support control. This is a new comfort feature and consists of a deflatable transversal cushion, on the seat back adjustable to each passenger's desirable waist support. Individual air outlet control is overhead.

In Economy Class, five seating zones are provided. Leg-room, standing-room and pacing-around-room are all there in abundance. The ceiling, eight-feet four inches off the deck, provides a feeling of space and airiness unknown in other types of aircraft. Soundproofing is also greatly improved over previous models.

The First Class is located in the upper-deck. Here there are twenty windows, as opposed to the six found in earlier 747 models, providing a panoramic view. Accessible through a spiral staircase, the elegant upper deck also has a private lounge for socialising, a refreshing drink, or merely friendly chit-chat.

A total of ten galley units (nine in Economy Class, one in First Class) provide easier and quicker serving of our varied and tasty menus.

Fourteen washrooms can be found in Economy Class, two in the upper deck, with a total of six dry-shaver stations equipped with mirrors and razor outlets.

Baby-care equipment, as described on page 24, is provided on all flights. That's an elementary

The view from the rooftop terrace of the Hotel London - SX-OAC 'Olympic Spirit' comes in to land. Compare this colour scheme to the one below. (*Spiros Papadopoulos Collection)*

acquaintance with our new 'Jumbo'-Jets! It's the best there is to offer in the 'Spacious Age' of the space age.

The first 747 to appear in Olympic colours was SX-OAA *Olympic Zeus,* which arrived on 22 June 1973 and was immediately put to work serving New York direct from Athína. The second 74 to arrive was SX-OAB *Olympic Eagle* which was delivered in December and was placed into service on the Athína - Singapore - Sydney route from 1 April 1974.

Introduction of the 747 was not without problems. The pilots' union continued to create frequent problems with familiar tactics: a literal interpretation of the labour agreement while making various economic demands and relying on soundbite slogans like 'fair management.'

Onassis wanted to put an end once and for all to these disputes and proposed that the pilots' union members' pay and working conditions be based on Swiss standards. This proposal was accompanied by a pension increase, which more

SX-OAB 'Olympic Eagle' in the later colour scheme. (*Spiros Papadopoulos Collection)*

A typicial scene on the ramp at Ellinikon, with a trio of 727s, a 707 and a 747. *(Spiros Papadopoulos Collection)*

With flaps lowered, *'Olympic Flame'* makes a low-level flyby.

Right: the famous spiral staircase to the upper deck of one of Olympic Airways' 747s.

than doubled members' benefits. Despite this assurance, the pilots' union countered that the salaries and working conditions of its French and Belgian counterparts were superior to those of the Swiss. In an attempt to finally put an end to this issue, Onassis proposed that the pilots' starting salary and working conditions be calculated based on the average earnings and working conditions of their colleagues in six nations: three from the Common Market and four from the European Free Trade Association, in addition to England. The pilots' union accepted this offer.

From that moment on, repeated lengthy meetings were held over the next two years. When these negotiations ended, only the issue of the salary increase had been settled.

As a result of all these delays, the dates that Olympic Airways had worked so hard to secure from TWA to ensure the training of approximately fifty Hellenic pilots on the Boeing 747 was in jeopardy. It seemed that the only way to keep the 747 introduction on track was to hire foreign pilots, something that Olympic was allowed to do under the terms of the labour agreement and because the need for more pilots arose as a result of the union's delaying tactics. Further complicating things, the delays also made the training of Hellenic pilots on the B.747 by TWA at it's Kansas City facility impossible. The pilots' union immediately complained to Onassis about this decision. They counter-proposed that Hellenic pilots covered the needs of the flight schedule by working for the maximum flight hours allowed under the foreign agreements, having previously spent weeks refusing to discuss a proposal based on the average flight hours logged by the pilots of six European airlines, even though these restrictions were forty percent lower than those that the pilots' union had been proposing. Clearly, the union was making every possible attempt to veto the hiring of foreign pilots.

Eventually the empassé was broken.

Chapter Six

OA In Hellas

Olympic Aviation
The most important human being in the world for Aristotle Onassis was his only son, Alexandros. For a Greek, any Greek, a son is a significant portion of himself. The fishing boat built, the house bought, the vines sown not just for the immediate needs of the family but for the future of the son. The son is his guarantee of immortality. For Onassis, with so much to bequeath and with an ego so overpowering, his son represented his imperishable destiny.

The son was Alexander 'Alexandros' Socrates Onassis (Greek: Αλέξανδρος Ωνάσης; b. 30 April 1948 – d. 23 January 1973)

The symbolic importance of Alexandros to his father did not ensure a comfortable relationship. Onassis never did manage to evolve a clear idea of how to bring up the heir to his vast fortune. Even before his parents' divorce, Alexandros had been a shy, introverted child with few acquaintances of his age.

Just as with his father Aristotle, much has appeared in print about the private life of Alexandros, most of which has little bearing on the story of Olympic Airways or its subsidiary Olympic Aviation. However, it is impossible to tell the story without looking into the tragic circumstances that led up the death of Aviation's creator.

By the time Onassis married Jackie Kennedy, Alexandros had already achieved a degree of emotional independence from him through a relationship with a woman old enough to be his mother. Baroness Thyssen-Bornemisza. She was the daughter of a British rear admiral and, as Fiona Campbell had achieved international fame as a fashion model. She married Baron Thyssen in 1955 and had two children, Francesca and Lorne. They were divorced nine years later. When she met Alexandros Onassis in the winter of 1967, she was thirty-five years old, and he was nineteen. For the next five years, she was, in her own words, 'his mistress, mother and priest confessor.' When Fiona first met Alexandros; she encountered a temperament that remarkably combined withdrawal with arrogance. In appearance, he was very like his father, though slimmer and slightly taller. He was also nearsighted and wore heavy, horn-rimmed glasses. His father had succeeded in indoctrinating Alexandros with an exaggerated concept of his importance, yet at the same time, he had hammered his personality into the ground until there virtually was none.

Alexandros Onassis at the controls of one of Olympic Aviation's fleet of aircraft.

It was clear that Aristotle, in his way, was very fond of his son and that Alexandros admired his father in return. Aristotle Onassis and Howard Hughes were the two heroes of Alexandros' cosmos, but for their achievements, not for what they were. That said, nothing embarrassed Alexandros more than his father in full extroversive flow. He was ill at ease in the Onassis business circus of sitting up all night drinking and driving bargains.

Alexandros felt trapped, eternally enmeshed in the Onassis business machine.

Olympic Aviation operated a small number of Britain-Norman Islanders for their inter-island services using the smaller airports. Here is SX-BFH. At some stage this aircraft was named *Isle of Karpathos (Richard Vandervord)*

He had no salary but an allowance. If he wanted a new car, he had to ask Aristotle. If he wanted a day off or even to go away for the weekend, he had to ask Ari. If he displeased his father, the money tap would be promptly tightened. He did not dare leave the office for an hour in case his father phoned, though in Monte Carlo at least he alleviated the problem by rigging the phones and training the operators so that, when Onassis called, he did not know whether he was talking to Alexandros in the office or his flat on the floor above.

The irony was that everything Onassis did to Alexandros was done to groom him for the succession and that most things he did were counterproductive. His egocentricity made it impossible for his thinking on the subject to accept a belief that the best person to inherit the empire of Onassis was Onassis. What he wanted of Alexandros was for Alexandros to be like him. It solved every conceivable problem. Still, he was able to perceive the necessity of increasing Alexandros' interest in the family business and to make concessions in that area, if necessary.

It became apparent that aircraft and aviation were Alexandros' consuming passion, whereas ships never would be, at least at the level of pushing markers around a map of the world in Monaco. Allegedly, as a result of this Aristotle gave him the air-taxi and helicopter division of Olympic Airways to play with.

Alexandros had learned to fly in 1968, being instructed at first by Captain Paul Ioannidis. Alexandros received further instruction from George and Dimitri Kouris, who served as Aristotle's private pilots.

By all accounts, Alexandros was as careful in aircraft as he was maniacal in cars and speedboats. As a pilot, he always flew by the book. The reason for his sobriety in aircraft was, apart from his vivid appreciation of the risks, due to his eagerness to be accepted as an equal by the men he most admired:

Another light aircraft used by Olympic Aviation was the Piper PA-28 Cherokee, represented here by SX-DBL *(Richard Vandervord)*

Alexandros Onassis, aged 21 at Ellinikon West Terminal with some Olympic Airways hostesses in 1969.
(Spiros Papadopoulos Collection)

Although apparently never officially 'on the books' of Olympic Aviation, the two Piaggio P.136-L2 amphibians were cared for by the company's maintenance crews.

Olympic Aviation operated the boxy little Shorts Skyvan in small numbers Here SX-BBN *Isle of Mykonos* is prepared for another flight. *(Richard Vandervord)*

Olympic Aviation also gained a lot of publicity from a somewhat unusual source: they allowed 'BBN to be used as the subject of an Airfix model kit.

the professionals. Supposedly it was one of the great disappointments of his life that he would never be able to qualify as a commercial pilot because of his poor eyesight, and he was one of the unfortunates who were unable to wear contact lenses.

Olympic Aviation SA was created on 2 August 1971 and was to be run by Onassis' son Alexandros, although its first Chairman was Stelios Papadimitriou, a close aide of Aristotle Onassis. Previously it was a division of Olympic Airways 'for light aircraft and helicopters', created by Alexandros from June 1968. Olympic Aviation's primary purpose was to link all the Hellenic islands - including the smaller ones that the 'Airways' fleet could not fly into - to the mainland, so it mainly operated a fleet of small turboprop aircraft, which could land in every airport of Hellas. Olympic Aviation began to function as a separate company rather than a department of Olympic Airways, although it used all the infrastructure and technical facilities of its parent. Nevertheless, it played a significant role for Olympic Airways, serving most domestic destinations of the parent company. The company was also responsible for charter flights in the Olympic Airways Group of Companies until the creation of Macedonian Airlines.

Alexandros did well with the enterprise, demonstrably better than his father was doing with Olympic Airways, but Onassis Senior seemed more inclined to pique than pride. *'Never forget...'* he is supposed to have admonished Alexandros, *'Olympic is only the leaves of the tree. The roots are the ships.'*

There were those at Olympic, where Alexandros was very popular who even hazarded the opinion - athough never with earshot of Aristotle Onassis - that

The Onassis family owned a pair of Piaggio P.136L-2 amphibians both of which came under the care of Olympic Aviation. The first, SX-BDB was eventually scapped due to severe corrosion. *(Spiros Papadopoulos Collection)*

Above: On the ramp at Ellinikon, Alexandros Onassis walks away from an OA 727. (*Spiros Papadopoulos Collection)*

Below: Piaggio SX-DBC ground-running outside the Olympic Aviation maintenance facility.
(OA via author)

the son was more in touch with the realities of modern business than the father. Alexandros felt that his father's 'caveman-style' approach to business problems was no longer useful in what was a broadly bureaucratic organisation.

One aspect of the activities of Olympic Aviation was the medical evacuation services it provided to the islands. Alexandros became something of a folk hero in this region of Hellas, often transporting the sick, injured or elderly for medical care on the mainland, sometimes in weather that was considered unsafe for normal flight operations.

There is one incident, enshrined in the annals of Olympic Aviation that tells of Alexandros flying in a Piper PA-31 Navajo to the island of Karpathos at night under deplorable weather conditions. The flight was to transport a local man whose hand had been blown off while he was fishing with dynamite. After arrival in Athína, the father of the fisherman thanked Alexandros for saving his son's life and gave him a tip. Despite Alexandros refusing to accept the money, the man insisted saying 'Αυτό είναι για ένα ποτό για την υγεία μας!' (This is for a drink to our health!). The next day Alexandros proudly showed his tip around the offices of Aviation as '*This is the first money I have ever earned in my life!*'

Another similar event occurred when a grateful father gave Alexandros a tip for flying his ailing son from a small island to the safety of a hospital in

To be photographed leaving or boarding a Learjet was almost the ultimate status symbol of the jet-set. Called by some the Ferrari of the skies, it was sleek, sexy and very fast. It was one of the trappings of luxury that Jackie Onassis adored. Originally manufactured by the Lear Jet Corporation Inc, the Learjet 23 was one of the first private, luxury jet aircraft. Olympic Aviation operated a number of the slightly larger Lear 25s which had a suave, sophisticated image that well suited the jet-set of Monte Carlo. (Spiros Papadopoulos Collection)

Athína. Alexandros did not have the heart to tell the father that he had just tipped the son of the wealthiest man in all of Hellas, so he merely managed to slip the money back into the man's pocket.

In February 1971, Alexandros received an emergency call from the island of Santorini, where a man had suffered severe injuries in a motorcycle accident and was near to death. The doctor said that the victim could not survive more than a few hours unless he were flown to Athína for hospital treatment. The weather was terrible, and all light aircraft were grounded, but Alexandros took off in high winds, picked up the injured victim, and got him back to Athína in time to save his life. Two weeks later, Alexandros returned to Santorini in marginal weather to save the life of another accident victim. His most publicised rescue flight was with his friend and flying instructor, Dimitris Kouris. The flight was to an outer island where the daughter of the Soviet ambassador to Greece lay close to death. They got the little girl to a hospital in Athína in time to save her life.

Apart from these mercy missions, Olympic Aviation's operation provided scheduled and charter air services to the islands, using small aircraft such as the Aztecs or B-N Islanders for those islands large enough to have some form of an airport, and Piaggio amphibians for those that could handle only seaplanes. Olympic Aviation extended the service to islands that had never seen an aircraft. Personally, Alexandros took good care of his customers, whether they could pay or not, and went out of his way to treat his personnel fairly.

It was not long before Alexandros, and his team had Olympic Aviation running well and earning a profit. In that sense, it wa doing better than the airline, although Aristotle Onassis claimed that he ran Greece's national carrier as a hobby and a public service which he did not expect to be profitable. But the labour relations and customer satisfaction were much better with the air—taxi service than at the airline, to say nothing of the highly favourable public relations impact of the island mercy flights.

The Loss of the Lear

In February 1972, Alexandros Onassis had been spending a few days in Monte Carlo. On 18 February Aristotle sent his two personal pilots in Learjet 25B SX-ACO to collect him and return to Athína. That

Above: the ill-fated Learjet 25 SX-ACO. Below: With the loss of SX-ACO, Aristotle soon replaced it with SX-CBM *(both OA via author)*

The Aérospatiale Alouette II was a French light helicopter. It holds the distinction of being the first production helicopter to be powered by a gas turbine engine instead of the conventional heavier piston powerplant. Olympic Aviation operated a small number, with SX-HAI seen here at Ellinikon. *(OA via author)*

Olympic Aviation also operated the larger Aérospatiale Alouette III for executive charter or Air Ambulance work. SX-HAC is seen here collecting a small group of passengers from a resort. *(OA via author)*

evening the aircraft crashed into the sea four miles short of the runway on approach to Nice-Côte d'Azur Airport, killing the brothers George and Dimitri Kouris who were piloting it.

According to the French accident investigation, the flight appeared utterly normal with a standard descent to 3,500 feet, where the jet was cleared for the final approach, which the crew confirmed by radio acknowledgement. Witnesses reported seeing the aircraft impact the sea at a shallow angle, about four miles from the start of the runway, having flown low over the town of Antibes.

The French authorities concluded that the probable cause was a 'classic optical illusion' caused by the total absence of light in the Baie des Anges before a well-lit town on a significant slope that could have resulted in the pilots misjudging their actual height above the water.

The main wreckage of the Lear was never found, and the cause of the accident, beyond a strong indication of pilot error, never established.

Slowly, theories of sabotage started to appear. Grigoris Kouris, another of the brothers, was convinced that there had been a bomb on board and that Aristotle or Alexandros Onassis were the targets. He urged Alexandros to search for evidence, and he and Fiona spent two weeks scouring the beaches of Antibes in a vain search for traces of wreckage. They even engaged the services of renowned French underwater diver Jacques Cousteau.

Alexandros often talked about the crash the previous summer of a British European Airways Trident airliner at Staines, near London Airport, in which all on board had died. The causes, which were

With their helicopter experience, Olympic Aviation did work on the Aérospatiale Alouette IIIs flown by the Hellenic Navy, as seen by these four machines lined up outside the maintenance facility alongside the West Terminal at Ellinikon early one morning in 1975. *(author)*

1972 how both Airways and Aviation were advertising themselves in the British holiday brochures dedicated to Hellenic travel destinations. Aviation in particular were strongly pushing the Air Taxi Experience 'with or without a pilot' and that payment could be made by credit card!

Olympic Aviation acquired a pair of YAK-40s, I-JAKE (above) and I-JAKI (below) on short-term evaluation from the Italian regional airline Aertirrena S.p.A for the 1972 summer season. Although the evaluation was largely a success, problems with the manufacturer meant that orders were never placed.

Left: Alexandros Onassis aboard one of the YAKs during a test flight.

Bottom: Alexandros Onassis and Captain Pavlos Ioannidis during the inspection of the YAK facility. In all the images of Alexandros, two things have always struck me - there is an air of melancoly about him and he always appears to dress much 'older than he really is! *(all Spiros Papadopoulos Collection)*

only now being established with certainty, were a perfect illustration, said Alexandros, of his theories about aircraft accidents: there was very rarely one single, primary reason for a crash; usually it was a matter of a lot of little things building up.

In the end, Alexandros had concluded that it had probably been a combination of circumstances that brought down the Lear: the younger, less experienced brother making his first night landing in tricky conditions at one of Europe's more challenging airports, a navigational error, and, perhaps, someone pulling the wrong lever at the wrong moment.

Buying Soviet Equipment?

In 1972 Olympic Aviation tested a Soviet-designed and built Yakovlev Yak-40, a small, three-engined airliner, that was the world's first commuter trijet.

The Yak-40 appeared to be an almost ideal airliner to put into service on some of Olympic Aviation's routes. It was a low-winged cantilever monoplane with unswept wings, a large T-tail and a retractable tricycle undercarriage. The passenger cabin was ahead of the wing, with the short rear fuselage carrying the three AI-25 turbofan engines each rated at 3,300 pounds of thrust, two mounted on short pylons on the side of the fuselage and a third in the rear fuselage, with air fed from a dorsal air-intake by an 'S-duct'. The airliner also was fitted with an auxiliary power unit to allow engine start-up without ground support, thus making savings on ground equipment.

There were a lot of similarities with the DC-3, a type that Olympic had only recently retired. The pressurised fuselage had a diameter of 2.4 metres. The pilot and co-pilot sat side-by-side in the aircraft's flight deck, while the passenger cabin had a standard layout seating twenty-four to twenty-seven passengers three-abreast, or thirty-two by switching to four-abreast seating. Passengers entered the aircraft via a set of ventral airstairs in the rear fuselage.

Most importantly, the Yak-40 was the first Soviet-built airliner designed to Western airworthiness requirements and was fitted with American-made instruments and electronics.

It seems that two aircraft - the Italian-registered I-JAKE and I-JAKI, from the Italian regional airline Aertirrena S.p.A - was supplied for extended flight trials around the Hellenic islands. Accounts are somewhat sketchy, but one of these suffered a landing accident, but was soon returned to Athína.

Paul Ioannidis and Alexandros Onassis visited Moscow to examine further the possibilities of ordering the jet. However to Soviets would not let them visit the factory where the airliner was manufactured, nor would they give any guarantee regarding availability and delivery of spares in the future. This was not a satisfactory state of affairs for any airline, so orders were not placed.

Replacing the Piaggio.

Alexandros's increasing self-confidence may have been related to his having decided what to do with the next stage of his life without consulting his father. He had concluded that the only answer was to get the academic qualification she lacked. Fiona, who encouraged him in the project, undertook to provide a financial safety net (she was moderately wealthy in her own right), and a whole floor had been set aside in her Swiss home where he could have lessons and pursue his studies at university level.

Alexandros did not tell his father of his intention,

The late 1960s and early 1970s was probably the peak of airline glamour, personified in Olympic's case by white-booted, miniskirted stewardesses dressed in chic Pierre Cardin uniforms flying the the Boeing 707s and later 747s.

It is not surprising that the airlines advertising department set up photo-shoot after photo-shoot for the world's media!

Olympic Catering was founded in 1970 as Marriott de Montis Airport Services but was renamed Marriott Hellas Airport Services in 1975. A year later it was renamed again and since then operated as Olympic Catering, aiming at supplying the company's flights with high-quality meals, a quality that was been recognised by millions of Greek and foreign passengers.

The company became one of the leading catering companies in Hellas, with a fully-organized food quality and hygiene control service. Apart from catering to OA flights they won the trust and dozens of other foreign airlines, offering banquets that cover national or religious requirements or needs for special menus. In addition, it supplied businesses, hospitals, industrial units and construction sites.

Olympic Catering also established and operated canteens and restaurants in many of the country's airports. In 1991, 49% of the company's shares were sold to a subsidiary of the international group Abella, who also consulted the management of the company, and in 1994 reverted to to being a subsidiary of OA.

In 2002 it was privatised (in the Everest Group) and has been operating since then as an independent company from the OA group.

OLYMPIC CATERING
INFLIGHT SERVICES

In what many regard as the golden days of Olympic Airways, different routes had different menus, and different faces on the menu cards using watercolour artwork from artist S Iossif that depicted traditiona costumes and historic locations.

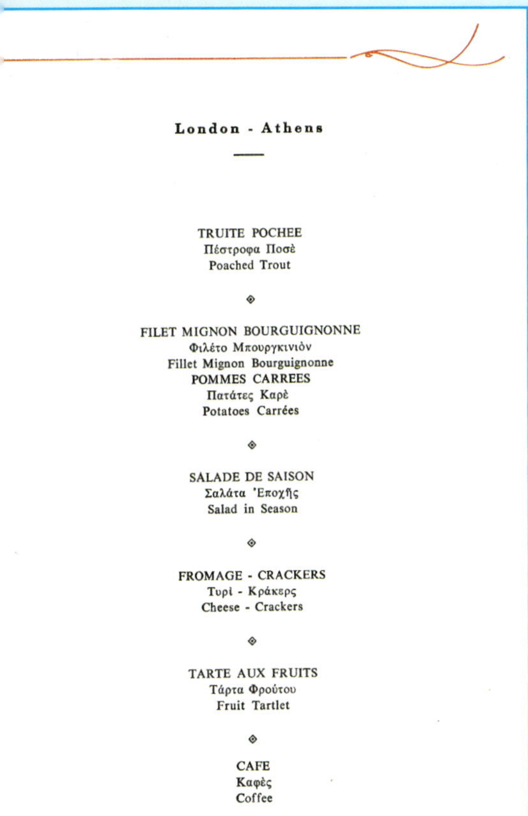

London - Athens

TRUITE POCHEE
Πέστροφα Ποσὲ
Poached Trout

FILET MIGNON BOURGUIGNONNE
Φιλέτο Μπουργκινιόν
Fillet Mignon Bourguignonne
POMMES CARREES
Πατάτες Καρὲ
Potatoes Carrées

SALADE DE SAISON
Σαλάτα Ἐποχῆς
Salad in Season

FROMAGE - CRACKERS
Τυρὶ - Κράκερς
Cheese - Crackers

TARTE AUX FRUITS
Τάρτα Φρούτου
Fruit Tartlet

CAFE
Καφὲς
Coffee

but they did meet to discuss - and agree on - increasingly essential subjects. He met with his father in Paris on 4 January 1973 securing an agreement on two issues that were important to both of them. Onassis had promised to replace the Piaggio amphibian, which Alexandros regarded as dangerous, with a helicopter.

There had been two Piaggios; the first, SX-BDB obtained in 1959 and served until well into the 1970s, when it was scrapped with excessive corrosion; a not uncommon event for a seagoing aircraft. The second machine, SX-DBC was delivered new in April 1967. Though nominally part of Olympic Aviation's fleet the Piaggios were used almost exclusively for ferrying Onassis and his guests between Skorpios or the Christina and the mainland. Alexandros was distrustful of amphibians in general and had once hit a log while landing the Piaggio in a storm off Saint Tropez, so was pleased by his father's acceptance of the safety arguments.

On the evening of 21 January 1973, Alexandros in Athína spent an hour and a half talking on the phone to Fiona in London. They made arrangements to meet in London the next evening. Alexandros explained

Olympic Aviations helicopter operations saw airlifts of equipment to the top of a number of mountains - often flown by Alexandros himself.

Some flights included to the very peak of Mount Olympus was the home of the gods who dwelt in fabulous palaces of marble and gold. Clearly the reality was not quite the same as described in Homer's Iliad!
(ΟΑ/ΠΟΛΚ.ΕΟΑ Collection)

Opa! Dancers and bouzouki players explode from the rear of an Olympic Aviation Skyvan for the innauguration of the service to Mykonos in 1972. The aircraft is almost certainly SX-BBN *Isle of Mykonos*. *(OA via author)*

that he had one important job to do before flying on to see her. Aristotle Onassis had announced his intention of taking the Christina across to Miami, and he wanted the Piaggio on board with a trained pilot (the helicopter which was to replace the Piaggio had not yet arrived). Unfortunately, the regular pilot of the Piaggio, Donald McGregor, a former BOAC captain, had been grounded while recovering from the effects of an eye operation. An American pilot, Donald McCusker, had been recruited, but though experienced with amphibians, he had never flown a Piaggio before.

Alexandros had devised an ingenious solution to the problem of how to train McCusker as quickly as possible. As the boss of Olympic Aviation, he was qualified to check McCusker's suitability as a charterer; he would take him up in the Piaggio on the following day to check him out as a legal formality, charter the aircraft to him, and assign McGregor to travel as a passenger for a week of familiarisation flights.

The man at his desk - one of the few photographs located of Alexandros Onassis without his glasses. *(Spiros Papadopoulos Collection)*

Alexandros Onassis de-planes from one of Olympic Aviations three Piper PA-23 Aztec aircraft. *(Spiros Papadopoulos Collection)*

Run-Up to Disaster

Don McCusker, the new pilot, was tired. He had spent the previous afternoon and night travelling from his home in Ohio in the USA to Athína, where he had arrived at 8 am on Monday. He and McGregor had spent much of the day sitting around fortifying themselves with coffee, waiting to hear what the plan was. It was his first taste of what it meant to be a personal pilot for Onassis. The reason Alexandros had had to recruit from outside was that there were no regular Olympic pilots who cared to volunteer for the job. None of them wanted to be up at all hours waiting upon the whims of their boss, more often than not far from home. They preferred the unglamorous but secure rostering of commercial flying when a man and his family knew when he would be where. Since McGregor was an integral part of the training scheme, Alexandros asked him to accompany McCusker and himself on the first flight. The subterfuge meant that both McGregor and

Piaggio SX-DBC starts a take-off run from the dock on Skorpios, escorted by a high-speed launch. It looks like Aristotle Onassis is in the co-pilot's seat. *(Spiros Papadopoulos Collection)*

McCusker needed tickets for the trip to keep everything legal. Olympic Ticketing issued these, listing their takeoff time as 3:15 that afternoon and their destination as 'Athína local.' The plan was for Alexandros to direct McCusker to fly to the nearby islands of Aegina and Poros where the American pilot would to do a few sea landings and takeoffs to demonstrate his fitness for the job, then return to base.

According to his secretary Kiki Feroudi Moutsatsos, Monday, 22 January 1973 was a cool, unremarkable day. The pair spent the morning in the Olympic Airways offices in the city centre. There were plans to have lunch at Antonopoulos, Alexandros' favourite fish taverna with two German friends to discuss business, but two hours before the appointment one of them called the office to say that he had a severe stomach problem and asked to postpone lunch until the next day.

So the two had a snack in the office. Kiri Moutsatsos takes up the story: *'I'm going to the airport now'. 'But you have not eaten any lunch' I reminded him. 'I'm not hungry,' he informed me, but I kept nagging him until he allowed me to order him a Coca-Cola and a plate of toast. He sat on the edge of my desk and nibbled at the toast and drank the Coke, but he was in a big hurry to get to the airport. I watched him quietly while he finished his small lunch, dressed as always in the dark navy suit with a stylish silk shirt and tie.*

When Alexandros finally got up to leave, I tried to stall him. I do not know why, but I did not want him to go. I knew he was meeting the American pilot at

Right: father and son together discussing a subject inside one of the hangars at Ellinikon.

Below: Piaggio SX-DBC aboard Onassis' yacht *Christina* in New York Harbor. *(both Spiros Papadopoulos Collection)*

the airport to train him to fly the Piaggio, but it was already after two. 'Why not train him tomorrow, when you can do it earlier?' I suggested. But he would not listen to me 'Kiki, I am leaving to the airport to fly' he told me. 'And if you need anything, after flying I will be at the Hilton. Otherwise, I will see you tomorrow'.

It was close to three o'clock when Alexandros arrived at Ellinikon. He immediately directed McCusker and 'Mac' McGregor out to the amphibian which was parked on the area of concrete between the Olympic Aviation maintenance area and the Domestic Terminal.

When the trio got to the Piaggio, they discovered that no-one had a set of checklists - the list of safety checks which a pilot is required to make before takeoff. Alexandros, anxious to avoid any further delay, felt that he knew the aircraft well enough to go through the checks from memory, and besides there was also McGregor in the back who knew the amphibian equally well and who could monitor their procedures. Alexandros went through the checks to his and McGregor's satisfaction, explaining the process to McCusker. Alexandros occupied the right-hand seat with McCusker to his left. He handed control over to McCusker, who taxied the Piaggio to the edge of the runway, where they held, awaiting permission to take off. An Air France 727 was ahead of them. While they waited, Alexandros carried out two more checks - the engine run-up and the 'before takeoff' check while McCusker lowered the flaps to twenty degrees - the takeoff position.

As the departing Air France Boeing 727 hurtled down runway Three Three, the Control Tower cleared the Piaggio for takeoff with instructions to turn left once it was airborne, allowing them to make their way directly towards Poros. Alexandros, who was handling all the radio calls, acknowledged the instructions and McCusker eased the Piaggio onto the runway. He accelerated to 100 mph and was airborne. Two seconds later, at less than one hundred feet altitude, the aircraft banked sharply to the right, hitting the ground with the right float. Still veering to the right, it spun off the runway onto the right wing tip. The aircraft then cartwheeled for another four hundred sixty feet, smashing the nose, the tail, and the other wing before coming to rest.

The Ellinikon Control Tower staff reacted quickly; activating the crash alarms and instigating rescue procedures. First on the scene were a number of United States Air Force emergency vehicles. Fortunately, there was no fire, but the three occupants were unconscious and bleeding profusely. When the rescuers reached the wreckage, Alexandros's head injuries were such that he was recognised only by the monogram 'AO' on the blood-stained handkerchief in his pocket.

Eustace Stroumpoúles, Alexandros' driver, pictured at Ellinikon during an interview in 2017. *(author)*

Eustace Stroumpoúlēs was Alexander Onassis' personal driver and he saw the entire disaster enfold. *'I took him out to the aircraft, but the technicians were not there, so I took his Mercedes out to the parking area and then came back. All three men got on board, they started the engines, taxied out to the runway and then took off. Then they crashed.*

Everyone was running, we were running, The Americans from the other side of the airport came running with an ambulance. We picked up Alexandros and put him in the ambulance and it went straight to KAT, the trauma hospital. Aristotelis was notified and I went to pick him up with the rest of the family and we went to KAT. Onassis was talking with the director of Neurology at KAT, and I heard the neurologist tell him after Onasiss asks the condition of his son, and the neurologist says, If I was in your seat, I would let him go. So Onassis says, let him go, because Alexandros was under life support with tubes everywhere'.

The rescue workers were able to get the pilots into the waiting ambulances quickly, and rushed them into medical care, 'Mac' McGregor to the Red Cross Hospital, with Alexandros and Don McCusker to the Kat Hospital in the suburb of Kifissia.

Both McGregor and McCusker's injuries were serious, but not life-threatening, but it was a much darker picture with Alexandros.

Almost everyone remembers the accident in a slightly different manner. At the Olympic Headquarters, the first to receive the news was the President, Costas Konialidis, who, with his staff set about locating and telling the family.

Aristotle and Jackie Onassis were in the United

States. Christina Onassis was in Brazil. Tina, Alexandros' mother and her husband Stavros Niarchos were in Switzerland. Fiona Thyssen was in London. The news, when it reached them could not have been worse - Alexandros' right temple had been reduced to pulp, his brain was apparently dead. Alexandros was placed in an oxygen tent on a life-support system after a three-hour operation to remove blood clots and relieve pressure on his brain.

At midnight a neurosurgeon arrived from London. The next morning Aristotle and Jackie Onassis came with a Boston neurosurgeon. A heart specialist came from Texas. Fiona Thyssen came from London and the Niarchos' from Switzerland. By the afternoon of 23 January, nearly twenty-four hours after the crash, it was clear that nothing more could be done. Onassis told the doctors to wait until Christina had arrived from Brazil to say goodbye to her brother, and then '...to torture him no more.' Christina arrived later that afternoon. Alexandros died at 6:55 P.M.

The aftermath of the crash - conspiracies galore!

Those are the cold hard facts; certainties as to what happened. Much has been enveloped in wild conspiracy theories that have made things much less clear, mainly due it must be said to lurid writings, incomplete primary source material and fantastic wild speculation.

In his grief, Aristotle Onassis was sure that the crash was no accident and that the main organisation behind it was the American Central Intelligence Agency, or was it his business rivals? It seems that somehow Onassis became convinced that that someone was following the old Balkan tradition of attacking the father, by killing the son and this inflicting far greater anguish on the family than by just killing the father.

So convinced was Onassis that sabotage was the cause that he offered a million dollars to anyone who could prove it: half a million to the informants and another half a million to the charity of their choice.

Reporting of the accident was not helped by Onassis making use of the services of Johnny Meyer, the former publicist for American billionaire Howard Hughes. Meyer made sure that his bosses views and opinions reached the broader world by any means possible - even if it formed part of the so-called 'Gemstone File' that was - or is - just about the most preposterous and far-fetched conspiracy theory ever promoted.

It is attributed to a gentleman called Bruce Porter Roberts. Initially distributed in 1975 by hand and mail in photocopy form, another document, *'A Skeleton Key to the Gemstone File'* appeared that was attributed to Stephanie Caruana. The 'Key' is purportedly a synopsis of Roberts' documents that presents a chronicle of interlocking

Viewed from the military area of Ellinikon Airport, the wreckage of Piaggio SX-DBC lies in the scrub between the runways *(Spiros Papadopoulos Collection)*

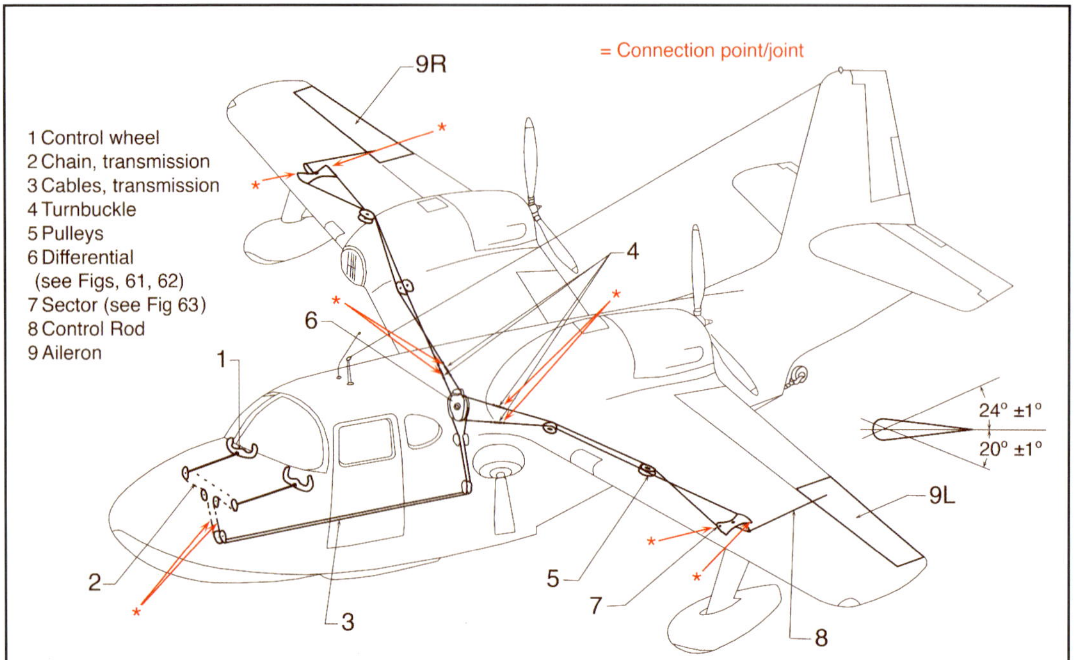

Fig 60 - Aileron Control

The aileron control circuit of the Piaggio, showing the cable 'runs' and pulley system. The stars in red show where each cable has a joint, the connection being made by screw adjustable turnbuckles. The drawing also shows the amount of 'up' and 'down' movement allowed in each aileron. *(author)*

conspiracies. It includes claims that almost every world event since the 1950s was shaped by suppressed information, the names of supposed shooters of President John F. Kennedy, and suggested connections between some political assassinations which occurred within a relatively short time frame. It has been called 'the original mega-conspiracy theory.' Roberts purportedly began gathering information in the file when Howard Hughes stole his invention for processing synthetic rubies, hence the title 'Gemstone'.

The File proposes that Aristotle Onassis, Joseph P. Kennedy, and other prominent figures were involved in various schemes to forward a vast global conspiracy, including the Mafia, corrupt politicians, brutal oil and drug cartels, rogue military operations, and more. It also claims that early in 1957, Aristotle Onassis had Howard Hughes kidnapped from his Beverly Hills Hotel bungalow. During the kidnapping Hughes suffered a massive brain injury, and that Hughes was subsequently a virtual prisoner of Onassis on Skorpios and regularly injected with morphine, while Onassis took over the operation of Hughes's considerable financial affairs, including airlines and U.S. defence contracting.

The Gemstone File portrayed Onassis as the main force behind the election of John F. Kennedy as President, and subsequently, Kennedy's assassination in 1963. According to the File, Lee Harvey Oswald was a patsy in the JFK assassination plan and was linked to the CIA, and to Mafia connections in New Orleans, with mobsters Aladena 'Jimmy the Weasel' Fratianno, John 'Handsome Johnny' Roselli, and Eugene 'Jim' Brading as the real shooters. The Gemstone papers claim that John F. Kennedy, Robert F. Kennedy and Joseph P. Kennedy were involved with both the Mafia and Onassis and when the Kennedy brothers attempted to break away, they were murdered.

Over the passing years, much has been made by conspiracy theorists when talking about the Alexandros Onassis accident of the fact that air force men predominated on the investigating team, the implication being that the military dictatorship wished to suppress the truth and that indeed the report was suppressed. Some authors have gone to the extreme in making lurid claims that Aristotle Onassis made use of his ties with the junta to actively suppress the report to cover things up. Indeed, the investigation was shrouded in the kind

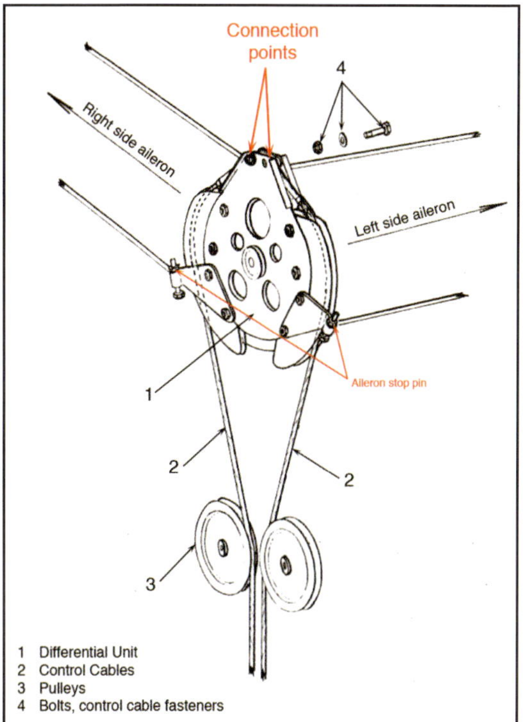

Fig.61 - Aileron Control - Differential

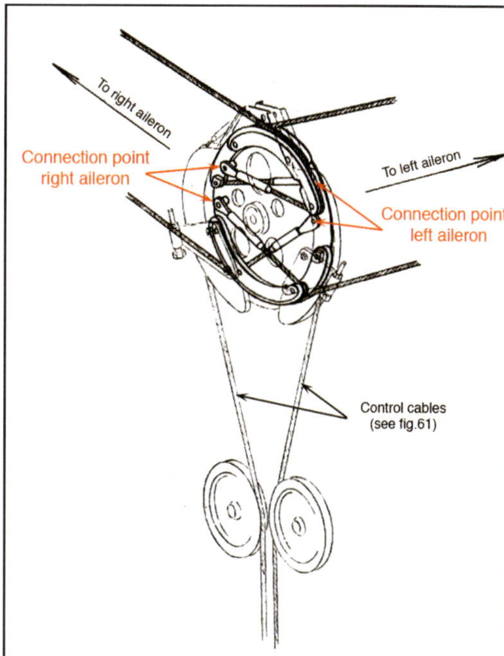

Fig.62
Aileron Control: Differential, transmission cable attachment

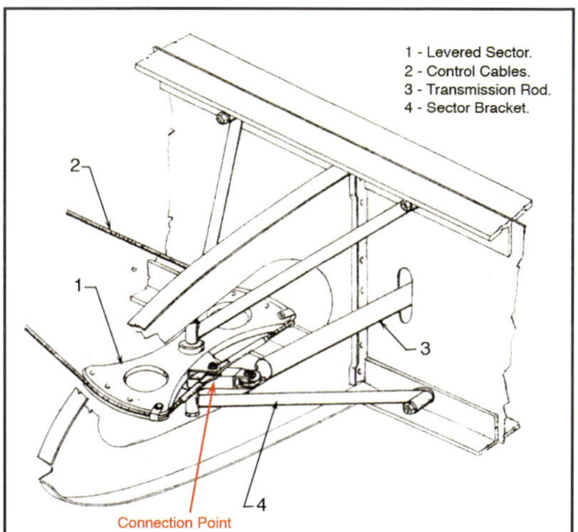

Fig 63 - Levered Sector on Rib No.19

Three detail drawings of aspects of the Piaggio's aileron circuit, showing how the cables were connected. The aileron control limit pins are adjustable bolts with locknuts on the Differential Unit. *(author)*

of heavy-handed cloak of secrecy which can only encourage such lively suspicions.

When one coolly and logically consider things it becomes clear that the appointment of men from the air force, the only repository of aviation expertise in Hellas apart from Olympic Airways, was entirely reasonable in a situation where Olympic and the Hellenic Civil Aviation Authority both had a vested interest. The Hellenic courts appointed a team of military personnel as impartial investigators to establish the cause and to see whether there were grounds for criminal proceedings.

Somewhat surprisingly, the same authors that claim suppression of the Official Report also stated that when the investigators delivered their report on 20 April 1973, they were unequivocal as to the cause of the accident. The connections between the control column and the ailerons had been crossed. The effect of this would be that when the pilot attempted to turn to the left - as McCusker would have done in obeying the control tower's request to do so after take off - the amphibian would have banked to the right. Then, when the pilot had taken the instinctive reaction to an unexpected banking to the right, namely the application of even more left wheel, he would only have made matters worse: increasing the right bank and so steering the aircraft into the ground. This explanation perfectly fitted the behaviour of the Piaggio, but McCusker, who had suffered amnesia as a result of his injuries, was unable to confirm or deny that

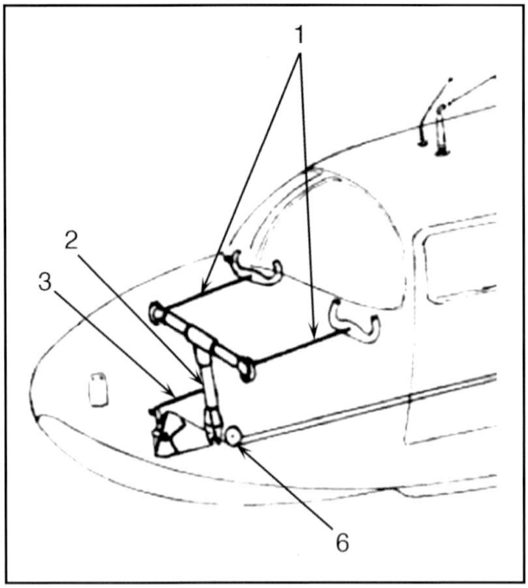

1 - Control tube from individual pilot's control wheel.
2 - Elevator control column.
3 - Rod, connection between column and elevator sector
4 - Elevator control cables.
5 - Aileron control cables.
6 - Pulley set.
7 - Levered sector, Elevator Control.

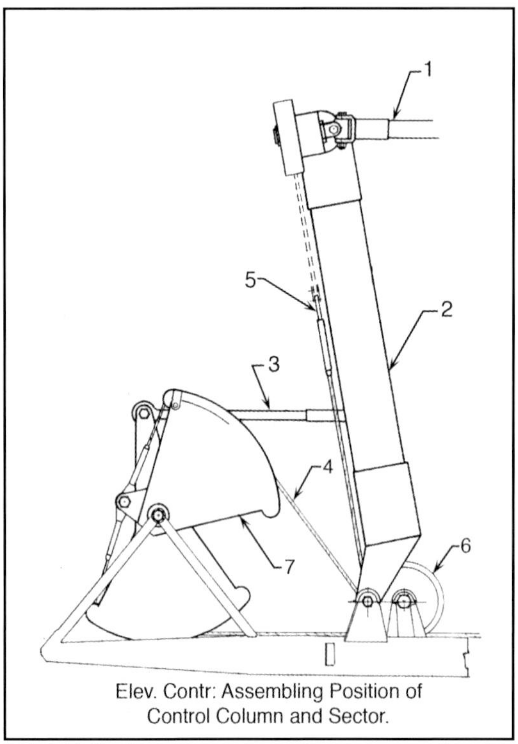

The general arrangement of the 'control column' in the P.136L2 showing the key components. The terminology used is Piaggio's, not mine. *(author)*

this was in fact what had happened. And it had all been over so quickly that McGregor, in the back seat, had not been able to see what was going on at the controls.

The Offical Report did little to clarify matters as far as Onassis was concerned. If anything, it provided an added impetus to his unshakable belief in sabotage. Who had crossed the controls, and when?

This contradiction - the claiming of suppression of the report while at the same time quoting exclusively from it - set me off on a search, in which I was only partially successful.

It took a lot of time and effort, but I finally located an English translation of the original document, which is reproduced in as full a manner as possible in Appendix 1. Much of what I expected to find in it was not there; things like the accurate positioning of the wreckage on the airport, where the aircraft was inspected, detailed pictures of items examined, all are 'missing'. Surprisingly, the precis of the Report is basically accurate, with some fundamental points of contention which I will attempt to explain here.

The control cables had been crossed the report concluded, but as to who did it - the same question was taxing the imagination of the top management of Olympic, but for somewhat different reasons.

So-called 'investigative reporting' by some journalists over the years have muddied the waters, rather than clarified them. Often, I am sure this has been done with innocent intent, but by people who have little to no technical knowledge or use of the correct terminology of 'things aviation'. A prime example of this is how the circumstances of the supposed 'crossed controls' originated. It has also not been helped by most of the primary source documentation not being available. Much of what follows, therefore, is secondary source material; that is taken from what others are supposed to have seen then reported on Almost all should be prefixed with the words 'It is alleged that...'

Sources report that on 15 November 1972 Olympic Maintenance made repairs to the Piaggio and, according to the OA records, '...both flight control columns together with their bases were removed due to time limit restrictions'. It seems that the manufacturer had placed a five-year 'life' on such items. Ten days later, on 25 November, the control columns were re-installed, along with their bases and the cables re-connected, some sources say by a different mechanic. Olympic Aviation then sent a written request to the Hellenic Civil Aviation Authority requesting the renewal of the

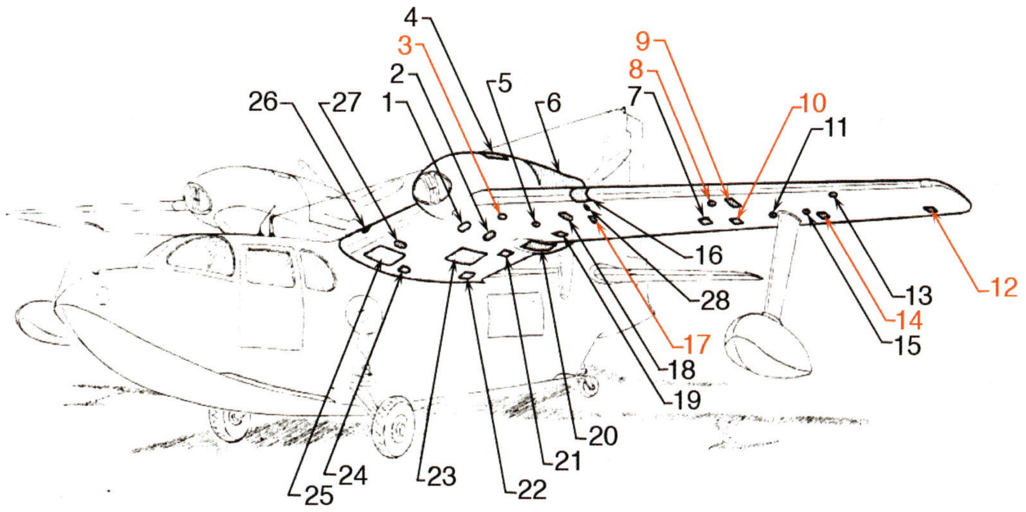

Fig.27 - Wing Port-Holes

Each wing had a number of removable inspection panels or 'port-holes; within it, some of which for use by the engineers when working on or inspecting the ailerons and their control circuits. The are the ones in red.

1 - Port-hole, inspecting wing skin riveting.
2 - Port-hole, inspecting division lever, flap control.
3 - Port-hole, inspecting aileron control pulleys
4 - Port-hole, reaching oil cooler.
5 - Port-hole, inspecting wing skin riveting.
6 - Engine cowl top rear, inspecting engine.
7 - Port-hole, inspecting outer flap hinge bracket
8 - Port-hole, inspecting levered section, aileron control.
9 - Port-hole, inspecting levered section, aileron control.
10 - Port-hole, inspecting aileron mount, bracket and control rod.
11 - Port-hole, dismantling and reassembling wing tip float.
12 - Port-hole, inspecting aileron hinge bracket.
13 - Port-hole, inspecting wing skin riveting.
14 - Port-hole, inspecting aileron hinge bracket.
15 - Port-hole, dismantling and reassembling wing tip float.
16 - Transparent shield, landing light.
17 - Port-hole, inspecting aileron control pulleys
18 - Port hole, inspecting flap control rocker lever.
19 - Port hole, inspecting outer wing flap hinge bracket and control rod.
20 - Port hole, inspecting engine.
21 - Port hole, inspecting inner flap hinge bracket.
22 - Port hole, inspecting inner flap hinge bracket and conrtrol rod.
23 - Port hole, inspecting CO_2 cylinder
24 - Port hole, inspecting flap control rocker lever
25 - Port hole, inspecting wing t hull attachment mounts and joints.
26 - Port hole, inspecting heater (left wing only)
27 - Port hole, inspecting heater (left wing only)
28 - Port hole, regulating landing light swivelling.

The under-surface of the Piaggio wing was a veritable swiss-cheese of holes. There were seven holes or hatches in just one side alone for working on the aileron circuit - these, plus the matching holes on the other wing would all have to be opened for any work to be done on it. To open up these to allow surreptitious sabotage to take place would have been virtually impossible in a busy aircraft hangar - and remember these are just the wing access hatches - it does not take into account the removal of all the interior seats and cabin trim to get to the aileron differential gear and the under-floor and behind the instrument panel connections! *(author)*

airworthiness certificate. The HCAA appointed one of its inspectors to do the job, and, in conjunction with the Olympic engineers spent two hours examining the amphibian. The HCAA Inspector recommended the renewal of the airworthiness certificate, according to some sources without first conducting any test flight. The C of A was issued for twelve months commencing 18 January 1972.

Nothing wrong with that you would think until a study is made of the Piaggio P.136L-2 Manual in conjunction with the Official Report.

The Piaggio did not have a control column in the usual sense; it had two control wheels, one for each pilot. A control column is an entirely different mechanical set-up to a control wheel. Secondly, from the Official Report, it is clear that it was not just the 'control column' that was replaced, but the entire aileron circuit due to a regular five year 'life' restriction placed on it - meaning it had to be routinely replaced every five years.

The fatal flight, therefore, was to have a dual function: it had been a C of A test flight, and not only McCusker but also the aircraft had been on trial.

If Onassis and the Olympic accepted this report, then at least the Olympic management was faced with two equally unpalatable alternative explanations. Either the controls had been crossed because the Olympic mechanic had installed the 'control column' incorrectly, or someone had been able to spend enough time un-noticed in the busy hangar subsequently to undertake the lengthy and skilled job of sabotage. Either explanation added up to some degree of negligence by Olympic. Onassis' offer of a reward provoked a furious row within the airline with the Olympic men arguing that it was tantamount to admitting to the travelling public that, when they flew Olympic, they were flying in aircraft not adequately protected from passing lunatics.

There is also a raft of speculation as to how Alexandros had missed anything quite so apparent as crossed controls during his preflight checks or that the inspectors had also missed it five days earlier - all of which is impossible to check one way or another with the passing of time.

Indeed, the crisis for Olympic Airways was threatening to become a major one. Not only did it seem probable that the airline was going to have to shoulder some of the responsibility for Alexandros' death, but Onassis himself, crushed with grief, had lost all interest in it. He refused to go anywhere near the airport or the offices of the airline. Its whole future, at least as a creation of Onassis, seemed in jeopardy. Onassis's private sabotage investigation was getting nowhere. The reward cffer had brought thousands of tips, mostly from cranks, but all had been painstakingly followed through with no result.

There was another possibility which Olympic's own flight safety department under Captain Xydis was pursuing. Could the Piaggio had taken off dangerously close behind the departing Air France Boeing 727? Calculations made by the Olympic Airways Safety Department which took into account the fact that the Piaggio had started its takeoff a third of the way down the runway thought to have been from Taxiway India - suggested that it would have reached the area of maximum turbulence created by the 727 only one minute and thirty-four seconds after the larger aircraft had passed. The most dangerous turbulence is that caused by the rotation of air currents around the wing tips of an aircraft as it

A closer, and different view of the wreckage of the Piaggio crash that took the life of Alexandros Onassis which in turn had such a dramatic impact in the story of Olympic Airways.*(Spiros Papadopoulos Collection)*

begins to experience maximum lift at takeoff. These vortices of spinning air persist for some time after the passage of the aircraft, and the bigger the machine causing them in relation to the size of another aircraft which runs into them, then the greater the danger that the smaller machine will be spun around on its axis like a top. A 727 is a giant in relation to a Piaggio, and the amphibian, because it had not started its run at the end of the runway, was closer to the heels of the big jet than it should have been. The behaviour of the Piaggio also appeared consistent with this explanation.

The problem with the 727 wake turbulance theory was that it was unverifiable. It also did not sit well with Aristotle Onassis. It shifted at least some of the blame onto Alexandros, for he should not have allowed McCusker to take off when he did. Onassis's conviction that Alexandros himself was entirely innocent of error was the one consistent element in his sabotage mania. By that stage, recalls an Onassis aide, '...he had built himself a whole edifice of suspicions and paranoia, the number of suspects and supposed motives, was almost limitless.'

It seems from the accounts of other authors the Olympic management asked Aristotle Onassis if he would commission an impartial outside investigation in the hope that it would resolve matters one way or the other. Onassis needed little persuading. He was prepared to spend his entire fortune and the rest of his life, if necessary, to find out how Alexandros had died. The Boeing Aircraft Company advised him that he could do no better than hire Alan Baird Hunter AFRAeS, the Principal Surveyor of British Aviation Insurance Co. Ltd.

Hunter, who was born in 1921, had previously served in the Royal Air Force from 1940 until 1946 before entering the world of aircraft insurance and crash investigation. The stories are that Hunter was on vacation at the time - the use of the word 'vacation' suggests this aspect originated from an American author - but Onassis had him tracked down and rushed to Athína under conditions of extreme secrecy. Nobody was to know who he was or what he was doing. Allegedly, only a handful of people at Olympic ever knew about Hunter's investigation.

Seemingly, Hunter's confidential accident report, dated 6 July 1973, did not tell either Onassis or Olympic what they wanted to hear. Not only were the contents of the report never made public, and its existence was never revealed, which is something of a contradiction; how could the contents become known if the report was never revealed?

According to more than one author, all of whom must be considered as quoting from the Hunter Report - or each other - the story goes that allegedly, Hunter produced incontrovertible evidence that the aileron controls had indeed been reversed. The official inquiry had got it right. He found something the air force men had missed: a line of small marks on the leading edge of the right aileron.

These marks aligned precisely with a line of small screw heads which protruded from the undersurface of the wing, facing the leading edge of the aileron. They could only have caused those marks on the aileron if the aileron had been up (that is, banking the aircraft to the right) at the moment of impact.

Errr.... no. 'Incontrovertable evidence' means that he found the actual crossed cables'. From item 26, section c of the Hellenic Air Force Accident Report, not even the investigators discovered that: *'The aileron control system and all its parts were in good condition. But the tests showed that its last position was the opposite of the correct one. The commission and the specialized technicians made this observation; they came to the conclusion that the reason for this was the fact that the control cables were connected wrongly in a reverse manner. These control cables begin from the floor of the cockpit and transmit the movement through pulleys to the ailerons on the aircraft's wings.'*

The wording here is very significant; *'...they came to the conclusion that...'* - this is not the same as they discovered that the cables were crossed. There is a big difference between the two.

Each aileron could only move up twenty-four degrees, and down twenty degrees according to the Piaggio's operating manual, for there were physical lock-stops on the differential gear that prevented any further movement. The only way it could have impact mark damage from the underside of the wing was after it had broken away from the structure.

From the quoted extracts it appears that Hunter's report did not presume to establish when the controls had been reversed or by whom, but he did state where it had occurred. He said that there are two parallel cables running back from the control column - one attached to either end of the control column chain and it was here the faulty connection was made. Again, I have difficulties with this, but it does give a location to consider. Look at Fig 60.

Item two on that list, situated in the nose of the aircraft shows the location of the two control wheels with the transmission chain, which join where I have drawn the red '*' in the vicinity of the pilot's feet. It would be impossible to cross these chains without it being noticed as they would scrape against each other, something that would affect the full and free movement of the aileron operation.

Onassis remained unable to accept the conclusions of the Greek inquiry and the Hunter report, although Olympic tacitly admitted liability by giving McGregor an ex gratia payment of damages for his injuries. A similar agreement was drawn up with McCusker, though Onassis refused to let the payment for him go through. 'Keep the case open,' he is supposed to cried whenever it was suggested that the settlement with McCusker should be made. 'Something might still come up.'Nothing ever did.

Despite the incomplete nature of all of the 'Report' material and the lack of primary source documentation, the accident comes down to three possible causes.

1 Sabotage by persons or persons unknown.
2 Crossed aileron control cables.
3 Wake turbulence from the 727.

Sabotage - theoretically possible, but in my view, highly unlikely. Nobody, not even Alexandros himself, knew he would be in the aircraft on its next flight until two days earlier. There was no possibility whatsoever that Onassis himself would be aboard the next flight of the Piaggio. It was to be a C of A flight, and the person who would perform it would most likely be McGregor, on his own. It was only because McGregor failed his eye test at the last moment that Alexandros was in the aircraft at all. It was just conceivable that if the saboteurs had been in collusion with one of the handful of people who knew of Alexandros's last-minute decision, they would have had time to undertake the long job of clandestine sabotage by reversing the aileron connections. One only has to look at Fig 27, showing the wing port-holes - the ones specific to the ailerons are marked in red. Anyone up to no good would be working on these in full view of others. If they wanted to work in more seclusion, this would be in the aircraft's cabin where either the rear wall of the cabin and the bench seat would have to be removed to expose the differential gear, or one of the pilot's seats would have to be removed to gain access to the transmission chains behind the instrument panel. Neither was a simple, quick task.

Crossed cables - The OA technicians denied this theory, and neither Onassis nor Olympic were inclined toward this explanation. Because this was a C of A test flight after replacement of either part of or the entire aileron circuit, this would have been the focus of any pre-flight checking, in particular by the OA ground engineers. Figures 60, 61 and 62 from the Piaggio handbook show just how hard it would be to cross the cables.

Wake turbulence - something that was not well known at the time, and even harder to prove. Interestingly, three years after the accident at Ellinikon, over in the USA the National Air and Space Administration conducted a series of wake turbulence tests using a Boeing 727. The B.727 was selected as the wake vortex generator aircraft because it constituted a large portion of the current air carrier service fleet, was expected to continue in airline service in significant numbers well into the 1980s, and because its vortex wake characteristics were not well documented. Part of these tests involved using a Piper Twin Commanche, (PA-30) as the aircraft following the 727, operated at remarkably similar speeds to the Piaggio.

As the pilot of the Twin Commanche said in the report: *'Severe upsets were occasionally encountered by the PA-30 at distances of up to four nautical miles behind the B.727. However, most of the time only light to moderate turbulence was found in the vortex wake at distances greater than two miles behind the B.727. It appeared as though there were patches of a high-energy wake behind the B.727. If the PA-30 got into one of these, the upset was severe. If not, the upset was like flying in light to moderate atmospheric turbulence. It should be pointed out, however, that I never could be sure what part of the wake I encountered. When the PA-30 got a severe upset, there was usually some very sharp acceleration changes followed by an uncontrollable rolling motion'.*

Today, in 2018 the tragic event is still shrouded in mystery, incomplete evidence, conspiracy theories, wild allegations and speculation. Indeed, in my view what is on the record seems a more than adequate explanation: possible reversed controls, takeoff before air turbulence had subsided, skimping of the preflight procedures, and a new pilot, tired after a night of travelling, flying an unfamiliar aircraft. There is no reason to believe that Alexandros' death was anything other than a tragically perfect illustration of his theories on the cause of accidents: usually, they are a matter of a lot of little things adding up.

Chapter Seven

Crisis - Reorganisation

If 1973 was a terrible year for Aristotle Onassis following the death of his son Alexandros, then 1974 was to be equally bad for Olympic Airways.

In July developments on the Hellenic political scene were taking place rapidly — Hellenic-Turkish relations took a turn for the worse because of a dispute over the continental shelf in the Aegean Sea and the tension that existed between the president of Cyprus Archbishop Makarios III and the junta. Rumors started to circulate about an upcoming coup d'état. On 2 July Makarios sent a letter to the president of the Republic General Phaedon Gizikis accusing the government of participating in a conspiracy against him and demanded that the officers serving in the Greek force stationed in Cyprus be recalled.

Three days later, Evangelos Averoff, the former minister of foreign affairs, informed the Cypriot embassy in Athína that the junta was planning a coup against Makarios in the coming days.

The coup was ordered by Dimitrios Ioannidis, a leading figure of the Greek junta, and Greek officers led the Cypriot National Guard to capture the Presidential Palace in Nicosia and establish the pro-Enosis nationalist Nikos Sampson as the dictator. The building was almost entirely burned down.

Enosis (Ενωσις, meaning union) is the movement of various Hellenic communities that live outside Hellas, for incorporation of the regions they inhabit into the Hellenic state. Widely known is the case of the Greek-Cypriots for the union of Cyprus into Greece.

Makarios narrowly escaped, fleeing the palace from its back door and making his way to Paphos, where the British managed to retrieve him in the afternoon of 16 July. They flew him from the British base at Akrotiri to Malta in an RAF Armstrong Whitworth Argosy transport and from there to London by a De Havilland Comet the next morning. On 19 July, he attended a United Nations Security Council meeting in New York and made a speech, in which he stated that Cyprus was invaded by Greece.

The newly established regime has been described as an extremist puppet regime of the Greek junta. On 15 July, between 8 am, and 9 am, the coup leaders proclaimed their victory on the state channel Cyprus Broadcasting Corporation, saying 'The national guard intervened in order to solve the problematical situation. Makarios is dead.' However, before his flight, Makarios announced that he was alive from a special broadcast in Paphos. The new government heavily censored the press and liberal newspapers stopped being printed. Only conservative newspapers Machi, Ethniki and Agon, continued publishing. Sampson did not openly announce his intention of enosis in the days following the coup but instead focused on suppressing any support for Makarios and massive propaganda to vilify his government.

In response, Rauf Denktaş, the leader of the Turkish Cypriot Administration, stated that he believed that the events were among Greek Cypriots and called for Turkish Cypriots not to go out, as well as for the United Nations Peacekeeping Force in

Left: Nikos Sampson, the dictator of the short-lived Hellenic Republic of Cyprus.

Right: President Archbishop Makarios III *(Spiros Papadopoulos Collection)*

Cyprus (UNFICYP) to take extensive security measures for Turkish Cypriots. The Cypriot National Guard made no attempts to enter the Turkish Cypriot enclaves but raided Greek and Turkish Cypriot homes alike in mixed villages to confiscate weapons. The Turkish government brought claims that ammunition was being carried to Cyprus by Olympic Airways to the attention of UNFICYP. Whether the Turkish Cypriots suffered as a direct result of the coup remains controversial.

As something of an aside here, a few months previously, on 8 May, the pilots' union issued its first announcement to its members, demanding that they strictly adhere to the existing labour agreement and to operate a strict flight schedule. The union added that *'...no deviation or change is allowed. The members are also asked to pass by the offices of the pilots' union to keep abreast of the issues.'* The secretary of the pilots' union E. Fasoulas signed the announcement.

On 27 May the pilots' union sent a letter signed by the pilots' union president E. Gakidis and the secretary E. Fasoulas to the flight operations department and copied it to the chief pilots of the 707, 720, 727 and YS-11A fleets, giving instructions for the composition of the crews during line training. The union's stated reason: in its opinion, the crew composition in effect up until then did not meet all the flight safety conditions. On 10 July the pilots' union issued yet another announcement demanding that they enforce both the labour agreement and Olympic Airways' agreements regarding Australia, etc. and that the flight schedule that was published monthly 'without any changes.'

Through these three announcements to its members, the pilots' union arbitrarily interpreted the articles of the labour agreement in effect as well as the Civil Aviation Authority's flight safety regulations and demanded that Olympic Airways and its pilots faithfully adhere to them. And so, a severe problem arose with the normal operation of the schedule and the progress of training.

Meanwhile, in Athína on 18 July - the chief of staff of the armed forces asked Olympic to make an emergency flight to Nicosia. However, due to the measures that the pilots' union had adopted, it was not easy for the management to find a pilot who was prepared to make the trip. Finally, K. Petrou, the chief pilot of the 727 fleet said he was ready to operate the flight.

He informed the secretary of the pilots' union E. Fasoulas of his intentions, but Fasoulas forbade him

Eleni Christidou along with four UMs - 'Unacompanied Minors', or children travelling alone as they are called within the industry - deplane from 727 SX-CBC *Mount Parnassus* at Thessaloniki. *(OA/ΠΟΛΚ.ΕΟΑ).*

Queen Of The Skies - one of the company 747s high about the clouds. *(OA/ΠΟΛΚ.ΕΟΑ)*.

to make the flight because of the work to rule that was in progress. Petrou ignored the pilots' union express orders and made the flight anyway. He did so after the Civil Aviation Authority's representative S. Vavaroutsos informed him that the flight was of national importance. Petrou picked up a dead body, injured persons, their families, and members of the United Nations' committee from Nicosia.

On return, he met with P. Paschaloudis and I. Katopodis, members of the board of the pilots' union, advising them that he considered it unthinkable for such measures to be in effect during this critical moment in the nation's history. In spite of his explanation, the pilots' union board started proceedings against him and unanimously expelled him from the union.

On 20 July Turkey invaded the island claiming that the action was compliant with the 1960 Treaty of Guarantee, taking control of the north and dividing Cyprus along what became known as the Green Line, cutting off about a third of the total territory. Sampson resigned, the military regime that had appointed him collapsed, and Makarios returned. The Turkish Cypriots established an independent government for what they called the Turkish Federated State of Cyprus, with Rauf Denktaş as president.

Olympic Airways was placed on standby for military service, and its crews were mobilised from 3:45 p.m. on 20 July. The Hellenic junta fell on 23 July, and Constantinos Karamanlis returned to Athína that same evening. The next day the first civil Hellenic Government was sworn in with the then president of Greece Phaedon Gizikis and Karamanlis as premier. Olympic staff were stood down from military service at 9:30 p.m. on July 24. With all this going on, most of the tourists stayed away (but not 'travellers' like me!), with disastrous effects.

One crisis after another

The 1973 oil crisis began in October when the members of the Organization of Arab Petroleum Exporting Countries (OPEC) proclaimed an oil embargo, targeted at nations perceived as supporting Israel during the Yom Kippur War. The first countries targeted were Canada, Japan, the Netherlands, the United Kingdom and the United States with the embargo also later extended to Portugal, Rhodesia and South Africa. By the end of the blockade in March 1974, the price of oil had risen from US$3 per barrel to nearly $12 globally; US prices were

OLYMPIC CARGO

From the very start of its services Olympic always carried cargo and freight. It was not long before Olympic established two major freight stations at Ellinikon and Thessaloniki, with the aim of continuously reducing the service times to the public, by using modern methods offered by the advanced technology and know-how.

By 1980 the cargo side of the business had built up to such a point where there was a need for separate cargo division and for an aircraft capable of carrying nothing but freight that could not fit in the underfloor holds, or be manually loaded through the passenger doors.

To solve this problem, one aircraft, Boeing 707-320 SX-DBO *City of Lindos* was converted with a roller floor and cargo door cut into the fuselage aft of the flight deck to allow oversized cargo to be easily loaded.

The OA cargo hub at Eleftherios Venizelos Airport was considered to be the largest in South-eastern Europe, with a surface area of 25,000 square metres, and could manage 1,400, 000 tons of cargo per year and served airlines such as British Airways, Singapore Airlines, Alitalia, Iberia, Gulf Air and others.

The cargo station had direct access to the airport runway. The black and white pages in this spread show the early days of the Cargo Division. The colour pictures depict the new hub at Eleftherios Venizelos Airport not long after it was opened. *(all OA files)*

Above: Shorts S.330 SX-BGA *Isle of Patmos* seen during a pre-delivery flight.

Left: the interior of the aircraft was bright and remarkably roomy, due in the main to the square-section fuselage which gave plenty of room for the overhead bins. *(both Spiros Papadopoulos Collection)*

significantly higher. The embargo caused an oil crisis, with many short- and long-term effects on global politics and the global economy.Like many other carriers, OA had had a bad year as a result of the rise in oil prices and the world recession. The increase in fuel costs dealt a decisive blow to the finances of Olympic, for it used around 150 million gallons of jet fuel annually. The price of fuel had increased about 30 cents a gallon over the previous five-year period, which meant that the total cost for fuel alone came to $45 million. All airlines tried to cut costs and were being pressured by banks because of prior commitments that they had made on their loans.

According to the Olympic Papers, the management calculated that the airline would have to downsize throughout the forthcoming winter schedule. The administration estimated the amount of severance pay for the termination of about 800 employees, as well as the money that could be saved if the entire staff were placed on a twenty-day suspension in intervals from 1 November through 31 March. During this period, the staff would receive fifty percent of their wages. Because Christmas bonuses were also handed out during this time, the company would withhold one and a half day's worth of salary per month - a figure comparable to that if they had downsized. The significant advantage was that there would be no job losses, and therefore, it would not incite the Federation of Civil Aviation Unions. Also, Olympic would not have to spend money on severance pay for the employees they would have fired - but almost undoubtedly re-recruited again for the 1975 summer programme!

Government ministers were advised - and they were in complete agreement with the decision - their only request was that this measure not take effect immediately, but be pushed back until the day after parliamentary elections, which had been set for 17 November. It was agreed that they would be implemented one week after the elections.

In the meantime, the pilots' union continued to follow its own standards. On 8 August Captain Th. Agiasofitis, a member of the pilots' union board, refused to fly the Athína-Zurich-Athína route because it was changed to Athína-Geneva-Athína to transport the deputy prime minister and Minister of Foreign Affairs G. Mavros to Geneva, where peace talks for the Cyprus issue were starting up. Captain I. Karatzas finally replaced Agiasofitis. During the last week of August of OA received a request from the prime minister's office for an airliner to transport Constantinos Karamanlis and his entourage to Thessaloniki for the opening of the Thessaloniki International Fair on 1 September. There were concerns regarding this, as less than a month had gone by since the fall of the junta and the government did not have complete control of the situation on the domestic front. The flight passed without incident.

During the summer, the pilot's union continued their disruptive tactics, creating severe problems with the flight schedule. Then, at noon on 21 September, matters escalated. A series of minor mechanical observations started being recorded in the technical logs of aircraft - likely upon the orders of the pilots' union. The observations were inconsequential to the aircraft's airworthiness, but the pilots claimed they would affect the safety of the flight. Consequently, they declared the aircraft unserviceable.

In response, Olympic requested that the Civil Aviation Authority conduct spot checks on the technical logs of individual machines on 23 and 24 September. The expert mechanics provided the airline with written verification that the specified observations did not have the slightest effect on the airworthiness of the aircraft, and that it was safe to use the airliners on their scheduled routes.

In light of this, the airline declared a lockout from 12:01 a.m. on 25 September. Announcements by both sides followed, and on 27 September the pilots' union held a press conference in which it stated that its sole demand was for the restoration of fair management of the pilots; demanding the replacement of Director of Flight Operations Panagiotis Kyrtatos and Paul Ioannidis, the Director-General. The union also demanded that Greek pilots be trained on the Boeing 747 to replace the foreign pilots who were serving as the crew on that aircraft. The other unions within the company expressed their strong displeasure with the

Left, from *Olympic Messenger: 'A chip off the Old Block. Ion Spyro Papadakis, son of Executive Director John Papadakis, is the son of his father, who at one time in his OA career served as a most effective sales manager. The 12-year old Papadakis, on overhearing his faculty at Leondios School was planning a class tour of france, immediately contacted Olympic's Manager-Greece Paraskevas Ioanides. The OA executive carried the ball and the movement of 45 students was undertaken by OA. The group left for a month's educational tour of France. Ion is near the bottom of the stairway in a striped shirt.*

Below: SX-DBL at London Heathrow. *(both OA files)*

Managing Director of Olympic Airways Pansyiotis Kortotos. both *(ΟΑ/ΠΟΛΚ.ΕΟΑ)*.

Striking workers march through the centre of Athína. The banner literally translates to ' THOSE THAT WERE FROM 1956 SUPPORT THE AIRPORT TODAY ROAD TO WHY?

Board members of Olympic Airways: The management of the public OA .. Avo Sterstron Donis, Koutsidis, Christodoulou and KubotosAvo Sterstron Donis, Koutsidis, Christodoulou and Kubotos. *(OA/ΠΟΑΚ.ΕΟΑ).*

airline over its decision to declare a lockout, as well as with the pilots' union over the position that the pilots had taken. But the pilots' union called for a particular strike, nevertheless.

Minister of Labour Costas Laskaris referred the matter to the First Administrative Arbitration Court of Athína since Olympic Airways had gone ahead with the lockout, following the implementation of the call for a strike.

Since the matter had been referred to court, both sides could not proceed with any measures for the 45-day period that followed until the case was decided. This happened on 1 November during a public meeting when the court threw out the dispute, ruling that the charges were unfounded. The formal decision was published on 14 November. The court published a statement that the special strike was decided upon and declared *'...to satisfy other demands besides those that were mentioned in the relevant document issued by the pilots' union and the referral by the Ministry of Labour. In light of this, the assertions to the contrary made by the pilots' union are hereby dismissed as groundless.'*

Three days later, on 17 November, Constantinos Karamanlis won the national election, gathering over fifty-four percent of the popular vote. The next day, Panagiotis Papaligouras, the minister of finance and George Vogiatzis, the minister of transportation summoned Paul Ioannidis to instruct him that Olympic should not move ahead with implementing the previously agreed measures for suspending the personnel. Olympic was given no choice - job cuts would have to be made, and letters of termination were sent out.

The government responded immediately. Law 206/ 74 was passed, forbidding Olympic Airways to fire employees or place them on suspension without previously securing the permission of the government. This law was retroactive, to negate the firings made on 20 November. Breaking this law became a criminal offence; it was deemed as '...obstructing transportation', and violators were to be arrested on the spot.

In the face of this development and numerous other factors, such as the cost of fuel, the unacceptable positions adopted by the pilots' union, and the government's decision to go back on its word and refuse to show any understanding on the issue, meant that something had to happen, for the airline was no longer capable of generating enough cash to keep its aircraft in the air.

The figures for 1974 were stark: Olympic carried 1,677,128 domestic and 786,276 international passengers, totalling 2,463,404 for a total of 3,088,242,000 passenger kilometres flown over 30,513 domestic and 11,299 international flights.

Onassis had never entirely regained his enthusiasm for Olympic Airways after Alexandros' death. The airline was run by Costa Konialidis, Aristotle's cousin, as an entity separate from the rest of the Onassis interests. For a time, no one dared tell Onassis just how bad things had become; when they did tell him, he decided to handle the matter himself in his usual blustering manner.

His first action was to make new demands of the Hellenic government - a substantial low-interest loan and exemption from fuel duty. The Karamanlis

727-234Adv SX-CBE *Dyonisus* comes in for another landing. *(OA/ΠΟΛΚ.ΕΟΑ)*.

administration was not impressed. Once again Onassis had seemingly miscalculated a fundamental change in attitude toward him. Karamanlis had been his confidant and friend when Olympic was created, but now the prime minister was in no mood to be bullied into concessions by a multimillionaire who was considered to have been closer than courtesy demanded to the military dictatorship.

On 10 December Onassis denounced the agreement that he had with the Greek government based on Article 25(a), and he invited the government to take over Olympic Airways. According to the terms of the agreement, the Greek government had six months to compensate Onassis for the aircraft, spare parts, facilities, personnel, and of course, the 'Olympic Airways' brand name. For the Greek government, receiving the rights of Olympic Airways by virtue of Article 25 triggered a series of developments that would prove to be financially very prohibitive: Olympic Airways would not have the right to continue its flight operations and passenger service because its international routes were based on various agreements and contracts that the airline had signed under Onassis' ownership.

These would no longer apply to Olympic Airways. The airline would be forced to stop its service until it could sign new bilateral agreements for all of the international routes flown by Olympic during the Onassis era. A large number of contracts regarding passenger service for its entire network of flights also had to be potentially re-negotiated and indeed signed anew. This would be a time-consuming task and a significant shortcoming facing the Hellenic state.

Of course, there would also be significant problems for Aristotle Onassis. If the government were to use up the six months of its deadline for taking over the airline, Onassis would be faced with an inestimable financial loss, stemming from the terrible state of disarray and economic burdens

SX-DBE *City of Pella* at Pearson International Airport, Toronto. *(OA/ΠΟΛΚ.ΕΟΑ)*.

arising from the positions adopted by the pilots' union and the already overwhelming cost of fuel.

The Greek government also knew that it would be taking over an airline that was dysfunctional, disparaged, and on the verge of coming apart. Nevertheless, it was in the government's interest to ensure that Olympic Airways operated as scheduled during the post-election period and holiday season, and so it wanted the deal for the acquisition of the airline to go as smoothly as possible.

The only way to make sure that flights on Olympic Airways' existing routes could continue unobstructed and without interruption was for the public sector to take over the airline as quickly as possible and to buy Olympic's shares from Onassis in instalments. This would avoid the financial consequences of taking over the airline following the cancellation of the agreement by Onassis.

Onassis' goal was to hand over Olympic Airways to the Hellenic state by 31 December so that the public sector would have to assume responsibility for the airline's management and finances as of 1 January 1975, but he was also aware that there were ways he could make more money out of the dealing.

In late November Onassis told OA management that there was a need to sell a pair of 707s, and the Olympic Papers reveal something of the web of intrigue that often surrounded aircraft deals.

Yes, two Olympic Airways 707s - SX-DBA and SX-DBB - were sold to Alia-Royal Jordanian Airlines, but it was not quite that simple. Onassis had exercised the clauses in the lease-purchase deal and sold the two airliners to Austral, a Panamanian company which he owned. The sale with Alia was

Left: *Olympic Zeus* is named.

Below: Few noticed that the last letter of the aircraft's registration was repeated on the nose, as seen in this head-on shot of Boeing 747 SX-OAC. *(both OA/ΠΟΛΚ.ΕΟΑ).*

727 SX- CBE *Mount Athos* seen surrounded by the normal airport ephemera at Zurich.*(OA/ΠΟΛΚ.ΕΟΑ)*.

then brokered in London via Euroworld so that the purchase contracts were then signed in London between Austral and Alia.

Against his doctors' orders, Onassis flew back to Athína, ostensibly to supervise the Olympic transition. Onassis' negotiations with the Hellenic government were compulsive, not systematic. He did not want to lose Olympic, and he used every stratagem in his arsenal to delay the takeover. By all accounts, many evenings and nights of negotiation were wasted over trivial matters. He was physically exhausted but maintained what seemed like an inexhaustible supply of quibbles, queries and delaying tactics. He ruined everyone's New Year by prolonging the business proceedings until almost midnight. His desire not to sign documents to which he had given verbal assent became so transparent that the government negotiators were forced into extraordinary strategies to pin him down.

At one meeting, George Theofanos from the Ministry of Transport, who was the Hellenic government's choice as Onassis' successor at Olympic, insisted that Onassis should deliver on his verbal agreement and sign the primary takeover document. It was already past midnight. 'But there are no secretaries to type up the deal,' Onassis is supposed to have exclaimed. Theofanos said he would type it out himself. 'I'm too tired,' Onassis replied and walked out.

Aristotle Onassis, Stelios Papadimitriou, Onassis' legal council and Mr Zobelos are heading to the Ministry of National Economy for its realization OA in public.

The legal proceedings on the future of the airline continued. At the request of the Greek government, the courts appointed a temporary eight-member board of directors to run Olympic Airways in mid-December. In spite of the efforts of Civil Aviation chief Elias Deros, this board never ended up being able to hold a meeting because two of Onassis' representatives did not accept their appointments. A series of lengthy negotiations followed.

During one session that was held at the Ministry of Coordination around Christmas, the Hellenic government suggested that Onassis be declared to have forfeited control of Olympic Airways. Soon, however, the government realised that this suggestion would only benefit Onassis because although he would have to pay the public sector a security deposit of $250,000, the government would then be compelled to purchase the airline from him in cash up front, not in instalments. Moreover, any dispute over the value of the carrier would have to be settled by an arbitration hearing presided over by the head of the World Bank, because the agreement had been cancelled before its specified date of expiration.

Paul Ioannidis: '*At that point, I more or less knew what Onassis was thinking and how he was going to react - as much as one could hope to predict what Onassis was thinking, of course. I want to note here what I believed he was planning deep in his mind. My thoughts on this have not changed to this day. First of all, I believe Onassis wanted to make certain that the Greek government would take over the airline as of January 1, 1975 to avoid the major financial hit that would take place over the next 160 days.*

Afterwards, knowing that the Greek state would be vulnerable after taking over the airline based on the terms of Article 25(a), he planned to negotiate with the Greek government and try to keep the airline. I believe that deep down he did not want to relinquish Olympic Airways. He found it flattering to own an airline. It was something in which he took deep pride. It was his accomplishment.

He was married to the sea, but Olympic was his mistress. We used to say that he would spend all the money he made at sea with his mistress in the sky.'

Some have argued that Onassis was aware that he was ill and that he might have known that he did

With the arrival of the Boeing 747, Olympic clearly saw itself entering the big league of carriers and featured the 74s on their timetables of the time.

Below: SX-OAB *Olympic Eagle* lines up for another departure. *(OA/ΠΟΛΚ.ΕΟΑ).*

OA's 747s carried a four-page safety card.

not have too much time left. Still, the fact is that people never lose hope. After his death on 15 March 1975, the Hellenic government signed a commitment letter to take over Olympic Airways on April 21, 1975, with its ownership retroactive to 1 January.

Professor Georgakis thought the loss of Olympic also resulted in the loss of Onassis's will to live: *'Emotionally and for his sense of grandeur, it was the*

Two views supposedly taken of boarding an Olympic 747, with a hostess standing on the upper deck stairs. These pictures are from a 1975 inflight magazine, and were often taken for publicity purposes by Boeing in their cabin mock-up at Seattle . *(OA files)*

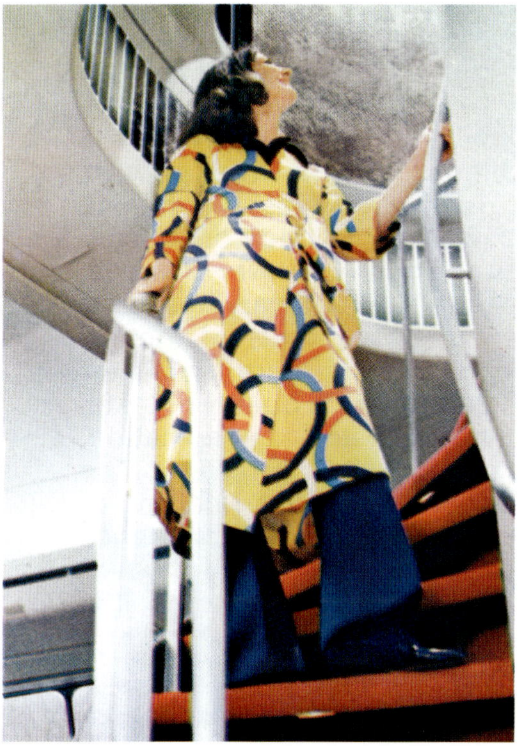

final blow. For once he was not begged to remain.'

To sidestep the consequences of taking over the airline based on Article 25(a) of the agreement, the Hellenic state had to purchase all of Olympic Airways' stock shares, that was held by a Panamanian company, Victoria Financiera S.A., a company controlled by Aristotle Onassis. The deal was made in the presence of Gregory Pantazoglou, the consul general of Greece in Montevideo, Uruguay, who acted as a notary public.

It is not hard for one to imagine the surprise of government officials over this development and the way they reacted when they heard that they had to buy the airline's shares from a Panamanian, not from a Greek company. This problem ended up being overcome by submitting the contract to Parliament for approval, which authorised the government to sign it. Parliament gave its support by passing the amendment on 26 July 1975, after which the related law 26/ 75 was published in the Government Gazette.

A week later, on 4 August 1975, the Greek government signed the purchase contract involving the full package of Olympic Airways' shares at the Ministry of Coordination. It was the end of Onassis' Olympic - the end of an era.

The official take-over was published in the Government Gazette on 24 July. Negotiations for the transfer were challenging, but eventually, the tycoon received $69 million, $34 million of which was earmarked to pay the airline's outstanding debts. Onassis was allowed to keep the company's real estate (worth $10 million), permitted to sell two 707s to Jordan for $9 million, and given a Learjet and two helicopters valued at $5 million.

Eustace Stroumpoúlēs who had been Alexandros Onassis' personal driver until his tragic death, continued to work for his father, Aristotle and was a first hand witness to his last days. *'From the moment Alexandros died, everything changed. At that time Onassis he lived in Glyfada, at Agios Konstantinos the house is still there, so, he lived there, we used to go there but after that, Onassis collapsed, and he gave us the order to take him to Scorpios. That's where Alexandros is interred in a lovely monument; they made out of marble that is still there., That's where his sister Christina is buried.*

When Aristotle got sick, we took him to Scorpios where he stayed for about a year, and then he became ill with the disease that attacked him from the top to the bottom. He couldn't open his eyelids, and he used to tell Christina to use sellotape to keep his eyelids open. He said to her - and we used to hear him because it was us that used to bring him back and forth, we did everything - 'with everything that I have,

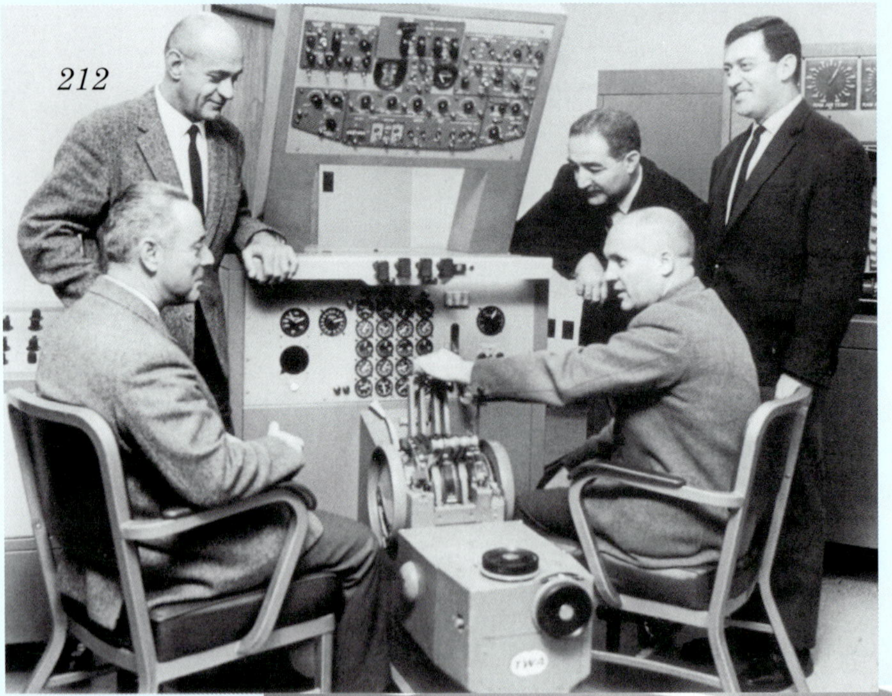

Left: The Boeing 707/720 procedures trainer, seemingly obtained from TWA if the sticker on the lower front is anything to go by - or maybe the picture was taken during training in the USA.*(all OA files)*.

Right: principals of the Pratt & Whitney JT8D engine that powered the 707, 720, 727, and early models of the 737.

Below: Flight attendant training - use of lifejackets and liferafts

The Boeing 737-400 full motion simulator.

TRAINING AT OLYMPIC

Olympic Airways' training centre was founded in 1978 and was a leading educational organization in Hellas in the field of air transport, providing complete services for the companies of OA. but also to other companies in the industry. The main mission of the training centre was the systematic improvement and enhancement of the knowledge and skills of the companies operating in the Hellenic air transport market through an integrated system of procedures that ensured the outcome of training and contributed to the improvement of business performance. All aspects of airline operation and service was covered in detail.

Above: YS-11 SX-BBK *'Isle of Zakinthos'* is seen during turn-around at the airport on Santorini in 1976. First hand experience showed that arrival at Santorini - then an unspoilt island that had not yet evolved into the parody it is today - during the Nihon years was somewhat 'interesting'. Letdown from cruising altitude was over the Naxos Non-Directional Beacon, followed by a low-level dash across the water flying almost straight at the huge hill near Kamari on Santorini. A rapid, almost 180 degree turn when the airport was off the right wing put the YS-11 on short finals over the nudist beach ready for landing!

Right: two views of the Roula Stathis-designed uniform. The knitted top creating the letters 'OA' and longer skirt was sometimes called 'retro-hippie'. *(OA/ΠΟΛΚ.ΕΟΑ)*.

if I give it all, I will never be the same again'. Those were the last words of Alexandros' father, Onassis.

Under New Ownership

Meanwhile Olympic Airways under its new owners were expanding: new routes were opened between Kirkira and Frankfurt, Kerkira and Dusseldorf, Kirkira and Vienna. There were also new routes from Thessaloniki to Vienna and heraklion - via Athína - to Frankfurt. On 17 May new services from Athína via Corfu to Munich and Paris were started.

Unfortuneately, even with the airline under new ownership, the attempted hijackings continued. En route from Athína to Mikonos on 27 September a Shorts SC-7 Skyvan was subjected to an attempted hijacking by a lone assailant holding a bottle of fluid he claimed to contain nitric acid. The man was overpowered by the crew and other passengers and was turned over to police when the little aircraft lands at its destination.

Although a deficit of US$40 million was forecast, Olympic Airways closed it's 1975 fiscal year at an almost break-even figure, taking into account the fact that a salary increase of US$9 million was granted to staff. The outlook for 1976 was optimistic with a forecast of an estimated increase in international traffic of over thirty percent and a domestic increase of between twelve to fourteen percent.

1976 was to be an even busier year. Olympic Airways announced the purchase of four 122-seat Boeing 737-200 airliners, bringing OAs Boeing jet fleet up to twenty-five. The airliners were delivered in June-July, October and November respectively. The fleet now included two B-747-284Bs, six B-707-284B/Cs, seven B-720-051Bs, six B-727-284s, three Shorts SC-7 Skyvans, and seven YS-11As.

Olympic Airways marked a 46% increase in international and domestic traffic over 1974 and a 19% growth in traffic over 1975. During the Greek Orthodox Easter season, Olympic Airways added 190 extra domestic flights and 52 international

The twenty-two contestants for the 1976 'Miss Europe' beauty contest de-plane from 747 SX-OAA at Ródos Airport. *(OA/ΠΟΛΚ.ΕΟΑ)*.

flights, 12 of the latter operated by Boeing 747 aircraft translating into 24.000 extra seats on domestic routes and 10,200 seats on the global network.

New Inter-island connections were established between Ródos and Kos for the summer season with a frequency of two flights per day, four times weekly. Olympic also commenced the route between Athína and Santorini on 1 July with a Shorts Skyvan on a daily basis. As of 1 November, the YS-11As started operating the Athína - Santorini route on a three-times weekly basis. Olympic Airways summer schedules in effect 19 April showed an increase of 18,7% domestically and 29,4% internationally on the available seating capacity over 1975 translating into 15, 606 seats over summer 1975 domestically and 9,852 seats available internationally over 1975.

On 5 June 1976 Olympic Airways carried twenty-two contestants aboard 747 SX-OAA to the Dodecanese island of Ródos for the 'Miss Europe Contest' that was won by Finland, Riitta Väisänen. Olympic Airways also launched new uniforms after a competition amongst designers for its air-ground hostesses and ticket agents. The winner was Hellenic designer Roula Stathis with a retro-hippie design.

Olympic's four Boeing 747s were the airline's flagships and named in a fashion to represent the Olympian ideal of heroic endeavour and honourable achievement. The airline's four Boeing 747s were named *Olympic Eagle, Olympic Spirit, Olympic Flame* and *Olympic Peace*.

The services offered to passengers as described in the inflight magazine in four languages - Greek, English, French and German - today reads as if it is from another time - which of course it is!

Fly in comfort: *To adjust the angle of your seat, use the knob positioned in the armrest. Please be sure, during landing and take-off, both your seatback and your integral table in front of you are in an upright position.*

Each seat has its individual reading light, air outlet, and hostess call-button, located directly overhead. Please pay attention to the 'Fasten seat-belts' and 'No smoking' signs whenever they are lit. An experienced traveller knows that it is advisable to wear loosely seat belts for the full duration of the flight.

Special attention for smokers and non-smokers: *Smoking is permitted on board, except when the 'No smoking' sign is lit. You will find an ashtray beside you in the arm rest. However, Olympic assures the comfort of non-smokers, as well, by*

Above: Boeing 737-200 SX-BCG *Phoebus* taxies past the camera in the Hellenic sunshine. *(Richard Vandervord)*

Right: the OA Safety Card for the 737-200. *(authors collection)*

reserving special rows for the exclusive use of non-smokers on all our flights.

Cabin facilities: *It is the cabin staff's job to assist you in every possible way. Our crew will be only too pleased to provide you with anything you may wish during your flight – newspapers, magazines, writing material, pillows, and blankets.*

For the jet-setting businessman, Olympic provides schedules of worldwide air services, available on all flights upon request

Baby care: *Cots for infants and also baby-food are available on every Olympic aircraft. Diapers, safety pins, and other necessities are available too, as well as puzzles and games for children's amusement.*

Don't hesitate to ask your hostess for any such items you may require. However, it is to your advantage to request the supply of such items when you first book your flight, since normally, only limited quantities are stored aboard. In case you carry along your own bottles of formula or jars of baby food, your hostess will gladly warm them.

Duty-free articles: *All of Olympic's aircraft carry duty-free articles available for sale. We regret, though, that due to weight restrictions and the limits certain countries place on the amount of tax-free goods that can be sold to passengers, we carry only a limited quantity of articles. According to*

IATA regulations, sales over the Atlantic are restricted to liquor, cigarettes, perfume, and lighters. No sales are made while the 'Fasten Seatbelts' sign is lit.

On a separate folder at the end of this booklet, you will find a price list of duty-free items on sale. May we point out, too, that as a result of the new and faster aircraft in our fleet, journey times have been reduced to such an extent that, especially on shorter routes, all passengers may not have time to obtain the duty-free articles they might wish to. We will, however, make every effort — as is our tradition — to meet the requirements of all passengers and to maintain the high standards of service to which all Olympic Airways clients are accustomed.

***Lavatory facilities:** The most modern and high-level hygienic facilities are available on board. There are more than sufficient washrooms on every aircraft. And an exclusive feature available on Olympic transatlantic and intercontinental services: throughout the flight a specially appointed cabin boy looks after the cleanliness of the aircraft and keeps everything shipshape.*

***Meals and beverages:** Our expert chefs will treat you to delicious meals. A full range of beverages — from vintage French wines to the traditional Greek ouzo and retsina — is served. These are complimentary to First Class passengers. Non-alcoholic beverages are served free of charge to*

Right: 1978 and the OA-Western Hellenic Airport / DEAM Workshop / Electronic Technicians: Christos Chondromatidis, Stelios Lasithiotakis, Christos Drosopoulos, Costas Vassiliou, Skourogiorgas, Vangelis Kampolis, Giorgos Pouladis, Pantelis Drossos, Yiannis Kritikos, Yiannis Tzannis, Andreas Gatsos, Christos Moschidis (foreman), Athanasios Lepetsos, Thodoris Palaiologou, Giorgos Leridis, Charalambos Karkalis is amongst the group. *(OA/ΠΟΛΚ.ΕΟΑ).*

Boeing 737-200 SX-BCG *Phoebus* comes in to land on Runway15 at Ellinikon. *(Richard Vandervord)*

all passengers. Light snacks, coffee, and tea are offered on shorter flights.

Olympic's Starlight Discotheque and Cinema: *On all Olympic's transatlantic, African and Far Eastern flights, you will enjoy outstanding entertainment. You may view a full-length feature film - one of the latest film productions - or choose the musical program of your particular preference from eight separate audio channels.' See your in-flight entertainment programs for complete details. The control units for in-flight music and film soundtracks, when available, are installed in the lower portion of your seat in Economy Class and at the base of the seat separator in First Class.*

Athína Kollas remembers one 747 flight that was slightly different than as described: *On a flight from Athína to Montreal and Toronto aboard a 747, it felt like you were in a Greek paniyiri. Forget the 'No Smoking' section; the whole cabin was one big cloud of smoke! When the food was being served, the bread baskets were passed along and over and sideways of the seats by the passengers in a 'help yourself' fashion.*

Clearly from some of the memories recounted, it is more than possible to imagine that on some flights the Captain really DID make a cabin announcement that '*...the galleys were at the front and rear of the aircraft, water and juices are in the fridges on the left, food in the shelves on the right and ice is in the freezer below. For first time passengers on our airline, as our experienced travellers will confirm, please do not depress the service button above your head. How would you like it if your sleep was disturbed for a Coke? You are not Kolos, and besides, you can avoid deep vein thrombosis, get up and fetch it yourself!*

Athena Kolias again: '*When I first came to Greece, I eventually got a job working for Grecian Holidays owned by a Cypriot called Takis Shakalis whose business was in Camden Town London. So it was a British charter holiday company (the company is now defunct, but I think the brand-name is still around), and they used British Airtours, Air Europe and Dan-Air (who my first serious Greek boyfriend worked for) His name was Tasos Dadiotis. I was a tour rep!*

OA was very good to their staff, but the management was, in the end, the downfall of OA. They had an Olympic Bus to pick up and drop off employees for their shifts, all around the Athens area. There was a Nursery School located at the East Air Terminal for children of Olympic employees. Olympic Catering was also found on the way to the East Terminal. My Aunt used this catering service many times for her personal home events, and she was forever flying all over the world with her mum and sometimes one of her brothers, for free! On many occasions, she would call the airport from her home (if she was going to be late for work) for a colleague to punch her employee card for her.

Shorts S.330 SX-BGC Isle of Paros arrives at Thessaloniki on the inagural flight of the type in 1973. *(OA/ΠΟΛΚ.ΕΟΑ).*

Above: SX-BGD *Isle of Naxos*. *(Richard Vandervord)*

Right: a number of Olympic staff in the dorrway of a Shorts S.330. The larger Shorts were obtained in 1973 to supplement the Skyvans. *(ΟΑ/ΠΟΛΚ.ΕΟΑ)*.

Of the four B747s *'Eagle'* was the oldest, being a -284B variant which joined Olympic Airways as a completely new airframe in December 1973. It seated 395 passengers, including 49 in Executive Class. The remaining three B747s were all -212B variants with a larger passenger-carrying capacity of 426 'pax', 382 of them in Tourist Class and entered service in 1984 and 1985, although all three were manufactured in 1979. The powerplant is the same for both variants, being the P&W JT9D-7.

The four B747s supplied Olympic's long-haul services to North America, Thailand, Japan and Australia. New York's John F. Kennedy Airport was Olympic's North American hub, from where the B747s continued on to Chicago, Boston, Toronto and Montreal. Destinations in Australia were Melbourne and Sydney. OA was always aware of the large Greek communities in Australia, Canada and the USA, therefore visiting relatives travelling to and from Greece made up a sizeable portion of the long-haul passenger traffic with much of the remainder consisting of tourists.

On 12 July Olympic Airways added to its network Benghazi, Dubai, Dhahran and Kuwait. Olympic issued commemorative envelopes for the Athína - Benghazi - Athína and Athína - Dubai - Athína services.

Olympic Airways participated in the 3rd Panhellenic Philatelic Exhibition held in Piraeus on 13 November, but it was also a month of tragedy. On 23 November YS-11A SX-BBR was operating flight OA830 from Athína to Kozani via Larissa. The flight proceeded directly to Kozani because of bad weather at Larissa at an altitude of 5500 feet. Last radio contact was at 09:45, when the pilot reported he was fifteen miles south of Kozani on a heading of 318 degrees, he was given the weather forecast. At 10:19 with nothing heard from the aircraft the airport declared an emergency and it was discovered that Flight 830 had flown into a mountain at a height of 4265 feet near the village of Servia, the mountains were covered in cloud. On board were four crew and forty-six passengers; there were no survivors. Investigation showed that the aircraft was on a heading of 310 degrees when it first struck the ground, it disintegrated over the next 200 metres before becoming shortly airborne again, finally crashing at the foot of another hill. Fire had broken out after the initial impact and continued to burn for

Boeing 737 SX-BCG *'Phoebus'* in the later colour scheme on the ground at Kerkira. *(author)*

several hours destroying the aircraft. At the accident site the mountain above 3000 feet was covered in cloud.

Olympic Airways inaugurated a new route Athína - Melbourne on Friday, 3 December creating the fastest service from Athína to Melbourne. Olympic on this occasion issued first flight covers commemorating this inaugural flight. Olympic's international route mileage at the end of the year reached 56,381 miles or 104,418 kilometres increasing its international destinations to twenty-seven and domestic destinations to thirty.

The arrival in 1976 of the first of the 'Baby Boeings' was the start of what was to become the most numerous type in service with Olympic in the early 1990s. The Boeing 737 was operated in two versions. Eleven Boeing 737-284s, seating 117 passengers, were introduced between June 1976 and July 1981 for short-haul services both internationally and domestic. OA had a long-established tradition of naming its aircraft to reflect the history and legends of classical Greece and this was no exception with the eleven 737-284s. They all bore the names of Greek gods and heroes except for the odd one out, SX-BCL, the last to enter service in 1981, which was named *Isle of Thassos*.

For a time this highly successful airliner, powered by two Pratt & Whitney JT8D-9A ducted turbofans, helped to replace five Japanese Nihon YS-11A twin turbo-props on some of the island servicess. However, although the 737-284 could competently handle the shorter runways on these islands, the company found that their pilots were of the opinion that a twin turboprop STOL aircraft was more suitable. Also, it was proving difficult to fill the 737s on a regular basis, passenger loads indicating that an aircraft with a capacity of between fifty and seventy seats would be more suitable.

Consequently, all of the 737-284s were operated on short-haul international routes although domestically they also served Ioannina, Thessaloniki and the islands of Corfu and Crete when passenger demands during the summer high season made it necessary. For the islands operation as a whole, however, they were replaced by the Alenia/Aerospatiale ATR-42 and -72 STOL twin turboprops.

Shorts S.330 SX-BGC *Isle of Paros* on finals during typical Hellenic evening light. *(Richard Vandervord)*

A busy scene at the Western Terminal stands. *(OA/ΠΟΛΚ.ΕΟΑ).*

Olympic's Boeing 737 fleet was increased with the introduction of seven 737-484s, which offered a passenger-carrying capacity of 150 seats and was powered by more economical and ozone friendly CFM International CFM56-3C-1 turbofans. Six of these aircraft arrived between September and December 1991 to reflect the first stage of Olympic's modernisation plan; a seventh being added in May 1993.

The airline was enthusiastic about this late-1980s development of Boeing's 737 family. *'The Boeing 737-400 is like a bus. It's a bus which has minimum requirements. It just flies in, flies out, flies in, flies out - non-stop. You have to realise that the 737-400 is only called a short-haul aircraft (when in fact) it's almost a medium-haul type. It can fly with a full payload more than 4.5 hours or something like that. It has given Olympic that flexibility'.*

The 737-484s were all been given place names from the province of Macedonia in the north. Macedonia is another area of concern for Hellas which might lead to a territorial dispute with its north-western neighbour, Albania. Olympic Airways, like other state-owned organisations in Hellas, likes to remind its customers in its own literature, such as its timetable brochure, that Macedonia has been, in its own words, 'Greek for

1978 - London: Donald McAfee, Lili Sgourou, Jimmy Onassoglou, Vangelis Strovalis, Kostas Dubros... We were on the premises of the then BOAC who were in the process of evolving into British Airways. We were there to learn BABS (British Airways Booking System). The reservation system bought by Olympic from the BA these six colleagues were taught the system, and were the pioneers of computers in Greece. The computer was FERRANTI brand, and made a lot of noise. *(Donald MacAfee)*

Above and below: Fresh fruit served about an Olympic Airways De Havilland Comet.

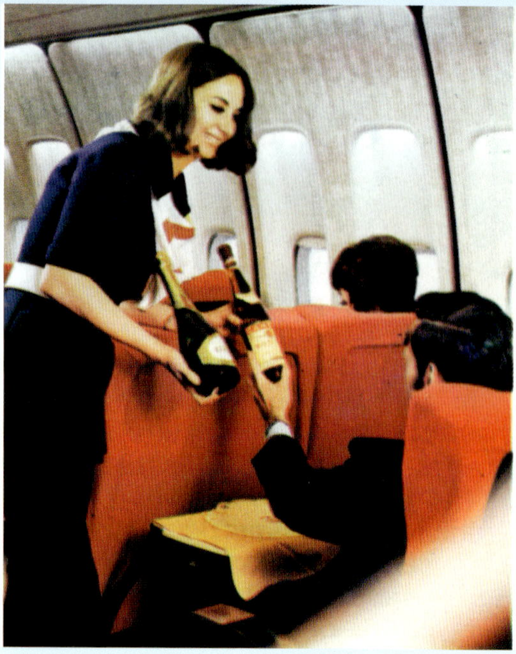

A choice of winE is offered to a First Class passenger on this OA 747. *(all OA/ΠΟΛΚ.ΕΟΑ)*.

THE CHANGING STYLE OF ONBOARD SERVICE

Below: from the 1975 Inflight Magazine comes this 747 interior shot.

Above and right: the year is 1980 and two scenes from aboard an A300.

Below: First Class on an OA 707.

A-300 F-ODRG *(Richard Vandervord)*

over 3,000 years'. To emphasise the Macedonian connection, in 1992 Olympic formed a new subsidiary called Macedonian Airlines. 'The object of this company', Olympic's official brochure stated, *'is to bring in charter flights from all countries in the world so that large groups of tourists will be able to visit Greece under the best possible conditions'*. The new 737-484s were partly operated on Macedonian's charter work, but were also available for scheduled services in Europe, the Middle East and North Africa.

All seven Boeing 737-484s were painted in the new Olympic Airways colour scheme which was regarded as far more pleasing to the eye than the old white top, dark blue trim and tail fin with natural metal under-surfaces. The new scheme retained the white top, but under-surfaces are light grey. Dividing them was a light blue cheatline over the windows bordered by thinner yellow and red lines below and a sky blue line above. The line swept up into an attractive sky blue tail fin on which Olympic's distinctive and multi-coloured logo of inter-linked rings was displayed.

The aircraft which the Boeing 737-484s replaced were the six Boeing 727-284s. Wisdom may come with age, but in aviation terms, so do higher operating and maintenance costs. The continued operation of these B.727s, all manufactured between 1967 and 1969, was becoming untenable for Olympic. They were not the last B727s to be operated by the airline, however. In 1990 three more were obtained from those retired by Lufthansa and used as stopgaps between the withdrawal of the earlier aircraft and the arrival of their replacements. Referred to by Olympic's staff as 'οι γερμανικές' the 'German ones', these three B.727s were all -230 variants powered by the P&W JT8D-15 ducted turbofan and were manufactured in the mid-1970s. Like the earlier six, they have been named after Greek mountains, apart from SX-CBI which is named after Macedonia's greatest historical figure, *Alexander the Great*. Perhaps it is no accident that this B727-230 was used exclusively for VIP flights and carries the Prime Minister of Greece on official visits to other countries.

1977 saw Olympic Airways launch a new weekly TV programme called *'Flight at 10,000 Meters'* featuring tourist sites of countries to which Olympic flew. On 15 April 1977, Olympic inaugurated new services between Athína and Geneva via Corfu. First

Prime Minister Andreas Papandreou on his way to London via Paris on 26 November 1981 for a two-day summit meeting of the heads of the then European Economic Community. (OA files)

flight covers were issued by Olympic Airways on the occasion of the first Corfu-Geneva route sector.

Olympic's domestic traffic recorded at 2,856,331 and International passenger traffic at 1,264,052 and 4,406,000 passenger-kilometres flown.

Baby John Danezis born on Olympic Airways aircraft on 24 February between Santorini and Athína fifteen minutes after take-off. An Olympic Airways Board Member and the pilot assisted in the christening of the child at a festive baptismal in Santorini.

Olympic participated in the '77-EPHILA' Exhibition of stamps from Greece and Cyprus, held at Zappeion Building in Athína, 15-24 November, with its collection of fifty-two First Flight Covers. Mrs Ioanna Tsatsos, the wife of the President of the Republic, opened the Exhibition.

1978 - On 28 March Olympic inaugurated its new link in the European network with a once-weekly service from Athína to Tirana. Albania, via Ioannina. Also reintroduced a flight between Ródos and Tel-Aviv on a once a week basis and, at peak season, twice weekly.

It was also a year in which a remarkable escape from disaster happened at Ellinikon. On 9 August Olympic Airways Flight 411, a Boeing 747-200 being flown by Captain Sifis Migadis and his crew blew an engine upon takeoff from Athína-Ellinikon International Airport heading for John F. Kennedy International Airport, New York. The huge airliner slowed to a dangerously low speed of 157 knots and was flying dangerously low over downtown Athína before Captain Sifis Migadis managed to gain enough speed and altitude to return the aircraft to Ellinikon on the remaining three engines.

In July 1978 Olympic signed an agreement with Airbus Industrie to purchase two A300B-4 airliners with options on a further three.. The expectation was

An almost classic image that portrays Olympic Airways so well for the period 1980-2000. Here a company 73 is seen on the turnaround for the runway 35 end at Ioannis Kapodistrias International Airport on Kerkyra. The picture was taken from the taken from the Café Kanoni, close to the Royal Boutique Hotel. *(author)*

that the new type - the only non-Boeing type in The Olympic Airways inventory of the time would be delivered in January and Frebruary 1979, and be put into operation on 1 April 1979. The plans went exactly to schedule when SX-BEB *'Odysseus'* innaugurated the daily Athína - London service. This eventually led to Eight Airbus Industrie A300B4s were delivered between 1979 and 1982 to gradually replace six Boeing 707-320s and five Boeing 720Bs on European, African and Middle Eastern routes. All were powered by General Electric CF6-50C2 turbofans and configured to carry 260 passengers, of which 232 are accommodated in Tourist Class while the remaining 28 are seated forward in Olympian Executive Class. Olympic introduced this recent new Class in 1991 for its medium- and long-haul routes. It replaced Business Class which in its turn had taken the place of First Class.

Mrs Helen Sophia Speronis, Olympic's Public Relations Manager, at Athína during this time explains; *'We thought that as far as Greece was*

Another first flight cover: this time Athína - Ioannina - Tirana by 737 on 23 March 1978.

concerned, not too many people required First Class. We decided that people would not be willing to pay that much, not even for flying for 11 hours. . . . But when we eliminated First Class we decided we should upgrade Business Class. This is what Executive Class was, a slightly improved Business Class'.

The introduction of newer aircraft meant there was a noticeable difference between what was on offer for passengers in Tourist Class, depending on which type they flew in. The A300B4s was 1970 s technology aircraft and their seating layout reflected the design thinking of those years and the early-1980s. The accommodation was relatively comfortable, but legroom limited. However, for the 3+ hour flight between London and Athína, this was acceptable.

Tourist passengers fared better on the new extended range Airbus A300-650Rs, four of which Olympic obtained. More comfortable seating and the introduction of video and hi fi earphones made their flights more relaxing and entertaining, especially as Olympic operated the A300-600s on longer routes. The single example in service, SX-BEK, linked Athína with Nairobi and Johannesburg. Powered by two GE CF6-80C2A5 turbofans, it carried 269 passengers. It also played its part in keeping the issue of Macedonia in the forefront of people's minds, for that was its name.

All eight of Olympic's A300B4s were purchased as -103 variants, but the airline became rightfully proud that its Technical Operations Department developed the capability to upgrade the Airbuses to -203 status. OA's Group Manager of Technical Operations, Panagiotis K. Makris, believed that not many airlines in the world had this capability which, in Olympic's case, earned it recognition from Airbus Industrie for the quality of its work. The A300B4s continued in service for

Billy Bo (Vassilis Kourkumelis), one of the most talented Hellenic fashion designers, ever (1954 - 1987) Olympic Airways used his uniform design from 1981 until 1987.

Below: A300 SX-BEC during pushback at London Heathrow in 1985. *(OA/ΠΟΛΚ.ΕΟΑ)*.

Above: The Billy Bo uniforms for the OA staff was 'launched' at a high-profile event where the designer and a number of selected guests were helicoptered in. Vassilis Kourkumelis - also known as 'Billy Bo' is fifth on the left.

Right: the face of the summer 1980 OA timetable. *(both OA/ΠΟΛΚ.ΕΟΑ).*

the best part of the 1990s, but their replacement was being planned; the purchase of further A300-600Rs was one option, but the introduction of the new generation A330 twin-jet widebody would provide Olympic with even greater carrying capacity over an even longer range if chosen.

The eight A300B4s maintained the classical Greek tradition, all of them being named after heroes from Homer's Iliad and Odyssey.

Olympic announced plans for the installation of a computer system for worldwide reservations and signed an agreement to use BABS, the computerised British Airways Booking System to introduce the reservation system by Spring 1979. Olympic announces the expansion of Airport building facilities to ease increasing passenger traffic with 60 million dollars budgetted over the next two years for building and construction projects.

1978 saw domestic passenger traffic reach 2,727,647 and international hit 1,156,288. A year later the figures had increased to 3,474,531 and 1,550,299 respectively.

During April 1979 OA inaugurated daily service to Milan with a Boeing 727s and on 11 of that month they begun a twice-weekly service to Jeddah on Wednesday and Saturdays with a Boeing 707.

Further expansion was planned, and so at the ordinary General Assembly of shareholders, it was announced that Olympic's capital would be increased by US$70.000.000. OA then ordered three Airbus A.300 aircraft and five Boeing 737s 1980 delivery, the A.300s arriving on 29 March, 18 April and 30 April 1980.

1981 saw further apparent increases in services. Olympic Airways issued first flight covers with commemorative stamps for its first flight from Athína to Lyon on 29 March, the same day it introduced a new Business Class section on its flights to Paris, London and Rome. Then OA inaugurated regular cargo services from Athína to Basle with its cargo Boeing 707, as well as to Tripoli, Libya and to Amsterdam.

The next day Olympic resumed non-stop flights to Istanbul three times weekly with Boeing 737s and once weekly on Mondays from Athína to Istanbul with a stopover in Thessaloniki. Finally, on 3 April Olympic uprated it's service to Nairobi and Johannesburg by replacing the 707 with a 747.

Throughout the latter half of the 1970s, Olympic Aviation was granted more scheduled domestic routes by its parent Olympic Airways until in 1980 the two companies were jointly providing inter-regional services on a regular basis. By this time, the surviving YS-11As had been transferred to the Hellenic Air Force, being replaced on domestic routes by Boeing 737-284s of Olympic Airways and Shorts 330s of Olympic Aviation. From 1980 on, Olympic Aviation grew rapidly, as it continued to renew its fleet through the purchase of new aircraft and helicopters, and was allocated a total of eighteen regular routes by the parent company. In 1985, Olympic Aviation S.A. was granted, by ministerial decision, a licence to provide technical maintenance, thus giving the company the opportunity to begin functioning as a self-sufficient, independent air carrier.

Two STOL (short take-off and landing) Shorts 330s - a 30-seater development of the earlier Shorts

Left: John Hili Snr (on the extreme right of the picture) used to be with OA from 1961 to 1987, *'I was the Conference&Incentives Manager in London and was responsible in organising the first charter flights from Dublin to Athens'.*

737 SX-BCH *Triton* is parked in front of A.300 SX-BEG at Ellinikon. *(OA/ΠΟΛΚ.ΕΟΑ).*

Skyvan - were taken on by Aviation for the islands with shorter runways and were subsequently joined by four more. At that time the plan was for the Boeing 737-284s to serve the larger domestic destinations with the Shorts 330s used for the smaller airfields. A good idea in theory, perhaps, but experience taught both Airways and Aviation that the Boeings' capacity was too large for this operation (they were rarely full) whereas the opposite was the case for the over-subscribed Shorts 330s. What was needed was an aircraft type with a passenger load mid-way between the two.

Enter the Avions de Transport Regional consortium founded by Aerospatiale of France and Aeritalia of Italy with its ATR-42 and ATR-72 airliners. Just as with the acquisition of the YS-11, the board of Olympic Airways studied a number of regional transport designs in addition to the ATR-42/72 series, including the De Havilland Canada Dash-8, the British Aerospace ATP, the Fokker 50 and the Saab 340. The Saab 340 was eliminated for being too small while the ATP and the Fokker 50 were still very much in the design phase.

Then, in 1983, they decided that the introduction of a suitable type offering a capacity in the 50-70 seat range was vital for the 1990s. What swung the the board of OA in the direction of the ATR-42 and-72 was the excellent STOL characteristics of the two aircraft, their ideal seating capacity and the fact that they were European aircraft which must have encouraged the funding support provided by the European Regional Development Fund of the EEC, of which Greece had become a member. By providing this support, the European Commission of the EEC acknowledged Olympic Aviation's multiple economic and social functions it was providing for the Hellenic populace and the hundreds of thousands of foreign tourists who visited the country annually.

As Liana Vassilaki, Senior Superintendant of Olympic Aviation's Sales Division said not long after the ATR was introduced: *'We're very happy for having chosen this aircraft. It's a money-maker, it's a very good aircraft, and it's very reliable. We have a very good after-sales service with product support. It has low maintenance costs and for our needs, it is the ideal aircraft'.*

'Not all our runways in Greece are good for bigger aircraft. For example, a B.737 would not land at Mykonos National Airport - it couldn't land there, for at 1900 meters long, there was not enough runway. The importance of Mykonos airport increased throughout the 1970's when the town of Mykonos became a centre of the hippie movement. Thousands of tourists thronged to this beautiful locale in search of peace and tranquillity. This resulted in Mykonos becoming an island with very good passenger traffic and using the Shorts 330s, we had to operate between thirteen and fifteen flights per day into there during the summer to meet passenger demand. Now we have the ATRs with greater capacity, so we have cut down on the frequency while carrying more passengers, which saves our costs. And it gives a better passenger service and better passenger appeal. Passengers prefer flying in a pressurised cabin instead of flying in the Shorts 330, which is a very good aircraft but is much noisier and less comfortable in comparison'.

The Shorts 330s were held in high regard by their pilots and maintenance crews who valued them for their dependability, ease of operation and their ability to withstand a high level of activity without needing frequent overhauls. That said, the type did not have that great passenger appeal when their looks were compared with the technologically advanced ATRs which were roomier, quieter and more relaxing.

With a total staff of 600, Olympic Aviation operated seven 68-seat, four 50-seat, and six 18-seat aircraft and served the following routes:

From Athína services were flown to: Mykonos - Santorini - Zakynthos - Cephalonia - Samos - Chios - Kozani - Kastoria - Karpathos - Skiathos - Ioannina

A stunning night-time picture of ATR-72 SX-BIF *(Richard Vandervord)*

- Limnos - Kalamata - Milos - Leros - Kythira - Paros - Naxos - Siteia - Ikaria - Astipalia - Preveza - Skyros - Syros.

From Thessaloniki services were flown to: Belgrade - Bucharest - Istanbul - Tirana - Chania - Chios - Heraklion - Limnos - Mikonos - Samos - Santorini.

Local Ródos based routes: Ródos - Kos - Ródos. Ródos - Kasos - Ródos. Ródos - Thessaloniki - Istanbul - Thessaloniki - Ródos. Ródos - Kastelorizo - Ródos. Ródos - Karpathos - Kasos - Karpathos - Ródos. Ródos - Karpathos - Siteoa - Karpathos - Ródos. Ródos - Kasos - Siteia - Kasos - Ródos

A number of other local routes were flown: Santorini - Heraklion - Santorini. Santorini - Ródos - Santorini. Ródos - Heraklion - Ródos. Mykonos - Santorini - Mikonos. Mikonos - Heraklion - Mykonos. Mytilini - Limnos - Mytilini.

A typical ATR-42 flight - OA50/51 - of the time could be described thus: Captain Jannis Frangos and First Officer Tilemachos Sinidros were operating ATR-42 SX-BIB *'Socrates'*. All of the ATR fleet was named after famous Hellenic philosophers. Captain Frangos' flying experience had been almost exclusively with Olympic Aviation on Dornier 228s, Shorts 330s and ATRs, but also some crop dusting, amounting to 6,000 hours in total. The flight was from Athína to the island of Zakynthos, the

The main passenger terminal at Zakynthos' Dionysios Solomos International Airport prior to its re-development. *(author)*

Below: On approach. The series of 'frying pan' turnarounds at each end of the runway shows how many times it had been extended.

ATR42 SX-BIA.*(Richard Vandervord)*

southernmost of the Ionian group and situated ten miles off the Peloponnese coast. Flight time with a load of thirty-five passengers, plus flight attendant, Angela Galaktdou, was estimated to be forty-five minutes.

With the Automatic Flight Control System (AFCS) pre-set by the crew before take-off, the flight departed Ellinikon Airport, climbing out over Athína before establishing a course towards Corinth and then a direct track to Zakinthos. First Officer Tilemachos had programmed the AFCS to take Socrates up to a cruise height of 16,000 feet with an indicated airspeed of 249 knots. The crew had uplifted 600 kilos of fuel, of which Jannis estimated 500 kilos would be used for the round trip.

Once at cruise height, it was possible to appreciate the ATR-42's very low noise level in the cabin, which made ordinary conversation very easy. Apart from when sitting near the engines, the ATR-72 was even quieter.

OA50 steadily crossed the Peloponnese with clouds capping the highest mountain tops before beginning a gradual descent towards Zakynthos' Dionysios Solomos International Airport. It was not long before the ATR was lining up on Zakynthos' single 2,220-metre Runway 34, having flown over Laganas Bay before making a 180-degree turn and a final approach over sunbathing tourists on the busy Kalamaki beach. As usual, the ATR encountered a slight amount of wind shear passing over the threshold, but nothing that caused *Socrates* any problems. Touch down was brisk but smooth the aircraft was soon back-tracking to the mid-way turn-off for the parking stands.

The turnaround was completed within twenty-minutes before the aircraft was on its way again, this time with just five passengers - which is not unusual for a mid-week flight. Around the islands, Fridays and Sundays were Olympic Aviation's busiest days throughout the year with most flights full due to VFR traffic - not Visual Flight Rules but Visiting Friends and Relations!

Being lightly loaded, the ATR positively leapt into the air on take-off, this time with Tilemachos at the controls demonstrating the aircraft's STOL ability within 600 metres. Now operating as Flight OA51, the ATR climbed out in a right-hand turn over the harbour of Zakynthos itself and the crew quickly established a heading for Athína, this time settling at a cruise height over the Peloponnese at 17,000 feet with 160 knots Indicated Air Speed helped by a slight tail wind.

As OA51 approached Athína, the radio traffic noticeably built up and both Captain and First Officer became very alert, constantly looking around the sky for the other aircraft we could hear but were, to my eyes anyway, invisible but very close by. The wind had changed since our departure nearly two hours earlier, and we were now ordered to make our approach over Athína itself, the vast expanse of the city filling the front screen of the cockpit with a myriad of high-rise flats and office blocks. A smooth, curving descent brought us into line with Hellinikon's runway and in no time at all, the ATR was down and turned quickly onto Olympic Aviation's apron at the West Terminal. For Jannis, it was his last flight of the day, but Tilemachos was just beginning his rota and had two more to make before he finished at midnight.

However, there were some domestic destinations in Greece for which even the ATRs were too large. This led to the introduction of the Deutsche Aerospace Do 228-201 light STOL transport, seating nineteen passengers and with a popular reputation worldwide as an excellent aircraft for third-level operations. Seven Do.228s served the Greek islands, exclusively, each one being named after the island to which it was designated. Their addition greatly increased Olympic Aviation's flexibility of operation through their heavy utilisation on charter work in addition to their daily scheduled work.

In the early 1990s, the remaining three aircraft in the Olympic Aviation inventory were rotary-wing and comprised two single-engined Eurocopter AS350B Ecureils and twin-engined Agusta Al09Mk 11 Plus. All three were available for private charter, 60% of their utilisation involves emergency medical services (EMS) roles. As Constantine Siappas, the Marketing Director of Olympic Airways explained: *'One of the burdens and one of the pleasures of Olympic is its social functions which, in the case of Olympic Aviation, is fulfilled by the use of its helicopters for medical evacuation of locals and tourists alike from the islands. They are crewed by ex-military pilots along with paramedics from the Greek Ministry of Health. The helicopters are often hired by foreign insurance companies for services to their members'*.

In January and February 1994, the two Ecureils were replaced by twin-engined AS355F Ecureil Ils.

The 1990s promised to be a very significant decade for Olympic Aviation, especially as the airline was granted autonomous status by its parent and was able to operate as a self-sufficient unit, although still owned outright by Olympic Airways. The inter-regional carrier branched out from its domestic network and began to fly international routes. Tirana, the capital of Albania, was the first in 1991; then, in April 1993, Istanbul in Turkey became the second. These and other international destinations were served by an ATR-72, but as traffic demands increased, Olympic Aviation considered moving into the jet age for the first time in its history. A regional jet of no more than a hundred seats was envisaged as

Left: More Olympic class! *(OA/ΠΟΛΚ.ΕΟΑ)*.

Below: ATR72 SX-BIL. *(Richard Vandervord)*

Left: Aerospatiale 350B Ecureuil SX-HBP.*(Richard Vandervord)*

Below: Piper PA-44-180 Seminole SX-BDZ. *(Richard Vandervord)*

being the largest type Olympic would wish to operate.

To support the main bulk of the domestic route network to the Greek periphery, in conjunction with the need to deal with the competition by operating at a profit, a strategically and critical decision was made by the Hellenic State and the parent company Olympic Airways to develop Olympic Aviation as a regional air carrier and to extend its activities to selected Balkan and European destinations. To serve these destinations, Olympic Aviation used Thessaloniki as its hub. To support this operation, it soon boasted a hangar, ATR simulator and a flying training school.

As Liana Vassilaki, Senior Superintendent of Olympic Aviation's Sales Division told the media: *'We are not competing with Olympic Airways', we work as a feeder for them as they do for us on certain routes. What we are trying to do is have a common front to the rest of the competition because two airlines are better than one - a second designated carrier leaves very little room for other airlines to enter the field'*.

Believing in the constant upgrading of our product, we have drawn up and are implementing a Business Plan for Olympic/Aviation S A., 1998 – 2002, revitalising its image so that we will be able to handle the new conditions of air transport deregulation on domestic routes dynamically and successfully.

For the past 30 years, Olympic Aviation has been the backbone of Greece's regional air transport system and has provided valuable services to local development carrying some 1,500,000 passengers annually on the domestic network'.

With the criterion of implementing this strategy, the decision was made to upgrade the Olympic Aviation fleet by introducing two regional jet aircraft, so in December 1999, Olympic Aviation was the first the company in Europe to incorporate into its fleet the 105-seat Boeing 717-200 - which were equipped with the most up-to-date technology systems and operational flexibility, as well as being environmentally friendly - to upgrade the services offered on regional flights.

As Petros Stephanou Chief Executive Officer told the media: *'With 17 aircraft and 700 employees, Olympic Aviation has achieved noteworthy successes in keeping its flights on time and has been rated as one of the top Greek companies in the field of flight safety.*

Olympic Aviation has an internationally certified repair centre, the only one in Greece, for aircraft such as ATR 42/72, Dornier 228 and helicopters. The quality control systems that we apply are also internationally certified.

The only school in Greece that can award commercial pilot's licence is Olympic Aviation's Flight Academy. To upgrade the level of education we provide, we have invested in a new two-engine Piper Seminole which has become part of the School's trainer aircraft at the same time and effort is underway to upgrade the Academy by transferring it to Thessaloniki.

With the cooperation of its employees and with your confidence and preference Olympic Aviation will keep making every possible effort to improve its services'.

Chapter Eight

New Challenges and the Politics of Change

In the ten years or so up to the turn of the millennium there was much debate over the reshaping of the airline industry across Europe and restructuring many of the heavily indebted national flag carriers. The European Commission sought to orchestrate this through a break up of monopolies in air travel and a tighter policing of state aid. The EU's agenda in air transport met with strong domestic opposition in the member states. Nowhere else was the resistance to reform stronger than in Hellas, where for a decade successive attempts to restructure or privatise Olympic Airways yielded only at best, partial success.

The capability of successive Hellenic governments to deliver substantive reform had long been in question, given the nature of state institutions, the power of vested interests, corruption and a political culture that brought about the exchange of services for the legislative support that often involved an implicit or explicit quid-pro-quo.

In politico-management-speak, this was 'clientelistic statism'. The so-called 'corporate logic' of the government was weak and factionalised, with differences of policy and political interest undermining its ability to act decisively. The transformation of Olympic Airways from a privately-run airline to a public utility following the sale by Aristotle Onassis opened a new chapter in the company's history. Political parties, state bureaucracy and a myriad of sectoral interests both in Hellas and abroad had, under the pretext of the Olympic Airways' 'national carrier status' sought to use Olympic as a tool for political expediency and easy money-making. Olympic Airways' position as a public utility made it almost impossible to monitor its financial position with any degree of accuracy. By

A company 737 outside the re-vamped OA international terminal at Ellinikon. *(DGR Press Agency)*

Airbus A.300 SX-BEB comes into land at London Heathrow. *(Richard Vandervord)*

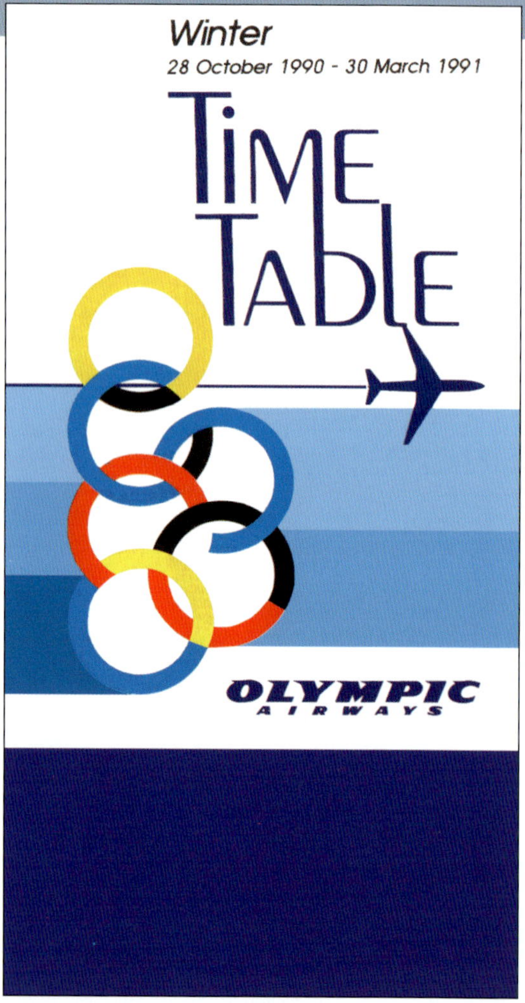

the mid-1980s it was already suffering heavy losses, the full extent never being fully appreciated as the company was not required to produce detailed accounts. The picture of the Olympic Airways' finances was further blurred by the state choosing not to pursue the company's colossal tax and national insurance arrears, and Olympic was not required to pay airport taxes and handling charges.

While the sole shareholder of Olympic Airways was the Ministry of National Economy, the supervision of the airline industry came under the aegis of the Ministry of Transport. The latter had always been a small and relatively weak ministry that lacked the expertise and human resources to perform its regulatory role adequately.

Nowhere else was the disruptive effects of clientelistic statism as practised by the government more vividly demonstrated than in the management of Olympic Airways. In the thirty years under state control, the Chairman and/or the CEO of Olympic Airways was changed an estimated thirty-two times, often filled with candidates with little or no industry experience. The changes occurred so frequently it was almost impossible to keep up with who was in post at any given time! The Board of Directors, filled with party-political appointees, ministry bureaucrats and union representatives in a non-executive capacity was regarded as a dysfunctional and unstable body. Membership of the board changed a distressing frequency, and most of its members did little to justify the substantial fee they received to attend meetings. The result was managerial paralysis with no Chairman or the CEO able to work with a Board that was directly or indirectly controlled by the government.

Despite all this, publically in its official brochure *'The World of Olympic Airways'*, the national airline was upbeat, declaring that *'During the decade leading up to the year 2000, Olympic Airways will be broadening its horizons and plans to renew its fleet with ultra-modern aircraft, improve its installations, adjust its service in accordance with customer demands and extend its network on five continents'*.

In 1993 that was a very confident declaration from a national flag carrier whose very existence was on the line two years earlier. The decade leading up to the year 2000 did just about everything it could to undermine and nearly wreck Olympic's modernisation plans, yet not only had the airline survived the worst crisis in its history, but it was also expanding, according to its Marketing Director, Constantine Siappas. 'We have new destinations. For example, we went to Boston, Chicago and Beirut. We started going to Naples. We hope we will be going to Sofia, in Bulgaria'.

Although Olympic Airways was been hit by the economic recession that was afflicting the world's airline industry as a whole (the International Air Transport Association reported to have estimated that the entire industry ended 1992 with a massive loss of US $ 7.5 billion), it faced an even more significant challenge: *'You wouldn't believe how critical it was in the period of the Gulf War...'* stated Mr Siappas. *'We almost disappeared. That was almost final '*.

Of course, the entire airline industry worldwide was drastically affected by the loss of traffic during the conflict to liberate Kuwait from Iraq, but because of its geographic location stood to suffer more than most. A considerable amount of trade takes place between Greece and its neighbours in the Middle East - as a significant number of Arabic, Asian and North African flag carriers sending their airliners to Athína' International airport at Ellinikon attested. In its turn, Olympic Airways regularly serviced Alexandria, Cairo, Tel Aviv, Damascus, Jeddah, Riyadh, Dubai and Kuwait City. Also, its long-haul flights to Bangkok, Tokyo, Melbourne and Sydney depend upon unrestricted airspace over Syria, Iraq and the Persian Gulf states. All of these major routes and destinations were placed in severe jeopardy during the Gulf War period.

With that major conflict out of the way and with its Middle Eastern routes restored, the last thing Olympic Airways needed was another war to threaten its services in Europe. However, that is precisely what it has had to contend with on the countries northern border. The war that raged in the former Yugoslavia meant that Olympic was denied three of its principle air routes to such major European cities as Vienna, London, Munich, Frankfurt, Amsterdam and Brussels. All civil airspace above Bosnia, Serbia and Croatia became restricted. Instead, Olympic had to use other routes over Hungary and Italy to fly round the conflict and, in so doing, had to compete for slot times with other airlines now also forced to use these increasingly congested corridors. It also had to contend with the activities of the American Air Force: I well remember a night jump-seat flight into Athína from London aboard a 737. At cruising altitude over France, four anti-collision lights drifted into our vision from the right and slightly above us. We followed the lights over Switzerland and down the Italian coast of the Adriatic. On our weather radar there were four 'blips' - just as they started a turn to the left, the lights flicked off. It was a flight of four B-52s beginning their bombing run - an utterly sobering view from the flight deck of an airliner with 170 holidaymakers heading for the sun down the back.

Despite these apparently overwhelming burdens, Olympic Airways forged ahead with its modernisation programme by obtaining new aircraft, opening new routes and preparing to undertake a large-scale renovation of its West Terminal at Hellinikon Airport.

Airbus A.300 SX-BEH parked awaiting the next flight. *(Richard Vandervord)*

Olympic Airways ended 1992 with a 23.3% increase in passenger traffic over the previous year's total, serving 40 destinations in Europe, North America, the Middle East, the Far East and Australia.

This increase reflected the restoration of passenger traffic after the Gulf War. To maintain its international services, Olympic had at its disposal a fleet of thirty-four short-, medium- and long-haul aircraft of four principal types. It also had a single Dassault Falcon 900 executive jet is operated exclusively for VIP flights while the company's long-serving Boeing 727-284s, purchased between 1968 and 1971, were retired.

Reducing the number of different types in service was necessary from the maintenance aspect, according to Panagiotis Makris. In talking to the media, it was clear that he would be happier if his Technical Operations Department had three types of aircraft to maintain instead of the existing five types. *'It's more difiicult if you have different aeroplane types' because you have different specialities, diflerent diplomas accepted by the Greek Aviation Authority which our technicians must have, plus a wide variety of difierent material'.*

Nonetheless, the 1,750 personnel under Panagiotis Makris' control found a way of putting their expertise to Olympic's advantage. *'In summer we try to take some work from a third party. There is no contract; it is done on an ad hoc basis. I cannot support any airline based on a contact- because I don't have the excess personnel. They ask us, do we have space? Everyone is saying we do excellent maintenance work and we are also competitive in the prices. We had a big advantage because our staff-hourly rate was lower than many countries in Europe. But it's not only the staff—hours because the labour is only 30% of the total cost, but the rest is also the material. We have a variety of types we can support, so there is another reason why they ask Olympic - say, for example, the Boeing 707 and 720. We have people who know how to maintain these aeroplanes, as well as the Boeing 727, 737-200, -300, -400, the Boeing 747 and two types of Airbuses. Our people know how to maintain a wide variety of aeroplanes '.*

Heavy maintenance on Olympic's own fleet was mostly carried out during the winter months; Olympic had always been a seasonal airline with the months from May to October seeing the maximum utilisation of its aircraft. Two large hangars dominated the apron next to the West Terminal at Ellinikon. These hangars accepted five aircraft at a time right up to the 747. Usually, four underwent heavy maintenance at any one time during the winter, with a fifth receiving minor checks alongside.

The complete strip-down of engines, however, was delegated to several maintenance centres in Europe which were also used by other major European airlines. Another legacy of using a variety of different aircraft types also meant that there was an even greater variety of engines needing servicing. Mr Makris explained that the number of engines of each model was not sufficient enough to be profitable to undertake full in-house overhaul, although interim checks and servicing was well within his staff 's capability.

Dornier 228 SX-BHO sweeps in for another landing. *(Richard Vandervord)*

Above: Dornier 228 SX-BHF *'Isle of Astypalaia'* waits between services at Ellinikon. *(Richard Vandervord)*

Right: the interior of the Dorniers were quite roomy, if somewhat spartan. It could also be quite noisy, especially when sitting directly in line with the props. *(author)*

By the 1990's the West Terminal at Ellinikon was started to look decidedly 'tired' so Olympic began the renovation of the southeastern wing of its Terminal, with completion planned for the commencement of the summer 1994 season.

Some form of 747 replacement became another important consideration for OA. Passenger density was an influence the choice of type. If a widebodied size aircraft was needed, then the B747-400 must be considered a favourite.

Flying in the Dornier 228.

A Olympic Dornier Do 228 flight could be regarded as something of an experience. All were of short duration - which was just as well that the flights are shorter because of the turboprop howl from the twin Garrett TPE-331-252D turboprops could be particularly penetrating in the cabin and took some getting used to for passengers who did not often use this type of aircraft. Locals who regularly flew in them merely relaxed with newspapers. They were in many ways similar to other Olympic Aviation services, but of a shorter duration and devoid of flight attendants.

My first flight in a 228 was 26 September 2000 - yet another crack of dawn trip out of Ellinikon, just before that airport closed. This time it was to the island of Paros, one of the Cyclades island group, which lies to the west of Naxos, from which it is separated by a channel about eight kilometres wide. It lies approximately one hundred and forty kilometres south-east of Ellinikon. Paros National Airport was located in the southwestern part of the island, about ten kilometres from the port of Parikia.

The airport was opened on 5 October 1982 on land made available by Nikolas Panteleou, hence its secondary name 'Panteleou Paros Airport'. Operation of the airport began as a municipal airport with a dirt runway and a small building covering 80 square meters. Three years later, in 1985, construction started on a paved runway. The terminal was initially a single story building, but in 1987 this was extended, and an additional floor was added, housing the Hellenic Civil Aviation Authority and the MHL (Meteorological Service). In 1989, the airport became a national airport. The airport has been replaced by the New Paros Airport - at a different location - which became fully operational on the 25 July 2016.

It was still dark when the fifteen passengers boarded a vast Mercedes shuttle bus that could easily have carried over one hundred people for the quick journey out to the aircraft. SX-BHD was operating OA060 that morning. On boarding, we were shown to our seats by a very polite First Officer who, once we were all seats walked the length of the cabin checking that we all had our seatbelts fastened. Two doors slammed shut — the rear cargo hold and the passenger door - before one of the ground handlers banged on the side of the fuselage twice - apparently a sign that all was good to go.

Both engines were started in short order, and we were soon moving out to the end of Runway One Five. I had been warned in advance about the internal noise of the 228 by someone who regularly flew with Suckling Airways in the UK, so had come prepared with a pair of foam earplugs. Acceleration seemed brisk, and we were soon airborne. Our course curved slightly to the left, then stabilised as we reached our cruising altitude of eight thousand feet overhead Lavrio. As dawn broke, the cabin lights went out. We flew out over the Aegean, abeam Kea, then overflew Kithnos, Serifos to just touch Sifnos before starting a slow descending turn to the left overflying Antiparos and then touching down on the high ground that was the airport. Backtracking down the runway, we arrived outside the gleaming white terminal building to be met by a pair of aircraft handlers and a Land Rover fire truck. The moment the turbines were off the brakes on the prop-hubs brought each propeller to a stop in no time at all.

The luggage was off-loaded onto a seemingly standard dark blue four-wheeled trolley that seemed to inhabit every aircraft parking apron in Greece and pulled by one man to an area outside the terminal. It seemed that here you did your own baggage-smashing as I discovered during the return trip on OAO73: after checking in I was expected to load my own bags on another OA trolley that was then wheeled out to Dornier SX-BHC *Isle of Leros!*

The return flight took a somewhat circuitous route - often the case when flying into Ellinikon when it was busy - for once we were airborne from Paros we flew over Siros and Giaros before crossing the coast of the mainland just to the south of Rafina, giving those on the left side of the aircraft a good view of the new airport then under construction. Of course, the aircraft was full, and I was sitting on the right-hand side! We then flew a convoluted path, finishing with an arrival overhead the capital on a heading which intentionally took the Dornier out to sea.

All aircraft were ordered to approach Ellinikon from the sea before lining up for landing, which in

Paros National Airport was opened on 5 October 1982 on land made available by Nikolas Panteleou, hence its secondary name 'Panteleou Paros Airport'.

Below: a Olympic Aviation Dornier 228 lands on the 850 metre strip. Since 2016 the airport has moved to a different location. *(both author)*

our case required the *Isle of Leros* to make quite a tight descending 180° turn over the bay which a couple of passengers on my flight unused to this kind of flying found a little disconcerting. However, the Domier was being flown well within its normal envelope, and such a manoeuvre was standard procedure for Olympic Aviation. Needless to say, any roll out on landing at Hellinikon was negligible.

Governmental intervention

The relationship between Olympic Airways' management and their political masters in the Ministry of Transport had always been one of convenience on one hand and subservience on the other. While the administration was expected to run the day-to-day business of the company, ministers were heavily involved in all major decisions affecting the future of Olympic, often with a blatant disregard for management's authority, experience and better judgment. The government's increasing reliance on external consultants to perform even the most routine management tasks within the OA group was indicative this regard. In the very few cases where the airline's management sought to assert its authority against the government, the latter was invariably quick to restore order by sacking those with a more independent disposition.

The relationship between government and the unions of OA, on the other hand, reflected the complexity, clientelism, corruption and conflict evident in the broader system of Hellenic labour relations. Within this system, interest mediation had always been characterised by 'rent—seeking' behaviour — with sectional interests competing for favours, resources and subsidies. Specifically within the OA group, a total of seventeen unions operated, reflecting the very diverse range of activities that included aviation, technical, handling and administrative duties performed by its numerous subsidiaries. All seventeen unions formed part of the Greek Federation of Civil Aviation Unions (Ελληνική Ομοσπονδία Συνδικάτων Πολιτικής Αεροπορίας ΕΟΣΠΑ/EOSPA), the umbrella union for the entire workforce of the OA group.

Traditionally, internal union politics were dominated by the divide between ground staff, on the one hand, and the pilots and cabin crew, on the other. Nevertheless, the OA's unions have been remarkably united in the fierce defence of their employment conditions and militantly opposed to the prospect of the flag carrier slimming down its operations or losing its state-owned character.

In the post-Onassis period, the unions' influence in the running of Olympic grew. Union leaders gained direct access to successive ministers, often without the knowledge of the OA Chairman/CEO's knowledge. Electorally, most of the OA current or former employees and their families lived and voted in the key second Athína constituency (Athína B) where forty-three of the three hundred members of the Hellenic Parliament stood for election.

During the 1980s union strength became all the more evident, as the famous — some said infamous — influential mistress and later wife of Prime Minister Andreas Papandreou, Dimitra, herself a leading figure in the flight attendants union, encouraged a more maximalist union agenda and rewarded her former colleagues with a number of extra privileges through what became known as the 'Dimitra-laws'.

Born Dimitra Liani in 1955 in the Macedonian town of Florina, she came from a well-connected family. Her father was a distinguished army officer, while her cousin George Liani was the

Left: Former Olympic Airways Flight Attendant and wife of Hellenic Prime Minister Andreas Papandreou, Dimitra 'Mimi' Lianni. *(DGR Press Agency)*

Right: Ignacia Loyola de Palacio y del Valle-Lersundi was a Spanish politician and Transport Commissioner for the European Union.

member of parliament for her home town.

Dimitra - popularly known as 'Mimi' in Hellas - was moving in high political circles long before she met Mr Papandreou. Her previous husband, Alexis Kapopoulos, was a prominent member of the Communist Party and they played a a full part in the Hellenic social circuit: parties, cruises and raucous weekends on Aegean islands.

It was, in fact, Margaret Papandreou who first noticed her. She helped Dimitra become a member of her husband's private entourage at Olympic Airways in 1985. She even used her influence to land this enterprising young woman the job of her dreams, her own chat show on television. One of the first guests on *Miso Miso* (meaning 'half and half') was the Prime Minister himself. The show may have flopped, but the love affair was in full swing.

Her public debut at the side of her future husband, Andreas, occurred at a European summit on Rhodes in 1988. At the time both were married to other people, and although Mr Papandreou had a reputation as a womaniser, he had never before appeared with a mistress in public, let alone at a state occasion. It caused a sensation. What was the Prime Minister of Hellas, then nearly seventy and recovering from major heart surgery, doing at an international meeting with a blonde air hostess less than half his age? Mr Papandreou, said the wags, had discovered a new sexual position: doing it with one foot in the grave.

After Rodos, she never left his side in public. Even PASOK's defeat in the 1989 elections failed to dent her resolve. One month later she was the third Mrs Papandreou.

Four years of opposition for PASOK were an invaluable apprenticeship for her. Once her husband was triumphantly returned to power not only did she take control of her husband's private office, controlling access of both people and documents, but she appeared to play a key role in his cabinet appointments.

Mrs Papandreou's cousin George became sports minister and Mr Papandreou's doctor, the health minister. By contrast Vasso Papandreou, the feisty former European Commissioner, unrelated to Andreas but widely believed to be an old flame of his, was left out of government altogether.

She won few points for helping break up Mr Papandreou's 38-year marriage to his popular American second wife, Margaret, and fewer still for provoking a damaging split in Mr Papandreou's PASOK party over her ambition to run for parliament.

Then, in 1994, a new law gave EOSPA two non- executive seats on the OA Board, allowing its unions direct and formal access to company management decisions.

The net effect, in strategic terms, was of the contest between ministers and the unions, with the latter as defacto veto players pursuing a reactive and defensive strategy. The government faced public opposition, but with uncertain solutions.

It is essential to understand just how the EU and its structure operated. As the EU's executive agency, the Commission had the task of regulating the internal market: an area in which it gradually extended its authority, supported by the European Court of Justice (ECJ). The Commission's role in the Union's 'competition policy' was complicated, and asymmetrical. While in some areas, such as theregulation of state aid, its institutional authority was supported by powerful compliance

Another London Hotel shot, this time of OA 747-200B SX-OAE with everything down and out about to land.

mechanisms, and in others, backed by legislation to enforce market de-regulation; in matters of the overall policy agenda, its capability rested on cooperation with the member states. It could thus insist or pull its punches on state subsidies, but it could only seek to build a consensus on specific solutions, such as privatisation. The role of the Commission combined specific areas of authority alongside a more comprehensive set of preferences and strategy based on softer mechanisms.

The Commission's competence to act in the air transport sector came from several sources: treaty provisions on transport, its powers to intervene on the market-distorting 'state aids', and the application of internal market liberalisation measures to the sector.

The liberalisation of air transport in the EU occurred in three stages: a package of measures adopted in 1987, a second in 1990, and a final and more substantive third package adopted in 1992 and applied as from January 1993. This 'third package' introduced the freedom to provide services within the EU and led in April 1997 to the privilege to present cabotage, i.e. the right for an airline of one Member State to operate a route within another Member State. It comprised: standard rules on the licensing of air carriers, rules on access for Community air carriers to intra-Community air routes, controls on fares and rates for intra-Community air services and the full application of the competition rules of the Treaty to the liberalised air transport market.

OLYMPIC GROUND HANDLING

The phrase 'ground handling' covers a multitude of topics; everything from refuelling the aircraft to emptying the toilets. For many years Olympic had the monopoly on ground services at all the Hellenic airports for not only their flights, but other airlines as well.

They provided baggage handling, cabin cleaners, aircraft tugs, transportation for passengers and crew alike to and from the terminals to the aircraft, flight planning, ground liaison... Almost every vehicle and item of equipment that surrounded your aircraft was marked Olympic/ΟΛΥΜΠΙΑΚΗ! *(author/OA files)*

In the general area of competition policy, the Commission's role was an exception from the more general norm: it had authority to act, and the objects of regulation were the national governments themselves. Within this framework, however, an essential element was the Commission's bargaining with governments concerning industry restructuring. The bargaining process required the Commission to elaborate its priorities, strategies and tactics, providing scope for interpretation and adjustment - something that was affected by changing political agendas and leadership personalities. By the 1990s, the emphasis was undoubtedly on deregulation and the abandonment of state aids distorting competition. Loyola De Palacio, the Transport Commissioner from September 1999 to November 2004, pursued her strategy with vigour, often heightening the sense of confrontation with member governments. She was a leading member of the centre-right Partido Popular in Spain, having served as

Below: The Olympic Airways offices in Othon Street: amongst those in this picture is Mr. Papadimitropoulos, Drosia Tsamadou, Sofia Zira, Mary Eugenides, Amalia Ziakri, Katia Andrizaki, Minos Hatzidakis, Gelly Psimogiannou, Alexandra Prokou, Irene Romanou and Minos Hatzidakis. *(OA files)*

Minister of Agriculture and as a member of the European Parliament. De Palacio was appointed as Vice President of the Commission, responsible for relations with the European Parliament, alongside the Transport and Energy portfolios, under President Romano Prodi. Previously, Neil Kinnock, former leader of the British Labour Party, held the Transport portfolio in the Commission of Jacques Santer, 1995-1999.

In addition to Olympic Airways, the Commission under Loyola De Palacio became embroiled in disputes concerning the restructuring of Air France, Alitalia and Iberia airlines.

Despite the fact that the Commission knew that political feathers would be ruffled if it were to call directly for privatisation in the sector to ensure that the national flag carriers were run on fully commercial lines, the Commission went as far as it could to structure the reform path. Loyola De Palacio, as the relevant Commissioner, was openly frustrated by the lack of reform and the lack of transparency in accounting by Olympic Airways. She outlined the Commission's approach on a number of occasions:

'*...Europe is airline industry and the economy was not strengthened by unquestioning national support for inefiicient national flag carriers and the building of national champions - on the contrary; it was weakened. We have seen how diflicult Olympic Airways and TAP* [Transportes Aéreos Portugueses - the Portuguese airline] *have found it to develop a successful long-term strategy in spite of state aid and restructuring plans...*'

The preferences of the Commission and the will to act was clear. The Commission's emphasis was on efficiency, competition, the abandonment of state aid and what they saw as a vibrant European marketplace.

Restructuring attempts

There was an attempt of the socialist PASOK government under Prime Minister Costas Simitis to restructure the ailing Olympic Airways, in parallel to the EU's agenda of market liberalisation of the air transport sector in the 1990s.

The two principal protagonists - the EU Commission and the Hellenic government - proclaimed compatible policy goals, but their respective institutional constraints prevented them from cooperating to achieve them.

There were two critical factors; the interaction between the EU Commission and the Hellenic government; and that between the Government

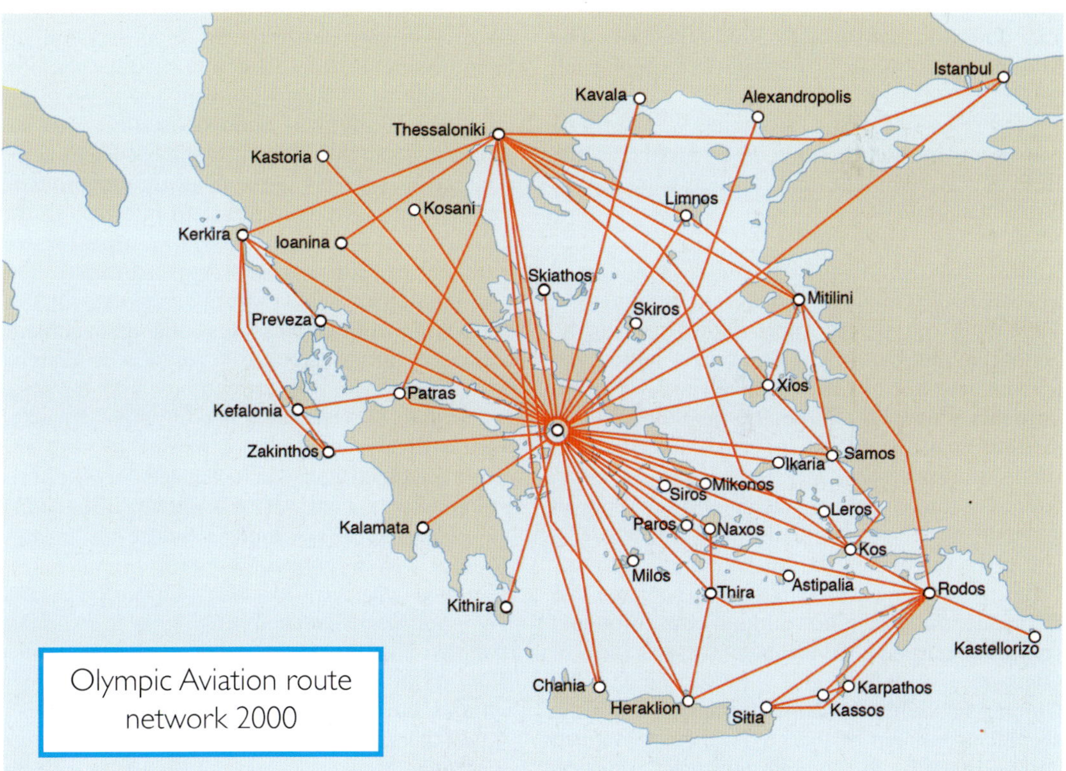

Olympic Aviation route network 2000

There are a number of airports in Hellas that are very photogenic in regards to taking action pictures of aircraft; the obvious one being Kerkyra and the terrace of the Café Kanoni, close to the Corfu Palace Hotel. Here A.300 SX-BED is captured 'over the numbers' about to touch down. *(author)*

and domestic actors with veto-potential. The Simitis government stood with a foot in each arena.

The role of domestic veto points was a crucial constraint on the options considered by the Hellenic government and on its capacity to implement change.

In October 1994 the PASOK Government of Andreas Papandreou and the Commission agreed to a rescue plan for OA. With this, the Commission sanctioned the second most significant airline bailout behind that of Air France. As part of the agreement, the Greek Government was forced to introduce a new law (2271/ 94) involving cuts in staffing costs, a rethink of OA's international routes transport package by the end of 1994. Crucially, the government also promised to put an end to its interference with the management of OA and grant the airline the full status of a private company. Implementation of the plan soon ran into difficulties following fierce union opposition and constant changes in the management structures of Olympic. Against this background, the Commission refused to authorise the release of the second instalment of the government's planned capital injection to Olympic worth €75 million (Δρχ 23 billion) in April 1996. In its decision, the Commission drew a distinction between its view of the actions of the government and those of the company. While the Commission stated that the airline had met the obligations imposed on it in the context of the 1994 agreement, the government had defaulted, by continuing to interfere in the management of OA and providing unauthorised state aid of €36 million (Δρχ 11 billion). The Commission appeared to accept that OA, with less political meddling and professional management, could be turned around - and it was thereby signalling a willingness to continue with the saga.

As late as October 1994 Olympic Airways were still allowing school parties to visit the airport and inspect their aircraft, as Lefteris Kaloterakis explains: *'My school class was visiting the airport of Thessaloniki because the airport director was a father of a girl in my class. He arranged for us to visit Olympic's A300 'Neoptolemos' which had just arrived from Athens and was waiting for passengers for the return flight to the capital. We passed through security without any checks and boarded the aircraft. Turnarounds in Olympic at that time were quite generous. Because we had the chance to visit the cockpit and meet the friendly captain and then walked across the plane and disembark from the back door. The stewardesses were using the break to have a cigarette using the passenger ashtrays.'*

Although the financial position of Olympic continued to deteriorate in 1996 and 1997, the Greek government made no serious reform attempt. The reform of Olympic only re-emerged in early 1998 within the context of Greece's effort's to convince its EU counterparts as to the merits of its membership of the European Exchange Rate Mechanism and its commitment to enforce fiscal discipline on its public utilities.

Right: Transport Minister Christos Verelis. *(DGR Press Agency)*

Below: the face of the summer 2004 timetable *(Olympic Airways archive)*

As with much appertaining to the 'grey men of Brussels' much of the subject is embroiled in 'legalise' and overly-complex jargon, but basically what happened was that following the government's refusal to claim back illegal subsidies it had granted to Olympic Airways, the European Commission referred the matter to the European Court of Justice. In December 2002, the Commission asked for the recovery of €194 million in what it termed as illegal state aid: *'Greece had two months from the notification of the Commission's decision to comply with it. By the deadline of 13 February 2003, the aid had not been recovered. The Commission has therefore decided to bring the matter before the Court of Justice.'*

Transport Minister Christos Verelis claimed that the problem, which he described as 'purely legal in nature' would not exist when the government carried out it's planned restructuring of Olympic's liabilities.

As part of its efforts to sell off the airline, the government said it would split Olympic into a new, healthy branch - which would be privatised - while dumping all the accrued debts on a company that will remain in state ownership. '*We believe we will forestall the court developments by the foundation of the new Olympic Airways'* said Verelis. *'This process had been heralded in advance and was to be expected. The Greek side has strong legal arguments and, as I have already declared, the matter is now purely legal.'* Verelis had responded to the December decision by claiming the Commission only wanted €41 million repaid, and described the 194 million as a figure cooked up by the international media.

Unfortunately, this led to a breakdown in the previous policy of tentative cooperation between Brussels and Athína, with an investigation by the Commission and a legal challenge in the ECJ - a process that took more than three years and eventually resulted in a legal victory for the Commission.

Born in Athína, Christos Verelis was the Minister for Transport and Communications from 13 April 2000 to 10 March 2004. Graduating from the German School of Athína, Christos Verelis studied chemistry at the Aristotle University of Thessaloniki and later on completed his PhD in the chemistry of natural products in Germany. In the general elections of 1996 and 2000, he was elected

SX-ECH was a Dassault Falcon 900B owned by the Hellenic Air Force, yet operated by Olympic Airways.

MP (PASOK) for Aetolia-Acarnania. His public sector career was impressive: From 1996 to 13 April 2000, Verelis was Deputy Minister for the Environment, Town Planning and Public Works. He was also Managing Director of the Hellenic Oil Refinery in Aspropyrgos, and president of the ASPROFOS company (1986-1989). President of the Public Petroleum Corporation (1993-1996); during his term, he recommended the merger of the group into a single company and a share issue. Chairman and managing director of the Public Gas Corporation (1993-1996). Chairman of the Greek Chemists' Union (1985-1993). Member of the PASOK Central Committee since 1996. President of the Greek Community in Heidelberg, and member of the Presidium of the Greek Communities in Germany. He had worked for large chemical companies in Germany and then in Greece until 1996. Christos Verelis was also a member of the Standing Committee on Economic Affairs. In May 2009, he resigned from the Hellenic Parliament out of political sensitivity over scandal allegations which, in May 2011, resulted in criminal proceedings that did not involve ministerial responsibility. In the October 2009 national elections, Christos Verelis did not run for a seat in the Parliament due to disagreements with his party leader.

The government pushed through Parliament a controversial new law (2602/98) in April 1998 on the restructuring of Olympic Airways. The new law entailed more flexible working practices and cost-cutting measures. Industrial relations within Olympic faced meltdown, and the airline was rocked by a continuous series of wildcat strikes during Easter and summer.

With these new measures, Athína requested from the Commission the release of the two remaining instalments of capital injection for OA that had been blocked since 1996. In the negotiations that followed, Athína was obliged to accept Commission claims of illegal state aid and to accept a deduction of €38.6 million (Δϱχ 11 billion) from the instalments. For its part, the Commission agreed to the immediate release of the second payment of €41 million (Δϱχ I4 billion) and authorised state loan guarantees of $378 million for the purchase of new aircraft. The release of the third and final instalment (worth €22.8 million/Δϱχ 7.8 billion), however, was made conditional on the successful implementation of the governments restructuring plan. Sceptisism and suspicion surrounded the process.

Against this background, the Commission, in May 1999, refused to authorise the release of the third instalment of the capital injection planned for OA under the 1998 plan.

Chapter Nine

Call Out The Cavalry... or Bring In The Clowns?

In a separate development, the Hellenic government attempted another solution for the Olympic Group by tying it to a strategic partner overseas. On 24 June 1999, a deal with British Airways via its consultancy subsidiary, Speedwing, was announced. *'British Airways sending senior BBC executive and the airline's most experienced Concorde pilot to rescue ailing Olympic Airways'* trumpeted the headlines.

Their appointment followed British Airways' success in winning a £6.3m management contract against fierce opposition from the US and Europe.

Speedwing had just thirty months to turn round Olympic. Leading BA's efforts was Rod Lynch, the BBC's £211,000-a-year chief executive of British Broadcasting Corporation resources. A former managing director of Air Europe, he was a senior executive at British Airways in the 1980s. Co-incidentally, Lynch had joined Air Europe in June 1989, replacing Roy Phillips just after The International Leisure Group, owners of Air Europe took the airline into the sceduled service market and when the British Airways' 'dirty tricks' campaign was gaining momentum against Virgin Atlantic and Air Europe.

At OA, Lynch was assisted by Peter White, former director of sales for British Airways and a member of its executive board until he retired in 1998, who was to serve as a commercial advisor. Captain William Dennis 'Jock' Lowe, at the time Concorde commercial manager, would serve as director of operations.

Rod Lynch, the new CEO of Olympic in 1999. *(Olympic Airways archive)*

Rod Lynch was appointed as Chief Executive of Olympic, and his management team was allocated two seats on the OA's thirteen-strong Board of Directors. At the time of the announcement, Lych was quoted as saying *'This is a challenge which any airline professional would relish, and I am very much looking forward to working with the team at Olympic to make the airline a real gold-medal winner in this industry.'*

If other media comments were anything to go by, he was going to be in for a rough ride. Greece's former foreign minister, Theodoros Pangalos, once joked that no logical person would fly Olympic.

Government officials had said the decision to hand Olympic's management over to a foreign organisation was a last-ditch effort to save it from bankruptcy after two failed recovery programmes and more than two decades in the red. An un-named transport official in Athína was reported as saying *'We expect Speedwing to introduce modern management methods and turn the company around. British Airways' experience in the field played a big role in choosing them'*.

Transport minister Tasos Mandelis said that the deal included a $1.5m success fee for meeting financial and commercial targets and a $2.5m premium for returning the airline to profitability.

It was clear that although the airline was 100% state-owned, the government

747 SX-OAC *Olympic Spirit* awaits the boarding of another load of passengers at the Western Terminal of Ellinikon in 1999. *(author's collection)*

was looking for a minority strategic equity partner from one of the major carriers - British Airways being the most obvious candidate given the Speedwings consultancy involvement. The government was also keen to put a substantial part of Olympic into private ownership, for the airline would need shareholder financing to implement its recovery strategy.

By the time the new management arrived, the situation in Olympic had once again become untenable. Many of the provisions of the 1998 restructuring plan had been efficiently cancelled by subsequent agreements between OA's former management and the unions, and the airline's losses for 1999 were estimated at more than €75 million, or 25 .9 billion drachmae.

As Rod Lynch said in a media briefing after being in post for a few days: *'In essence, Olympic was bust, and the European Union made it clear that an approved recovery plan had to be implemented or discussions would 're-open' on the debt forgiveness programme that could see the airline having to repay $l.5billion. The only way for Olympic to survive in the new airline situation in Europe was for it to become a free-standing commercially viable operation. The problem is very much one of finance; the airline generates enough cash to pay its bills but not to advance as it needs to - regarding fleet renewal, training programmes to raise service levels, and the move to the new airport. While the fundamentals of the operation are good, some of the processes are questionable, in many cases, the service levels are woeful, although this is, in part, due to the aged fleet.'*

Bring In The Consultants!

A team of highly-paid 'aviation management consultants' were called in, and the blueprint of the BA managers for the future of Olympic was finally published in October 1999; it was, in effect, the third restructuring plan since 1994.

When each successive report appeared, each ran to hundreds of pages, and each suggested basically the same thing; the complete re-arrangement of the company. Each report was built on the findings of the previous, all using the 1978, 1988 and 1998 sets of cost structure published in percentage terms by the Financial Department of

Olympic Airways' in the Annual Report.

	1978	1988	1998
Labour	41.50	35.00	38.00
Fuel	16.90	9.81	12.27
Financial	2.09	13.78	5.88
Aircraft Related	6.58	7.25	8.27
Sales, Promotion and Advertising	8.13	7.46	11.23
Other	24.80	26.701	24.35

Each report highlighted the fact that labour costs represented nearly forty percent of the companies total expenditure and even at their lowest level of thirty-five percent in 1988, it was higher than the carrier's chief rivals. This was regarded as being particularly significant given that this had been a critical area of focus for reducing costs as part of the two restructuring plans. Fuel was also a huge component of the airline's operational costs. The

Airbus A300 SX-BEM *Kreta* seen through the myriad of reflections in the double glazing and bathed in sodium lighting of Terminal Two, London Heathrow ready to board the last passengers of the day back to Athína. *(author)*

Left: from 1987 until 1992 Olympic Airways wore uniforms designed by Aspasia Jerel. *(ΠΟΛΚ.ΕΟΑ)*

Above: passengers deplane from the forward door of 737-484 SX-BKE *Stagira* at Samos.

Below: Samos Terminal building seen from Kilo Echo. *(both author)*

airline's management could not influence the price of crude oil, but they could control fuel costs through the adoption of more sophisticated fuel-buying strategies, more efficient fuel management policies, and obtaining - either by buying or leasing more fuel-efficient aircraft.

Since 1975, Olympic Airways tended to obtain many airliners together in short periods of time. Thus, in 1991-1992, Olympic Airways obtained

737-484 SE-BKA *Vergina* poses for it's pre-delivery portrait in front of Mount Hood, Washington State, USA.

Cabin crew in the Aspasia Jerel uniform (both ΠΟΛΚ.ΕΟΑ)

six Boeing 737-400 and two A300-600 and in 1999, four Airbus A340-300 and eight Boeing B737-400s. This acquisition pattern caused the financial costs to increase enormously in some years. A similar pattern was the cause of the high costs in 1988.

The aircraft-related costs for the airline rose in the last few years of the reports due to the increased maintenance and leasing costs. It was regarded by the consultants as being due to the absence of any fleet commonality by the carrier. These costs were expected to increase further because the price of aircraft insurance had been rising internationally. The move of the carrier to the new Athens International Airport from the Ellinikon airport, in the form of higher parking and landing fees, was expected to increase aircraft costs further.

'Other Costs' in the reports included Information Technology support, ground handling, infrastructure, administration, and passenger related costs. They were a significant proportion of the carrier's cost structure, comprising of a steady 25.3 percent average of total costs, with very little fluctuation over the thirty year period.

In summary, it was clear that the consultants thought that Olympic Airways should emphasise controlling all the cost areas to improve its financial position and to achieve viability. The carrier should establish a monitoring system that examined its costs on a daily basis and compared them with carriers having similar route structures and operational characteristics to determine whether specific cost categories were consuming excessive resources.

The report's authors thought it was clear that the monitoring and controlling of the labour costs were necessary regardless of whether the Olympic Airways management decided on a cost leadership strategy or whether it choose to adopt a differentiation strategy, because the company was in such a weak financial position

The carrier's costs would have to be considerably reduced by the management and the state to improve the carrier's financial and market position.

A synopsis of all the additional detailed analysis conducted and reported on by the army of management consultant *malakas* amounted to the following:

- Labour costs.

These costs involved employee wages, overtime, staff insurance, away from base allowances, crew hotel accommodation, and so on. Therefore, it was essential to address all these elements to control and decrease the total labour costs.

A study of the accounts showed that labour costs were highest in 1990, 1993 and 1997 and were the most important reason for the introduction of the two restructuring plans in the following years, aiming to assist OA to reduce labour costs. However, since their second peak in 1997, they had steadily decreased to their lowest level since 1990.

The 1993 labour cost increases were as a result of the state intervention in the carrier's operation, where the frequent management changes during the election year led the firm to lose control of costs. The 1997 rise was as a result of the significant wage increases and the compensation to redundant employees.

Although the two restructuring plans lead to a decrease in the number of employees, the labour cost per employee actually increased during the same period. Overtime was a significant contributing factor, as a large part of the carrier output was produced through overtime, as well as other expenses, such as away from base allowances, which were out of the management control. The generous wage increases were given to gain the support of employees and their unions also contributed.

The Restructuring Reports stressed that OA should adopt more efficient labour cost management practices to control these costs better. Although, Olympic Airways has a significant cost advantage over its main scheduled rivals due to lower staff wages, the carrier had not exploited them, as had been done by the Asian airlines, who offered an attractive, superior product. This would be particularly important looking towards the future as Olympic Airways was starting to compete with low cost and charter carriers who were beginning to dominate in the Hellenic market offering lower fares.

Each Report went into details regarding the employee Unions, stating that the workforce was highly unionised at almost ninety-nine per cent. Three groups of employees were dominant through their strong unions and their bargaining power, each pressing the carrier's management for more benefits. The pilots union represented the permanent force in the Olympic Airways power structure, in effect controlling many of the airline's functions and they would - and did - resort to strike

Left: the new terminal building at Kithira National Airport in 1998. The pan-tile roof of the old building that was little more than an open-faced bus shelter can just be seen on the extreme left.

Below: Olympic Aviation's Dornier 228-201 SX-BHE *Isle of Leros* awaits the re-loading of both bags and passengers. *(both author)*

Above: Kithira National Airport 'Alexandros Aristotelous Onasis' as seen just at the point where the new facilities were about to be completed in 1998. As with a number of other Hellenic airports, one does not so much make a descent onto the runway, it's more that the runway comes up to meet the aircraft! The airport has considerably expanded since then.

Left: OA were never shy in using images of the country for promotional purposes. Here sunset at the temple of Posidion is shown. *(ΠΟΛΚ.ΕΟΑ)*

Below: Olympic Aviation's Domier SX-BHE taxies out at Kithira for the start of the return flight to Ellinikon *(both author)*

action whenever their position was threatened. Pilots away from base allowances and hotel accommodation were a significant contributor to the carrier's high labour costs.

Thus, pilots, through their strong union, pressed the management to open, and to retain, unprofitable long-haul routes because they earn more from away from base allowances and hotel accommodation. The flight attendants, who also have significant bargaining power, also pushed the management on the same issue, for the same reason.

Both reports cited the Olympic Airways pilots and flight attendants flying to New York, Johannesburg and Australia who remained away from base for four, five and ten days respectively earning significant compensations, while their colleagues from other carriers stayed away from their stations for only half this time. These away from base allowances and hotel accommodation were a significant contributor to the carrier's high labour costs.

Olympic Airways management needed to control these costs through better flight scheduling of its aircraft, pilots and flight attendants to reduce the away from base days. The contracts with these two groups of employees should also be renegotiated and unprofitable long-haul routes should be re-examined.

Mechanics also pushed the carrier's management, mainly through work slowdowns, to earn significant amounts of overtime pay. The solution of outsourcing for maintenance should be examined by the carrier's management in some cases.

The Report's authors felt that the level of Olympic Airways labour costs had not allowed the carrier to adopt a cost leadership strategy. Thus, the airline did not manage to exploit its lower labour wages compared to its main rivals and stated that management should focus on this advantage.

- Sales promotion and advertising costs

OA spent more on sales promotion and advertising in the period 1990-1993 than in subsequent years due to the state support of the carrier via significant subsidies. However, the international competition was restricted, and they had a monopoly in the domestic market. Therefore, spending on sales promotion and advertising was less critical than in the following years. Since 1994, these costs declined as a consequence of the implementation of the first restructuring plan, except for a small increase in 1996 when the competition started to increase in the international markets and some private Greek carriers appeared in the domestic market. Thus Olympic Airways had to offer significantly discounted fares and spend money on advertising campaigns to promote this. The lowest level for sales promotion and advertising costs was in 1998 during the implementation of the second restructuring plan. From 1999, these expenses increased due to the intense competition in both domestic and international markets. Also, since 1999 the more intense competition - mainly in the domestic market - led Olympic Airways to invest more in differentiation strategies, to maintain or to improve its financial and market position. The majority of these expenditures were directed at advertising in the press, offering more facilities to the frequent flyers and at improving the quality of the timetables. Olympic Airways' promotional and advertising campaigns were targeted to inform the carrier's current and potential travellers and to promote new routes, improvements to existing routes, the carriers Frequent Flyer Programme (ICARUS), new discounted fares, and new services offered.

The company undertook common campaigns with other organisations, by providing complimentary tickets, or onboard advertising and such like in co-operation with the Greek National Tourist Office (GNTO) and the new Athens International Airport (AIA). Adopting this policy offered a way of minimising its spending on advertising and promotion while increasing the effectiveness of its campaigns.

The key strength of Olympic Airways is that it has a significant advantage over its competitors through its strong brand, which is easily recognised by travellers around the world and it was suggested that this would assist the carrier, through the right promotional and advertising campaigns, to achieve a higher penetration of the market.

- Costs for On-board Passenger Travel

Food and drink on board are some of the most important attractions for the passenger. Meals, refreshments, plates, cutlery, newspapers and magazines and other consumables can significantly differentiate the airline's offering product.

In the cost section for On-Board Passenger travel, the company such items as catering, refreshments, newspapers and magazines and all other onboard amenities that included complementary gifts given to passengers, such as blankets and pillows, gifts for children, etc., but did not include flight entertainment.

The main proportion of this is catering cost. OA offered Mediterranean cuisine on-board, and

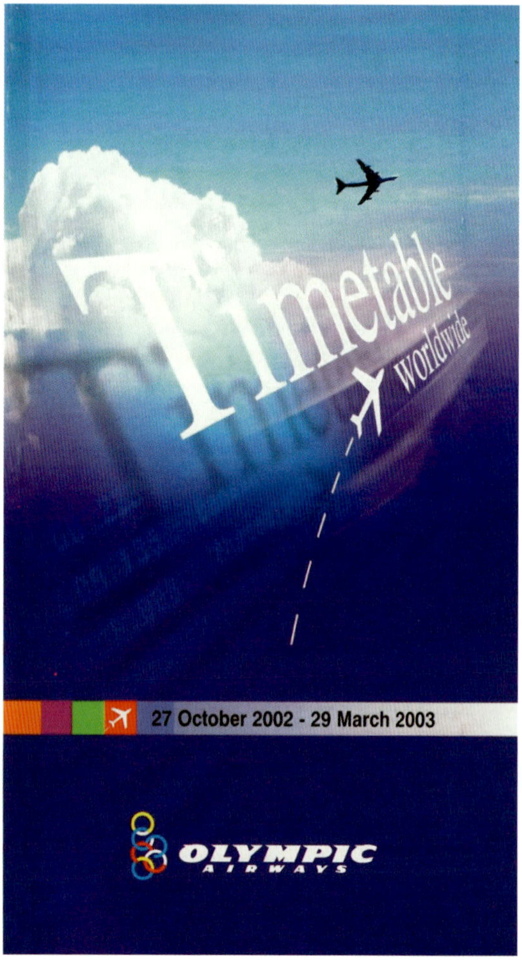

The Technical Base for Olympic Airways at Ellinikon was usually a hive of activity.

Kleanthis Tratsa, trade union member of the facility remembers the hangars at Ellinikon well: *The airlines Technical Base, at its peak had a turnover of 120 million and we were serving tens of foreign airlines. A few years ago it was full of life, but now has evolved into a huge, empty warehouse after being used as a technical storage facility for the 2004 Olympic Games.*

OLYMPIC ENGINEERING

(all photos *ΠΟΛΚ.ΕΟΑ)*

Boeing 717-200SX-BOB on finals. It's Douglas DC-9 heritage is obvious. *(Richard Vandervord)*

its leading provider was a company subsidiary named Olympic Catering, which had recently gone through privatisation. It also provided upgraded meals for executive travellers and meals for specific passengers groups such as children, diabetics, vegetarian, etc. All the refreshments are provided free of charge to both business and to economy passengers, which is not the case with most other charter airlines, who charge for drinks offered to economy class passengers and is very different to the low-cost carriers, who charge for everything extra that they provided on-board.

Regarding newspapers, Olympic Airways offered most of the Greek and international newspapers and magazines free of charge, with priority to the business passengers. The extras amounted to a significant differential advantage over low-cost carriers, many charter airlines as well as some scheduled airlines, who also offered less than Olympic Airways, but of course also added to the carrier's costs.

OAs on board passenger travel costs increased from 1990 but have also showed two periods of reduction between 1993-1995 and 1997-1999 due to the carrier's management strategy towards cost minimisation brought about through the introduction of the two restructuring plans. These cost reductions were achieved, through the carrier's management decision to re-design the food tray, removing some items and decreasing the size of some others to 'economise some funds and simultaneously not to change too much the image of the carrier's well-known food tray'.

Given the success of this differentiation strategy, Olympic Airways should continue to invest in upgrading its onboard service to achieve a differentiation advantage over its competitors. However, this investment should be combined with investment in other onboard facilities such as advanced flight entertainment, improvement of flight crew behaviour, upgrading aircraft's interior design, and so on, for the carrier to achieve a coherent advantage. It will also require the close and continuous monitoring of what the competitors do regarding their onboard services to maintain this. Finally, this needed the airline to inform its passengers about the advantages offered, the quality and quantity of onboard catering and refreshments provided, through advertising campaigns. This will, of course, have the effect of increasing both the onboard passenger travel costs as well as the promotion and advertising costs. However, the subsequent increase in passengers travelling on the higher price tickets should compensate.

Airbus A.340 SX-DFB *(Richard Vandervord)*

OA looked after not only their own aircraft, but also airliners for other companies.

Routine engine work was done in the Technical Base, but as with many other airlines, full engine overhaul was done at specialist companies elsewhere.

(all photos ΠΟΛΚ.ΕΟΑ)

Makis Tselios; fashion designer and artist from the Ionian Islands. He was born on the island of Ithaki. He created his own history through his innovative designs and unprecedented fashion shows which featuring international models. His designs for Olympic Airways uniforms were worn from 1992 until 1998. *(ΠΟΛΚ.ΕΟΑ)*

- In-flight entertainment costs

The costs associated with the video and radio facilities offered by Olympic Airways to its onboard travellers could not be under-estimated. For most of the 1990-1997 period, it was stable but increased in 1992-1994. This was caused by the introduction of video and audio equipment into the carrier's airliners and the purchase of two A300-600ER and one B737-400 with advanced audio and video facilities. In the following three years the airline did not spend as much because all the aircraft that were used for long flights already had advanced in-flight entertainment facilities.

The first restructuring plan and the lower competition mainly in the domestic network also contributed to this drop in costs between 1995 and 1997. The introduction of more modern and newer airliners such as the A340-300 at the beginning of 1999 with advanced technology video and audio facilities and the intense competition lead Olympic Airways to increase their investments in these services.

The improvements made in its in-flight entertainment on its long-haul routes, accompanied with the lower fares that the carrier offered was thought to be an attractive differential advantage over its competitors which would hopefully lead to increased load factors. Whether the increased revenues from adding these services to these routes would cover the higher costs remained to be seen.

Also, to achieve this differential advantage over competitors, Olympic Airways was going to have to spend more on this direction to compete with the other domestic competitor carrier, Aegean Airlines, which already offered an excellent in-flight product. This would further impact on costs and the likelihood of breaking even.

The Reports authors also stressed that in-flight entertainment alone did not make a difference. This service had to be backed up by courteous, friendly and helpful cabin crew which would add to training costs.

- Uniform Costs

Although this cost was not too high, the effectiveness of any uniform change is important, and any cutting of the expenses in this area should take place with due care as the appearance of an airline's employees is directly connected with a customer's image of that carrier.

Employee uniforms should not be considered in isolation; they must be combined with the appropriate customer-oriented behaviour.

Throughout the 1960s and 1970s, OA invested heavily in changes to the employee uniforms, particularly in Onassis era, and history shows that the staff were proud to wear outfits designed by fashion designers. This trend that was not continued in the 1980s with a resultant drop in morale. In the domestic market, Olympic was the dominant carrier during this period and in the more international routes the competition was limited, therefore, the airline just spent enough to keep its staff uniforms up to standard.

There was a significant increase in 1992, due to a campaign run by the carrier's management to improve its ground employee uniforms and to change its flight crew uniforms. In the following years, the airline significantly decreased these costs except for the years 1996 and 1997, when some additional money was spent re-designing the flight crew uniforms. In the years 1999 and 2000, this cost started to increase again due to increased competition, which has forced Olympic Airways to spend more money on its staff appearance in line with the competition.

The management consultants who prepared the Reports strongly suggested that Olympic Airways should, at a minimum, match the spending of competitors, to put forward a consistent message across its cost areas, and view expenditures on staff uniforms as means of showing that the carrier is interested in its employee's appearance, to improve the carrier's staff low morale. This should, in turn, mean that the staff offer a better service to its passengers.

- Reservation costs

A sophisticated computer reservation system (CRS) is an important marketing tool for airlines. Reservation costs are the money a carrier spends on maintaining and upgrading its CRS system as well as the booking fees that a carrier pays to the global distribution systems (GIDS).

In the dates covered by the early period of the Reports - 1990-1992 - there was nothing listed; just because the costs were too small. With the purchasing of the Swissair's CRS, a yield management system from Sabre in 1992, and of AIRFARE, a pricing system from SITA, by Olympic Airways this led to an increase in these costs from 1993 to 1997. The carrier also upgraded its own CRS, HERMES I, to the more advanced HERMES II in 1995, and, since October 1997, has invested more to promote its position in the global distribution systems (GDS).

The improvements in the CIRS allowed OA to implement new pricing policies that, through the appropriate yield management, contributed to an increase in the carrier's revenues. Despite the investment in the systems, they did not offer superior reservation services to its passengers and did not

From 1998 until 2005 Olympic wore uniforms by Artisti Italiani.(*ΠΟΛΚ.ΕΟΑ)*

achieve a differentiation advantage through their reservation services.

To be effective, an airline's reservation system had to be combined with fully trained and experienced members of staff to offer a superior service to travellers. Significant investments in the management needed to be directed to improve the service that this group of the employees provided to the carrier's passengers. These employees were the first point of contact for the carriers' customers. The Reports stated that OAs telephone reservations department appeared to offer opportunities for improvement: the number of 'not answered' calls were too high and, during peak season, the time waiting to be answered was also too long, a situation created by the shortage of qualified staff available since a large number of experienced personnel were made redundant in 1999, instead making use of temporary team who have had little training. In turn, this had a significant effect on company image and customer relations.

Planning for the extensive use of e-ticketing and reservations was at the embryonic stage at the turn of the century.

- Customer Complaints

This included passengers' compensation due to delayed and cancelled flights, lost baggage and ticketing/reservation mistakes. There had been a gradual, but constant increase, mostly due to the imposition of EU regulations since 1992 in favour of the customer.

Within Olympic, the majority of these compensations were caused by long flight delays, cancellations and missing baggage. Much less was caused by reservation and ticketing problems. The Reports authors suggested that improvements on the punctuality of its flights - especially international long-haul - and its baggage tracing and handling system would significantly help to reduce costs.

Also, compensation was typically paid a long time after a complaint - which generated more complaints about this delay - instead of being given at the airport when the passengers face the problems. Those compiling the restructuring reports thought this could be partly explained by the shortage of staff at Customer Services.

- Training Costs

Within the group, training was divided into two areas - technical and the area where human contact between the line personnel and consumers, the attitude, courtesy, and friendliness of flight crew, ticketing personnel and reservation staff can be more important to customers than the quality of food and entertainment served on board.

On the technical side, a reader of the restructuring reports got the impression that the management consultants somewhat regretted the significant funds spent in training flight crews on the new technology in the carrier's new airliners. Thus, when the carrier acquired or leased new aircraft flight crews were trained on the airliners new technology. The same happened with the carrier's engineers. Following the initial training abroad, a large number of educational programmes took place in Olympic Airways two aeroplane simulator centres, in Chania for Boeing 737-400 series and one in Thessaloniki for ATR.42 and 72s turboprops.

All type of training assisted employees to improve their abilities and deliver higher quality service to travellers. The training costs increased in 1999 when two educational programmes took place. The first one aimed to train all the managers who had recently taken their positions, to improve

A.300 SX-BED in an all-white scheme, with just company titles and logos. *(Richard Vandervord)*

their management abilities. The second plan was dedicated to educating all the airport staff in readiness for the transfer to the new Athens International Airport (AIA) in 2001. Thus, 2,134 employees were trained on the new facilities that the new airport provided such as passenger boarding, and the baggage handling system, etc. at the cost of 118 million drachmae.

The consultants strongly recommended that OA should offer its front-line employees more training to provide a higher level of service. The reports went on to state that this exercise should be used to motivate OA personnel to enhance their productivity and their morale.

Digesting the Reports - and Action?

Central to the vision of the new management was the drive to win back passenger numbers. Rather than placing all its attention on cutting costs and shrinking the airline's activities, the 1999 plan provided for the expansion and modernisation of Olympic's fleet, a thousand-strong increase of its workforce' and an aggressive restructuring of its network aiming to make Athína a significant transit route within the region, whilst retaining its long-distance routes. To finance this expansion, Speedwing were planning a mixture of borrowing and asset selling.

'There was a desire for change within the airline...' claimed Captain Gregory Konstantellos, General Secretary of the Pilots' Union, *'...We are very much behind the proposals put forward by the Speedwing team. Something had to be done, and it was clear that the existing management structure, with its levels of political interference, was not capable of forcing through the necessary changes. The BA management team is the last chance for Olympic Airways survival, and it has to identify where the problems have occurred in the past to make sure that they are not repeated. We do not have a dogmatic view on the question of privatisation – it holds no fears for us. We had to change the bad financial and organisational position and so it is only right to give these people, who know aviation, a chance.'*

The targets the Group was aiming for included:

- Development of Athens into a main Eastern Mediterranean hub.
- Development of Thessaloniki into Olympic's secondary hub.
- Improvement of Olympic's presence in the North Atlantic and Asian markets.
- Strengthening of Olympic's position in the main European markets.
- Penetration into new Middle East markets.
- Increase the commercial agreements with other airlines.
- Admission of Olympic into one of the major global alliances.

The emphasis on expansion afforded Rod Lynch a precarious truce with the influential pilots (EXPA) and flight attendants (EISF) unions (but not OSPA) and the full support of the Minister of Transport Tasos Mantelis. However, Speedwing's plans for expansion were met with scepticism by the Commission, which regarded them as a departure from the 1998 plan and the agreed aid. The Commission's advisors also expressed concern that they considered the forecast increases in the OA's revenues were 'too optimistic' and could not

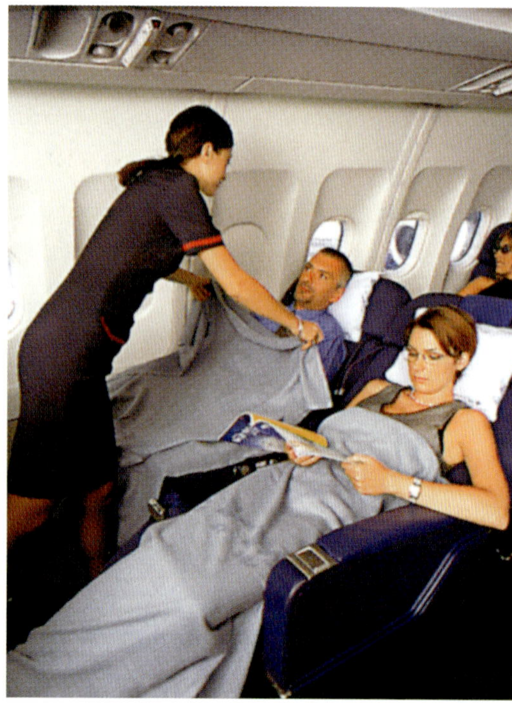

ensure the viability of the airline in the long run. With a general election less than six months away, Lynch had little time to prove whether his gamble would pay off.

Fleet renewal and route expansion

One of the major problems faced by Olympic was that of old equipment - a look at the fleet list by the Speedwing team revealed that many of the aircraft have been in service for over twenty years. Indeed, some of the Boeing 737s dated back as far as the late 1970s, and it is only with the introduction of the Srs 400 B737s in the mid-1990s, and latterly with the introduction of some Airbus A340s - that Olympic has started to make real progress with fleet renewal. The next stage would be the replacement of the Srs 200 B737s

The pictures on these pages come from the 'Company Profile' and show both aircraft interiors and the Business Class lounge at AIA. *(all ΠΟΛΚ.ΕΟΑ)*

and the Airbus A300s (by 2002); the two leased (from GE Capital Aviation Services) A300B4s were to be returned while the newer -605s were planned to be refurbished as part of the revitalised long-haul fleet.

The 737s served a wide range of European destinations, linking business centres and tourist destinations. However, as the Speedwing team revealed; *'The age of many of the Boeings means that we will need to look at a fleet renewal programme and to that end, we are in talks with Boeing regarding Next-Gen 737s and Airbus regarding the A320 family of aircraft. No decisions have yet been taken, and there are strong arguments to support each case.'*

The Boeing 747s were to be retired by the beginning of 2000, so giving the long-haul element an all-Airbus look. The airline had options on a further two A340s, and as its route structure plans continued to develop it was in a position to decide if, and when, these will be required.

Rod Lynch speaking to the media: *'On the long-haul route structure the intention is to consolidate our existing routes but increasing frequencies, for example, a double-daily Athens to New York. The number of other routes will increase to daily, and a few new routes will be added: for example, from next summer an Athens to Boston and Toronto via Manchester, although this may be code-shared with British Airways. We already have the traffic rights to Boston and are presently negotiating with the Canadians.'*

The long-haul fleet was expected to grow to around eight to ten aircraft. While this is not a large number for a major airline, with Olympic's impressive European route structure and feeder network - which became more effective with the

move to the new Athens International Airport in March 2001 - it was one with growth potential.

Meanwhile, Olympic Aviation was also in the process of fleet renewal and has recently acquired its first two jets - Boeing 717s, although it was thought that these possibly would not be in service long and would be disposed of when their three-year lease expired as the airline looked towards employing Regional Jets from 2002. Indeed, the acquisition of the 717s was seen by some within the carrier as a wrong decision made by the previous regime and one that was been followed through because of political pressure. Decisions on the future of the ATRs and the Do 228s depended on how the Olympic/Olympic Aviation feeder/hub concept developed at the new airport: the primary

Boeing 717-200 SX-BOB seen at Munich *(Richard Vandervord)*

intention was to offer morning and afternoon connections throughout Hellas. It was only with the more efficient, and reliable, two-runway arrangement at the new airport that the hub concept could be genuinely developed and it was one that was central to Olympic's plans.

Competition by deregulation

Early in 1999, the deregulation plans let the way open for aggressive start-up airlines such as Cronus, Air Greece and Aegean Airlines - the latter two of which were to merge under the Aegean title.

Aegean Airlines was founded as Aegean Aviation in 1987. It was originally a VIP/business air operation specialising in executive and air ambulance services. On 17 February 1992, it became the first airline to be issued with a Greek independent air operator's licence. After it was acquired by Vasilakis Group in 1994, Aegean Aviation commenced VIP flights from Athens all over the world with a Learjet aircraft. The Aegean Airlines name was adopted with the start of scheduled passenger services at the end of May 1999, flying from Athens to Heraklion, Crete and Thessaloniki with two brand-new British Aerospace Avro RJ100 BAe.146. In December 1999 Aegean also acquired Air Greece an airline that was established in 1994 by Cretan businessmen and started operations in the same year using two leased ATR72 turboprops on domestic routes. In April 1997 a third ATR72 was added to the fleet, followed by the lease of two Fokker 100's in May and June 1999. Delivery of the Fokkers marked the international expansion of the company and new routes to destinations in Germany were opened.

In 1999, passenger ferry company Minoan Lines acquired a 51% stake in Air Greece. However, at that time Air Greece was facing stiff competition from Aegean Airlines, Cronus Airlines and Olympic Airways, forcing it to begin a cooperation with Aegean which ended in a full takeover by Aegean in December 1999. During 2000, Air Greece's original owners made an unsuccessful attempt to launch Cretan Airways as its successor.

Cronus Airlines was established in 1994 by retired Air Force fighter pilot Captain Theodore Kokmotos, who started operation in 1995 with a single aircraft that flew flights targeting expatriate traffic between Hellas and Germany as well as chartered flights to popular tourist destinations. Two years later, Cronus leased more aircraft and expanded its network, gradually becoming the largest privately owned airline in Greece. In late December 1998, the Laskaridis family who owned a large fleet of refrigerator ships acquired a controlling 55% stake in Cronus. In spring 2001, a codeshare agreement was signed with Aegean Airlines, and a few months later Cronus' aircraft were painted in Aegean's livery carrying an AEGEAN Cronus logo. Eventually, Cronus was fully acquired by Aegean in October 2001, and its owners obtained a minority share in Aegean.

After an agreement in March 2001 to merge Aegean and Cronus Airlines, the company operated for a while as 'Aegean Cronus Airlines' until full integration. From 2005, the airline was in partnership with Lufthansa, offering participation in the Miles & More programme, and its flights, in addition to its A3 code also have the Lufthansa LH code. In March 2006, Aegean Airlines also entered into a co-operation agreement with TAP Portugal. In December 2008, Aegean Airlines announced its co-operation with Brussels Airlines.

The success of these airlines, most of which operated more modern equipment than that of Olympic, affected the national carrier's regional market share. Rod Lynch: *'We obviously keep an eye on all competition, but the market position in*

OA PEOPLE

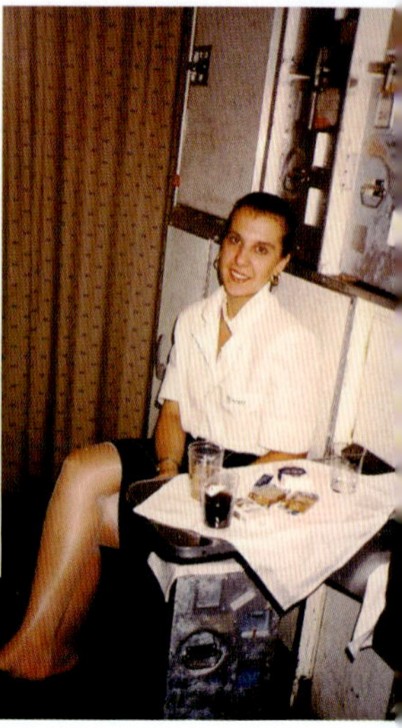

(all photos ΠΟΛΚ.ΕΟΑ)

this region, especially for low-cost operations, is unstable and immature and I am not convinced that there is much of a long-term future for such competition as it is likely that some of these start-ups were based on the assumption that Olympic had no real future and that they would, therefore, pick up the pieces.

There is, however, probably enough market share for one such efficient regional operator.

The international situation is somewhat more complicated, and Olympic does not see any threat in this market as in addition to the 'new look' Olympic (and its potential strategic partner and proposed alliance membership) there are enough active international competitors, especially Lufthansa, Alitalia and Austrian, to make this a very risky venture '.

Parliamentary elections were held in Hellas on 9 April 2000. The ruling Panhellenic Socialist Movement (PASOK) of Prime Minister Costas Simitis was narrowly re-elected, defeating the conservative New Democracy party. This brought to Simitis' new cabinet some fresh faces, including the new Minister of Transport and Telecommunications, Christos Verelis. A supporter of Premier Simitis, Verelis was keen to prove his modernising credentials to his new boss.

Olympic sell-off?

Within weeks of his arrival in the Ministry, Verelis announced the government's intention to sell off a stake in Olympic Airways to the private sector and it offered BA a 45-day deadline to exercise its option, under the 1999 deal, to buy a 20% share in the airline. The Minister's relationship with the British managers, however, was already showing signs of discord. Leaks suggested that Verelis was critical of Speedwing and that he doubted the sincerity of BA in acquiring a stake in Olympic, particularly in the aftermath of Rod Eddington's appointment as BA's CEO in May 2000. Thus, BA's announcement, on 2 June 2000, that it was no longer pursuing the deal with Olympic came as no surprise.

To his opponents, however, Verelis had made a huge miscalculation. Many blamed him for being too easily convinced by the unions' complaints of Speedwing's management and too ready to pass judgement on its performance. Even if the Minister was dissatisfied with Lynch's management, the 1999 agreement gave the Greek government the right to ask for his replacement (by BA), an option that was never used. Above all, Verelis stood accused of torpedoing the deal with BA without having secured a viable alternative. In the early 1990s, the Greek flag carrier had repelled the possibility of an alliance with Lufthansa, now it had lost another suitor.

Less than a year afier his arrival in Athína, Rod Lynch's Olympic adventure was over as Speedwing's managers were given two months to vacate their offices and leave the Greek airline. The departure of the BA management marked a new stage for OA and a clash of interpretations. For Verelis, the termination of the BA deal was a natural conclusion of what he regarded as inept management and a lack of commitment on behalf of BA.

In response to new situation, Verelis moved

OA went through a phase of putting their aircraft in special colour schemes, such as 737 SX-BKC...
(Richard Vandervord)

... or 737 SX-BKD *'Amphipoli'*also in the 2004 Olympic scheme. *(Richard Vandervord)*

quickly to announce the sell off of a majority stake of the whole Olympic Airways group - including subsidiaries - to a private investor who would also be solely responsible for the management of the airline. In an attempt to entice potential investors, Verelis also floated the idea that the government might be willing to assume all of Olympic's debts. In the meantime, Verelis announced that an independent consultant - Price Waterhouse Coopers - would undertake a financial audit of Olympic to offer transparency before the international tender for the sale of OA scheduled for late 2000. The new rescue plan for Olympic was received with dismay by the unions which feared that the government was planning further job cuts and accused Verelis of trying to sell off the airline 'on the cheap'.

As Verelis battled with the OA's unions at home, the reaction to his rescue plan in Brussels was mixed. The Commission criticised the Greek government over its compensation to Olympic for the move to the new Athina airport - scheduled for 1 March 2000 - and refused to release the third instalment of capital injection foreseen in 1994 restructuring plan. However, in the aftermath of Verelis' meeting with Commissioner for Transport, Loyola De Palacio, in October 2000 the Greek Minister appeared confident that the Commission would be willing to accept the write-off of OA's debts provided that such a move would lead to the transfer of the Greek flag carrier to private hands. Encouraged by what he perceived as the Commission's silent consent to his plan, Verelis pushed ahead with the publication of an international tender for the sale of the OA group in December 2000. The bid referred to the purchase of a majority stake in OA on condition that Olympic would: (a) continue to operate as an airline; (b) be based in Athina, and (c) keep the same name and logo. In exchange the Hellenic government undertook to cover all past debts of the airline and, crucially, to absorb any 'excessive OA staff' by re-employing it in other services in the wider public sector. The latter was a significant concession from the government's original proposals in the summer of 2000: Athina was making a big pitch for a sell-off.

Faced with a disappointing response to the international tender and confronted by mounting industrial unrest, the government, in July 2001, announced its decision to start negotiations with its preferred bidder Axon Airlines, a small private Greek airline owned by Thomas Liakounakos, while also continuing to talk with the other two shortlisted bidders. The government's hopes for a quick sale of Olympic Airways were soon to be dashed by the events of 9/ 11 and the subsequent global crisis that engulfed the airline industry. By February 2002 negotiations with all three shortlisted bidders had failed, leaving the Greek government in limbo. During the same period, pressure by the Commission also began to mount. Following a series of complaints by Olympic's competitors, the Commission announced its intention to launch a new investigation into state aid to Olympic and threatened that the Greek flag carrier might have to return to the government all state aid authorised since the 1994 restructuring plan, worth more than €31.5 billion.

As relations with the Commission continued to deteriorate, the government announced in February 2002 yet another plan for the rescue of Olympic. Acknowledging that the potential suitors of Olympic Airways were 'too small' to buy the entire OA group (including all its subsidiaries),

Verelis was now ready to accept a 'salami slicing' strategy for the privatisation of Olympic. According to the plan, the most profitable non-aviation subsidiaries of the OA group would be sold separately to private investors. At the same

Macedonian Airlines SA was a wholly owned subsidiary of Olympic.It was created in 1992 to operate charter flights to and from the Macedonian region of the country, using a pair of 727 and 737s leased from the parent. During the summer of 1999 a third 737 was leased from Pembroke Capital to operate not only charters but also sheduled services on behalf of OA.The fleet was repainted in 1999, with a yellow sun logo painted in the blue vertical fin.

Above: a crew poses on the stairs of their aircraft, whch bears the titles 'subsidiary of OLYMPIC AIRWAYS' below the cheatline.

Right: the 2001 holiday brochure for Macedonian.

Below: SX-CBH comes in for a landing.
(all photos ΠΟΛΚ.ΕΟΑ)

737 SX-BMA in the earlier Macedonian colours. *(Richard Vandervord)*

time, all aviation services performed by Olympic Airways and its subsidiaries would be merged under one company and sold off. To entice potential investors, the government also promised to terminate OA's loss-making route to Australia and absorb any staff that would not be needed by the airline's new owners.

Under the threat of a new Commission investigation and the possibility of being forced to return vast amounts of illegal state aid to the Greek government, the interest of potential investors in the purchase of Olympic was predictably limited and confined predominantly to a small group of Greek businessmen. In December 2002, Golden Aviation, a consortium led by Greek shipping tycoon Stamatis Restis, was announced as the government's preferred candidate to buy Olympic.

The initial optimism, however, that the final deal could be finalised within two months was shattered following the publication, in December 2002, of the Commission's decision on state aid to Olympic. In there, the Commission produced a damning report of the handling of Olympic's 'restructuring' since 1994. Whilst falling short of asking Olympic to return all state aid it had received from the Greek government since 1994 (worth over €1.5 billion), the Commission concluded that such aid was 'incompatible' with common market rules as the conditions (i.e. the restructuring of the airline) upon which it was initially authorised were never met.

Focusing on fresh allegations of illegal state aid since 1998, however, the Commission concluded that the Greek government should recover from Olympic the sum of €153 million that the airline received as aid in the form of preferential tax treatment over the period 1998-2002 as well as asked for the return of €41 million that Olympic collected in the summer of 1998 as part of the second instalment of the 1994 rescue plan.

The Hellenic Minister of Transport responded angrily to the Commission's decision and accused De Palacio of trying to shut down Olympic at a time when the government was negotiating its sale. Verelis insisted that the government would resist the Commission's decision all the way to the ECJ and that the new owners of the airline would not be burdened with €194 million that the Commission had asked OA to return to the Hellenic state. In the meantime, the carrier would continue to operate as usual. Despite Verelis' protestations, however, the cloud that the new Commission decision cast over the future of OA fatally undermined negotiations between the Hellenic government and Golden Aviation which, in February 2003, announced it was no longer interested in buying Olympic.

With the OA privatisation process in tatters and his relations with the Commission suffering a complete breakdown, Verelis then announced that the government would now seek to implement a solution for Olympic, similar to that for Swissair. He proposed a new company, called Olympic Airlines, which would take over all aviation activities of Olympic Airways. The new airline would service the full network of the 'old' Olympic, but it would be much smaller than its predecessor. It would employ a total of 1,850 staff (out of the 5,000 employed in the aviation side of the 'old' Olympic) all of which would have to sign new revised collective agreements with the new airline. These agreements would provide for salary cuts, and a much tighter employment regime in the new airline and they were designed to replace the complex and generous network of 240 sectoral and ad hoc agreements signed between the union and the management of the 'old' Olympic. Crucially, Olympic Airlines would be free from all debts of the 'old' Olympic which, by the end of 2001, had reached €500 million. These debts, together with the staff that would not join the new airline, would remain in the 'old' Olympic which would oversee an early retirement (or redeployment) scheme for excess personnel before eventually been closed down. The new plan also provided for the privatisation of all subsidiaries of the Olympic Airways group which, it was hoped, would generate enough proceeds to finance the OA's early retirement scheme as well as the return of €194 million of illegal state aid from the old Olympic to the Greek government (if Greece lost the case in the ECJ)

The travelling public's View of all this became a rebranding exercise, with the marketing consultants pushing the new vision in a document called 'Company Profile:

OLYMPIC AIRLINES, born out of the historical OLYMPIC AIRWAYS, established in 1957 by Aristotelis Onassis, incorporates the flight operations of Olympic Airways, Olympic Aviation and Macedonian Airlines.

Our fleet consists of 41 aircraft, connects Greece with 75 domestic and international destinations and our network is expanding with commercial agreements and codeshares with other major companies.

Since 1957 'our world turns around you', and the six Olympic circles carry the Greek spirit around the world.

From the times when flying used to be a wonderful adventure for the few, until nowadays, when air transportation is a popular and common way of travelling, Olympic has been close to every passenger, with affection and the most responsible care for transportation with absolute safety.

OLYMPIC AIRLINES have been valuated by international organizations as one of the safest airlines globally, a fact that is certified by the results of repetitive checks performed by both national and international authorities.

We apply strict and modern training programs for our flight crews, and it is known that our pilots are the most experienced ones.

Focusing on Olympic tradition and principles and especially on your transportation needs, we create our flight schedules in a way to allow your connection with every corner of the planet. OLYMPIC AIRLINES facing the challenges of the aviation market is targeting its continuous development.

Olympic celebrated 40 years with the launch of a hot-air balloon at a number of locations around the country. (OA files)

Within it, the company described it's new services - first, the 'Olympic Club' domestic flights: *'We created the 'Olympic Club' which ofiers you unique privileges. Park your car free of charge in the airport parking lot for 24 hours and take advantage of the luxuries offered by our VIP lounge. Have a light snack on your flight and enjoy the relaxation of our new Business Class Convertible seats that set new standards for modern aesthetics and comfort.*

It went on to describe 'Business Class' International flights for short, medium and long-range destinations: *'Olympic Airlines welcomes you to 'Business Class the Executive Class for International flights. Your travel is accompanied by a complete program of services, introducing you to maximum privileges.*

Sit comfortably on our Boeing B737 aircraft with their upgraded interior decor, where we have introduced a new type of roomier, convertible seat in Business Class, with height-adjustable headrests, deep seatback recline and footrest.Your privacy is ensured because you are separated from your neighbour by a wide cocktail table.

Become acquainted with our ultra-modern Airbus A340-300 fleet with special seat-beds, personal video screen, satellite phone and fax'.

Enjoy our enriched in-flight entertainment program featuring the most recent Hollywood movies.

Depending on your destination, we will serve you a meal comprising of many nutritious and healthful Mediterranean dishes.

Our menus are renewed every ten days, and our Mediterranean cuisine is adjusted to the tastes of your destination country. Olympic Airlines gives you the luxury of choosing from three diflerent, delicious menus, making sure that the options always include a light meal.

If the above suggestions do not cover your dietary needs, you may select your meal from specialised menus (e.g. vegetarian, low-fat etc.) when you make your reservation.

With the move to the new Athens International Airport, the new airline found itself able to offer *Business-Class passengers and holders of an Icarus Gold Card have the exclusive right to enjoy our VIP Lounges at all destinations abroad, and of course in Athens and Thessaloniki.*

In fact, at the Athens International Airport, we provide two luxury lounges with upgraded facilities and services, including:

- *Fully equipped Business Center with office services (conference rooms, computer use, e-mail and Internet access, telephones, faxes, photocopiers, etc.).*
- *Specially designed quiet areas with comfortable sleeper seats for enhanced comfort and relaxation.*
- *Dressing rooms and showers.*
- *Greek and international newspapers, library and reading room.*
- *Coffee, soft drinks, a selection of alcoholic beverages, known wine labels and tasty snacks.*
- *Areas designated for smokers and non-smokers.*

Economy Class passengers had not been overlooked: *'Welcome to Economy Class International, Olympic Airlines hospitality includes a program of services that will ensure you a pleasant flight, whatever your destination.*

Our modern aircraft, with improved cabin interior, ofler unique comfort by ensuring a distance of 32-34 inches between seats, a footrest and large seat back recline.

On the Airbus A340-300, the seats are equipped with personal video screens so that you can select your own program or latest future film on intercontinental flights.

Our new in-flight entertainment will provide information about your destination and will entertain you as well. Our international passengers will also be given a chance to learn some basic words and sentences in the Greek language.

You can expect a real treat at mealtime. Our top chefs have created dishes that will impress you from the first glance to the last mouthful. Mediterranean cuisine at its best....

In the aftermath of Verelis' announcements, the government came under a barrage of criticism from the OA unions. Despite the fact that the new plan did not refer to compulsory redundancies, the proposed salary cuts and job losses met huge opposition, particularly from the pilots union and the flight attendants union. The mathematics of the exercise were challenging. The 'old' Olympic had a total of 649 pilots and 1,100 flight attendants whereas the new plan provided for 420 and 600 vacancies respectively.

Captain Virgil Komnénó is just one example of those who got caught in the trap: *'I started 1969 employed as ground staff at Thessaloniki Airport. At that time we had DC-6s flying Athens - Thessaloniki. A bit later on we had the Boeing 727 flying once a week flying Athens - Thessaloniki - Frankfurt and back, which started with a big ceremony for it was an international service for us. Later on, they introduced a 707 from Athens - Thessaloniki - London. I was there until the end of 1971. For six months I was a Steward, and then in 1973, I got my flight licence.*

After that, I came back for an examination of candidate pilots in support of Olympic Airways sending me off to air training school. At that time the training manager was a Captain that I knew from the 727 when I was ground staff at Thessaloniki Airport. I came down to Ellinikon, over to the flight operations for an interview. I told them I had obtained an FAA licence in the USA. He said me I had to take the same examinations as all the other candidate pilots, but I was worried because I had away from the learning process for eight years or so.

Finally, I found work in Kinshasa down in Africa, flying a DC-4 for Societe Generale d'Alimentation - known as SGA. One of their aircraft, SX-DAG, had previously been operated by Olympic Airways. SGA was the most extensive food wholesaler and retailer in the region who sold cargo space on their aircraft when available. I also

Thessaloniki Airport - also known as Diethnis Aeroliménas Thessaloníkis 'Makedonía' dates back to World War I when the area that the airport currently occupies was used as an airfield and it continued operating as an airfield during World War II. At the time of the German occupation of Greece, major projects took place, such as the creation of a 600 m runway, while in 1948 the airport started operations as a civil airport for the first time. *(OA files)*

Right: Captain Virgil Komnénó seen during an interview in June 2017.*(author)*

flew a YS-11 down in Kinshasa and a CL-44. I got my captaincy on the DC-4 in 1976, a year later on the CL-44, and then in June 1977 I got a phone call from Olympic - I left with two suitcases, and came back to Greece. First on the YS-11, then 720, then four and a half years on the 727, the 707, eleven months on the Airbus A.300 as co-pilot, then back onto the 727 as Captain, then 737-400, Airbus 300-600, 747, then Airbus 340.

At the end of 2003, quite a number of us pilots were kicked out. I was a bit older than most of them; they owed me 50,000 euros. The plan was to calculate how many years each pilot had to reach the retirement age of 60. They estimated the basic salary, minus the pension - the balance they called 'loss of income'.

The move to the new airport.

Athens International Airport 'Eleftherios Venizelos' commonly initialized as 'AIA', began operation at 15:00 hours on 28 March 2001 for aircraft landings and at 00:01 hours on 29 March for both landings and take-offs. It is the primary international airport that serves the city of Athens and the region of Attica. It is Greece's busiest airport and it serves as the hub and main base of

Dash 8 SX-BIO. *(Richard Vandervord)*

Aegean Airlines as well as other Greek airlines.

AIA is located between the towns of Markopoulo, Koropi, Spata and Loutsa, about 20 km to the east of central Athens (30 km by road, due to intervening hills). The airport is named after Elefthérios Venizélos, the prominent Cretan political figure and Prime Minister of Greece, who made a significant contribution to the development of Greek aviation and the Hellenic Air Force in the 1930s.

The airport was constructed to replace Athens (Ellinikon) International Airport, as the latter had reached its saturation point with no physical space for further growth. Studies for a new airport had been carried out from as early as the 1970s, with as many as nineteen different locations being looked at before an area close to the town of Spata was chosen as suitable. Athens Airport SA, a state-owned company, was established in 1978 to proceed with the plans. However, after delays and slow development, the project was revived in 1991 with the then government launching an international tender for the selection of a build - own - operate - transfer partner for the airport project, with Hochtief of Germany being selected.

In 1996, Athens International Airport S.A. (AIA) was established as a Public/private partnership with a thirty-year concession agreement. That same year, the €2.1 billion development finally began with an estimated completion date of February 2001.

Work started at the site in July 1996, the earthmovers arriving the following month to carry out landfill operations and to slice the tops off two hills on the runway approach paths. One of these,

One of Olympic's leased 737, SP-LMD. *(Simon Peters Collection)*

from which forty metres had to be removed, proved to contain an important archaeological site - the Neolithic fortified site at Zaghani - and this had to be fully excavated and recorded before earthmoving could take place. The same is true of a number of other sites within the airport boundary, one of which proved to be the remains of a road that connected two of the Classical (5th century BC) sites in the area. The church of the Holy Apostles Peter and Paul - which dates from the fifteenth century was located in the area where the western runway was to be built, so this was moved in its entirety to a site outside the new aiport boundary. There is a small museum in the airport terminal that displays some of the artefacts.

Two parallel runways, both northeast/south-west (37/217 degrees) have been built at the airport, the easterly one being 4,000 metres and the westerly 3,800 metres long and both 45 metres wide, the one and a half kilometres between them being linked by taxiways and 'air bridges' over the central highway that bisected the site.

Construction was completed five months ahead of schedule but was delayed opening a month due to surface connections to Attiki Odos - the nearby motorway system - not being achieved.

The airport received approval from the European Aviation Safety Agency and the Federal Aviation Administration for take-offs and landings of the biggest passenger jet worldwide, the A380.

Olympic planned the move to the new airport to occur in stages. Ron Lynch of Speedwing, who were running Olympic at the time explained: *'Our intention was to be up and running at Spata on the pre-arranged 1 March 2001 opening date while running a full service from Ellinikon right up until changeover day. In order to do this we had to pre-position support elements there ready to be able to be in a prepared position. We were then able to move other elements, such as machine shops, by road to the new airport in the following months'.*

It was vitally important that as one airport opened the other closed, not only because the movement of personnel and equipment from one location to the other, but possibly of greater importance was that the approach patterns for one airport was at roughly ninety degrees to the other and there could be no traffic signals to control 'crossing traffic'!

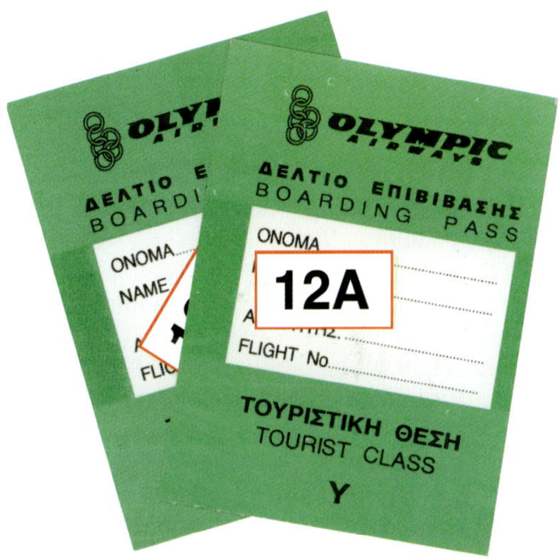

Right: with the advent of todays e-ticketing and the like as was introduced at the new airport, boarding cards such as these are a thing of the past.

Below: 'Eleftherios Venizelos' Airport starts to take shape. One of the two runways runs across the picture, with the terminal buildings and control tower off to the left. Olympic's new Technical Base is being built to the right of centre. Athens lies over the hills in the background.

‘Eleftherios Venizelos’ Airport. The port of Rafina is in the distance, with Marathonos off to the top left. The motorway, with railway in the middle of it is coming into the airport from the front left. *(Olympic Air)*

In actuality, for a period of nine hours - from 15:00 until 24:00 on 28 March both airports were open. On the night of 28/29 March the roads of the Attica basin were flooded with traffic as around five hundred trailer trucks moved equipment and material from Ellinikon to AIA.

Some 150 platform-trailers, 100 trucks and more than 200 other motorised vehicles created a special type of 'convoy' that rumbled through the streets of the capital on the Varis - Koropi road.

The new airport was opened officially in a ceremony on 27 March 2001, attended by the President of the Hellenic Republic Mr Konstantinos Stephanopoulos, the Prime Minister Mr K. Simitis, Archbishop Christodoulos of Athens and all Greece, virtually the entire Cabinet, political party leaders, officials and a large crowd.

The site of the new airport was decorated to welcome the guests. Giant screens permitted them to watch the ceremony from all points in the hall. An emotional recording of the voice of Eleftherios Venizelos was played at the opening ceremony explaining his vision of the growth of air transport in Hellas, and a small exhibition was opened containing some of Venizelos’s personal objects and manuscripts.

Outside, the opening ribbon was 'cut' by an Olympic Airways aircraft that sent it flying off into the air. The first Olympic Aviation aircraft, an ATR from Kythera, landed at the new airport at 15:10 on 28 March.

The next day the new airport was in full, regular operation, with aircraft taking off and landing but there were teething problems that had to be sorted out. A week after the 'Eleftherios Venizelos' opened, it found its pace; flight delays were limited and then gradually eliminated. The new airport did a splendid job of handling the increased passenger traffic in the period around the Easter holidays and was soon handling the summer tourist traffic perfectly normally.

A New Type and a new base

Back in 1998 Olympic Aviation started negotiations for the lease of a pair of airliners from Bavaria International Aircraft Leasing Company. Eventually, the first two 717-200 airliners on lease from Bavaria for Olympic Aviation were handed over in a ceremony at the Boeing Long Beach Division on 6 January 2000. Olympic was the first operator of the twin-engine jetliners in Europe.

The Boeing 717 was a twin-engine, single-aisle jet airliner, developed for the 100-seat market. The airliner was designed and marketed initially by McDonnell Douglas as the MD-95, a derivative of the DC-9 family from the 1960s. Capable of seating up to 134 passengers, the 717 had a design range of 3,815 km. It is powered by two Rolls-Royce BR715 turbofan engines mounted at the rear of the fuselage.

After McDonnell Douglas was acquired by Boeing in August 1997, most industry observers expected that Boeing would cancel development of the MD-95. However, Boeing decided to go forward with the design under a new name, Boeing 717. While it appeared that Boeing had skipped the 717 model designation when the 720 and the 727 followed the 707, the 717 name was the company's model number for the KC-135 Stratotanker tanker aircraft. 717 had also been used to promote an early design of the 720 to airlines before it was modified to meet market demands. The lack of widespread use of the 717 name left it available for rebranding the MD-95.

Painted in a distinctive livery featuring colourful interlocking rings on the aeroplane tail sections, the airliners were scheduled to enter passenger service by the end of January 2000.

Petros Stefanou, the chief executive officer of Olympic Aviation, said the airline planned to expand its route network regionally, using the 717s from Thessaloniki to Amsterdam, Berlin, Brussels, Munich, Paris, Stuttgart, and Larnaca, Cyprus. Olympic Aviation is configured its 717s with 34 seats in business class and 71 in economy.

Jerry Callaghan, director, 717 programs, told an audience of employees, leasing company and airline officials, *'Olympic Aviation will provide the first regularly scheduled service for the 717 outside the United States. We believe the flying public in Europe will embrace the airplane's quiet and clean performance as well as its high comfort level as enthusiastically as travellers here in this country.'*

Karsten Sensen, managing director of Bavaria International Aircraft Leasing Company, said, *'The 717 is based on the robust design of the Douglas twinjets, and it incorporates modern technology and new engines. I am pleased to see it is proving itself in service, and I believe it will meet all our*

On 6 April 2001The ATR-72 SX-BIL *Melina-Ellada* captained by Mr Vas. Katiniotis, director of Flight Simulation, with co-pilot Mr. St. Zacharakos, and passengers Mr Petros Stephanou CEO of Olympic Aviation, and Mr. Alex. Thanopoulos, its General Director of Flight Operations made the first test flight into the new Athens International Airport. *(Olympic Air)*

On 28 January 2001, Olympic Aviation took delivery of a third B.717-200 aircraft; however, the christening ceremony - where it as given the name *'Iridanos'* did not happen until 2 April 2001 at the company's new Technical Base at the 'Eleftherios Venizelos' airport, was attended by many people including the political leadership of the Ministry of Transport and Communications, the administration of the Olympic Airways Group of companies, general directors of its subsidiaries, the management of the Civil Aviation Service, the management of the Eleftherios Venizelos international airport, a large number of working people and multitude of guests.

Left: Christos Verelis 'cuts the ribbon', delcaring the facility open. *(both Olympic Air)*

expectations with Olympic Aviation.'

The official opening of Olympic Aviation's new technical installations at the new Athens International Airport in Spata took place on 2 April 2001 at the same time as the christening ceremony of the third Boeing 717-200 to be incorporated into the Company's fleet. The plane was christened 'Iridanos' by Minister of Transport and Communications, Christos Verelis.

The Olympic Aviation building complex at Eleftherios Venizelos airport covered an area of

7500 square metres and had roofed areas of 17000 square metres of which 4500 square metres belong to the Technical Base, which has an opening of 100 metres, a depth of 45 metres and a height of 13.60 metres, and is capable of servicing aircraft including ATRs, B717s , B737s and A320s.

The hangar is adjacent to a three-storey office building which has a total area of about 12, 500 square metres, in which all Olympic Aviation services were accommodated. The working areas were spacious, meeting all specifications for airline services and equipment, with the modern aesthetics and provisions necessary for the smooth operation of the company.

The construction of the new Olympic Aviation building was awarded, under the design-construction system after public competition, to the lowest tender, to the construction company GEK S.A. The relevant contract was signed on 26 June 2000 and provided that the project, which had a budget of 3,200,000,000 drachmas, would be completed in two phases: the first included the delivery of the Technical Base before the new airport went into operation. The second phase included the office complex, in which the company's administrative and financial services would be housed, which is expected to be completed within the year.

Nine months after the signing of the contract, the Olympic Aviation Technical Base was completed and operating, not only to serve Olympic Aviation but also contributing to the smooth operation of the new airport, with its modern installations and specialised personnel.

With this building complex, Olympic Aviation has acquired its own model installations, for the first time in its history, which will house the entire company's organisation and operation. The role and goals of Olympic Aviation have changed to keep pace with the new competitive environment, as stressed by Mr Petros Stephanou, Olympic Aviation's CEO.

He also added that, over the past three years, the company has evolved in accordance with the 1998-2003 Business Plan. From an exclusive air carrier for remote islands, it gradually developed into an international regional air carrier with a profitable prospect, with the goal of covering the domestic and new international regional network, to the benefit of the entire Olympic Airways group.

The new Olympic Aviation Technical Base was certified as a Maintenance Organisation in accordance with European legislation when the new airport entered into operation, thus constituting a significant project on a nationwide level. It is one of the basic infrastructure works not only for Olympic Aviation and the OA Group, but also regarding the entire airport.

Present at the official opening ceremony, in addition to Mr Christos Verelis, Minister of Transport and Communications, was the Olympic Aviation management, the management of the new international airport, many employees and, a multitude of guests.

Pride within the company.

In spite of the roller-coaster ride the employees of the Olympic Group had been forced to travel by their political and financial masters, there was still a tremendous pride and spirit within the airline - that sense of φιλότιμο (philotimo) - which is considered the highest of all Greek virtues, the standards for family and social living; the core concept is that of respect and walking in right paths. In its simplest form, the term means 'doing good', actions that ensure that a person's behaviour be exemplary and demonstrate his personality and the manner in which he was raised. Philotimo to a Greek is essentially a way of life. Stella Rapti waxed lyrical in a piece in *Messenger*, the Olympic house magazine:

Olympic Airways: Priority, the happy Customer.
'A passenger is always the oficial guest who deserves and is entitled to the best possible service. This was also the ultimate goal of creating all the Olympic Airways subsidiaries: Olympic Tourism, Macedonian Airlines charter flights, Olympic Catering and Olympic Aviation.

Since the days of airliners flying over the Alps and the passengers literally froze from the cold, when many people wanted to carry their animals in the cabin as hand luggage, a lot of water has passed under the bridge. The passenger is the centre of all the Olympic Airways flights. Impeccable service both in the air and on the ground remains the only priority.

Other people and passengers, for their part, prefer Olympic, they love it. They love her people; they love to accept their care. Aristotle Onassis did not hesitate to provide the best for the travelling public. On European routes, he had demanded that the food was served with gold-plated cutlery and where possible a candle on the tables created a romantic and lightweight atmosphere.

As long as Onassis owned the company, he intended to put a piano on the B.707 and the B.747. From his experience in the world's most expensive and expensive resorts and hotels, but also from his travels with competing airlines, he knew that what would difierentiate Olympic Airways would be the behaviour of the staff who, as he used to say, 'it

A company A.340 taxies over an airbridge that gives the motorway and railway access to the airport.*(OA files)*

had to smell Greece'. Care and warmth was the slogan. A smile by the staff at the top of the steps at the time of boarding and a polite 'thank you' at the end of the trip.

The feeling that you read clearly in the confident and accountable behaviour of well-trained staff helps passengers feel safe and secure. This is because the Olympic Airways' personality is not only selected with strict criteria but above all because it is regularly updated with all new air traffic data. Certainly, it is no accident that Olympic is considered by the most trustworthy and carefree companies in the world. Great success is not only due to the capability of pilots but also to the high level of technical services of the company.

Throwing glimpses in the past, making a stop in the present and guiding the future, in those fifty years of her life, Olympic Airways has shown that everything returns to the same core: Man. He proved not to be a cranky, cold companion, but a living organism, a living chain, which consists of links inseparably linked to one another, each of which has reason to exist.

In front of the tireless efforts of the Olympic Airways employees, in front of their own psyche for the company's progress, which they consider to go along with their own, they lure the the passengers which in turn increases the numbers of growth.

On 16 September 2008, the Government announced a significant restructuring of Olympic Airlines, using the 'Pantheon Airways' plan to relaunch Olympic as a private airline. Pantheon would operate parallel to Olympic Airlines until April 2009, when Olympic Airlines would be shut down, and Pantheon would take over most of its routes. Pantheon would then be renamed using the 'Olympic' brand name and its six-rings logo. The new Olympic Air would not be a legal successor to Olympic Airlines or Airways, taking up none of the former employees or assets directly.

In February 2009, an international tender concerning the sale of the three companies and the assets of the Olympic Airlines Group (Flight Operations, Technical Base, Ground Handling Operations) and Pantheon Airways collapsed, as the offers presented by the candidates were deemed not satisfactory by the government. After the collapse of this attempt to sell the company, former Transport Minister Kostis Hatzidakis extended an invitation to financial groups to proceed to direct negotiations for the sale of the Group.

Chapter Ten

Towards the End Game

By February 2009 Olympic Airways was in deep trouble, having accumulated more than €2.7 billion of debt.

First to respond to Transport Minister Kostis Hatzidakis invitation was the Marfin Investment Group (MIG), who were seen as the most significant investment fund of Greece, and who submitted an offer to buy the flight operations and technical base of the Group. Also, Swissport, a Swiss aviation services company who provided airport ground and cargo handling services, headquartered in Opfikon, Switzerland, sent an offer to buy the ground handling operations. After three weeks of negotiations with MIG, on 4 March 2009, Aegean Airlines and the Greek-American consortium operating under the umbrella organisation of Chrysler Aviation headquartered at Southern California's Van Nuys Airport, also submitted offers to buy the Group. However, Aegean Airlines‘ offer was not accepted as the new airline would control over 95% of domestic routes, while the government's financial advisors could not determine whether Chrysler Aviation was in the financial position to support its bid.

The situation was more pressing than ever and Marfin Investment Group (MIG), Greece's largest holding and buy-out company, seemed to be the last and only white knight. While Olympic had more than five decades of experience, it was seen to have an extremely bloated workforce of about 8,000 employees. The most recent attempt to sell the carrier was approved by the European Commission that agreed to suspend action over illegal state subsidies if a sale went ahead.

But Minister of Transport and Communications Kostis Hatzidakis, finally admitted: '*The tender was void. We did not receive the offers we hoped for. We are moving to a new stage for the sale of Olympic*'.

The Group was facing the prospect of an unbecoming death spiral if a local private investor does not come to the rescue by injecting capital, appointing better management and applying an appropriate strategy to turn it around.'

The Greek government's final gambit was to appeal to local businesspeople to enter into direct negotiations to acquire the ailing airline after its spectacular failure to sell it to an international group.

'*MIG decided to respond to the Greek privatisation committee's call and was to conduct direct talks so that Olympic could continue to operate as a Greek enterprise*', MIG said in a filing to the Athens Stock Exchange. Dubai Group,

Left: Hellenic Transport and Communications Minister Kostis Hatzidakis He served from 2007 to 2009 and then as Minister for Development in 2009.

Right: The lawyer turned businessman - Marfin Investment Group (MIG) president Andreas Vgenopoulos. He was later to fall from grace surrounded by scandals.

A.320 SX-OAT comes in to land. *(Richard Vandervord)*

the Gulf state's investment arm, held a seventeen percent stake in Marfin.

MIG submitted a somewhat complicated binding offer of €45 .7 million for the transport services of the airline, €16.7 million for the maintenance unit of the carrier and €70 million for Pantheon Airways, the company that held the rights, names and trademarks of Olympic. It was reported in the Hellenic press that if MIG wished to acquire the carrier's aircraft it had to raise its offer by 90.3 million euros, but it was thought that they were more likely to opt for new machines. Additionally, Swissport has placed a 44.8 million euro offer for Olympics' ground handling services.

The media reported that all of the debt liabilities of the airline were to be undertaken by the Hellenic state which would also be paying for a voluntary redundancy scheme for any employees that MIG did not need. They, the employees, would get some substantial payoffs or re-appointments to other public service jobs.

The total offer for all the segments of the airline stood at €77.2 million which sources close to the government were reported as claiming that it was close to the asking price. Nevertheless, some details still needed to be resolved - like how the company would be restructured to become profitable and the intentions of the bidder regarding adjusting the Olympic's business model.

MIG appeared to have an excellent chance to acquire the carrier given the absence of any other serious interest for Olympic, for it was doubtful that the Greek government would get another chance to sell the airline under the then current market conditions unless they accepted the offer of entrepreneur and MIG Vice-President, Andreas Vgenopoulos.

Dimitris Anastassakos, an investor relations officer at MIG, told the media: '*...we will be making some proposals to the state that we want to be accepted, and we will be exploring the detailed conditions of the state's privatisation process*'. He went on to state that MIG had in place a team of experts to analyse the potential investment. *'If we buy Olympic, we will be doing so without its current debts, legacy costs and staff. Some of the staff may be asked to remain but on new terms and conditions and the rest of the current workforce will have to be dealt with by the state since that won't be our responsibility,'*

There was severe pressure on the Hellenic state to complete the deal quickly to offload the continuing losses as well as removing the growing impatience of the European authorities. Politicians had previously claimed that for every day that Olympic operated in its current state the Hellenic taxpayer was burdened with another one million euro of costs.

Just like Onassis before him, Vgenopoulos metaphorically wrapped himself in the blue and white flag by referring to his patriotic duty to promote Greece's image and hold the flag of the national carrier up high in the clouds. *'Olympic's operations are of vital importance to the Hellenic tourism industry, employment, national sentiment and Greece's status in the international investment community,'* he said. Nevertheless, Vgenopoulos was careful to avoid generating any political controversy over the acquisition. He met with the principal opposition socialist party president, George Papandreou, and was given enough assurance and a low key blessing for his initiative political sources were supposed to have said. At the time, it was said that Vgenopoulos was supposed to be open to a partial re-nationalisation of the carrier if socialist PASOK came to power.

Analyst Panayiotis Kladis of National P&K Securities, considered to be a foremost expert on Marfin took a more cautious view of MIG's intentions regarding Olympic. *'Given MIG's track record I find it hard to believe that if they do invest that they will hold onto Olympic for very long. MIG tends to emphasise a trading as opposed to buy and hold strategy'*.

He went on to say that he suspected that this was partly a communication exercise to improve MIG's relations with the state, as well as raising their favourable profile with the Greek public. This sentiment was rebutted by MIG's Dimitris Anastassakos, saying this was not the case for significant holding company investments. He

It could only be one airport - Skiathos 'Alexandros Papadiamantis' . This is on a small Greek island in the northwest Aegean Sea. Skiathos is the westernmost island in the Notthem Sporades group, east of the Pelion peninsula in Magnesia on the mainland, and west of the island of Skopelos. The runway was built by reclaiming land from the sea between Skiathos and the smaller island of Lazareta (a former leper colony) effectively joining the two islands into one larger island.

Left: a View from the sea looking up the runway (author).

Below: A320 SX-OAU comes in to land at Skiathos. *(Richard Vandervord)*

DHC Dash 8 SX-OBG comes in to land. *(Richard Vandervord)*

thought the market had misunderstood and judged MIG rather harshly because previously they were in effect forced to dispose of their considerable interest in Greek Telecom group Οργανισμός Τηλεπικοινωνιών Ελλάδος Α.Ε. - Hellenic Telecommunications Organisation S.A., or OTE due to indiscriminate regulatory blocking action.

Panayiotis Kladis speaking at the time: '*As a strategy, entering aviation will not be easy for MIG because at the moment they don't currently have the deep skillset necessary to run an airline, they may be looking for the right executives to manage Olympic. Furthermore, aviation is a business with significant challenges and not one that is easy to make profits in*'.

There were also rumours that MIG was asked to close the deal by that autumn, giving them enough time to prepare for revamping the fleet and the operational management.

Expert sources reported that MIG had about €800 million in cash and it has access to another €200 million in capital from its subsidiaries. Therefore, buying Olympic would not stretch its balance sheet and was unlikely to make a massive impact on its operating performance. But MIG may eventually buy the carrier in a consortium with several Greek shipping magnates where others take minority stakes.

The ruling New Democracy government was secretly praying that high profile former lawyer Vgenopoulos would pick up where the Onassis legacy left off after Olympic was run into the ground through past government nepotism and corrupt permanent public service appointments. The government knew that the sooner it was out of public hands - the better.

Kladis added: '*In my view buying Olympic is a risky bet for MIG. Let's all hope that the bet comes to fruition and pays off*' *because otherwise, we could lose a historic Hellenic icon*'.

On 6 March 2009, Hatzidakis announced the sale of the flight operations and the technical base companies to MIG. The negotiations with Swissport continued for another week, to facilitate a hoped-for commercial agreement between MIG and Swissport. However, a deal was not reached, and MIG announced it would take over Olympic's ground handling operations as well. As a result, after thirty-five years of state control and ten years of failed sale attempts, Olympic returned to being a private corporation. The new owners planned to secure approximately 4,000 of the 8,500 jobs of the Group.

As part of its deal with the Greek state, MIG purchased the assets of Pantheon Airways, some of the valuable slots of Olympic Airlines in New York, London, Paris, Rome, Frankfurt, Brussels and Bucharest, as well as exclusive rights to the 'Olympic' brand name and the six rings logo. It also acquired the right to use the two hangars, the cargo unit of Olympic Airways Services and other facilities at Athens International Airport for twenty-five years. The new airline planned to only retain 65% of the flight operations compared to Olympic's flight operations in summer 2008, following a rule imposed by the EU during the approval of the sale. It also had to give up its monopoly on the currently operated state-subsidised island routes, and equally share them with other Greek airlines.

The Birth of Olympic Air

The world did not have long to wait to see MIG's plans. There was a flurry of announcements: Olympic Handling, as the new ground handling company was named, commenced its operations on 29 June, followed by the new technical base company, Olympic Engineering and finally, on 29 September, the new airline, officially called Olympic Air. As Olympic Air's CEO Antonis Simigdalas, formerly with Aegean Airlines said *'You can't throw away a brand as strong as Olympic.'*

The new name of the company was announced during a solicitation exercise calling for tenders to modernise and redesign the logo of the new airline. This bid followed a previous one that called for fashion designers to submit their designs for the new uniforms of the carrier. Shortly after the deal was struck, MIG announced the recruitment process for the three new companies, as well as new tenders for the acquisition or lease of new aircraft.

Olympic Air ordered eight new next-generation Bombardier Q400 during the 2009 Paris Air Show, four of which will be the Q400 NextGen, with options on a further eight which were set to cover domestic and Balkan routes with delivery dates commencing in July 2010. Olympic leased fourteen Airbus A320 airliners for its entry into service in September 2009.

One of the European Union's stipulations for the privatisation of Olympic was the removal of 35% of the old airline's available seat kilometres (ASKS). Accordingly, Olympic Air ceased intercontinental flights and began life as a significant regional carrier.

In a press conference on 17 September 2009, MIG president Andreas Vgenopoulos announced new codeshare deals and stated that Olympic Air also planned to join SkyTeam in the future.

Vgenopoulos appeared to have grandiose plans: he wanted to make the company a regional leader, and later, one of the largest airlines in the world. Olympic Air planned to employ around five thousand staff, some of which included staff employed under the state carrier, with newly negotiated contracts. Furthermore, Vgenopoulos stated the company would honour its commitment to give the new government three months to re-nationalise Olympic if it desired. Vgenopoulos also noted that a new aircraft order would be announced soon, to replace the current aircraft once their leases ran out.

A symbolic 'inaugural flight' took place on 1

'OA 456 line up and hold' DHC Dash 8 SX-OBG at Kefalonia Airport 'Anna Pollatou'. *(Richard Vandervord)*

DHC Dash 8 SX-OBC at Kefalonia Airport 'Anna Pollatou'. *(Richard Vandervord)*

October 2009, during which MIG president Andreas Vgenopoulos stated that Olympic Air still held the exclusive rights to the Macedonian Airlines brand name, and plans to relaunch the airline as a subsidiary of Olympic Air. The new subsidiary would begin offering scheduled services from Thessaloniki to Moscow, London, Paris, Amsterdam, and a German city, starting by April 2010.

Vgenopoulos went on to tell the media that the airline's chief agenda was working to change the image many still hold of Olympic as an *'unfriendly, delay-plagued, loss-making carrier. That's why Olympic Air has started an international marketing campaign emphasising our new image.'*

MIG won the bidding for Olympic last March with an offer worth €177.2 million, beating main domestic rival Aegean Airlines and US-based Chrysler Aviation. The agreement followed the conservative government's public appeal to investors, after a previous tender - the sixth attempt to privatise the ailing flag carrier - failed to attract sufficiently high bids.

Under 35 years of state management, the former Olympic had become a tragic figure, weighed down by accumulated debts estimated at €2.7 billion and was losing €1 million a day.

Antonis Simigdalas signs a deal with Bombardier for acquring a number of the new Q400s. *(Olympic Air)*

The 'opening party' for Olympic Air at Elefthérios Venizélos Airport on 15 October. *(OA files)*

Olympic Air has already negotiated several partnership arrangements, with Air France-KLM, Delta Air Lines, Etihad Airways, Flybaboo, and Cyprus Airways. Long-haul services may be added at a later date, though. 'We have some initial plans, but they are modest - and some way off,' the CEO revealled.

Summing up the philosophy of Olympic Air with an underlying message of optimism, Antonis Simigdalas said, *'We are an example of how airlines right across Europe can cooperate with each other.'* Europe's newest flag carrier was officially launched on 15 October at a huge glitzy party in a hangar at Athens International Airport. More than 8,000 people attended with entertainment provided by 2005 Eurovision Song Contest winner, the Swedish- Greek Elena Paparizou, and members of Cirque du Soleil, whose fitting performance involved hoops symbolising Olympic 's six-ring logo.

In something of a sustained media blitz following the launch, CEO Antonis Simigdalas stated that Olympic was carrying around 10,000 passengers a day with a domestic market share of about thirty percent; the new Olympic Air was about thirty-five percent smaller than the old Olympic Airlines, that they were planning its long-haul flights, within the next twelve months and that they were expecting to make their first profits in 2012. He claimed Olympic Air's load factors were around 60% with 'decent' yields, but, what's paramount at present is to operate with efficiency and a high level of service. *'We are already transporting 10,000 passengers daily and trying just to do basic things, fly on time, and smile at people.'*

Less than two months later he was telling Flight International that Olympic Air's domestic market share had grown to forty-seven percent by December 2009 and that the airline was predicted to break even in 2011.

On 6 December 2009, Olympic Air announced that it has been chosen as the official carrier of the Hellenic Olympic Committee for three years from 2010 to 2012. Through this sponsorship, Olympic Air has committed to provide free transportation of Greek Olympic delegations to the 2010 Winter Olympics in Vancouver and 2012 Summer Olympics in London. On 10 December 2009, the company announced that mobile phone check-in was now available for flights departing Athens Airport, making Olympic the first Greek airline to offer this service. As part of its corporate responsibility programme, Olympic announced *'A Day at the Museum'*, transporting 3500 students from Cyprus to the new Acropolis Museum in Athens, starting from 29 January 2010.

Olympic Air had already negotiated several partnership arrangements, with a number of other carriers. As Antonis Simigdalas told the media: *'Long-haul services may be added at a later date, though. We have some initial plans, but they are modest - and some way off'*. The next year Olympic Air announced the start of a premium economy service on its fleet of Bombardier Q400 aircraft for domestic and selected international flights, in addition to its business class service.

Dash 8 to Kalymnos

Many claim that the domestic island services should be regarded as PSOS — Public Service Obligation flights. That may be the case, but they do save a lot of that most precious commodity, time. The services have also freed many of the islands from the strangulation of that most dreaded means of travel — well for me anyway, for I did more than my fair share of island-hopping back in the 1970s - the inter-island ferry! A typical example of this was a trip I took to the island of Kalymnos. I had two options open to me; from home via central London to Gatwick, a low—cost carrier cattle—truck flight to Kos, coach transfer to Kos town, an overnight stay there until catching the midday ferry across the channel to Pothia, the capital of Kalymnos and another coach transfer to where we were staying. It would have been a twenty-nine-hour journey.

The alternative - which was much more appealing to me - was to sample an Olympic Air DHC Bombardier Dash 8-100 flight direct from Athens Eleftherios Venizelos Airport to Kalymnos National Airport. This entailed a journey from home via London to Heathrow, to catch a scheduled service Aegean Airlines A321 flight to Athens, with a four-hour sojourn in the 'MacDonalds Lounge' at Eleftherios Venizelos (seasoned travellers to Hellas know all about this delightful if discrete lounge on the upper level) before checking in for the Dash 8 flight scheduled to depart at 06.10. This resulted in a door-to-door transit time of slightly under thirteen hours!

We had been checked in and cleared along with our bags direct through to Kalymnos National at Heathrow, so we remained airside at Athens Eleftherios Venizelos until the gate for flight OA12 was announced - the 'Gate' in this instance being a loading lounge for a shuttle-bus out to the remote stands and the waiting Dash 8 - SX-BIR. Boarding was quick and straightforward, and as the sky started to lighten on the horizon, our Captain started the pair of Pratt & Whitney turboprops, and we taxied out over one of the airbridges crossing the E62 highway for the long trek down the taxiway to the start of Runway 03L.

Sunrise over Athens Eleftherios Venizelos as Dash 8 SX-BIR climbs steeply away in the early morning light. Central in the picture is the remote parking stands, used by Olympic Air for their Dash 8s and ATRs. Off to the left is the hangar complex built for Olympic Airways. *(author)*

The take-off was swift and steep, using not half of the runway as the sun rose, showing the Dash 8 making a right-hand turn just before reaching the port town of Rafina. We soon reached our cruising altitude. It was time for the single air hostess, Despina Doxopoulou, to serve the traditional orange juice and pack of biscuits. It was not long before Captain Theodordatos started a gentle descent using part of the Kos Approach pattern to overfly the airfield then visually make a curving left-hand turn, overflying the island capital Pothia. Once over the harbour, he lined up with Runway 03. Glancing out of the window, the approach seemed a little high as he took us down what appeared to be a relatively broad valley as the ground reared up either side of us. We started bouncing around in the turbulence. By now Miss Doxopoulou - who had strapped herself into the rearward-facing crew jumpseat on the forward bulkhead was beginning to look just slightly nervous.

Kalymnos Island National Airport is 'interesting' to say the least. Aircraft do not descend to land on it; as can be seen it is more that the land comes up to meet the pilots! The approach is usually from the left of the picture below on to the 28 end of the 1,035 metre long runway. Pilots tend to use the Potmoi road out of Pothia (above right) as an approach marker! *(author)*

Up and Away! SX-BIO launches into the air from the seaward end of Kalymnos Island National Airport.

The view from onboard as the aircraft leaves the ramp. *(both author)*

Looking almost straight down out of the window I suddenly saw the road we appeared to have been following for the last few moments change into a rocky hillside that rapidly climbed up to reach us despite the aircraft appearing to hold the same rate of descent, then in a flash we were over the runway turnaround and thumping down on the runway, the props quickly changing to reverse pitch - welcome to Kalymnos Island National Airport!

A quick back-track down the runway followed by a left-hand turn, and we were parking on the apron by the small terminal building. Although it was not yet 7 am, the air was already hot. It took less than ten minutes to get our bags, and we were then on our way with friends to where we were staying.

The return trip aboard OAl5, flown by SX-BIO was just about as quick - the 'launch' off the end of the runway at Kalymnos was akin to departing from an aircraft carrier! The transfer at Eleftherios Venizelos was faster, there only being ninety minutes to wait before boarding the Aegean A321 back to London Heathrow.

Attempted merger with Aegean Airlines

In February 2010, initial shareholder discussions took place to consider cooperation between significant competitor Aegean Airlines and Olympic Air, fueling rumours of a possible merger. On 22 February 2010, Olympic Air and Aegean Airlines announced that they had agreed to a merger. The new airline would carry the Olympic name and logo, after a transition period in which both airline brands would be used in parallel. The Aegean brand would cease to exist after the transition. Furthermore, Olympic Ground Handling and Olympic Engineering would become subsidiaries of the new company.

The sole shareholder of Olympic Air, Marfin Investment Group, and the main shareholder of Aegean, the Vassilakis Group, would have an equal shareholding of 26.6% in the combined entity, while the groups of Messrs Laskaridis, V. Constantakopoulos, G. David and L. Ioannou, as well as Piraeus Bank, would all maintain their proportional equity participation in the form of a 46.8% stake in the new company, thus giving Aegean an 73.4% stake overall in the new company that would be listed on the Athens Stock Exchange. A decision on the merger was initially expected be given from the European Competitions Commission by the end of September 2010.

According to press releases by Aegean and MIG, Aegean Chairman Theodoros Vassilakis and Olympic Chairman and CEO Andreas Vgenopoulos were expected to lead the new company. Vassilakis stated that the merger was brought on by the size of their competitors in the EU, which made it necessary for Greece's two leading airlines to merge to create a national airline champion with an increased presence in the European market as well as seamless coverage of even the most remote Greek islands. Vgenopoulos further stated that the merger also would preserve and strengthen the Olympic brand name, an integral piece of Greek national tradition.

At the time of the merger announcement, Aegean was in the process of becoming a full Star Alliance member, while Olympic Air was forging ties with SkyTeam pre-merger. Despite this, it was announced that Aegean's Star Alliance process would continue with the airlines working to guarantee a smooth transition of the merged carrier into the Star Alliance, who welcomed the proposed merger in a press release: *'The integration teams from both sides will soon meet to assess the necessary steps, in order to guarantee a smooth transition of the merged Aegean Airlines and Olympic Air operations into the Star Alliance network'*. At Aegean's welcome ceremony into Star Alliance on 30 June 2010, Star Alliance CEO Jaan Albrecht confirmed that the enlarged entity would be a full Star Alliance member if the planned merger gained regulatory approval.

After an initial review of the merger, the European Competitions Commission expressed doubts on 30 July 2010 that the merger met competition regulations, citing 'serious competition concerns' in the domestic market and on several international routes. The EC further stated that it had 'serious doubts' that the merger met requirements regarding ground-handling at Greek airports as well as the provision of Public Service Obligation (PSO) routes, which would bring together the 'two strongest and most credible bidders' on these routes. The commission chose to open a ninety-day inquiry into the proposed merger to further assess the effects of the partnership. The EC was expected to give their final ruling by 7 December 2010. In an interview with Air Transport World in August 2010, Dimitris Gerogiannis, managing director of Aegean Airlines, stated that their main goal at the time was making the merger work, saying that merging with Olympic Air was a matter of viability, driven by 'economic and business realities'. Gerogiannis was certain that Hellas was unable to sustain two full-service airlines, pointing out other European countries and airlines as examples. Later that month, Aegean posted its first losses in years, thus

The line up of Olympic Air A320s ready to be returned from lease.*(Olympic Air)*

A line up of Aegean Airlines A.320s and 321s at AIA. *(Aegean)*

backing up Gerogiannis' thoughts and further displaying an urgent need for the merger.

Despite a given deadline of 7 December 2010, Olympic and Aegean were hoping for a decision from the EU earlier. The two airlines expected to hand over all details and documents to the EU as requested by the end of September. Olympic and Aegean were hoping for an early decision to allow them to synchronise the 2011 flight schedules, ideally by November 2010 as is the industry standard, so as to reap the benefits and synergies of the merger as soon as possible. The airlines claimed a later decision would hurt them both economically and competitively against other carriers and delay full benefits from the merger until 2012.

On 24 September 2010, it was announced that Olympic Air had won the European Regions Airline Association Silver Award: Airline of the Year for 2010/2011. Olympic was praised for operating one hundred and ninety daily flight within two months of starting operations, despite having been re-launched during an extreme economic crisis in Greece and against a backdrop of a troubled past.

On 21 October 2010, the EU commission announced that they would delay their decision on the merger until 12 January 2011. Commissioner Joaquin Almunia Amann, the Spanish-born politician, also cited difficulties with the two companies holding almost all the domestic market in Greece. Almunia had previously been chief economist of the Union General de Trabajadores, a Spanish trade union affiliated to the Socialist Workers' Party (PSOE), from 1976 to 1979. He was an economist at the Council Bureau of the Spanish Chambers of Commerce in Brussels from 1972 to 1975.

The EU gave no specific reason for the delay but, according to publications, the commission typically defers decisions when companies offer to take steps that would ease concerns. On 17 November 2010, Commissioner Joaquin Almunia confirmed that the two carriers still faced some difficulties in their efforts to overcome anti-trust concerns over the merger, but stressed that they had weeks ahead of them to find an adequate solution until the planned 12 January 2011 decision. However, on 10 December 2010, it was reported by Greek media that the European Commission bureaucrats had pushed back their ruling date, this time with a new tentative date being set for 2 February 2011. Then, on 26 January 2011, the European Commission blocked the merger between the two airlines, citing anti-competition concerns.

The commission stated that the merger would have created a quasi-monopoly in the local air transport market, with the combined airline controlling more than 90% of the Hellenic domestic air transport market. The EC further stated its belief that the merger would lead to higher fares for four of the six million passengers flying to and from Athens each year, with no realistic prospects that a new airline of sufficient size would enter the market to restrain the merged airline's pricing. Additionally, commissioner Joaquin Almunia stated that the merger would have led to higher prices and lower quality of service for passengers travelling between Athens and the islands, where the merged airline would have a near total domination between Athens and

Thessaloniki, and between the capital and eight island airports.

Welcome to the world of Planet EU!

Despite both carriers offering remedies in an attempt to ease concerns, the EU believed that they would not be enough to protect travellers adequately and ease competition concerns.

EU competition commissioner Joaquin Almunia then came out with the remarkable statement that the airlines could have won approval if they offered to sell part of their fleet to a potential competitor or let another airline use one of their brand names, per EU suggestions. One has to wonder which planet these bloated Brussels bureaucrats live on!

Aegean Airlines called the brand-name proposal unacceptable - which is probably the understatement of the decade - with vice-chairman Eftihios Vassilakis stating that the brand names have a colossal value which both airlines had worked hard to build. Furthermore, Vassilakis noted that the brand name and fleet remedy was utterly unprecedented in the history of airline mergers.

Commenting on the developments in a joint press release, Aegean Airlines chairman Thodoros Vasilakis stated *'Throughout last year we presented to the European Commission the benefits of the merger for our companies, our passengers and our country's economy. We also offered important commitments to safeguard consumers as well as measures to facilitate the entry of new competitors in the domestic market. Unfortunately, the EC decided to prohibit the agreement. An important opportunity for a consolidated representation in the European aviation market has been lost. We will adjust and continue. Our track record shows that we can succeed through challenging times.'*

Olympic Air chairman Andreas Vgenopoulos echoed Vasilakis' thoughts on moving forward, also stating *'The EC Decision will have negative consequences for consumers as well as our country's economy while it will benefit foreign competitors. Obviously, we, as well as Aegean, will continue to do our best for the benefit of our staff, our shareholders and our passengers'*.

Both airlines stated that they would study the block report issued by the EU, and after careful analysis and discussion with their advisers would decide whether to appeal.

Following a shake-up of its board of directors, on 2 March 2011 Olympic Air announced that they planned to appeal the EU ruling with Aegean Airlines, and also announced a series of route network changes as a part of their strategy adjustment, which included the cancellation of most of their western-European routes and additions of domestic and regional routes.

In separate developments, MIG's Andreas Vgenopoulos, who at the height of his success had acquired a string of businesses including Marfin Popular Bank, the Attica Group, a passenger shipping firm, one of Greece's largest food companies Vivartia, a private clinic, a minority

Aegean Chairman Theodoros Vassilakis. *(Aegean)*

On Parade! An Aegean Airlines crewand their aircraft. *(Aegean)*

shareholder of soccer club Panathinaikos as well as Olympic Air was vilified as the man who precipitated Cyprus' banking crisis in 2012, which led to an EU bailout and a one—time levy on all uninsured bank deposits over €100,000. He was also accused of corrupt lending practices, first in Cyprus and then in Hellas.

On 21 October 2012 Aegean Airlines announced that it had struck a deal to acquire Olympic Air for a sum of €75 million, pending approval by the European Commission. Contrary to their previous merger attempt, both carriers would continue to operate under separate brands after the acquisition. As part of the deal, Aegean Airlines paid Olympic Air €20 million up front. If the European Commission did not approve the agreement, Olympic Air would still retain the money, with Aegean Airlines owning a 17% stake in the company.

European Commission sources said that Aegean Airlines' second attempt to buy Olympic Air would be approved by the Commission; it was understood that Olympic Air would be forced into bankruptcy proceedings if the merger was not allowed to go ahead. The buyout was approved by the European Commission on 9 October 2013.

Vgenopoulos, who had been a champion fencer in the 1970s and early 1980s and competed in the 1972 Olympics was also involved for a time as a minority shareholder of soccer club Panathinaikos. He died early 5 November 2016 from a heart attack.

As of 1 February 2014 Olympic Air became a service provider for parent company Aegean Airlines, with all the international flights carrying the latter's flight prefix. The carrier continues to operate the domestic routes(some of them in co-operation with Aegean). Some Aegean international flights are operating by Olympic Air

Chapter Eleven

Bearers Of The Olympic Flame

Athina's Ellinikon Airport closed on 28 April 2001. As the city's air traffic moved to the new Eleftherios Venizelos Airport, Ellinikon went quiet, just at a time when the Olympic group of companies were going through a rapid number of changes.

In 2004, the site of Ellinikon Airport became an Olympic Games venue, with two baseball stadiums going up and a hangar converted into a basketball and handball arena. Later, the government housed thousands of refugees seeking temporary shelter in some of the airport buildings.

In June 2017 when I made a three-day visit to the site the main impression is abandonment. Between the concrete segments of the aircraft stands, grass was growing - and even small trees. Debris was strewn around. A storm had destroyed some windows of the Eeno Saarinen-designed eastern terminal building, designated a heritage landmark.

Since the closure of the airport there have been architectural contests and master plans, but nothing has ever come to fruition. One investor was supposed to have been prepared to spend €37 billion to develop the site - along with some of the surrounding area that included the now-decrepit Aristotle Onassis mansion on Poseidonos - into one of Europe's biggest coastal resorts. However the whole Ellinikon area seems to have inexorably descended into a depressing catatonic morass as the plans became enmeshed in politics and bureaucracy.

However, the Olympic Airways flame has not yet been finally extinguished. This is due to the unstinting efforts of men like Vassilis Tsatsaragos, who heads the non-profit Cultural Society of Employees of Olympic Airways; known under the initials of POLKEOA.

Since 2003, its members have been trying to establish a museum devoted to Olympic Airways. They have been doing it largely on their own - the best they can expect, given the dire economic

The original hangar that was removed from Kerkyra and brought to Athens. The plan is to eventually move it to a new site and use it for the Museum. *(author)*

straits in which Hellas finds itself.

In the former departure hall of the Western terminal, they have laid out a small collection of artefacts, a small fraction of the about twenty thousand or more original pieces the association has amassed. Most are not on display, as these treasures are believed not to be safe in the old terminal. *'Some time ago we had a fire here, an arson attack probably...'* Tsatsaragos told me during my visit.

Former aircraft mechanics have taken shifts to stay on location overnight to protect the collection against vandalism. Finally, they had a big metal gate built from their own money, which now better protects the place against theft.

'The area of Ellinikon airport is double that of Berlin-Tempelhof Airport. This place, here in the terminal, with a history of sixty-five years, should be preserved as a museum and can't just be torn down,' Tsatsaragos said. *'We don't demand a*

Hristoforos Stafanidis the author and Antonis Tzimos outside the offices of Cultural Society of Employees of Olympic Airways at the old Western Terminal of Ellinikon in June 2017 (author)

Just some of the documentation preserved by *ΠΟΛΚ.ΕΟΑ. (author)*

single cent from the Hellenic government. This is about private initiative. The Onassis Foundation and even the EU has given us hope for money to build a proper museum. Because Olympic's history started here, this is the right place to do it.'

In the old terminal, parts of the glorious era of the Hellenic airline have already come alive. That airline is inextricably linked to one name: Aristoteles Onassis. Not only does the museum boast photographs of the aircraft and equipment from the Onassis era, but there is also Onassis's original desk and portraits of the Patriarch. The fledgling museum also boasts mannequins wearing the extravagant and glamorous uniforms created by world-famous fashion designers like Pierre Cardin for the Air and Ground Hostesses, as well as silver bowls with crystal glass inserts, used to serve caviar on board.

Left: sometimes vandalism has its benefits! Ellinikon Airport may have closed in 2001 but some of the signage dated back earlier to a time when prices were still in drachma - like this one for taxi tariffs dated July 1 1998.

The enginless airliners await the creation of a museum at Ellinikon. *(both author)*

In the 1960s and early 1970s, the glamour of Olympic Airways rivalled that of Pan American World Airways. The artifacts in the old west terminal proves the point - an eclectic mix of aircraft models, photos, old telephones, and computers from the 1980s, as well as original signage advertising flights that went from Athina all the way to Sydney, Australia.

While the small exhibit is open for visitors who make appointments, the major attractions of the future museum are to be found a few kilometres away, in a fenced-off corner of the vast empty ramp of Ellinikon. Nobody is officially allowed in, but I was granted access to the site. Here is a unique collection of old Olympic Airways aircraft that the association had acquired in 2003, a British Aircraft Corporation 1-11, and some smaller aircraft.

It was following the expansion of Ellinikon Airport to the east with the opening of the Eero Saarinen-designed East Terminal in 1969 that Aristotle Onassis decided that something had to be done to promote the Olympic Airways brand and expand its market share as an air carrier.

Onassis knew that the new East Terminal - one of the last works by the world-renowned Finnish-born American architect Eero Saarinen whose headquarters were in Birmingham, Michigan would attract worldwide attention. Saarinen had already gained international recognition for the elegant expressionism of the TWA passenger terminal in New York and the Dulles International Airport near Washington DC.

The object of his design was to create a building that would be representative of 20th-century technology and express the Greek spirit as well.

Onassis proposed to the Olympic Board that some form of advertising sign be erected in a prominent spot and so, after a study, space search and international competition for the construction of a sign. The order was given by Konstantinos Konialidis, President of Olympic Airways to the manufacturer, Mr Votsis.

Construction began in 1973 - at the junction of Avenue Vouliagmenis and Avenue Alimou - and was completed

I SAW THE SIGN

with the help of wooden scaffolding and a special crane, for the suspension of the steelwork, which was a particularly large construction for that time and cost 980,000 drachmas

The sphere has a diameter of 10 metres, and its overall height is 26 metres. Its total weight is 11.5 tonnes. Its first design depicted an aircraft named Olympic Airways but it was soon changed to the design seen today.

With the demise of the airline, the sign fell into disrepair and eventually became something of an eyesore. In 2016 *ΠΟΛΚ.ΕΟΑ* along with numerous other organisation decided that it needed preserving and so set about renovating it. A grand 'switch on of the illumination system' happened on the night of 10 May 2017 in what is now a mini-park, attended by a huge crowd, which were addressed by Yiannis Konstantatos, the mayor of Hellenic - Argyroupolis.

'The Olympic brand is a landmark not only for our city but for Athens as well, since it has been a reference point for citizens throughout Athens since 1973.

The generation of the four-year-olds, to which I belong, has many events and incidents to be told with reference to the Olympic brand. Back then we did not have mobile phones and Facebook, and so we made an appointment on the weekends to meet at the 'Sigma'.

Illuminating the sign will remind us of memories of an earlier era. An era in the positive elements of which Greece should return'.

Just some of the collection of airline aphemira collected over the years. (author)

'In 2003, Olympic sold the Boeing 747 to an American-Israeli junk dealer, and he removed the worthy parts...' Tsatsaragos told me as we walked around. *'He sold an engine for US$300,000, the equivalent of what he had paid for the whole aircraft. Then we, the former Olympic staff, put together money and raised $100,000 to have him leave the aircraft here for the future museum.'*

The vintage Boeing 747-284B 9 (*Olympic Eagle* SX-OAB), was Olympic's second wide-bodied jet, having been delivered new from the factory in December 1973. Olympic deliberately requested the registration to be SX-OAB. *'OA stands for Onassis Aristotelis, B for the second aircraft,'* said the association's head.

Despite being engineless the 747 - which operated long-haul routes such as Athens - Singapore - Melbourne - Sydney before being grounded in 1999 - is still an impressive sight. Even the cabin, with ornaments on window blinds and wall covers showing Hellenic monuments are well preserved.

The other airliners on site are a Boeing 727-284 (*Mount Olympus* - SX-CBA). This was Olympic's first 727-200, delivered in December 1968, and retired in 1992. Also, Olympic's first Boeing 737-284 (*Apollo* SX-BCA), delivered in June 1976 sits on the ramp.

A BAC 1-11, delivered originally to Aloha Airlines in 1966 purchased by US Airways and earmarked for a new airline called Hellenic. However, the airline never started operations, and the Greek Civil Aviation Authority used the jetliner for training purposes after taking possession of it.

This impressive collection of Olympic Airways aircraft and artefacts is in need of urgent support. *'The present parking area for our aircraft has only provisionally been assigned to us...'* Tsatsaragos said. *'Nobody knows when a possible new buyer of the property could take over, and what then would become of us.'*

But, with Greece's economy in such difficult shape, there's not much hope that these sturdy veterans will find support for this project that is so close to their hearts.

Perhaps now it is time for all those wealthy Greek-Americans and Greek-Australians to step up to the plate, put their hands in their pockets and help out!

To everyone at ΠΟΛΚ.ΕΟΑ I say this... Συνεχίστε την καλή προσπάθειά με το έργο σας και να παραμένετε στη ζωή μας. (roughly translated: Continue your good efforts with your work and stay in our lives.)

Appendix One

The Hellenic Air Force Accident Investigation into the accident of Piaggio 136 SX-DBC

Explanatory notes.

The original report into the accident from the Hellenic Air Force was written in Greek and was, for many years, allegedly surpressed from publication. This english translation came my way from a fellow researcher who wishes to remain anonnymous. The document was located in a US library and contains some interesting signs that it could well have been 'tampered with' from the original.

Translation from Greek into English is never precise; however, with this document there are a myriad of signs that it was done by an American with little knowledge of aviation. Many words have been 'Americanised' with US spellings - 'ized' instead of 'ised - and with date presentations the wrong way around - Month - Day - Year instead of Day - Month - Year.

There are also instances of strange uses of words. One example of this is the use of the phrase 'parking lot' for aircraft stand in Section 3, Paragraph 31, item c.

Does this all matter? Probably not, but in the interests of accuracy it deserves pointing out to make the reader aware from the onset that is is certainly not a word-for-word representation of the original Air Force Report. What follows is the report, followed by my own interpretation and conclusion.

Findings under the evidence as regards the accident of the Piaggio 136 Aircraft SX-BDC of Olympic Airways on January 22, 1973.

I. COMMISSION

President: Group Captain M. Tsingris (Pilot)
Members: Squadron Leader D. Papageorgiou (Pilot)
Squadron Leader M. Saharides (Engineer)
Flight Lieutenant D. Mpiniaris
Sergeant-Major M. Katsikis

II. INVESTIGATION ORDER

On January 25, 1973, the members selected by Police Lieutenant A.P.D. Kakouli were instructed to proceed with the investigation.

III. SEQUENCE OF EVENTS

1. On January 22, 1973, at approximately 15:00 (3 p.m.) local time, the Piaggio 136 amphibian aircraft of Olympic Airways, with Alexandros Onassis as the pilot, had been scheduled for flight from the Athína Airport to the area of Poros Isle. The aircraft was scheduled to make a number of water takeoffs and landdings before it returned to the airport.
2. The pilot of the aircraft submitted the flight schedule in accordance with the regulations before the flight. In this schedule, among other things, were the names of two people reported as passengers. These two people were the foreigners McGregor and McCusker.
3. The pilot in command entered the aircraft and sat on the right-hand side of the cockpit. McCusker sat in the left seat, and the third person, McGregor, sat in the back seat.
4. After the engines were started and the aircraft was ready to take off, the pilot received via radio the relevant clearance from the control tower. The aircraft slowly moved towards the runway where they

stopped to perform the necessary procedures and final checks before taking off. After this, the pilot was permitted to enter the runway from the taxiway. Once the aircraft was on the runway, the pilot set the engines to full power and the aircraft accelerated to takeoff. The control tower gave them information regarding wind velocity and direction. It also informed the pilot about other aircraft traffic on the airport.

5. After the aircraft accelerated for approximately 570 meters it left the ground and immediately it turned to the right. This sudden turn caused the aircraft's right wing to strike the runway surface, thus causing the aircraft to crash between the runway and the taxiway. The time of the crash was estimated at 15:20 (3:20 p.m) local time.

6. The control tower immediately ordered the rescue teams into action for immediate assistance of the passengers and crew of the crashed aircraft. The pilot and the two other occupants of the aircraft were taken out badly injured and were immediately transported to the hospital. After a few days the pilot of the aircraft died due to his serious injuries.

IV. INVESTIGATION

1. The commission, which was organized three days after the crash, went to the scene of the accident on January 25, 1973. They found the following facts:

2. The aircraft crashed within the airport about 84 meters away from the runway. The aircraft's engines were still running at full power.

3. In examining the aircraft's remains, the commission came to the conclusion that once the plane was off the ground and at a right angle to the runway, the right wing came in contact with the ground, forcing the plane to crash nose-first. Then the plane spun to the right for about 300 degrees, because the engines were still at full power. Due to the fast spinning motion, the aircraft's left wing also hit the ground, forcing it to fold in half.

4. The plane's cabin was completely destroyed at both the front and rear end. This was due to the repeated contacts with the ground during the final phase of the crash.

5. Due to the severe impact at the front of the aircraft, the cockpit and the passenger seats were also crushed, thus causing the serious injuries of the pilot and passengers.

6. It was also observed that the wheels of the landing gear were in the landing position, and only the steel legs holding the wheels appeared to be damaged. The right leg indicated harsh contact with a rough surface. The tail wheel was locked in the neutral upward position as it is supposed to be according to the takeoff procedures. This wheel also showed contact but with a dirt surface.

7. The aircraft's doors were cut and removed by the rescue team in order to extricate the trapped occupants.

8. Both the aircraft's wings were destroyed at the ends, but the propellers were completely undamaged.

9. Although the wings were mostly destroyed, the wing flaps were in perfect condition and were found in the 'up' position.

10. The right aileron was also destroyed, while the left aileron was undamaged but not functioning due to damage to the part of the wing to which it is attached.

11. The elevators were found in the aircraft's horizontal tail section, but were also badly damaged from the crash and spinning of the plane.

12. The surface of the rudder, found in the vertical tail section, was damaged in the upper left section, also as a result of the crash.

13. The left wingtip float of the aircraft was still on the wing, sustaining minor damage due to contact with the cement surface of the runway, while the right one was detached and was found close to the aircraft.

14. Although the cockpit was badly damaged by the crash and by the rescue teams efforts, the experts were still able to study the instrument panel and the positions of the levers and switches. The seat belt mechanisms were in the locked position but the belts were cut by the rescue team in order to free the three occupants. The instrument panel and the pilot's seats had been compressed and moved to the right due to the angle of the contact with the ground.

15. The lever controlling the landing gear was found in the 'landing gear-down' position. The lever controlling the wing flaps was in the 'up' position. The wing flaps, in accordance with the position of the lever, were up, and this is not the proper position for takeoff procedure.

16. Both the aircraft's control columns were found in the leftward position, the last position they were in before the crash. This was worthy of note since the whole structure of the plane was distorted completely to the left.

17. The elevator trim tabs were observed to be in the '6 degrees up' position. Again this position is not appropriate for taking off.

18. The levers controlling power and fuel were found in the position appropriate for full engine power, in accordance with takeoff procedure.

19. The fuel tanks were undamaged and full.

20. Inside the aircraft were various documents, logbooks, maintenance manuals, fuel reports, and the aircraft's Certificate of Airworthiness.

21. A tape containing the live conversation between the aircraft and the control tower was also given to the commission.

22. Based on the tape, the commission came to the conclusion that the pilot, Alexandros Onassis, was the one handling the radio throughout the flight.

23. From both the control tower's records and the tape, it was apparent that an Air France Boeing 727 had taken off shortly before the Piaggio did. The accident took place approximately two minutes later.

24. An identical Piaggio aircraft was furnished to the commission by Olympic Airways for the purpose of testing and studying the aircraft's engines. The commission transferred the engines of the crashed aircraft to the second Piaggio for testing purposes. They were found to be in perfect condition and operated normally in all respects.

25. The laboratory reports stated that the hydraulic, electronic, and fuel systems were in good condition and there were no indications of malfunction.

26. From the study of the aircraft's controls the following observations were made:

    a. The rudder's pulley, cables, and the rest of the rudder's gear were tested and found in good condition and without any kind of malfunction.

    b. The elevator assembly was also found to be in good condition and responded correctly to all tests. It was observed that the elevators, responsible for causing the aircraft to climb, were in the completely 'up' position due to the final impact of the plane's tail section. The elevator trim-tab lever was found at a position of 6 degrees up, which was not in accordance with the aircraft manual's instructions for takeoff procedure.

    c. The aileron control system and all its parts were in good condition. But the tests showed that its last position was the opposite of the correct one. The commission and the specialized technicians made this observation; they came to the conclusion that the reason for this was the fact that the control cables were connected wrongly in a reverse manner. These control cables begin from the floor of the cockpit and transmit the movement through pulleys to the ailerons on the aircraft's wings.

    d. It was further noted that the control cables were made of 5/32 carbon, but the one connected to the right aileron was of 3/16 stainless steel.

27. The prevailing weather conditions at the airport when the accident occurred were good. The pilot received all relevant infor- mation regarding wind and current runway traffic from the con- trol tower. Wind velocity and direction were clearly within safety limits for the safe takeoff of the Piaggio aircraft.

28. The occupants of the crashed aircraft were Alexandros Onassis (pilot), foreigner McCusker occupying the left-hand seat, and the second foreign passenger McGregor in the back passenger seat. The commission came to the following conclusions based on the evidence:

    a. The pilot of the aircraft, Alexandros Onassis, was an authorized 'B' class license holder (serial no. 719). He had been submitted to the proper medical testing and was granted a medical certificate which was valid until May 9, 1973. By the order E1/A/ 1 9899/ 355 7/ 6-7-72 of the Civil Aviation Authority, he had been granted the authorized license to examine pilots to qualify them to fly amphibious aircraft like the Piaggio 136. His total flying time was 896 hours, 51 hours of which were in the Piaggio aircraft. His last flight in this kind of aircraft prior to the accident was on August 27, 1972. In his personal file there is a reported incident regarding a regulation violation, as to which he submitted an apology to the Civil Aviation Authority. Further details are unknown.

b. As regards McCusker, who was sitting in the left front seat, no information was found concerning his flying experience or medical certificate.

c. As regards the third person on board, McGregor, evidence was supplied by Olympic Airways that he was a certificated airline pilot. However, his pilot certificate had expired as of November 9, 1972, due to the expiration of his medical certificate. He had been originally recruited by Olympic Airways as a Boeing 707 pilot, but later transferred to the amphibian section of Olympic Airways as a pilot of the Piaggio 136. He had 166 hours of flight time on that type of aircraft.

29. According to the flight schedule, the flight was local and the estimated time of flight was 2 hours and 30 minutes.

30. According to the records of Olympic Airways, the purpose of this flight was to familiarize McCusker with this type of aicraft by making a number of takeoffs and landings on the water in the vicinity of Poros Isle.

31. According to the statement of McGregor, the following was reported:

a. All the relevant pre-flight checks were done by Alexandros Onassis. He then started the aircraft's engines and made further checks, while simultaneously explaining the procedures to McCusker.

b. McCusker taxied the aircraft from the parking lot to the beginning of the runway.

c. All further testing of the engines, up to the point of taking off, was done entirely by Alexandros Onassis.

32. From examination of the aircraft's log books it appears that the load being carried was within limits, and that the fuel and other fluids were adequate for this scheduled flight.

33. Further examination of the aircraft's records shows that permits were granted for its operation by both Olympic Airways and the airport authorities.

34. The aircraft was acquired by Olympic Airways on December 22, 1967. It bore manufacturer's serial number 97.

35. The previous Certificate of Airworthiness of the amphibian aircraft had expired on November 29, 1972. The new certificate, which was issued on January 18, 1973 by the Civil Aviation Authority, had an expiration date of January 18, 1974.

36. From the time the aircraft was built to the moment of its destruction it had been flown for a total of 1081 hours. It had undergone a general overhaul on December 1, 1970.

37. The last flight prior to the accident took place on October 2, 1972, from Skorpios to the Athens Airport.

38. During the aircraft's stay at the Athens Airport, considerable maintenance and overhaul work was done to it. The following were reported:

a. Some parts were replaced with new ones according to the instructions in the aircraft manual, and some test flights took place, according to the aircraft's logbook.

b. On November 15, 1972, again according to the aircraft's logbook, the ailerons were removed along with their control systems since they had exceeded the estimated life period (5 years).

c. Ten days later, on November 25, 1972, the records of additional work noted that a re-installation of the ailerons and their control systems was made.

d. On November 11, 1972, the aircraft was taken out of operation because of the expiration of the Certificate of Airworthiness, and this was noted in the daily service forms from that time on until January 19, 1973.

e. In the daily service form O00/A16-9/5/69 of January 17, 1973, apart from the repeated observation that the aircraft was out of operation due to expiration of the Certificate of Airworthiness it was noted that the Certificate of Airworthiness had been renewed.

f. However, in the daily service form of January 19, 1973 as well as in the daily service form of January 21, 1973, the observation continued to be noted that the aircraft was out of operation due to expiration of the Certificate of Airworthiness, without any other comment or observation.

g. Apart from the above, the Certificate of Airworthiness itself showed that it was renewed on January 18, 1973. Therefore the observation about renewal of the Certificate of Airworthiness entered in the daily service form of January 17, 1973 was not correct, although that observation was correct for January 18, 1973.

39. Through document No. TD/ 1—3030/2622/ 3-11, Olympic Airways applied to the Civil Aviation Authority (C.A.A.) for renewal of the Certificate of Airworthiness of the Piaggio on November 29, 1972. This document noted that the said aircraft was fit for safe flight under the responsibility of Olympic Airways.

40. The C.A.A., through its message No. 6617/ 10.11.72 on November 10, 1972, informed Olympic Airways that for the renewal of the Certificate of Airworthiness, two aeronautical engineers were appointed: G. Papademetropoulus (3rd Grade) and E. Mavroforos (5th grade), both employees of the C.A.A.

41. Then, Olympic Airways, through its message to the C.A.A. dated December 4, 1972, applied for the granting of a special license to carry out test flights for the renewal of the Certificate of Airworthiness.

42. Through a message dated December 14, 1972, the C.A.A. approved the carrying out of the requested flight tests, on condition that under the responsibility of Olympic Airways, said aircraft would be fit for safe flight.

43. By document dated January 18, 1973 addressed to the C.A.A. Department of Aircraft Airworthiness, one of the appointed airworthiness inspectors, E. Mavroforos, submitted an inspection report of the aircraft SX-BDC according to which the aircraft was considered 'fit for flight.' The Certificate of Airworthiness of that aircraft was renewed for one year, from January 18, 1973 to January 18, 1974.

44. Please note here that the test flight requested by Olympic Airways was not carried out.

45. From investigation of the form relating to daily inspection of the aircraft on January 22, 1973, which was the day of the accident, it emerged that this document carried the signatures of the authorized maintenance technicians who confirmed that the aircraft was in good condition and had been cleared for flight, despite a noted observation that the Certificate of Airworthiness had expired.

46. The maintenance of Olympic Airways' aircraft as well as the inspection and control of the maintenance work carried out by technical personnel was the responsibility of Olympic Airways.

V. ANALYSIS

1. Before the takeoff from Athens Airport for a domestic flight of 2 hours and 30 minutes on January 22, 1973, the pilot of the aircraft, Alexandros Onassis, had submitted a flight plan and was briefed on the prevailing weather conditions. The meteorogological conditions of that day were suitable for flight.

2. The purpose of the flight was to familiarize McCusker with this type of aircraft, by making water landings in the area of Poros Isle.

3. Before the flight, the required briefing of McCusker was made by the pilot, Alexandros Onassis, according to McGregor's statement.

4. The technical check of the aircraft before the flight was made by the authorized maintenance personnel of Olympic Airways, who signed the appropriate inspection documents confirming the fitness and

readiness of the aircraft for flight; however, the investigation showed that the aircraft was not at all fit for flight.

5. The pilot, together with the two foreign nationals, took possession of the aircraft and boarded, with the pilot taking the seat on the right. McCusker took the left seat while McGregor sat behind McCusker. The pilot started the engines and carried out the checks and the taxiing process from memory, given the fact that no checklist was used, nor found, as required. At this point one of the items on the checklist is the check of the ailerons for free and correct movement.

6. Then, in accordance with the instructions of the control tower, the aircraft taxied to the second connecting taxiway of Runway 33. At this point a test of the engines was made, which confirmed their proper functioning (according to McGregor's statement). At this point the pre-takeoff checks were carried out, also from memory. In accordance with the checklist, the first of these is a test of the ailerons. The flaps were positioned at 20 degrees down (according to McGregor's statement) and the other levers and controls were positioned at the proper settings.

7. Around 15:12 hours (3:12 pm.) local time, the pilot of the aircraft told the control tower that he was ready for takeoff. The control tower instructed him to wait.

8. At 15:18 hours (3:18 p.m.) the Air France aircraft took off from Runway 33.

9. At 15:19 hours (3:19 p.m.) the pilot of the Piaggio requested permission to enter the takeoff runway. The control tower granted permission and also gave the latest information on air traffic and wind velocity, which at that time was at 8 knots from 240 degrees, that is, from the left side of the aircraft. The pilot acknowledged reception and understanding and began to taxi for takeoff at 15:20 hours (3:20 p.m.).

10. The time lapse between the takeoff of the Boeing 727 and of the Piaggio, measured with the assistance of the control tower tape recorder, was estimated at about 2 minutes.

11. Here it should be clarified that in the case of successive takeoffs, the control tower grants takeoff permission, but it is up to the pilot in the command of the aircraft about to take off to decide whether it will take off and with how much separation, in order to avoid entering air turbulence caused by the preceding aircraft.

12. The commission cannot determine with certainty who was handling the aircraft at the critical time of the takeoff. If what is reported by the passenger McGregor is correct, the takeoff was executed by McCusker, sitting in the left seat, under the supervision of Alexandros Onassis.

13. The aircraft accelerated normally on the runway and took off at a speed of about 100 miles per hour. At takeoff, the aircraft banked to the right. As a consequence of this bank to the right, the right-hand wingtip float came into contact with the runway, with the result that the aircraft veered to the right of the takeoff point. As a result of the increasing bank, the right tire came into skidding contact with the runway. This caused a short bounce, and the aircraft exited from the right side of the runway, maintaining a bank to the right while climbing.

14. At this point, it is presumed that the flaps were retracted. It is highly probable and reasonable to assume that the pilot of the aircraft at that moment presumed that the continuous and intense bank to the right was due to a disparate position of the flaps. This action, however, resulted in further loss of stability and climbing ability of the aircraft, the right wing of which impacted rough ground outside the runway.

15. At this point, the banking increased further, and due to the contact of the wing with the ground, the nose of the aircraft came down and followed a circular motion of about 300 degrees to the right, in which the nose, affected by the movement to the right on the one hand and the propulsion of the engines on the other hand, crashed to the ground. The cockpit and passenger cabin were crushed and as a consequence those on board were severely injured, particularly those sitting in the front, McCusker and Alexandros Onassis.

16. The latter, Onassis, due to the fact that he was sitting on the right side, and due to the fact that the impact of the crash was from the left to the right, came under the greatest force of impact, and suffered the most serious injuries.

17. After the collision of the nose of the aircraft with the ground, with the nose coming down low and the right wing banked, the aircraft crashed and came to a stop on the ground resting on the left wing and tail section of the fuselage.

18. From the investigation that followed, it appeared that the functioning of the ailerons was the opposite of the correct function, due to the reverse connection of the aileron control cables. This work was conducted on November 25, 1972 (see Technical Section, Part V).

19. If the ailerons were correctly connected and the aileron control system were operating correctly, the correct position for a turn to the left is that when the control wheel is turned by the pilot to the left, the left aileron rises while the left wing declines, and thus the aircraft makes a turn to the left. In this case, with the turning of the control wheel to the left, the left aileron, instead of rising, was declining, with the natural result that the aircraft performed a move opposite from the normal, that is, a right turn. Therefore the continuous right turn of the aircraft after takeoff, under the above-mentioned circumstances of the reversed connection of the ailerons, is fiilly explained.

20. It is here judged by the commission as appropriate to note the quality of the maintenance work carried out by the personnel of Olympic Airways on the aircraft in question.

a. The whole process of replacing the aileron control system of the aircraft, that is, its removal on November 15, 1972 and its reinstallation on November 25, 1972, during which operation the movement axis of the aileron pulleys and the separation ring were found in improper positions and the aileron links were found in the reversed positions; and

b. the presence of wrongly connected aileron control cables; and

c. the preparation and inspection for flight of the aircraft in question by the maintenance personnel despite the written observation on the daily service forms of November 21 and 22 concerning the expiration of the Certificate of Airworthiness, and also the signed certification of the authorized technicians that the aircraft was fit and cleared for flight; indicated that in the execution of maintenance on the aircraft in question, the necessary attention and care due to such work was not duly paid.

21. The technique of takeoff under cross-wind conditions, as in this case, requires for all types of aircraft the turning of the control wheel toward the side from which the wind is blowing, at the start of taxiing for takeoff until the point of leaving the ground. This is done for the purpose of counteracting the tendency of the wind to tilt the wing into the ground. When the aircraft is in flight and after it gains airspeed, the ailerons become active and the turning of the control wheel into the wind is gradually reversed by the pilot.

22. During the takeoff run, the Piaggio aircraft encountered the effect of the wind from the left, and immediately after its take-off, because of the reversed connection of the ailerons, instead of finding itself in the position of correcting for the wind drift, it was turned the wrong way, with the result that the right wing dropped and turned the aircraft even further to the right, followed by the striking of the right wing float, the forceful contact of the right wheel, the right wing striking the ground, and finally the crash.

23. The persistent increase of the bank to the right was due to the reaction of the pilot, who, when he first realized the bank to the right, attempted to correct with a left turn of the control wheel. This action increased the bank to the right and evidently created the impression of an irregular deployment of the wing flaps, which he raised. The bank to the right increased, the pilot turned the control wheel completely to the left and at the same time pulled the control wheel back to gain altitude. Due however to the excessive increase of the bank to the right, the loss of lift from the raising of the wing flaps, and the contact of the right wing with the rough ground, it became impossible to maintain altitude despite the continuous operation of the engines at fiill power.

24. The commission examined and ruled out the suggestion that the accident was caused by the effect of the turbulence created by the preceding takeoff of the Boeing 727 aircraft, because the phenomenon of turbulence by a preceding aircraft begins to appear from the moment that an aircraft takes off from the ground. The Boeing 727, which was larger and heavier, took off at a longer distance from the take-off point of the Piaggio, and therefore the Piaggio, at the point of take-off at least, was not inside the area of the turbulence of the preceding aircraft and was not affected by it.

25. Also ruled out was the suggestion of failure or malfunction of an engine, given that the engines were not damaged during the accident, and when tested they operated normally. Moreover, both engines operated at full power even after the crash and immobilization of the aircraft on the ground. Additionally, the passenger McGregor, who is experienced on this type of aircraft, testified to the normal operation of the engines.

26. Finally, also ruled out was the loss of sufficient airspeed of the aircraft at takeoff, given that the aircraft was at an airspeed of about 100 miles per hour at takeoff. which is within the safe level for takeoff.

27. The commission believes it is its obligation at this point to refer to the actions of the pilot of the aircraft in the takeoff phase. The actions taken by him were the appropriate and required actions assuming that the ailerons were properly connected, and not connected in reverse as was the case here. However, as the fact of the reverse connection of the ailerons was not known to the pilot, and because the aircraft was flying at low ground speed in the takeoff phase, it was not possible for him to react otherwise.

VI. CONCLUSIONS

Following the investigation and analysis it carried out, the commission came to the following conclusions regarding the circumstances and cause of the accident.

1. The accident was not the result of poor technique or mistake of the pilot of the aircraft at the time of the accident.

2. The main cause of the accident was the mistakes of the maintenance personnel of Olympic Airways which consisted of:

   a) The reversed connection of the ailerons during the work for the replacement of the controls of the aircraft, and

   b) The inadequate inspection by the inspector of Olympic Airways of the workwhich had been carried out on the aircraft.

3. Contributory causes of the accident are believed to be the following:

   a) The faulty operational check of the aircraft by the authorized official of the Civil Aeronautics Authority for the renewal of the Certificate of Airworthiness.

   b) The omission by the pilot to use the checklist and as a result the omission by the pilot to carry out the required check of the ailerons before takeoff, which resulted in the failure to notice the reverse connection and operation of the ailerons,

Signed at Athens on April 20, 1973, by the President and each Member of tbe commission:

President: Group Captain M. Tsingris
Members: Squadron Leader D. Papageorgiou
Squadron Leader M. Sabarides
F ligbt Lieutenant D. Mpiniaris
Sergeant—Major M. Katsibis

Appendix Two

The Fleets

Note: this should not be regarded as a definitive fleet list for the Olympic Airways Group, or it's predecessor or successor companies. Information on the early days is far from complete, and for long periods of time aircraft were 'exchanged' within the group with little regards for the paperwork. Likewise, the dates of some or the details are to be regarded as suspect, again for the paperwork was not always completed 'on the day'. It should also be noted with aircraft on lease, especially during the latter timeframe aircraft were allocated to different 'holding companies' such as Phoenix Aviation before being allocated to different airline operations. This is particularly true for the early 2000 period.

It should be also noted that some, but not all aircraft carried their name in English on one side, and in Greek on the other side of the aircraft nose.

Elliniki Etaireia Enaereon Synkinoion AE (EEES)

Junkers G.24he

Regn	c/n	Reg date	Remarks
SX-ACA	962	2.11.31	Cert of Regn 001. Captured by Germans 27.4.41.
SX-ACB	963	2.11.31	Cert of Regn 002. Captured by Germans 27.4.41.
SX-ACD	964	2.11.31	Cert of Regn 003. Captured by Germans 27.4.41.
SX-ACE	965	2.11.31	Cert of Regn 004. Captured by Germans 27.4.41.

Junkers Ju.52/3m

SX-ACF	5984	17.09.38	Cert of Regn 012. To Hellenic State 2.11.40. Captured by Germans 27.4.41 Captured by Allies .45 and operated as VM980. Cancelled 11.3.46.
SX-ACH	6004	17.09.38	Cert of Regn 013. To Hellenic State 2.11.40.
SX-ACI	6025	17.09.38	Cert of Regn 014. To Hellenic State 2.11.40.

Hellenic Air lines

Consolodated Liberator II Series LB.30

SX-DAA	55		Previously with Scottish Aviaton Ltd, Preswick.
SX-DAB	50		Previously with Scottish Aviaton Ltd, Preswick.

Douglas DC-3

SX-BAA	12677	25.4.47	From TWA. To TAE National Greek A/L 1951.
SX-BAD	9491	29.5.46	From RAF stocks by Iranian AW. To TAE National Greek A/L 1951
SX-BAG	26880	26.9.47	From RAF stocks via Iranian AW. To TAE National Greek A/L 7.51
SX-BAK	26095	8.3.49	From RAF stocks via Iranian AW. To TAE National Greek A/L 7.51
SX-BAL	25923	8.3.49	From RAF stocks via Iranian AW. To TAE National Greek A/L 7.51.
SX-BAM	20184	1948	From Matrad Corp. To TAE National Greek A/L 7.51. To Airwork Ltd 23.5.54.
SX-BBA	12373	1.3.48	From Scottish Aviation. To TAE National Greek A/L 7.51
SX-BBB	12332	9.3.48	From Scottish Aviation. To TAE National Greek A/L 7.51
SX-BBC	12304	1.3.48	From Scottish Aviation. To TAE National Greek A/L 7.51
SX-BBD	13012	15.2.48	From Scottish Aviation. To TAE National Greek A/L 7.51
SX-BBE	26459	30.5.49	From FIAT SpA. To TAE National Greek A/L 7.51

Douglas DC-4

SX-DAC	27336	9.50	From American Overseas Airlines. Named 'Hellas' To TAE National Greek A/L 7.51

TAE

Early, incomplete records suggest that TAE operated at least three De Havilland Moths: SX-AAE, AAI and AAK, along with Fairchild Argus II SX-AAJ. Some reports suggest that the Argus was transferred to the Olympic Airways fleet, but was not scrapped until the mid-1970s.

Douglas DC-3

SX-BAA	12677	1951	From TWA. To Hellenic Gvmt 6.55. To Olympic A/W until 6.4.57
SX-BAB	18981	9/1946	From TWA. Crashed near Hassani 3.9.47.
SX-BAC	19274	4.9.46	From TWA. Named 'Nile'. To Hellenic Gvmt 6.55. To Olympic A/W 06.04.57.
SX-BAD	9491	7.7.51	From Hellenic Air Lines. To TAE National Greek A/L 1954. To Hellenic Gvmt 6.55. To Olympic A/W 06.04.57.
SX-BAE	12351	8.3.49	From RAF stocks via Iranian AW.
SX-BAF	12322	29.3.49	From RAF stocks via Iranian AW. Damaged beyond repair Hassani 23.4.49
SX-BAG	26880	7.51	From Hellenic Air Lines. To Hellenic Gvmt 6.55. To Olympic A/W 06.4.57.
SX-BAH	26565	23.9.47	From RAF stocks via Iranian AW. Named 'Epirus'. To Hellenic Gvmt 6.55. To Olympic A/W 06.04.57.
SX-BAI	12162	5.11.47	From British Aviation Services. Crashed Malacassa, Attica, 6.6.49.
SX-BAL	25923	7.7.51	From Hellenic Air Lines. To TAE National Greek A/L 1954. To Hellenic Gvmt 6.55. To Olympic A/W 06.04.57.
SX-BAN	9187	9.11.49	From British Aviation Insurance. To Hellenic Gvmt 6.55. To Olympic A/W 06.04.57.
SX-BBA	12373	7.7.51	From Hellenic Air Lines. To TAE National Greek A/L 1954. To Hellenic Gvmt 6.55. To Olympic A/W 06.04.57.
SX-BBB	12332	7.5.51	From Hellenic Air Lines. To Field Aircraft Services 31.10.53
SX-BBC	12304	7.5.51	From Hellenic Air Lines. To TAE National Greek A/L 1954. To Hellenic Gvmt 6.55. To Olympic A/W 06.04.57.
SX-BBD	13012	7.5.51	From Hellenic Air Lines. To TAE National Greek A/L 1954. To Hellenic Gvmt 6.55. To Olympic A/W 06.04.57.
SX-BBE	26459	7.5.51	From Hellenic Air Lines. To TAE National Greek A/L 1954. To Hellenic Gvmt 6.55. To Olympic A/W 06.04.57.
SX-BBF	4860	31.12.49	From Fokker ex-PH-NDV. To TAE National Greek A/L 1954. To Hellenic Gvmt 6.55. To Olympic A/W 06.04.57.

Douglas DC-4

SX-DAC	27336	7.51	From Hellenic Air Lines. To TAE National Greek A/L 1954. To Hellenic Gvmt 6.55. To Olympic A/W 06.04.57.

Olympic Airways

Douglas DC-3

SX-BAA	12677	6.4.57	From Hellenic Gvmt. To Hellenic Air Force 30.01.63.
SX-BAC	19274	6.4.57	From Hellenic Gvmt. To Hellenic Air Force 30.01.63.
SX-BAD	9491	6.4.57	From Hellenic Gvmt. Crashed Tanagra, Athens, 29.10.59
SX-BAE	12351	6.4.57	From Hellenic Gvmt. To Hellenic Air Force 30.01.63.
SX-BAG	26880	6.4.57	From Hellenic Gvmt. Registration cancelled 31.10.72. To All World Aviation (Air Libya) 1977.
SX-BAH	26565	6.4.67	From Hellenic Gvmt. Registration cancelled 31.10.72. To All World Aviation (Air Libya) 1977.
SX-BAK	26095	6.4.57	From Hellenic Gvmt. To Uganda Air Services 1972.
SX-BAL	25923	6.4.57	From Hellenic Gvmt. Wfu 1970. To All World Aviation 2.1972.
SX-BAN	9187	6.4.57	From Hellenic Gvmt. To Hellenic Air Force 30.01.63.
SX-BBA	12373	6.4.57	From Hellenic Gvmt. To Hellenic Air Force 30.01.63.
SX-BBC	12304	6.4.57	From Hellenic Gvmt. To Hellenic Air Force 30.01.63.
SX-BBD	13012	6.4.57	From Hellenic Gvmt. To Hellenic Air Force 30.01.63.
SX-BBE	26459	6.4.57	From Hellenic Gvmt. To Weather Engineering 1971.
SX-BBF	4860	6.4.57	From Hellenic Gvmt. Wfu1970.

Douglas DC-4

SX-DAC	27336	6.4.57	From Hellenic Gvmt. Named 'Hellas'.
SX-DAG	42995	8.7.58	

Douglas DC-6

SX-DAD	45539	25.7.58	Named 'Isle of Rhodes'.
SX-DAE	45540	8.8.58	Crashed Mt Pan, Keratea, 21 miles north of Athens 8.12.69.
SX-DAF	45543	22.8.58.	Damaged on take of for training flight due to premature retraction of undercarriage 30.3.59. To Aero Factors Corp.
SX-DAH	43124	15.7.59.	Leased from Transair. To Boreas Corp 8.12.65.
SX-DAI	45544	12.12.58	From Hughes Aircraft. Named 'Isle of Kreta'. Wfu 5.11.70 due to hard landing.

SX-DAM	44087	1.5.64	From Swissair. Named 'Isle of Lesvos'.
SX-DAS	45218	16.9.66	From Fairchild Hiller. Named 'Isle of Chios'
SX-DAQ	44871		From UTA. ex- F-BGSN. Named 'Isle of Limnos'
SX-DAR	45224	19.11.67	From Fairchild Hiller. Named 'Isle of Samos'
SX-DAS	45223	2.2.68	From Fairchild Hiller. Named 'Isle of Kos'
DH.106 Comet			
SX-DAK	6437	26.4.60	Named 'Queen Frederica'. To BEA 24.3.69
SX-DAL	6438	14.5.60	Named 'Queen Olga'. To BEA 1.4.69
SX-DAN	6440	14.7.60	Leased from BEA. Named 'Queen Sophia'. To BEA 27.3.69
SX-DAO	6447	25.3.61	Leased from BEA. Named 'Princess Sophia'. To BEA 2.4.69
Boeing 707			
SX-DBA	18948	11.5.66	Named 'City of Athens'. Sold 6.3.75 via Euroworld to Alia.
SX-DBB	18949	21.3.66	Named 'City of Corinth'. Sold 6.3.75 via Euroworld to Alia.
SX-DBC	18950	18.6.66	Named 'City of Knossos'. Sold 1.4.90 to Israeli Aircraft Industries.
SX-DBD	19760	5.6.68	Named 'City of Sparta'. Sold 1.4.90 to Israeli Aircraft Industries.
SX-DBE	20035	18.12.68	Leased from Aircraft Leasing Co. Named 'City of Pella'. Sold 1.4.90 to Israeli Aircraft Industries.
SX-DBF	20036	23.1.69	Leased from Aircraft Leasing Co. Named 'City of Mycenae' Sold 1.4.90 to Israeli Aircraft Industries.
SX-DBO	19164	26.3.73	From Northeast Airlines. Named 'City of Lindos'. Leased to EAS Cargo Phoenix Aviation. Sold 1.4.90 to Israeli Aircraft Industries.
SX-DBP	19163	5.73	From Northeast Airlines. Named 'City of Thebes'. Sold 1.4.90 to Israeli Aircraft Industries.
Boeing 720			
SX-DBG	18352	25.2.72	From Northeast Airlines. To Northampton Panama SA, leased to Olympic named 'Axios River'. Purchased by Olympic 26.7.79. Withdrawn from service 6.81 and scrapped.
SX-DBH	18353	25.2.72	From Northeast Airlines. To Northampton Panama SA, leased to Olympic named 'Achelios River'. Purchased by Olympic 26.7.79. Withdrawn from service 6.81 and scrapped.
SX-DBI	18355	25.2.72	From Northeast Airlines. To Northampton Panama SA, leased to Olympic named 'Pinios River'. Purchased by Olympic 26.7.79. To Omega Air 13.12.84
SX-DBK	18356	25.2.72	From Northeast Airlines. To Northampton Panama SA, leased to Olympic named 'Strimon River'. Purchased by Olympic 26.7.79. Withdrawn from service 6.81 and scrapped.
SX-DBL	18420	6.2.72	From Northeast Airlines. To Northampton Panama SA, leased to Olympic named 'Evros River'. Purchased by Olympic 26.7.79. Withdrawn from service 6.81 and scrapped.
SX-DBM	18687	28.76.72	From Northeast Airlines. To Northampton Panama SA, leased to Olympic named 'Aliakmon River'.Purchased by Olympic 26.7.79. Withdrawn from service 6.81 and scrapped.
SX-DBN	18688	18.1.73	From Northeast Airlines. To Northampton Panama SA, leased to Olympic named 'Nestos River'. Purchased by Olympic 26.7.79. Leased to Air Tanzania. Sold to AeroNica 25.2.82
Boeing 727			
SX-CBA	20003	19.12.68	Named 'Mount Olympus'. Scrapped Athens 1998.
SX-CBB	20004	16.1.69	Named 'Mount Pindos' Scrapped Athens 1998.
SX-CBC	20005	7.2.69	Named 'Mount Parnassus' To Aero Controls 1998
SX-CBD	20006	7.2.69	Named 'Mount Helicon' Scrapped Athens 1998.
SX-CBE	20201	24.10.69	Named 'Mount Athos' Scrapped Athens 1998.
SX-CBF	19536	28.6.71	Named 'Mount Taygetus' Scrapped Athens 1998.
SX-CBG	20918	3.90	Leased from Lufthansa. Named 'Mount Menalon'. To Macedonian Aviation 30.6.98.
SX-CBH	20790	1.4.90	Leased from ATASCO. Named 'Mount Vermio'. To Macedonian Aviation 26.6.98.
SX-CBI	20791	12.3.90	Leased from ATASCO. Named 'Mount Dirfis'. WO in heavy landing at Thessaloniki 12.8.97.

N9233Z	18366	4.76	Leased from Boeing Aircraft Corp. Returned 31.10.76
N9234Z	18368	4.76	Leased from Boeing Aircraft Corp. Returned 31.10.76

Boeing 737-200

SX-BCA	21224	23.6.76	Named 'Apollo'. Stored Athens.
SX-BCB	21225	30.6.76	Named 'Hermes'. Sold to Indonesia for spares 10.03.
SX-BCC	21301	13.10.76	Named 'Hercules'. Sold to Indonesia for spares 10.03.
SX-BCD	21302	19.10.76	Named 'Hephaestus,' later 'Ajax'. Sold to Indonesia for spares 10.03.
SX-BCE	22300	25.6.80	Named 'Dyonisus'Sold to Indonesia for spares 12.03.
SX-BCF	22301	24.7.80	Named 'Poseidon'. Sold to Indonesia for spares 10.03.
SX-BCG	22338	21.8.80	Named 'Phoebus'. Sold to Indonesia for spares 12.03.
SX-BCH	22339	26.8.80	Named 'Triton'. Sold to Indonesia for spares 10.03.
SX-BCI	22343	11.9.80	Named 'Proteus'. Sold to Indonesia for spares 10.03.
SX-BCK	22400	10.6.81	Named 'Nerus'. Sold to Indonesia for spares 10.03.
SX-BCL	22401	16.7.81	Named 'Atlas'. Scrapped.

Boeing 737-3/400

SX-BKA	25313	12.9.91	Named 'Vergina'. To AirSale Inc 29.12.10.
SX-BKB	25314	20.9.91	Named 'Olynthos' To Garuda Indonesian AW 10.08.
SX-BKC	25361	30.9.91	Named 'Phillipi'. To AirSale Inc 29.12.10.
SX-BKD	25362	17.10.91	Named 'Amphipoli'. To AirSale Inc 29.12.10.
SX-BKE	25417	14.11.91	Named 'Stagira'. To AirSale Inc 29.12.10.
SX-BKF	25430	12.12.91	Named 'Dion'. To AirSale Inc 29.12.10.
SX-BKG	27149	3.6.93	To AirSale Inc 29.12.10.
SX-BKH	24703	3.6.98	Leased from ILFC. Returned 5.11.09.
SX-BKI	24704	6.6.98	Leased from ILFC. Returned 3.9.09.
SX-BKK	25371	23.5.98	Leased from ILFC. Returned 3.06.
SX-BKL	24915	1.7.98	Leased from Malaysian Airways. Returned 28.3.09.
SX-BKM	24709	14.7.98.	Leased from ILFC. Returned 29.7.09.
SX-BKN	26281	3.7.98	Leased from ILFC. Returned 27.8.09.
SX-BKT	25377	12.6.07	Leased from ILFC. Returned 5.11.09.
SX-BKU	25764	1.8.08	Leased from WFBN. Returned 2.10.09
SX-BKX	27000	24.7.07	Leased from ?. Scrapped 28.8.10.
SX-BLA	28869	6.4.98	To BouAS 3.05.
SX-BLB	25015	5.6.02	Leased. Damaged when blown 90 degrees at AIA 27.7.02. To Germania 3.3.04.
SX-BLC	26303	25.6.04	Leased from ILFC. Returned 2.2.10.
SX-BLD	25071	8.08	Leased from ?. Returned 21.7.09.
SX-BMD	25765	24.10.08	Leased from WFBN. Returned 28.9.09.

Boeing 747

SX-OAA	20742	21.6.73	Named 'Olympic Zeus'. To TWA 11.4.85
SX-OAB	20825	7.12.73	Named 'Olympic Eagle' Leased to Aerolineas Argentinas 16.4.96. Returned 15.7.96. Stored.
SX-OAC	21683	1.9.84	Formerly with Singapore Airlines. Named 'Olympic Spirit'. Broken up.
SX-OAD	21684	1.4.85	Formerly with Singapore Airlines. Named 'Olympic Flame' Stored Bruntingthorpe UK.
SX-OAE	21935	23.12.85	Formerly with Singapore Airlines. Named 'Olympic Peace'. Scrapped.

Boeing 717-200

SX-BOA	55056	29.12.99	To Spanair as EC-KFR 14.6.07.
SX-BOB	55053	21.12.99	To Spanairlink as EC-KHX 11.7.07
SX-BOC	55065	26.1.00	Named 'Iridanos' To Spanairlink 1.07.

Airbus A300

F-BUAP	052	15.5.85	Leased, returned 11.11.85.
F-ODRF	048	19.10.84.	Leased, returned 14.6.85.
SX-BEB	046	25.2.79.	To Grand Air as RP-X8882 13.5.95.
SX-BEC	056	15.2.79	To Translift. 5.96.
SX-BED	058	28.3.80	To TMG 4.6.00.
SX-BEE	103	21.4.80	To TMG 22.5.00.
SX-BEF	105	30.4.80	To Finova 14.4.99.

SX-BEG	148	29.7.81	Named 'Diomedes'. To l'Aeropostale 1.99.
SX-BEH	184	8.4.82	To l'Aeropostale 17.3.99.
SX-BEI	189	17.5.82	To l'Aeropostale 18.3.99
SX-BEK	632	7.8.92	To Iran Air 1.3.05.
SX-BEL	696	4.10.93	To Iran Air 1.3.05.
SX-BEM	603	2.4.00	Named 'Creta' To Onur Air 26.10.08.

Airbus A340

SX-DFA	235	29.1.99	Named 'Olympia'. To AAG 12.11
SX-DFB	239	29.1.99	Named 'Delphi'. To AAG 12.11
SX-DFC	280	14.10.99	Named 'Marathon' To AAG 12.11
SX-DFD	292	25.10.99	Named 'Epidaurus'. To AAG 12.11

Airbus A319/320

SX-OAF	3895	7.7.09	Leased. Returned ?.?.??
SX-OAG	3950	7.7.09	Leased. Returned ?.?.??
SX-OAH	3316	22.7.09	Leased. Returned To Aegean Airlines.
SX-OAI	3162	17.8.09	Leased. Returned 25.9.09
SX-OAJ	3905	30.6.09	Leased. Returned ?.?.??
SX-OAK	3316	22.7.09	Leased, Returned 11.10
SX-OAL	3252	25.9.09	Leased, Returned 11.10.
SX-OAM	3990	6.10.09	Leased, To Aegean Airlines ?.?.??
SX-OAN	1727	12.9.09	To Aegean Airlines 17.4.11.
SX-OAP	4065	20.10.09	Leased. Returned ?.?.??
SX-OAO	1880	22.9.09	To Aegean Airlines 21.4.11
SX-OAQ	3748	25.8.09	To Aegean Airlines
SX-OAR	3812	25.8.09	To Aegean Airlines
SX-OAS	4094	12.11.09	Leased. Returned ?.?.??
SX-OAT	4190	5.2.10	Leased. Returned ?.?.??
SX-OAU	4193	3.2.10	Leased. Returned ?.?.??
SX-OAV	3142	18.9.09	Leased. Returned 7.4.10.
D-ANNB	1240	21.5.09	Leased from Blue wings. Returned 12.09.

Olympic Aviation
NAMC YS-11

SX-BBG	2136		Named 'Isle of Cephalonia'. To Hellenic Air Force 10.80.
SX-BBH	2137		Named 'Isle of Ithaca'. To Hellenic Air Force 1981
SX-BBI	2143		Named 'Isle of Samothrace'.To Hellenic Air Force 1981
SX-BBJ	2104		To LN-MTA
SX-BBK	2144		Named 'Isle of Zakinthos' To Hellenic Air Force 1981
SX-BBL	2145		Named 'Isle of Delos' To Hellenic Air Force 1981
SX-BBM	2106		To JA758
SX-BBP	2153		Named 'Isle of Andros'.To Hellenic Air Force 1981
SX-BBQ	2155	26.3.71	Named 'Isle of Kalymnos'. Written off on approach to Athens 21.10.72.
SX-BBR	2156	28.4.71	Named 'Isle of Milos'. Written off 23.1.76 when crashed into a mountain 25 miles south of Kozani.

Shorts SC7 Skyvan

SX-BBN	SH1869		Named 'Isle of Mykonos'
SX-BBO	SH1870		Named 'Isle of Skiathos'
SX-BBT	SH1866		
SX-BBW	SH1847		

Shorts SD3-30

SX-BGA	SH3043	23.5.80	Named 'Isle of Patmos' Broken up 6.97
SX-BGB	SH3048	28.6.80	Named 'Isle of Kastelrizo' Broken up 6.97
SX-BGC	SH3065	7.4.81	Named 'Isle of Paros' Broken up 6.97
SX-BGD	SH3066	7.4.81	Named 'Isle of Naxos' Broken up 6.97
SX-BGE	SH3083	14.5.82	Named 'Isle of Alios' Crashed Samos 3.8.89 in bad weather
SX-BGF	SH3084	4.6.82	Named 'Isle of Tinos' Broken up 6.97

Britain-Norman BN2 Islander

SX-BBS			Named 'Isle of Kythira'

SX-BFC	316	5.78	Leased from Arkia, returned 1.79.
SX-BFG	316	5.80	Leased from Arkia, returned end of summer.
SX-BBX	334	5.75	Leased from Arkia, returned end of summer.
SX-BFA	399	3.76	Leased from Arkia, returned 10.76
SX-BFD	399	5.78	Leased from Arkia, returned end of summer.
SX-BFF	399	5.79	Leased from Arkia, returned end of summer.
SX-BFB	403	3.76	Leased from Arkia, returned 10.76
SX-BFE	435	4.79	Leased from Arkia, returned end of summer.
SX-BBZ	435	7.75	Leased from Arkia, returned end of summer.
SX-BFH	461	10.81	Named 'Isle of Karpathos' Leased from Loganair. Returned 21.6.85

ATR42/72

SX-BIA	169	11.1.90	Named 'Plato'. To Willis Lease Finanace Corp. 12.11
SX-BIB	182	24.4.90	Named 'Socrates'. To Willis Lease Finanace Corp. 12.11
SX-BIC	197	18.7.90	Named 'Artistotle'. To Willis Lease Finanace Corp. 12.11
SX-BID	219	15.5.91	Named 'Pythagora'. To Willis Lease Finanace Corp. 12.11
SX-BIE	239	28.6.91	Named 'Thales'. To Willis Lease Finanace Corp. 12.11
SX-BIF	241	1.8.91	Named 'Democritus'. To Willis Lease Finanace Corp. 12.11
SX-BIG	290	10.4.92	Named 'Homer'. To Willis Lease Finanace Corp. 12.11
SX-BIH	305	11.6.92	Named 'Herodutus'. To Willis Lease Finanace Corp. 12.11
SX-BII	353	2.4.93	Named 'Hippcrates'. To Willis Lease Finanace Corp. 12.11
SX-BIK	350	11.6.93	Named 'Archimedes'. To Willis Lease Finanace Corp. 12.11
SX-BIL	437	9.6.95	Named 'Melina-Ellada'. To Willis Lease Finanace Corp. 12.11
SX-BIM	337	10.12.02	Named 'Kostas Tsiklitiras'. Returned to ATR.
SX-BIN	291	28.11.02	Named 'Spiros Louis' Returned to ATR.
SX-BIX	020	30.5.89	Leased, returned 5.10.89.
SX-BIY	021	30.5.89	Leased from ATI, returned 4.1.90
SX-BPA	033	10.10.08	Scrapped 8.12

Dornier 228

SX-BHA	8010	8.83	Returned to Dornier 11.83.
SX-BHB	8009	29.11.83	Returned to Dornier 5.84.
SX-BHC	8030	30.5.84	Named 'Isle of Leros'. To Nemisis GmbH/Kaskasi Aviation 25.5.07
SX-BHD	8034	12.7.84	Named 'Isle of Skyros'. To Dolphin Air 14.6.05
SX-BHE	8050	10.5.85	Named 'Isle of Kasos'. To Dolphin Air 21.11.05
SX-BHF	8057	15.5.85	Named 'Isle of Astypalea' Reportedly to Kenya as spares.
SX-BHG	8061	12.7.85	Named 'Isle of Amorgos' Damaged beyond repair at Paros 2.5.97.
SX-BHH	8079	30.4.86	Named 'Isle of Kythira' WFU 18.10.03 Reportedly to Kenya as spares.
SX-BHI	8080	28.5.86	Named 'Isle of Karpathos'. To Logistic ApS/Air Traffic 7.5.07.

Cessna 152

SX-BDG
SX-BDP
SX-BDR
SX-BDQ

Piper PA-23 Aztec

SX-BDE	27-2962
SX-BDL	27-5081

Piper PA-28 Cherokee

SX-BDF	28-25626
SX-BDK	28-25010
SX-BDM	28-25007

Piper PA-31 Navajo

SX-BDD	31-252

Piper PA-44-180 Seminole

SX-BDZ

Learjet

SX-ASO	25-174	6.6.71	Crashed 18.2.72. Hit sea near Antibes on final approach to Nice Airport.

SX-CBM	25-094	11.72	Sold as VR-BFV.

Piaggio _136L-2

SX-BDB	242	1959?	Formerly HB-LAV. Aircraft scrapped at Athens.
SX-BDC	246		Crashed Athens 22.1.73

SA318 Alouette 2

SX-HAC	01
SX-HAH	2042
SX-HAI	2230
SX-HAN	2352

Aerospatiale Super Frelon

F-OCMF	116

AS350B Ecureuil

SX-HBI	1482	-	To F-WQDV
SX-HBK			
SX-HBP	1652	-	To F-GPUM

Augusta A109Mk.II Plus

SX-HDA

Olympic Air
DHC-8-1/4

SX-BIO	330	3.10.03	Leased. Named 'Katerina Thanou'
SX-BIP	347	22.10.03	Leased. Named 'Voula Patoulidou'
SX-BIQ	361	30.10.03	Leased. Named 'Kahi Kahiasvili'
SX-BIR	364	28.8.03	Named 'Kostas Kenteris'
SX-BIT	4148	25.9.09	Leased.
SX-BIU	4152	15.9.09	Leased.
SX-OBA	4267	23.8.09	Leased
SX-OBB	4268	9.9.09	Leased.
SX-OBC	4276	6.11.09	Leased.
SX-OBD	4311	26.5.10	Leased
SX-OBE	4314	14.6.10	Leased
SE-OBF	4318	20.7.10	Leased.
SX-OBG	4321	1.12.10	Leased.
SX-OBH	4327	1.12.10	Leased.

Macedonian Aviation.
Boeing 727

SX-CBG	20918	30.6.98	Transferred from Olympic Airways. Named 'Mount Mendalon'
SX-CBH	20790	26.6.98	

Boeing 737

SX-BMA	27171	19.5.99	Named 'City of Athens'. To Air One 16.7.04
SX-BMB	27213	19.5.99	Named 'City of Thessaloniki' To Futura International AL 3.6.04
SX-BMC	27143	3.8.00	Named 'City of Alexandros' To Euro Aviation 21.5.10.

Appendix Three

Glossary

Romanised Greek	Modern Greek	English
Athína	Αθήνα	Athens
Aristotélēs	Αριστοτέλης	Aristotle
Agrínio	Αγρίνιο	Agrinion
Alexandroupoli	Αλεξανδρούπολη	Alexandroupolis
Alexandros	Αλέξανδρος	Alexander
Chaniá	Χανιά	Chania
Dráma	Δράμα	Drama
Ellinikon	Ελληνικόν	Hellinikon
Iraklion	Irákleio	Heraklion
Kalamáta	Καλαμάτα	Kalamata
Kavala	Καβάλα	Kavala
Komotini	Κομοτηνή	Komotini
Kythira	Κύθηρα	Kithira
Kastellorizo	Καστελλόριζο	Castellorizo
Kefalonia	Κεφαλονιά	Cephalonia
Kerkyra	Kérkyra	Corfu
Lesbos	Λέσβος	Lesvos
Lefkáda	Λευκάδα	Lefkas
Paros	Πάρος	Paros
Ródos	Ρόδος	Rhodes
Samos	Σάμος	Samos
Thira	Σαντορίνη	Santorini
Thessaloniki	Θεσσαλονίκη	Salonika
Volos	Βόλος	Volos
Yannena	Ιωάννινα	Ioannina
Xios	Χίος	Chios
Zakinthos	Ζάκυνθος	Zante